Neopragmatism

Neopragmatism

Interventions in First-Order Philosophy

Edited by
JOSHUA GERT

OXFORD
UNIVERSITY PRESS

Great Clarendon Street, Oxford, OX2 6DP,
United Kingdom

Oxford University Press is a department of the University of Oxford.
It furthers the University's objective of excellence in research, scholarship,
and education by publishing worldwide. Oxford is a registered trade mark of
Oxford University Press in the UK and in certain other countries

© the several contributors 2023

The moral rights of the author have been asserted

All rights reserved. No part of this publication may be reproduced, stored in
a retrieval system, or transmitted, in any form or by any means, without the
prior permission in writing of Oxford University Press, or as expressly permitted
by law, by licence or under terms agreed with the appropriate reprographics
rights organization. Enquiries concerning reproduction outside the scope of the
above should be sent to the Rights Department, Oxford University Press, at the
address above

You must not circulate this work in any other form
and you must impose this same condition on any acquirer

Published in the United States of America by Oxford University Press
198 Madison Avenue, New York, NY 10016, United States of America

British Library Cataloguing in Publication Data
Data available

Library of Congress Control Number: 2023936449

ISBN 978–0–19–289480–9

DOI: 10.1093/oso/9780192894809.001.0001

Printed and bound by
CPI Group (UK) Ltd, Croydon, CR0 4YY

Links to third party websites are provided by Oxford in good faith and
for information only. Oxford disclaims any responsibility for the materials
contained in any third party website referenced in this work.

Contents

Acknowledgements	vii
List of Contributors	ix

I. INTRODUCTION

1. What Is Neopragmatism? Joshua Gert	3

II. TIME, CAUSES, AND SCIENCE

2. Time for Pragmatism Huw Price	23
3. A Neopragmatist Approach to Modality Amie L. Thomasson	70
4. Neopragmatism in the Philosophy of Perception? The Case of Primitive Color Mazviita Chirimuuta	98
5. A Neopragmatist Treatment of Causation and Laws of Nature John T. Roberts	118

III. LANGUAGE, TRUTH, AND LOGIC

6. A Pragmatic Genealogy of Rule-Following Philip Pettit	141
7. Neopragmatism and Reference Magnetism Joshua Gert	170
8. Realism Rehabilitated Claudine Verheggen and Robert H. Myers	189
9. What Is Linguistic Interpretation? José L. Zalabardo	210
10. Neopragmatism and Logic: A Deflationary Proposal Lionel Shapiro	235

IV. VALUE AND PRACTICE

11. Pragmatism in Practice *Simon Blackburn*	261
12. Pragmatism and the Ontology of Art *Robert Kraut*	275
13. The Subject Matter of "Subject Matter" and General Jurisprudence *Stefan Sciaraffa*	303
14. Pragmatism and the Prudential Good *Diana Heney*	328
Index	349

Acknowledgements

This volume began its life at a conference at William & Mary, held in the Fall of 2018, at which most of the contributors presented earlier versions of the papers that appear here as chapters. I am very grateful for the funding for that conference, which came from the Rachel and E.W. Thompson Philosophy Endowment and the Foradas Philosophy Department Speaker's Series Endowment. Thanks also to the support of my colleagues at William & Mary, for helping to make the conference a success.

List of Contributors

Simon Blackburn, Bertrand Russell Professor of Philosophy Emeritus, University of Cambridge

Mazviita Chirimuuta, Senior Lecturer in Philosophy, University of Edinburgh

Joshua Gert, Leslie and Naomi Legum Professor of Philosophy, William & Mary

Diana Heney, Assistant Professor of Philosophy, Vanderbilt University

Robert Kraut, Professor of Philosophy, The Ohio State University

Robert H. Myers, Professor of Philosophy, York University

Philip Pettit, Laurence S. Rockefeller University Professor of Politics and Human Values, Princeton University

Huw Price, Bertrand Russell Professor of Philosophy Emeritus, University of Cambridge

John T. Roberts, Professor of Philosophy, University of North Carolina-Chapel Hill

Stefan Sciaraffa, Professor of Philosophy, McMaster University

Lionel Shapiro, Professor of Philosophy, University of Connecticut

Amie L. Thomasson, Daniel P. Stone Professor of Intellectual and Moral Philosophy, Dartmouth College

Claudine Verheggen, Professor of Philosophy, York University

José L. Zalabardo, Professor of Philosophy, University College London

PART I
INTRODUCTION

1
What Is Neopragmatism?

Joshua Gert

1. A Broad Overview

Most broadly speaking, neopragmatism is an approach to philosophical questions that have traditionally been addressed by metaphysicians and epistemologists: questions about such things as numbers, possibilities, free will, truth, moral properties, and our capacity to know anything about them. Rather than taking such questions at face value, as many metaphysicians and epistemologists do, the neopragmatist emphasizes the fact that human language—the language in which these perplexing questions arise—is a naturalistically explicable phenomenon. That is, it views language use as the production and consumption of sounds, signs, and marks by creatures capable of learning very sophisticated practices with them, and passing those practices on from generation to generation.

The 'pragmatism' in 'neopragmatism' indicates an emphasis both on the idea that language in *general* is a social practice, and on the idea that what makes the details of a *particular* practice intelligible is a clear view of what that practice allows us to do. The 'neo-' prefix will be addressed in the following section, which sketches some of the ways in which it is related to classical pragmatism. I myself think of neopragmatism as a kind of theory: a theory about how language works, its relation to the world, and how we should think of truth and reference, among other things. It is also possible to think of it not as a theory but, as Robert Kraut (Chapter 12) puts it, as 'a set of directives for the construction of theories'. Given that some neopragmatists will think of many theoretical-sounding assertions as doing—in some important sense—the same job as directives, there is probably no bar to thinking of neopragmatism in both ways.

If one views language as a naturalistically explicable phenomenon, a number of other claims become immediately plausible. One is that, to the degree that language serves our everyday needs, we should regard it as in perfect working order. So we should look with suspicion on any philosophical view that has very surprising implications regarding our first-order claims. For example, any view that disallows truth-assessments of moral claims takes on a significant burden. And a second is that, just as we definitely do not need to appeal to any substantive notion of truth or reference to explain the social practice of baseball, or chess, we should not assume from the get-go that those semantic notions will bear explanatory

Joshua Gert, *What Is Neopragmatism?* In: *Neopragmatism: Interventions in First-Order Philosophy*. Edited by: Joshua Gert, Oxford University Press. © Joshua Gert 2023. DOI: 10.1093/oso/9780192894809.003.0001

weight in explaining how language works. Indeed, neopragmatists end up endorsing deflationary accounts of 'true', 'refers', and other semantic notions. That is, they endorse views on which to say '"*P*" is true' is just another way of asserting that *P*, and on which to say '"*X*" refers to *Y*' is just another way of asserting that *X* is *Y*.

Perhaps surprisingly, neopragmatists—like most other philosophers—tend to focus on assertions, rather than commands, questions, exclamations, and so on. One exception is Amie Thomasson, who—following Michael Halliday—emphasizes that assertion is in fact a rather late arrival in the linguistic repertoire of children. A possible explanation for the focus on truth and assertion is that neopragmatists are often trying to demystify the sorts of truth-apt claims that get traditional metaphysics going. That is, by keeping the naturalistic facts of language use firmly in view, neopragmatists seek to explain why there is no distinctly philosophical mystery in our asserting such things as 'lying on your résumé is wrong', 'three plus four is seven', 'the election could have gone either way'. Normative words, number words, and modal words are all *words*. We can explain how we use them without having to appeal to anything particularly mysterious. In the language Jose Zalabardo uses in his contribution (Chapter 9), the neopragmatist will hold that an account of what grounds the *meaning* of these sorts of claims preempts the need to offer an account of what grounds their *truth*. Nor is there any distinctly philosophical mystery in our using words like 'fact' or 'know' in connection with such claims. After all, our practices with these words do not differ in any deep metaphysical way from our practice with words like 'lemon' or 'yellow'. If all of this is right, then there is no distinctively philosophical problem about the nature of moral properties, or numbers, or unrealized possibilities, or our knowledge about these things.

It is true that much of our everyday talk is about observable objects and their observable properties. And it is also true that our knowledge of these things depends on our having some causal connection with them. But, neopragmatists tend to argue, this picture can be extremely misleading when we use it as a model for other sorts of talk. As I emphasize in my own Chapter 7 on reference magnetism, there is a difference between what we can say about *the reference* of a certain term or class of terms, and what we can say about *reference* in general, thought of as a uniform relation between words and what they refer to. Neopragmatists deny that there is a robust reference relation. But the endorsement of such a deflationary view of reference does not, of course, prevent neopragmatists from using the word 'refer'. Nor, therefore, does it prevent them from holding that *the reference* of certain terms are the entities that play a distinctive causal role in our use of those terms. Failure to appreciate the distinction between innocuous talk of *the reference* of a term, and confused talk of *reference* in general may be part of what makes it so tempting to take a theory of the reference of names of physical objects and properties as a model for reference in general. And once one succumbs to this temptation it can seem difficult to maintain that we *really* refer to numbers, or unrealized possibilities, or even to moral properties.

As Huw Price emphasizes in his contribution (Chapter 2), neopragmatism is necessarily *global* in nature. No matter what the topic of our theorizing, neopragmatism give us the same overarching advice: look at how the words that are central to that topic are used, and try to provide a naturalistic explanation of a practice in which words are used in that way. One way of thinking about this—by no means new—is to think of neopragmatism as a global version of the sort of *local* expressivism that is well known from the ethical case. Local ethical expressivists explain why we use ethical terms as we do—what our practice with these terms allows us to do. And they also explain why ethical discourse takes a form grammatically similar to the simple truth-apt discourse with which we attribute physical properties to physical objects. The neopragmatist can accept all the positive explanations these ethical expressivists offer. But the neopragmatist declines to make—much less to emphasize—a contrast with claims about, for example, the location of the nearest grocery store. They decline, to use a term that is becoming standard, to endorse a *bifurcation* thesis: the thesis that there is *genuinely truth-apt* discourse, about *real* things, and, alongside it—mimicking its superficial grammatical form—merely *quasi-realist* discourse (see Kraut 1990).

In rejecting the bifurcation thesis, neopragmatists hold that *all* truth-assessments are performing a uniform function. So there is no distinction between the genuinely truth-apt and the merely quasi-truth-apt. What is that uniform function? Huw Price (forthcoming) describes it in the following way: sentences that take the form of assertions—as opposed to exclamation, orders, questions, and so on—open speakers up to the pressures of truth-assessment by others. These pressures play a crucial role in getting a linguistic community to converge in the psychological states expressed by those assertions. This uniform explanation of the existence of truth-apt discourse is—as Price (2004) emphasizes—consistent with an important pluralism in connection with the psychological states at issue. Some states might be attitudes toward the punishment of certain actions. Others might be dispositions to produce the counting-numbers in a certain order. Still others might be functional models of the layout of the physical environment. Thomasson's and Chirimuuta's contributions to this volume (Chapters 3 and 4, respectively) both emphasize this sort of pluralism, as well as the temptations to overlook it and the dangers of doing so. What unites all the states we express with assertions—what makes them all apt for expression in that particular way—is (1) the usefulness of having the members of a community converge on them, and (2) the fact that truth-assessments can in fact influence them in the direction of convergence.

Neopragmatism can be seen as a form of meta-metaphysics, in that it gives us second-order advice. That is, it tells us how to go about understanding and addressing ontological questions. But it is a commonplace these days that one cannot distance oneself from first-order issues simply by using the prefix 'meta'. So it is certainly possible that neopragmatism will have first-order implications: that it will not merely tell us what we are doing when we talk about justice, but that it will also push us to classify some practices as just, and others as unjust. Diana Heney's Chapter 14 takes this possibility very seriously, and argues that pragmatist methods yield first-order constraints on what counts as a person's prudential good, and what counts as a human right. And Simon Blackburn's contribution (Chapter 11) is, largely, an exploration of the question of the relation between a neopragmatist perspective and various first-order ethical and political issues. His characteristically Blackburnian conclusion is that the issue is complicated. One complication stems from the psychological fact that the first shocking exposure to the metaphysically deflationary implications of neopragmatism can lead to a fatal sense of moral "unshackling"—at least in those who are disposed to move in that direction in the first place.

2. Historical Connections

The roots of neopragmatism lie, unsurprisingly, in the earlier pragmatism of Dewey, James, and Peirce. What makes the word 'pragmatism' apply to these thinkers is at least in part the role that *usefulness* plays in their theories. Only James (1907) might be regarded as having defined the true as the useful, and even that is probably unfair. But all three of these classical pragmatists wrote in ways that suggest, at the very least, that the true might be *defined* in a way that relates truth to our practical aims. The neopragmatist, on the other hand, does not offer a *definition* of truth at all. Rather, the goal is to describe the use of the word 'true', and its cognates, in a linguistic practice. And just as we can describe the use of words like 'hello' without appeal to a referent, or truth-conditions, so too can we characterize the meaning of 'true'. Claudine Verheggen and Robert Myers, in their contribution (Chapter 8), describe traditional pragmatists as having an overly epistemic conception of truth: one on which truth cannot outrun our capacities to know. This leads to *definitions* of truth in terms of inquiry. Verheggen and Myers reject such a conception, describing it as objectionably antirealist. But they also reject a conception that is so radically non-epistemic that it allows room for global skepticism of the Cartesian sort. They find, in the work of Donald Davidson, a neopragmatist conception of truth that sails between these two shores.

Another source of contemporary neopragmatism is the later Wittgenstein, who emphasized the central role of linguistic *practices*—what he sometimes called 'language games'—when we are trying to understand how language works. This emphasis was meant to displace a more traditional focus on the *referents* of the terms we use. Since it is natural to describe linguistic practices in terms of people following rules, one of Wittgenstein's enduring legacies is a concern with the phenomena involved in rule-following. He tries repeatedly to undermine the idea that true claims are made true because they reflect the way things are with the referents of terms they employ. But replacing talk of referents with talk of rules doesn't advance his project very much—indeed, it undermines it—if rules are regarded as strange sorts of entity, and if rule-following is a matter of our acquaintance with them. The natural thing for Wittgenstein to do, therefore—and what he actual does do—is to turn the same pragmatic lens on our talk of rules and rule-following that he tells us to use when talking about numbers, colors, sensations, and other traditional topics of metaphysical theorizing. Philip Pettit (Chapter 6) and Stefan Sciaraffa (Chapter 13) develop this Wittgensteinian project. Pettit's goal is to explain how it might be that we humans come to behave in ways aptly described using the language of rules and rule-following. And Sciaraffa highlights the fact that we need guidance in determining what the rules for use of a term are, in token instances, before we can know whether or not two people using the same term ought to be regarded as talking about the same subject matter. That is, it is not always clear whether or not we ought to regard two people as talking past each other. This would not be an issue if the rules of use for any given term were open to view—but they are not: rules are no more visible than unrealized possibilities.

Diana Heney's Chapter 14 also helps bring into view the continuities between classical pragmatists and neopragmatists. Heney herself places more emphasis on the classical pragmatists. In describing the distinctive features of their mode of inquiry, she offers us '(1) an emphasis on lived experience, (2) the demand to own uncertainty, and (3) the opportunity to build consensus'.[1] How do these features of classical pragmatist accounts of inquiry relate to the contemporary neopragmatist project? I think we can see the following counterparts.

(1′) A rejection of a metaphysics that includes entities and properties that would have no intelligible impact on lived experience.

(2′) An explicit acknowledgement that mastery of a concept is a skill, and that even complete mastery of a skill need not fix a unique way of deploying it—especially in novel circumstances.

(3′) An explicit acknowledgement of the practical importance of consensus of certain sorts, as distinct from any suggestion that consensus is an indication of truth, much less that it constitutes it.

These paraphrases might not seem perfectly apt to Heney. In particular, (2′) has more to do with the open-ended nature of practices, and less to do with the sort

---

[1] My numbering.

of humility and fallibility that Heney wants to emphasize. Still, it is an important insight of neopragmatism—and one with which I think Heney would agree—that since some of our most important concepts have their origins in our complex and contingent nature, they will resist any neat sort of reductive analysis, and will yield areas of dispute in which there will often fail to be a unique right answer. Of course, that does not rule out theories—even systematic theories—of, say, morality. But the systematic part of such theories will "bottom out" in such normative concepts as rationality, reasons, harm, and benefit.[2] And *those* basic concepts will not be further reducible.

Let me mention one final set of historical connections. Mazviita Chirimuuta's views on color are part of the cutting-edge of neopragmatism. But one of the things Chirimuuta stresses in her Chapter 4, as part of her criticism of my own views on color, is that that cutting-edge can and should be sharpened by contact with some theorists from an earlier era. In particular, she draws attention to phenomenologists such as Heidegger, Merleau-Ponty, Husserl, and Cassirer. These theorists provided insights into the role of the human perspective in scientific inquiry—insights that Chirimuuta argues ought to be taken up by contemporary neopragmatists. In particular, she suggests that some neopragmatists—including the author of this introduction—remain in partial thrall to the idea of a mind- and human-independent world. This idea has served science well as an idealization, but should not be taken literally even there.

3. Theoretical Starting Points

One of the recurring themes in Wittgenstein's later work is our failure to notice certain ubiquitous features of our environment: features that in fact help to explain why we have the linguistic practices we have. As he puts it:

> What we have to mention in order to explain the significance, I mean the importance, of a concept, are often extremely general facts of nature: such facts as are hardly ever mentioned because of their great generality.   1953: note on §142
>
> What we are supplying are really remarks on the natural history of human beings; we are not contributing curiosities however, but observations which no one has doubted, but which have escaped remark only because they are always before our eyes.   §415

A number of the contributions to this volume provide vivid examples of this technique. Perhaps the most vivid is Huw Price's attention to the fact that we have

---

[2] My (2012) is just such a theory, and is explicitly neopragmatist.

a "temporal viewpoint" (Chapter 2). To say this is to try to make salient such platitudinous facts as that we remember the past but not the future; that we have *expectations* about the future but not the past; and that our linguistic acts are both effects of what has happened in the past and causes of things that will happen in the future. Price's chapter starts from a place where the temporal viewpoint is harder to ignore—an explanation of temporal indexicals like 'now' and 'yesterday'. But from there he takes five further steps, each rising to a higher level of generality. At the end of this ascent, he has widened our view to take in virtually all language. And from the resulting viewpoint, Price helps us see the temporal background to it all.

Pettit too focuses on features of human beings that are so basic and ubiquitous that their significance can be hard to appreciate (Chapter 6). The first is that we humans, like pigeons and other even less sophisticated animals, have evolved to respond differentially to different stimuli, and to have the capacity to acquire, via reinforcement, new dispositions of the same sort. The second is that we humans, unlike most other animals, have a quite general capacity for joint action. This involves a certain amount of mind-reading, in the sense that we can attune ourselves to the dispositions of other people. And the third is that we offer and receive correction in training or being trained in new practices.

Another obvious but frequently overlooked feature of the human condition is that we live with and talk to other people. A failure to see the relevance of this to philosophical theorizing may be the ur-error of those who reject neopragmatism. Without realizing that they are idealizing away the whole basis for a satisfactory explanation of the nature of human language, some philosophers seek to understand what members of a linguistic community mean by considering what a lone individual might mean. But one might just as well try to understand the flocking of birds by studying the behavior of a single starling. It is easy to see how this methodological error would leads to theoretical errors. In taking away other people, and with them any hope of a clear view of our linguistic practices, what else remains besides the referents of our words or thoughts to determine what we mean when we speak or think?

Of course it will not be possible to complete a first-order application of neopragmatism while relying on nothing but extremely general facts of nature that are always before our eyes. My own (2017) account of color relies on facts from color science that were hard won. And Thomasson's account of modals is informed by work in systemic functional linguistics: work that is far from everyday knowledge. What is important is that none of these starting points is at all puzzling from a *philosophical* point of view. It is by using only philosophically uncontroversial starting points that neopragmatists seek to put certain distinctively *philosophical* worries to rest: worries about the nature and existence of entities and properties have seemed hard to fit into a naturalistic world. That still leaves plenty of mysteries. It even leaves some mysteries that might be regarded as distinctively philosophical, such as why there is something rather than nothing, or how it is that there is such a thing as conscious phenomenal experience.

4. Genealogy

As I have been repeatedly stressing, neopragmatism focuses on our linguistic practices. It seeks to describe them accurately, of course, but it also seeks to explain how they came about. In this way neopragmatism is a bit like the theory of biological evolution. In neither the biological nor the linguistic case can we actually observe the processes of evolution, so we rely instead on a combination of plausibility, stray empirical clues, and so on, in hopes of coming up with a plausible genealogical story. Philip Pettit's Chapter 6 is perhaps the most explicit in taking the goal of his theorizing to be the production of a plausible genealogy. He uses this technique in order explain the acquired skill of following rules. This basic feature of our social lives is essential to the use of language, so the neopragmatist needs to explain it, and needs to do this in a way that does not appeal to any substantive notion of reference or representation. This is what Pettit does.

Pettit himself might not—currently—wish to be held up as one of the standard-bearers in neopragmatism's struggle against forms of realism that it does not find intelligible. But he still counts as a neopragmatist hero. Not only does he tackle the problem of rule-following using the neopragmatist technique of genealogy, but he is also explicit in stating that *all of the most basic properties* of which we are aware, and in terms of which we can think, correspond to 'patterns summoned to view under the pressure of practical concerns'. Moreover, he is equally explicit in saying that the 'pragmatist aspect of the model [does not] count against it', since 'it allows us still to embrace an important form of realism—pragmatic realism'.

One important difference between Pettit's genealogy and the genealogies offered by other neopragmatists is that Pettit is not explaining the emergence of a specifically *linguistic* practice. Rather, he is explaining how the practice of rule-following—of which language use is of course a prime example—might have emerged. Other instances of neopragmatist genealogies might have a more explicitly linguistic focus: they might seek to explain our practice of using words like 'true' and 'false', or normative language, or the language of necessity and possibility. The comparison with biological evolution is again useful here, in making it clear that there should be no presumption that the results of the process are optimal. Evolutionary explanations are constrained by the fact that each step in the process needs to have been made possible by some small mutation. And the survival of the resulting trait depends on the contingent circumstances that were prevalent during the crucial time period. Similarly, there may well be a vocabulary that would do a better job achieving the sorts of things that moral vocabulary achieves. But that is completely irrelevant to the truth of our moral claims.

The rules for use of moral vocabulary are what they are, and those rules determine what is relevant to determining whether a particular sort of act is morally acceptable or not. Of course, just as it is possible to engage in genetic engineering, it is possible to engage in conceptual engineering (see Burgess, Cappelen, and Plunkett 2019). But the results of such engineering will be *new* concepts. Neopragmatists, on the other hand, have primarily been interested—in the first instance—in *reverse-engineering* the concepts we *already* have (see Queloz 2021; Köhler 2022; and Thomasson 2022). That may be a prelude to offering some replacement concept, but the two projects should still be kept distinct.

Now, offering a genealogy is theorizing in a natural science, even if it is armchair theorizing. And it is perfectly reasonable to be suspicious of armchair science. But there are a pair of considerations that should mitigate such suspicion in the present case. The first is that the goal is, often, merely to tell a naturalistically plausible story: to say what *might* have happened, that would explain our ability to think and talk about normative properties, or counterfactuals, or whatever, without the involvement of any mysterious metaphysics. Proof-of-concept is often the only goal of a neopragmatist story. And if our explanations are plausible and appealing, then, at the very least, we've undermined—to some degree—the attraction of more metaphysically heavyweight accounts.

The second consideration that should help dispel worries about the neopragmatist's armchair linguistic anthropology is that the basic empirical starting points to which a neopragmatist appeals are meant to be completely uncontroversial—to the point, noted above, of being invisible to many theorists. Unlike, say, the view that every event has a cause, the neopragmatist's starting points concern the world of human beings, where we can be more sure of our premises. We can be quite sure, for example, that human beings can hurt or kill each other, that many of them have children, and that children learn a lot from their elders: such things are not a matter of the least philosophical or scientific controversy. It is also worth stressing that all the neopragmatist often needs are *general* truths. For example, when theorizing about the emergence of color language, we do not need it to be true that *everyone* would arrange color chips in the *very same* way. We only need that most people would arrange them in quite similar ways. That is enough for stories about language teaching and learning to get going, since we also have a story about how we come, sometimes, to treat outliers as *wrong*.

Let us return to the analogy between linguistic evolution and biological evolution once more. In the case of biology, before Darwin's theory was available, belief in a designer was quite a reasonable response to the existence of such exquisitely complex and well-calibrated bits of organic machinery as eyeballs and hearts. Now, however, most philosophers—including those who believe in God—take biological evolution to provide a correct account of the amazing features of animal bodies. But when it comes to our talk of things that are not the objects of empirical science, many philosophers still seem to be stuck halfway between pre- and post-Darwinian perspectives. What I mean by this is that, when it comes to such things as numbers, or values, or sensations, they recognize only three options: (1) to fit them into the world of fundamental physics by means of reductive accounts; or (2) to countenance a host of mysterious non-natural properties and entities; or (3) to deny facts that had seemed undeniable. The third of these is a natural stopping point as the difficulties with the first two become clearer. This is why, as Blackburn points out in his Chapter 11, 'an exalted view of [a] subject matter, be it a metaphysical view or an a prioristic view, readily tips into skepticism'.

5. Demystification

According to the neopragmatist, one of the three theoretical options above is in fact very close to correct. The correct view results from simply taking the word 'mysterious' out of option (2)—at least once one has provided a plausible explanation for the existence of a linguistic practice that makes use of the relevant terms.[3] The neopragmatist draws attention to the existence of perfectly non-mysterious naturalistic explanations of our talk of, say, numbers, and of our assessing some numerical claims as literally true, and others as literally false. Language use is, again, a naturalistic phenomenon: a bunch of hairless apes making and listening to noises as they go about various tasks. The idea that we need to go further than an explanation of the naturalistic phenomenon itself—to determine, for example, what the resulting talk is really *about*—is a mistake. The goal of demystification is manifest in the title of Thomasson's (2015) manifesto *Ontology Made Easy*. It is also the goal of the sort of genealogies described in the previous section. Matthieu Queloz explicitly links genealogy with demystification: 'an explanation of why certain needs would naturally lead us to go in for certain conceptual practices can also perform a *demystifying* role: it can dispel the air of mystery about the entities referred to in those practices' (2021: 28). Pettit, too, in his book-length genealogy of ethics, makes the same point. The goal of such a genealogy, he says, 'is to demystify our ethical concepts naturalistically by explaining how corresponding concepts might have emerged in a naturalistically unproblematic way' (2018: 54). And Shapiro, in earlier work, expresses the same point in connection with a tendency to see logical vocabulary as giving rise to mysteries:

> A central motivation for expressivism about logic has been to avoid a view of logical vocabulary as serving to map the layout of a special domain of facts whose bearing on discursive practice remains mysterious. Logical expressivists

---

[3] As Wittgenstein (1953: §195) writes in a closely related context, 'Really the only thing wrong with what you say is the expression "in a queer way"'.

adopt, instead, a pragmatist stance: they seek to explain the role of logical vocabulary in terms of discursive practice. 2018: 179

Of course metaphysical realists who plump for the second of the three options listed at the end of the last section will not be content with this explanation of the difference between their views and the neopragmatists'. They will want to say that their non-naturalist realism is quite a different animal from the view to which neopragmatism leads us—even if the neopragmatist lets us say all of the very same things. Some non-naturalist realists might even wish to disavow the use of the term 'mysterious' in characterizing their own views. Perhaps they will say that our everyday use of numbers and normative reasons and such things renders them unmysterious.[4] Still, I think it is up to such a theorist to clarify what it is they want that the neopragmatist fails to deliver.

6. Social Practices

Given the focus on *explaining* our linguistic practices, neopragmatist theorizing is almost always going to look to the development, over time, of those practices, rather than simply describing, in more static terms, what happens in isolated uses of a given vocabulary. As Amie Thomasson puts it in her Chapter 3, what we want 'is a good naturalistic story about [1] why such forms of vocabulary would have evolved as they did, and [2] why they would have stuck around in our language.'[5] The first of these naturalistic stories is essentially the sort of genealogy discussed in the previous section. It concerns processes that take place over evolutionary time. But the second sort of story includes an account of the transmission of linguistic practices from one generation to the next.[6] So it is no surprise that neopragmatists will also concern themselves with the processes by which neophytes first come to acquire competence in those practices. That is, they will take facts about language acquisition in children to be of relevance to their philosophical project. Pettit's contribution (Chapter 6) can be characterized this way. One of his central points is that correction by language teachers is essential to an appreciation, by language learners, that they are fallible. And appreciation of fallibility is essential to the practice of rule-following.

Attention to the processes of language acquisition is also very prominent in Thomasson's Chapter 3 on modals.[7] Drawing on the resources of systemic

---

[4] This seems close to the position of the so-called "relaxed realists," such as Scanlon (2014). Such theorists would, I suspect, reject the label "metaphysical realist," but would not want to endorse neopragmatism either. For an assessment of the comparison with mathematics, see McGrath (2014).
[5] My numbering.
[6] In Gert (2012), I call these 'the question of origins' and 'the question of inheritance'.
[7] For another instance of this sort of attention, see Gert (2002).

functional linguistics, as developed by Michael Halliday (2009), Thomasson takes into account the development of children's capacity to use modal language. She notes that when modal language first appears—in such locutions as 'I can eat candy before dinner'—it may serve a relatively limited set of functions. Later on, speakers acquire grammatically distinct ways of expressing what philosophers might have thought of as the same "modal fact": that I have permission to eat candy before dinner. But, Halliday argues, the new grammatical forms allow speakers to do more complex things with their utterances. As a result, Thomasson makes the insightful point that even neopragmatists should not take the question 'What is the function of modal discourse?' at face value. As formulated, the question contains the assumption—almost certainly false—that each "flavor" of modal discourse (deontic, alethic, epistemic...) serves a single unified function.

Thomasson's focus on language as a practice allows her to make a useful general point regarding certain arguments for—or against—the existence of traditionally philosophically troubling entities, such as possibilities. In particular, she argues, in many cases it is a fundamental error to approach ontological questions by appeal to the sort of abductive arguments that David Lewis (1986) offered in support of the existence of possible worlds. Inference to the best explanation, Thomasson argues, is simply out of place when it comes to theorizing about the existence of possibilities. Why? Because the function of modal discourse involving nominalizations of auxiliary verbs like 'can' and 'might'—that is, the function of nouns like 'permission', 'possibility', or 'chance'—is simply not to *explain* anything: it is to *do* various things, many of which are essentially social.

The emphasis on social practices is also salient in John Roberts's Chapter 5. Roberts offers us a neopragmatist take on what he calls 'the natural modals', which include causation, laws, counterfactuals, and dispositions. For Roberts, pride of place in explaining these modals goes to the notion of *basic responsibility*. This sort of responsibility is quite distinct from moral responsibility; one could be basically responsible for the car being parked in its current location even though—let us grant—that fact has no moral significance at all. Basic responsibility is to be understood in terms of the social practice of *holding responsible*—something that is, again, not to be understood in a moralized way. For Roberts, when we make causal claims, we are therefore engaging in a social practice that makes it clear who is to be, or who would be, held responsible for what. So, as in Thomasson's account, we are reversing a direction of explanation: rather than explaining the appropriateness of holding people responsible for an outcome by asking whether or not they caused it, Roberts is explaining the meaning of causal claims by reference to our practices of holding responsible. As I will explain in the next section, this reversal of the direction of explanation is characteristic of neopragmatist accounts, and is part of what contributes to their characteristic quietism about metaphysical questions.

7. Quietism

'Quietism', like 'neopragmatism', is a name for a family of perspectives on philosophical topics that have typically been the focus of debates between realists and non-realists. As Chirimuuta understands it, following Alexander Miller (2019), quietism is the denial 'that there can be such a thing as substantial metaphysical debate between realists and their non-realist opponents'. Neopragmatism entails quietism, since the neopragmatist provides an explanation of all the sorts of vocabulary with which such a realist would like to mark the difference between their realism and the neopragmatist's position. After all, the neopragmatist will say that it is *true* that murder-for-hire is wrong, that there are many modal *facts*, that we can have *beliefs* and indeed *knowledge* about numbers, and so on. Given this, neopragmatists will see difficulties for self-described realists who want to deny neopragmatism.[8]

A second way of understanding quietism is that it is a refusal to take up questions about the representational accuracy or adequacy of a linguistic framework as a whole—say, the framework of color talk, or number talk. The quietist is happy to answer questions about the existence of this or that color, or this or that number, using the linguistic frameworks that provide methods for answering them. And indeed they may well be happy to answer questions about the existence of colors or numbers in general—though they will think the answers to those questions are trivial and obvious: if there is an even prime number, then numbers exist. But to ask whether the frameworks of color language or number language are concerned with *real* things or not—where the italics are gesturing at something beyond the trivial—is to make the characteristic mistake of metaphysically minded philosophers. Quietism is a self-conscious commitment to avoiding this mistake.

One danger to guard against when discussing neopragmatism—whether to defend it or attack it in a non-question-begging way—is to yield to the temptation to depart from its quietism. In providing its explanations of our ways of speaking about numbers, or colors, or moral properties, or possibilities, the careful neopragmatist should take their job to be done when the philosophical itch that initially prompted metaphysical theorizing has faded. Internalizing the neopragmatist perspective should be like taking an antihistamine—providing immunity from whatever caused the itch in the first place—rather than like scratching, which ends up making matters worse. But, as we all know, the temptation to scratch can be hard to resist. And once you are itching, taking an antihistamine can seem to take too much time to provide relief. Finally—to stretch the analogy to its

---

[8] This difficulty is, in essence, what Jamie Dreier (2004) calls 'the problem of creeping minimalism'. It should be clear that it is only a problem for a certain kind of theorist.

breaking-point—for some people antihistamines produce an unpleasant feeling of disorientation, as if they had lost direct contact with reality.

Mazviita Chirimuuta, in her contribution to this volume (Chapter 4), criticizes my (2017) neopragmatist account of color as insufficiently quietist. She thinks— and she may be right—that I have been seduced by the picture of a mind-independent world that is at work in the hard sciences, but that should not be taken literally even there. She is certainly right that my position is that colors are mind-independent properties that explain our color experiences. I think she might also say that Davidson, as Verheggen and Myers present him, goes wrong in endorsing an externalism according to which it is informative to say that 'what is believed is determined, to a significant degree, by how things are'. On one natural reading, this claim goes against a view that Chirimuuta endorses— methodological non-realism—according to which theorists should avoid any appeal to the 'way the world is, independent of human minds and conceptions'. This methodological principle is very closely related to points made in section 3 above, on theoretical starting points.

Chirimuuta's complaint about metaphysically minded philosophers who reject neopragmatism is that they take scientific explanation to be the model for all philosophy. That seems right to me. But it is important to note the dual nature of the error Chirimuuta identifies: they take the notion of an explanatorily potent mind-independent world in a wrong way, *and* they apply it as a model in too many areas. So it is possible that I might escape Chirimuuta's criticism if I can show that my notion of an explanatorily potent mind-independent world is unobjectionable. As Chirimuuta notes, 'the logical empiricists before Hempel rejected the idea that science explains anything as being too metaphysically loaded'. But surely there is a sense in which science does explain things. Non-scientists look for scientific explanations of puzzling phenomena all the time, and sometimes they find them.

Given the availability of neopragmatist accounts of 'scientific explanation', perhaps my account of color does not in fact depart from metaphysical quietism. Still, Chirimutta's discussion undoubtedly shows that even if one does not actually succumb to the temptation to scratch at one's metaphysical itches, it is easy to appear to be doing so. In this connection, consider even Price, in his contribution to this volume (Chapter 2), when he writes that 'distinctions that other views take to be elements of temporal reality, such as a distinguished present moment, are better regarded in a neopragmatist spirit as manifestations of our own natural and practical perspective'. It might easily seem, to an itchy reader, that Price is *denying* that the present moment is an element of temporal reality, and denying a metaphysical claim is scratching an itch. In fact, and unsurprisingly, Price is not really scratching. This is apparent a moment later, when the focus is again on *how concepts are explained*, and not on whether or not they are concepts of elements of reality. Indeed, he explicitly advises us not to scratch toward the end of the chapter, writing that 'Neopragmatism does not tell us what our words say, but how our words are used'.

Lionel Shapiro, too, thinks many neopragmatists go wrong in a way that might also be regarded as itch-scratching. In his Chapter 10, he argues that neopragmatists should, but do not, 'apply to *propositional content* the same strategy of linguistic ascent they apply to *moral wrongness*' (my italics). That is, they should not attempt to say what propositional content *is*—not even in terms of psychological states. To take such a question seriously is to itch, and to give an answer is to scratch. Instead of doing either of these things, Shapiro argues that neopragmatists should focus on what we are doing in making a claim of the form 'the propositional content of *S* is *p*'. This question is similar to the parallel question as to what we are doing in making claim of the form '*S* is true'. Shapiro's deflationary strategy allows him to offer an ingenious new account of logical vocabulary that makes sense of what we are doing with logically complex sentences, and what we mean in saying that one sentence logically follows from another. And he offers us these things without requiring us to *identify* anything as *the content* of a sentence in such a way that the content of a logically complex sentence is a function of the content of its parts.

8. Conclusion

Neopragmatism, or something very much like it, is not an entirely new arrival on the philosophical scene. I think the later Wittgenstein could aptly be given this label. And the first edition of Price's book came out in 1988. Robert Brandom (1984, 1994) and Michael Williams (2006) have defended neopragmatist views. Simon Blackburn, though sometimes ambivalent, has been well aware of the position, both to defend it and to express worries about it, since the 1980s (Blackburn 1984). But in general, the neopragmatist position seems only to be visible to other philosophers when the issue between neopragmatists and their opponents is framed at the highest level of abstraction, as an account of how language works. When it comes to debates in metaethics, or in philosophy of mathematics, or time, or color, or art, a *general* representational realism becomes the only visible position, and the only representative of neopragmatism is its cousin, a local expressivism that is developed against such a representationalist background.

The point of the present collection is to bring neopragmatism to bear on more first-order issues. A handful of successes there would strengthen the case for the neopragmatist perspective as a *general* perspective, of course. But they would also show that there is a real choice to be made, before one even begins to investigate any philosophical issue. That is, the more instances there are of successful first-order neopragmatist theorizing, the less acceptable it should seem simply to take the representational perspective on language as the default—which, at present, it certainly is taken to be. In my view, if this were generally recognized, then a host of positions that currently are taken seriously would be very seriously threatened. For example, non-naturalist realism about normative properties is perfectly acceptable from a neopragmatist perspective, as are versions of non-naturalist realism about colors and numbers. Indeed, I think that it is only neopragmatism that can provide a successful grounding for such views. But there are theorists who put forward versions of non-naturalist realism about this or that, but who also would deny neopragmatism. I think that such theorists are pushed into these sorts of heroic views because they have a clear-sighted appreciation of the difficulties that naturalistic views would face, and also of the difficulties that one would face if one were pushed to deny that claims about these things are *really* true or false. If the representationalist view of language were not so standard, the natural move in the face of these difficulties would be toward neopragmatism.

Collecting together more "localized" applications of neopragmatism to first-order issues has another theoretical benefit, beyond simply strengthening the case for the more general view. Rather, a neopragmatist account of one first-order issue will almost certainly make use of some concepts that, though unexplored in that account, could (of course) be the target of a distinct neopragmatist account. Call the explicit target of a piece of first-order neopragmatist theorizing the *mentioned* concept, and the other concepts—the ones used in doing that theorizing—the *used* concepts. An interesting question then arises, as to whether an explicit neopragmatist account of a particular used concept dovetails with the account of the mentioned concept. For example, Verheggen and Meyers offer a Davidsonian version of neopragmatism that takes truth as one of the mentioned concepts. But their Chapter 8 makes significant use of the notion of causality in discussing the Davidsonian notion of triangulation, which is crucial to his account notion of truth. So the interesting question is whether a neopragmatist account of causation, such as the one that John Roberts provides, could be used to understand that notion as Verheggen and Myers employ it. Similarly, it is an interesting question whether the skill of rule-following for which Pettit provides a genealogy fits with other neopragmatist accounts that make use of the notion of a rule or a social practice. And, finally, virtually all neopragmatist accounts of anything make use of modal language. So it would be interesting to follow the trails that Thomasson begins to blaze in her Chapter 3, to see if they arrive at places that make sense of those uses.

The possibility of the sort of consilience just described gives neopragmatism significant theoretical resources. As Shapiro notes, citing Sellars' expansion of Lewis Carroll's list, we "talk of many things": not only cabbages and kings, but finger-snaps and forces. What Shapiro does not specifically draw attention to is that we often talk of these things at the very same time. That is, we combine number words with normative words and causal or explanatory words, and every other kind of word, all in the same conversation—often all in the same sentence. For the neopragmatist, this places constraints on the use-based accounts of the meaning of those words. We must be able to count not only eggs, but moments, transgressions, and shades of blue. We must be able to grant permissions to individuals and to groups, and we must be able to index them to times and places. These constraints are not to be regretted, however. They are clues that point us toward the ultimate goal of the neopragmatist: an account not only of this or that language game, but of the whole amusement park of human language. For now, and in lieu of a ticket to that philosophical nirvana, I invite you into the smaller arcade made up of the thirteen chapters that follow. Enjoy!

References

Blackburn, S. (1984). *Spreading the Word: Groundings in the Philosophy of Language*, Oxford: Clarendon Press.

Brandom, R. (1984). 'Reference explained away', *Journal of Philosophy* 81, 469–92.

Brandom, R. (1994). *Making It Explicit: Reasoning, Representing, and Discursive Commitment*, Cambridge, MA: Harvard University Press.

Burgess, A., Cappelen, H., and Plunkett, D. (eds.) (2019). *Conceptual Engineering and Conceptual Ethics*, New York: Oxford University Press.

Chirimuuta, M. (2017). *Outside Color: Perceptual Science and the Puzzle of Color in Philosophy*, Cambridge, MA: MIT Press.

Dreier, James (2004). 'Meta-ethics and the problem of creeping minimalism', *Philosophical Perspectives* 18, 23–44.

Gert, J. (2002). 'Expressivism and Language Learning', *Ethics* 112, 292–312.

Gert, J. (2012). *Normative Bedrock: Response-Dependence, Rationality and Reasons*, Oxford: Oxford University Press.

Gert, J. (2017). *Primitive Colors: A Case Study in Neopragmatist Metaphysics and Philosophy of Perception*, Oxford: Oxford University Press.

Halliday, M. (2009). *The Essential Halliday*, ed. J. Webster, London: Continuum.

James, W. (1907). *Pragmatism: A New Name for Some Old Ways of Thinking*, London: Longmans, Green, and Company.

Köhler, S. (2022). 'What is (neo-) pragmatists' function?', *Australasian Journal of Philosophy* 1–17. DOI: 10.1080/00048402.2022.2034904.

Kraut, R. (1990). 'Varieties of pragmatism', *Mind* 99, 157–83.

Lewis, D. (1986). *On the Plurality of Worlds*, Oxford: Blackwell.

McGrath, S. (2014). 'Relax? Don't do it! Why moral realism won't come cheap', in R. Shafer-Landau (ed.), *Oxford Studies in Metaethics*, Vol. 9, Oxford: Oxford University Press, 186–214.

Miller, A. (2019). 'Realism', *The Stanford Encyclopedia of Philosophy*, <https://plato.stanford.edu/archives/win2019/entries/realism/>.

Pettit, P. (2018). *The Birth of Ethics: Reconstructing the Role and Nature of Morality*, New York: Oxford University Press.

Price, H. (2004). 'Immodesty without mirrors—making sense of Wittgenstein's linguistic pluralism', in M. Kölbel and B. Weiss (eds.), *Wittgenstein's Lasting Significance*, London: Routledge.

Price, H. (forthcoming). *Facts and the Function of Truth: New Expanded Edition*, Oxford: Oxford University Press.

Queloz, M. (2021). *The Practical Origins of Ideas: Genealogy as Conceptual Reverse-Engineering*, Oxford: Oxford University Press.

Scanlon, T. M. (2014). *Being Realistic about Reasons*, Oxford: Oxford University Press.

Shapiro, L. (2018). 'Logical expressivism and logical relations', in O. Beran, V. Kolman, and L. Koreň (eds.), *From Rules to Meaning: New Essays on Inferentialism*, New York: Routledge, 179–95.

Thomasson, A. (2015). *Ontology Made Easy*, New York: Oxford University Press.

Thomasson, A. (2022). 'How should we think about linguistic function?', *Inquiry* 1–32. DOI: 10.1080/0020174X.2022.2074886.

Williams, M. (2006). 'Naturalism, realism and pragmatism', *Philosophic Exchange: Annual Proceedings* 37, 56–71.

Wittgenstein, L. (1953). *Philosophical Investigations*, trans. G. E. M. Anscombe, New York: Macmillan.

PART II
TIME, CAUSES, AND SCIENCE

2
Time for Pragmatism

Huw Price

> Ours is the eyes' deceit
> Of men whose flying feet
> Lead through some landscape low;
> We pass, and think we see
> The earth's fixed surface flee:—
> Alas, Time stays,—we go!
>   Dobson, 'The Paradox of Time' (1886)

1. Introduction

In this chapter, I explore the connections between neopragmatism and time. These connections run in both directions, but in keeping with the theme of this volume, I'll frame the central issue from the neopragmatist side. How is time, and its philosophy, relevant to the concerns of neopragmatism? I'll offer an answer in six steps:

1. Temporal indexicals
2. Further features of 'manifest time'
3. The 'temporal modalities': probability and causation
4. 'Future-facing' properties and concepts in general
5. The trans-temporal character of language
6. Predictive processing and the future-facing character of mind.

There will be some overlaps, and also a natural progression. Treated as a stairway, these steps lead in the direction of generality. One of my goals is to show that approaching neopragmatism from this direction reveals senses in which it is necessarily a *global* viewpoint, applicable throughout language and thought.

In this respect, I will thus be defending what I have elsewhere called a global pragmatism, or global expressivism. My central message is that the human temporal perspective turns out to be deeply implicated not merely in our temporal notions themselves, but in many other conceptual categories—arguably, in fact, in all of them, and in the nature of language and thought. In this way, reflection on our own temporal character vindicates James' famous slogan for a global pragmatism: 'The trail of the human serpent is thus over everything' (James 1907: 64).

The chapter goes like this. In the next section (section 2) I'll explain what I take neopragmatism to be. In section 3, I turn to indexicals, which here do double duty. As a category as a whole, they serve to illustrate what I mean by neopragmatism; while in their temporal manifestation, in tensed language, they take us on the first step of our main project. They introduce the idea that distinctions that other views take to be elements of temporal reality, such as a distinguished present moment, are better regarded in a neopragmatist spirit as manifestations of our own natural and practical perspective.

The second step, in section 4, then follows very naturally. It simply broadens the message to some other aspects of what rival approaches see as elements of the nature of time, to be investigated by physics or metaphysics. Broadening again, the third step (section 5) applies a similar lesson to a different set of traditional concerns of metaphysics, that of modal notions such as chance and causation. The neopragmatist message here is that the temporal character (among other things) of these notions is best explained, not as some sort of primitive or even derivative feature of things in the world, independent of the perspective of us users of the concepts in question, but as a reflection of our own epistemic, agential, and (especially) temporal viewpoint.

This third step is still 'local', in the sense that it concerns only a comparatively small class of categories, the temporal modalities. In section 6 the fourth step, by contrast, takes the underlying insights about the human temporal perspective and applies them to a much broader class of properties and concepts—arguably, as we'll see to all of them. It links what I'll characterize as a Humean pragmatism about dispositions with a Sellarsian and Brandomian inferentialism about concepts in general. I don't mean that it treats these as the same thing, but merely that they belong in a similar place when our interest is in highlighting the role that our own temporal character plays in both.

The fifth step (section 7) makes a point about the temporal character of language—not a deep point, as we'll see, though one linked to issues about rule-following that I have long taken to be central to the case for global neopragmatism. The sixth step (section 8) turns from language to thought. Sketching recent ideas from the literature on 'predictive processing', I point out that this approach puts the human temporal situation even more deeply at the core of an understanding of mind and language. Citing recent work by Daniel Williams and Daniel Dennett, I note that this, too, seems to have pragmatist implications.

Dennett's remarks will lead us back to Hume, and in section 9 I discuss the relationship between global neopragmatism, Humean naturalism, and natural science itself. I close (section 10) by identifying three demarcation issues, whose clear delineation will I hope be helpful in guiding future work on these topics.

2. Pragmatism, Neopragmatism, and Expressivism

2.1 Terminological Issues

As often happens in philosophy, there are both too few and too many terms in use in this area, and clarification is needed before we begin. On the side of scarcity, there is a variety of views calling themselves pragmatism, not necessarily compatible with one another. My own favorite is what in recent years I've been calling Cambridge Pragmatism. Here 'Cambridge' refers not to the intellectual home of the great American Pragmatists, such as James, Peirce, and Dewey, but to the *ur*-Cambridge, seat of a one-hundred-year pragmatist lineage I take to stretch from Ramsey and Wittgenstein to Bernard Williams, Edward Craig, Simon Blackburn, and myself. In two recent books, Cheryl Misak (2016, 2020) has shown us how much Ramsey and hence Wittgenstein owed to the original Pragmatists, especially Peirce.

Ramsey is famous as a pioneer of subjectivism about probability—the view that the philosophy of probability begins with the psychology of decision. Less well known is his analogous view about causation, sketched in one of his last pieces (1929a; hereafter GPC). In 1913, Bertrand Russell had dismissed causation altogether. Physics, he argued, shows us a time-symmetric world of bare associations. Why then do we think that we can affect the future but not the past? Russell attributes it to 'the accident that memory works backward and not forward' (1913: 20).

In GPC, Ramsey doesn't mention Russell,[1] but his investigation of lawlike generalizations leads him into similar territory. He agrees with Russell that we shouldn't count causes among the furniture of the world. As with probability, the interesting questions are matters of 'psychology', as Ramsey says, not metaphysics. The interesting question isn't what causation is, but why we humans come to think and talk in causal terms.

This shift from metaphysical questions, on the one hand, to psychological or linguistic questions, on the other, is what I take to be the distinctive Cambridge pragmatist move. We find the same orientation in many later Cambridge philosophers, many of whom wouldn't regard themselves as pragmatists. Examples include D. H. Mellor's work on tense and chance, Craig's account of knowledge, and Blackburn's views on morality, modality, and other topics. (We find the same orientation in other places, too, of course—I was being chauvinistic in claiming it as *Cambridge* Pragmatism!)

I suggested that 'pragmatism' is a case of terminological scarcity—one term being conscripted for too many jobs. I have been explaining my use of 'Cambridge

---

[1] He seems to have taken the issue from Eddington (1928); see further below.

Pragmatism' as a way of distinguishing the variety that has interested me from other claimants. I see *neopragmatism* as a welcome (and, happily, less chauvinistic) way of doing the same thing. I propose to use it for the same view.

There is also a problem of terminological excess, to which I'm aware that I have contributed. As noted above, I have also referred to my view as a form of global *expressivism,* and used this label interchangeably with global pragmatism. My justification was that I wanted to mark strong continuities with not one but two existing uses of 'expressivism', by writers such as Blackburn and Gibbard on one side, and Brandom on the other. One of my interests was to connect these major philosophical projects, which had tended to proceed independently of one another, despite obvious affinities (see, e.g., Price 2011c).

Like 'pragmatism', though to a lesser extent, the term 'expressivism' also suffers from the 'too many uses' problem. Many writers think of expressivism simply as a view in metaethics, for example. Again, my use has been the broad one, a fact which goes some way to explaining both how I equate it with a kind of pragmatism, and how I can take it to be a global view.

2.2 The Expressivist Recipe

In recent work (Price 2022b, 2022d, forthcoming), I have been attempting to distinguish all the major components in contemporary expressivism, as I use the term. I characterize expressivism as a recipe with about five main ingredients. The first ingredient is what I term a *use-first* approach to meaning. Expressivism focusses on how words are *used,* rather than what they are *about.* I have a rather broader conception of the factors the relevant accounts of use are allowed to involve than many expressivists. I think it is unhelpful to restrict them to psychological states, as opposed to more general aspects of speakers' circumstances.[2]

The second ingredient is a program that presents itself as an alternative to metaphysics, or ontology. It may be motivated in the same way by so-called 'placement problems'—that is, in their typical form, questions about the 'place' of some seemingly problematic subject matter (e.g., morality, modality, meaning, or the mental), in the kind of world revealed to us by science. But expressivism combines an insistence that these be regarded as *primarily* linguistic or psychological

---

[2] This means that the term 'expressivism' is in some ways unhappy, a point in favor of 'neopragmatism'. See Price (forthcoming: ch. 11) for discussion of this issue, as well as of different conceptions of the proper form of an account of meaning in terms of use—I contrast the approaches of Schroeder (2015) and Williams (2010, 2013), for example. Schroeder thinks of the relevant use conditions simply as assertibility conditions, whereas Williams' 'explanations of meaning in terms of use' (EMUs) offer something considerably broader. Among other things, they involve 'downstream' language-exit rules, as well as 'upstream' language-entry rules—certainly an advantage in the present context, where our eye is on the future-facing character of language and thought.

issues—Why do we talk or think this way?—with a renunciation of the 'representational' moves that lead from there back to metaphysics (e.g., that of seeking 'referents', or 'truthmakers', in some non-deflationary sense).

The third ingredient—closely linked to the first and second—is an explanatory program. It aims, roughly speaking, to account for the *existence* and *practical relevance* of the vocabularies in question; typically the former in terms of the latter, in some way. Why do creatures like us employ these terms and concepts? And why do these terms and concepts exhibit distinctive links to various aspects of our practical lives? I have called the latter question the *Practical Relevance Constraint* (Price and Weslake 2010; Price forthcoming: ch. 11), and argued that it is often a great advantage of neopragmatism over various rivals that it meets it so easily—much more on this below.

The fourth ingredient, closely linked again to the third and first, rests on identification of *features of speakers*—typically features of practical or 'pragmatic' significance—that play characteristic roles in expressivist accounts of particular vocabularies. I have called these features the *pragmatic grounds* of the vocabularies in question (Price 2019a: 146).

The fifth ingredient, finally, is a kind of perspectivalism, with the pragmatic grounds of a vocabulary playing the role of the perspective from which the users of that vocabulary speak. I link this ingredient to the Copernican metaphor familiar from Kant, noting how well it characterizes the sense in which expressivism provides an alternative to metaphysics. What we took to be in need of *metaphysical* investigation is instead explained as a perspectival matter, in which features of our own situation carry the main explanatory burden.

2.3 Neopragmatism as Subject Naturalism

As I say, these are what I take to be the major ingredients of expressivism, as I use the term, or equivalently of neopragmatism. I want to emphasize that I take it to be a thoroughly naturalistic program, although not in the sense that many self-styled philosophical naturalists have in mind. In Price (2004a), I draw a distinction between two kinds of naturalism—roughly, two views of how philosophy properly defers to science. The first kind, the view often called simply 'naturalism', is the view, as I put it, 'that in some important sense, all there is is the world studied by science', or that 'all genuine knowledge is scientific knowledge' (2004a: 185). I call this view *object naturalism*. It implies that in so far as it is concerned with ontology, or the quest for knowledge, philosophy must in some sense be under the umbrella of natural science, for there is nowhere else to stand—no other object of inquiry.

I contrast object naturalism with a second view:

> According to this second view, philosophy needs to begin with what science tells us *about ourselves*. Science tells us that we humans are natural creatures, and if the claims and ambitions of philosophy conflict with this view, then philosophy needs to give way. This is naturalism in the sense of Hume, then, and arguably Nietzsche. I'll call it *subject naturalism*. 2004a: 186

I take neopragmatism to be a subject naturalist project. It is continuous with natural science in the sense that it is asking first-order scientific questions about natural creatures (mostly but not exclusively ourselves). Typically, for example, it is seeking an understanding of some aspect of the psychology or linguistic behavior of creatures like us.

Next, a word about the relation between neopragmatism and Sellars' famous distinction between the *manifest image* and the *scientific image* (Sellars 1962). A neopragmatist about a given topic—say, color—is among other things someone who is inclined to regard the subject matter in question as part of the manifest image, not the scientific image. But it goes beyond this in one important respect, in thinking that the interesting questions in such cases are not metaphysical questions—e.g., what is color?—but what Ramsey called the psychological questions: why do creatures like us see, conceptualize, and describe the world in these terms? By contrast, it is easy to find examples of philosophers who agree that color is part of the manifest image—a secondary quality, rather than a primary quality, to use an older terminology—but who nevertheless see the job of philosophy as being to say what color is. Their answer might be that it is a 'response-dependent' property, to use some influential terminology from the 1990s (see, e.g., Haldane and Wright 1993). Some writers (e.g., Johnston 1993) who put their view in these terms think of it as a kind of pragmatism, but as I noted in Price (1993), it differs from neopragmatism in trying to answer a different question.

A crucial issue for neopragmatists concerns the scope of the program. Is neopragmatism a local view, applicable to some vocabularies but not to others? Or is it, as I have argued, a global view? One of my goals in this chapter is to explain why thinking about time leads a pragmatist to the global conclusion. This is not the only path to the global conclusion, but it is an interesting one. By thinking about the respects in which James' human serpent is a temporal serpent—among other things, a structured, extended entity in spacetime, interacting with its surroundings—we can come to see why there is no part of our language and world view that escapes the mark of the snake.

Is there now a tension between James and Sellars? In other words, can global neopragmatists still represent their program in terms of Sellars' distinction between manifest and scientific images, or does that distinction depend on a pragmatism that shuts up shop when it gets to the investigation of science itself? This is a very nice question, to which I'll return briefly toward the end of the chapter (in section 9). For now, let's take the first step on our stairway. It concerns 'now' itself, and its linguistic cousins.

3. Temporal Indexicals

> Indexicals are linguistic expressions whose reference shifts from utterance to utterance. 'I', 'here', 'now', 'he', 'she', and 'that' are classic examples of indexicals. Two people who utter a sentence containing an indexical may say different things, even if the sentence itself has a single linguistic meaning. For instance, the sentence 'I am female' has a single linguistic meaning, but Fred and Wilma say different things when they utter it, as shown by the fact that Fred says something false, while Wilma says something true.　Braun (2017)

As these examples demonstrate, indexicality is far from exclusively a temporal matter. Within the temporal domain, it is involved in a wide range of expressions in addition to 'now' and its synonyms: terms such as 'yesterday', 'today', and 'tomorrow', for example, as well as the phenomenon of tense. All these expressions enable us to indicate the temporal location of something with respect to our own temporal location at the time of speaking. Other kinds of indexicals do a similar thing with respect to space, or personal identity.

What do indexicals have to do with neopragmatism? It is easy to answer this question with the recipe of the previous section in front of us. Imagine a different view, holding that when we talk of the *here* or the *now,* we are talking about distinctive features of the world, features whose nature a metaphysician might properly set out to investigate. That might seem a highly implausible view in the case of 'here', but it is familiar in the temporal case—as is an alternative, one that often compares 'now' with 'here', arguing that they should be understood in the same way. With the recipe in front of us, it is easy to see that this alternative counts as a case of neopragmatism. Here is Brandom, calling attention to most of the ingredients we need.

> As a somewhat fanciful example, consider someone who is puzzled about what is represented by indexical...vocabulary. Are there indexical...*facts,* over and above those expressible in nonindexical terms? If not, why aren't indexical terms freely interchangeable with nonindexical ones (as [Perry's] essential indexical...shows they are not)? If so, what are these peculiar items?
>
> The fact that we can formulate rules sufficient to specify the correct use of indexicals (at least for ordinary, spatiotemporally located speakers)...entirely in nonindexical terms should be enough to dispel any concern that there is something spooky or mysterious going on...If the practices themselves are all in order from a naturalistic point of view, any difficulties we might have in specifying the kind of things those engaged in the practices are talking about, how they are representing the world as being, ought to be laid at the feet of a Procrustean semantic paradigm that insists that the only model for understanding meaningfulness is a representational one.　Brandom (2013: 86–7)

As the work of Anscombe (1975), Perry (1979), Lewis (1979), Ismael (2007), and others has shown us, indexical beliefs have a distinctive *pragmatic* role. They connect to our practical life in particular ways, ways that any proposal to introduce 'indexical facts' would be obliged to explain. If there is a real 'now', for example, as some philosophers of time maintain, why should beliefs about it be relevant to action? Indeed, how would we *know* when the relevant fact obtained—'How do we know it is now now?', as Braddon-Mitchell (2004) says.

These questions provide examples of what our third ingredient above termed the *Practical Relevance Constraint*—in my view, a very general and powerful piece of the neopragmatist machinery. The neopragmatist avoids such problems by *beginning* with the feature of speakers of immediate practical relevance, and building out from there. We will meet several more examples below. For *now*, as it were, the lesson we need is simply that a distinguished present moment is a central element in the manifest image of time, paradigmatically amenable to the neopragmatist machinery. That's our first step.

4. What Makes Time Special?

Our second step generalizes the issue about time to which this familiar account of 'now' provides one part of the answer. Craig Callender (2017) puts the issue like this: what makes time *special*? In particular, what distinguishes time from space?[3] Posed this way, the question certainly doesn't presuppose a neopragmatist answer, but it turns out to invite one. Much of what belongs to our ordinary view of time turns out to be best thought of as belonging to the manifest image of time, interpreted in neopragmatist terms.

What are the features of time in question? We have just observed that many writers have thought that one key distinction between time and space is that the world we inhabit requires a distinguished present moment, but no comparable distinguished place—an objective *now*, but not an objective *here*. This view is typically linked to the claim that time is also distinguished in several other ways. It is said that time flows, or passes, in a way not true of space; that time has an intrinsic direction, again in a way not true of space; and the past and future are importantly different, the one fixed and the other open. These claims are not always well distinguished from each other, though in principle they are independent, to a large degree.

As a point of entry to these issues, let's begin with the passage from Arthur Eddington's *The Nature of the Physical World* in which the term 'Time's Arrow' makes its first appearance:

---

[3] My usage here is slightly different from Callender's. He asks the question 'What makes time special?' after he has set aside what he takes to belong merely to the manifest image of time.

Time's Arrow. The great thing about time is that it goes on. But this is an aspect of it which the physicist sometimes seems inclined to neglect. In the four-dimensional world...the events past and future lie spread out before us as in a map. The events are there in their proper spatial and temporal relation; but there is no indication that they undergo what has been described as "the formality of taking place" and the question of their doing or undoing does not arise. We see in the map the path from past to future or from future to past; but there is no signboard to indicate that it is a one-way street. Something must be added to the geometrical conceptions comprised in Minkowski's world before it becomes a complete picture of the world as we know it.   Eddington (1928: 34)

Here already we can distinguish two kinds of elements, both of which Eddington takes to be missing from Minkowski's four-dimensional picture of the world, in which time and space are treated in much the same way. One is what Eddington elsewhere calls 'happening', or 'becoming', or the 'dynamic' quality of time—the fact that time 'goes on', as he puts it in this passage. Time seems *in flux*, to use a much older term, in a way in which space is not, and Eddington is objecting that this aspect of time is missing from the four-dimensional picture.

The second missing ingredient—which Eddington himself doesn't distinguish from the dynamic aspect of time, but which is usefully treated as a distinct idea—is something to give a *direction* to the time axis in Minkowski's picture; something to distinguish past from future, as we might say.

The neopragmatist strategy is to explain all of these things as aspects of the manifest image, rather than the scientific image. This is most contentious, I think, in the case of the direction of time. In this case there is a strong tradition of writers who regard themselves as robustly scientific about time, who don't mess with presentness or passage, but believe in direction (Earman 1974 is an example). But I think even these folk would allow that some aspects of the intuitive distinction between past and future, such as the fixed past/open future contrast, is psychological in origin.

My own view is that direction, too, is a thoroughly perspectival matter. As Boltzmann put it in the 1890s: 'For the universe, the two directions of time are indistinguishable, just as in space there is no up and down' (Boltzmann 1964: 447). Boltzmann was merely entertaining the possibility at that point, noting that it would be a natural thing to say in the context of a particular cosmological proposal, one he credits to his assistant, a Dr Schuetz.[4] However, the idea doesn't

---

[4] Boltzmann is considering the question of why the entropy of our universe in the present era is so much lower than its maximum possible value (a circumstance that his own work can be argued to render extremely improbable). The suggestion he attributes to Schuetz is that if the universe is infinitely old, such low entropy phases are bound to occur occasionally, simply by chance. If we add that life such as ourselves could only exist in such a phase, there is no longer any mystery in what we observe. Boltzmann notes that such a random 'dip' in the entropy curve slopes upwards in both

seem to have been proposed explicitly before this, which makes the remark a significant step in intellectual history—'one of the keenest insights into the problem of time', as Reichenbach (1956: 128) put it—and all the more so, of course, if the proposal turns out to be correct, as I think it does.

Indeed, in my view (see Price 2011b), it is very hard to make sense of *what it would be* for time to have an intrinsic direction, at least if we want to have some prospect of connecting that fact to our ordinary dealings with time, in physics and in ordinary life. In comparison, it is very easy to explain why temporally oriented creatures such as ourselves—all of us, as it happens, sharing the same orientation—should come to think of this as an entirely objective feature of their environment, just as our ancestors did with up and down.[5] Recognition of the perspectival element has its usual Copernican advantages, avoiding a need for structure *in the world* by explaining the appearance of structure as an artifact of our viewpoint.

As I say, this view about the direction of time is controversial.[6] Not all writers on the topic, by any means, agree with me about the bleak prospects for non-perspectival accounts. I mention the case here with two lessons in mind. First, I think it provides a very clear idea of the *potential* of the general recipe—in particular, its potential for avoiding difficulties that arise when issues are addressed in other keys. Second, it illustrates some significant points about the contemporary philosophical landscape. In a case like this, part of the argument for neopragmatism rests on criticism of rival approaches. These rival approaches are typically defended by writers who, as specialists in fields such as metaphysics and the

---

directions, away from the lowest point. If we add finally that our sense of past and future is linked to this entropy gradient, then we have Boltzmann's conclusion. Creatures on the two sides of the 'dip' will have different views about which direction is past and which future, with no objective sense in which one side gets it right and the other wrong. This is the analogy with up and down, assessed on opposite sides of the planet. (For details, see Price 1996: ch. 2, 2010, 2011b, and Barbour 2020a, 2020b.)

[5] I'll say some more below (section 9) about what our own temporal orientation involves. For the moment, let me emphasize that I am not suggesting that there is no objective temporal asymmetry at all, independently of our own temporal characteristics. On the contrary, there is at least the thermodynamic asymmetry that Boltzmann himself had in mind (cf. fn. 4). But important as this may be in explaining the existence of creatures such as ourselves, it turns out to be a poor candidate to provide a fundamental direction of time. One of the difficulties, as the Boltzmann-Schuetz hypothesis already recognizes, is that like the gravitational field at a point on the Earth's surface, this asymmetry may turn out to be a local rather than a universal feature of our universe. (Again, for details, see Price, 1996: ch. 2, 2011b.)

[6] Though not as controversial as it may seem at first sight. Some writers who take there to be a direction of time are merely following Reichenbach (1956), in taking the phrase to refer to the temporal asymmetry described by the second law of thermodynamics (see, e.g., Rovelli 2022a). This is simply a terminological disagreement. These writers agree with me, and with Reichenbach himself, that there is no intrinsic direction *to time itself*. As I put it in Price (1996), this view holds that the *contents* of the universe are temporally asymmetric (at least in our region), but not that there is any asymmetry to the container itself, in its temporal aspect. Concerning the choice of terminology, I follow Earman (1974), in thinking that anything worth calling a direction *of time* should be universal. Once again, there is no guarantee that this is true of the thermodynamic asymmetry, as the Boltzmann-Schuetz hypothesis recognizes (cf. fn. 5).

philosophy of physics, are likely to have little familiarity with the ins and outs of neopragmatism. For their part, most neopragmatists will have little sense of the issues within metaphysics and philosophy of physics, and hence will be poorly placed to evaluate the potential advantages of their own methodology in those fields. So the two sides tend to fail to engage—thereby missing, I think, important insights from both points of view.

Indeed, describing it as a matter of just two sides may be understating the degree of difficulty. From a neopragmatist perspective what needs to be explained is in large part the *psychology* of time. But here both sides in the philosophical debate tend to be underequipped, to say the least. (There are some honorable exceptions, including Callender 2017.)

One writer who does seem to have appreciated the sense in which these become psychological questions is Ramsey. In the remarkable piece I mentioned earlier, one of the questions Ramsey touches on is the difference between past and future:[7]

> It is, it seems, a fundamental fact that the future is due to the present...but the past is not. What does this mean? It is not clear and, if we try to make it clear, it turns into nonsense or a definition.   129a: 145

Ramsey soon steers this toward a psychological question:

> What then do we **believe** about the future that we do not believe about the past; the past, we think, is settled; if this means more than that it is past, it might mean that it is settled *for us*,...that any present event is irrelevant to the probability for us of any past event. But that is plainly untrue. What is true is this, that any possible present volition of ours is (for us) irrelevant to any past event. To another (or to ourselves in the future) it can serve as a sign of the past, but to us now what we do affects only the probability of the future.
>
> This seems to me the root of the matter; that I cannot affect the past, is a way of saying something quite clearly true about my degrees of belief.
>
> 1929a: 146; bold emphasis added

As we shall see, Ramsey's point turns on the fact that for the agent herself, whether she acts a certain way is not an epistemic matter—'not...an intellectual problem'

---

[7] As I note in Price (2022a), Ramsey may have got this puzzle from Eddington. Eddington's book, *The Nature of the Physical World*, was published in November 1928, and was soon a bestseller, reprinted several times by the summer of 1929. Ramsey certainly read it; his notes survive among his papers. Eddington (1928: ch. 14) discusses causation and the apparent difference between past and future, including the puzzle of why causation seems to work only in one direction (even though the underlying physics is time-symmetric). Eddington doesn't have a solution, but he ventures two possible approaches. Ramsey's phrasing in GPC suggests that he is briskly dismissing one, while putting his finger on the crucial element needed for the other. See Price (2022c) for further details.

(1929a: 142). 'In a sense', as Ramsey puts it, 'my present action is an ultimate and the only ultimate contingency' (1929a: 146).

For the present, what matters is the stance that Ramsey's view embodies. He is explaining what we take to be a fundamental difference between past and future as a manifestation of the epistemic perspective of a deliberating agent. It is a classic example of a neopragmatist alternative to what other approaches treat as a metaphysical issue. Moreover, it occurs in passages in which Ramsey is explicit in adopting the same stance with respect to causality. This brings us to our next step.

5. The Temporal Modalities: Probability and Causation

At the previous step we were concerned with neopragmatist approaches to the manifest image of time. We now turn to what we might call the temporal or time-laden modal categories of causation and probability. The neopragmatist again treats these, as Ramsey says, as questions for psychology. The project is to explain them as useful cognitive architecture for non-omniscient agents, burdened with a concern for their own future.

Ramsey's neopragmatism about both probability and causation amounts to the view that a philosophical account of either topic needs to begin with the psychology of choice. The difference between probability and causation turns mainly on the fact that it makes a difference to a decision maker whether she takes herself to be able to act in the world, able to fix the value of certain variables at will. That's where causal thinking comes in. As Ramsey puts it, 'from the situation when we are deliberating seems to me to arise the general difference of cause and effect' (1929a: 146).

5.1 Practical Relevance for Probability

Ramsey is well known as one of the founders of so-called *subjectivism* about probability. We need to be careful with this term. Subjectivism about probability is sometimes characterized as the view that probabilities are degrees of belief. That should be seen as a mistake, in my view, by neopragmatist lights. Neopragmatism isn't interested in the *metaphysical* question as to what probabilities *are,* but in the *psychological* question as to why creatures like us think in those terms—and that's where the degrees of belief come in. Of course, this is only the beginning, and the neopragmatist's goal should be to elaborate from this starting point into a theory for why we model the world in terms of probabilities, or chances, which look for many purposes like 'regular' objective features of reality.

When the view is developed in this way the subjectivism becomes more subtle. We can no longer say simply that probabilistic claims are *about* our degrees of belief. A good way to keep the central issue in view is to focus on the Practical

Relevance Constraint. As in other cases, we can highlight the issue by asking the *Euthyphro* question. Is it the fact that there is a high probability, or chance, that *P* that makes it reasonable to hold a high degree of confidence that *P* (and act accordingly, in our choice of betting odds)? Or is the meaning of the claim that there is a high probability that *P* somehow *constituted by,* or *grounded in,* the psychological state of being confident that *P*. These options may reasonably be termed *objectivism* and *subjectivism,* respectively.

I have phrased the Practical Relevance issue this way to connect to some important discussions in the metaphysics of chance and probability, where writers sympathetic to objectivism have recognized the importance of subjectivist insights. One such writer is D. H. Mellor (1971), who defends a version of what we are here calling the subjectivist option, calling it 'personalism'. Following (Kneale 1949), Mellor insists that personalism is compatible with the view that chances are real and objective—it is just that in saying what they are, we need to begin with rational degrees of belief, or credences.

> [C]an we not analyse full belief that the chance of heads on a coin toss is 1/2 without reference to some supposedly corresponding partial belief that the coin will land heads? The reason for denying this is the fact to which Kneale himself draws attention (p. 18) 'that knowledge of probability relations is important chiefly for its bearing on action'. It follows as Kneale says (p. 20) that 'no analysis of the probability relation can be accepted as adequate...unless it enables us to understand why it is rational to take as a basis for action a proposition which stands in that relation to the evidence at our disposal'. Similarly with chance. It must follow from our account that the greater the known chance of an event the more reasonable it is to act as if it will occur. This concept of a quantitative tendency to action is just that of partial belief [i.e., credence] as it has been developed by the personalists. It is thus available to provide in our account of chance that necessary connection with action on which Kneale rightly insists. *A great difficulty facing other objective accounts of chance, notably the frequency theories, has been to build such a connection subsequently on their entirely impersonal foundations.* Mellor (1971: 3; emphasis added)[8]

---

[8] In later work, Mellor makes other moves that seem to me to suggest neopragmatism about chance. He says that the reason 'it has proved so hard to frame an acceptable account of objective chance' is that 'people naturally feel that, if chance is objective, it must make true beliefs with some characteristic content,...supposing that the only objectifying job facts can have to do is making beliefs true' (Mellor 1982: 247). As I noted in Price (1981: 5/17–18, 6/15), this is strikingly similar to Toulmin's view that 'there is no special "thing" which all probability-statements must be about, simply in virtue of the fact that they *are* "probability-statements"' (Toulmin 1950: 50). And Toulmin links it explicitly to what would once have been called a non-cognitivist account of probability judgments. In Toulmin's view, 'to say "Probably p" is to assert, guardedly and/or...with reservations, that *p*' (1950: 61). In Price (1981)—my Cambridge PhD thesis, written under Mellor's supervision—I was citing Toulmin as an ally for my own proposed 'non-truthconditional' account of probability claims (i.e., what I would now call a neopragmatist or expressivist account).

Kneale's point, too, can be traced back to Ramsey. As Misak has recently pointed out, one of Ramsey's objections to Keynes' theory of probability as a logical relation is that such relations 'would stand in such strange correspondence with degrees of belief' (Misak 2020: 144; quoting from notes by Ramsey), and hence with betting behavior. In other words, Keynes leaves it mysterious why probability should matter in the way that it obviously does.

Lewis (1980) also defends a form of subjectivism. Like Mellor, he takes chance to be objective, but takes it to be definitive of chance that it plays a distinctive role in guiding credence. As he says, he is 'led to wonder whether anyone but a subjectivist is in a position to understand objective chance!' (1980: 84). Returning to this theme in later work, he criticizes rival approaches on the grounds that they pay insufficient attention to this connection between chance and credence: 'Don't call any alleged feature of reality "chance" unless you've already shown that you have something, knowledge of which could constrain rational credence', he says (1994: 484).[9]

5.2 Practical Relevance for Causation

In the case of causation, however, the parallel point is far less well known. Everyone agrees that causality and rational means-end deliberation go hand-in-hand, in normal circumstances. Putting it roughly, *A* causes *B* if and only if, other things being equal, it would be rational for an agent who desired *B* to *do* or *bring about A*, in order to realize *B*. Again we can ask the *Euthyphro* question. Is it the causal connection between *A* and *B* that makes it rational to do *A* to achieve *B*? Or is the meaning of the claim that *A* causes *B* somehow *constituted by* or *grounded in* the psychology of agency? As the probability case, let's call the first option the objectivist view, the second the subjectivist view.

In this case, it is hard to find the equivalents of Mellor and Lewis—leading metaphysicians of causation who recognize the need to build in its practical face from the beginning.[10] On the contrary, two influential arguments have seemed to many writers not only to mandate the objectivist view, but to do so on the basis of the intuitive connections between causation and rational decision. In our present terminology, both can be read as attempts to use the Practical Relevance Constraint *against* subjectivism and neopragmatism.

---

[9] It is worth quoting the full passage in which Lewis makes this remark:

Be my guest—posit all the primitive unHumean whatnots you like...But play fair in naming your whatnots. Don't call any alleged feature of reality 'chance' unless you've already shown that you have something, knowledge of which could constrain rational credence. I think I see, dimly but well enough, how knowledge of frequencies and symmetries and best systems could constrain rational credence. I don't begin to see, for instance, how knowledge that two universals stand in a certain special relation N* could constrain rational credence about the future coinstantiation of those universals.   Lewis (1994: 484)

[10] We do find it in the work of Pearl (2000) and Woodward (2003), but even here it comes from a computer scientist and a philosopher of science, respectively.

One of these arguments is Nancy Cartwright's famous (1979) claim that realism about causation is required to ground the distinction between effective and ineffective strategies—e.g., to explain why moving a barometer needle is an ineffective strategy for controlling the weather, despite the correlation between the two. Cartwright argues that it is an objective matter which strategies are effective and which ineffective. Such an objective matter calls for explanation, one that it seems that laws of association simply cannot provide. Hence, Cartwright concludes:

> [C]ausal laws cannot be done away with, for they are needed to ground the distinction between effective strategies and ineffective ones... [T]he difference between the two depends on the causal laws of our universe, and on nothing weaker.   1979: 420

The second argument arose from the literature concerning so-called Newcomb problems (Nozick 1969). These are decision problems that seemed to some writers to provide *counterexamples* to the usual association between causation and rational means-end reasoning—in other words, cases in which it makes sense to do A because A provides strong *evidence* for a favorable outcome B, without being a cause of B. 'Evidentialists' try to make the case for such counterexamples, while 'Causalists' oppose it. The two sides thus disagree on what the rational choice is in Newcomb problems, with Causalists insisting that it is determined by the causal facts of the situation. In this way, they commit themselves implicitly to the objectivist answer to the *Euthyphro* question. For the subjectivist, after all, the causal facts could not be settled in advance of the question about rational choice, in difficult cases.

In my view, both of these influential arguments—Cartwright's argument, and the Causalist case in Newcomb problems—are vulnerable to the neopragmatist's usual Practical Relevance challenge. In both cases, the neopragmatist can point out that objectivism simply leaves it mysterious why causation should *matter* to rational decision, in the way that it is crucial to both arguments to claim that it does.[11] Subjectivism can do much better, for a reason that depends on another of Ramsey's insights in GPC. For the response to Cartwright, the crucial point is that evidential dependencies are *different* from an agent's perspective, as she considers possible actions, than they are from a third-person perspective. As Ramsey puts it in the passage I quoted above:

> What is true is this, that any possible present volition of ours is (for us) irrelevant to any past event. To another (or to ourselves in the future) it can serve as a sign of the past, but to us now what we do affects only the probability of the future.
> 1929a: 145

---

[11] I develop this argument in Price and Liu (2018).

(After that we get the remark that 'my present action is an ultimate and the only ultimate contingency.')

What does Ramsey have in mind here? I think it is what has since become known as the thesis that *deliberation crowds out prediction* (DCOP). As Isaac Levi puts it, 'deliberation crowds out prediction so that a decision maker may not coherently assign unconditional probabilities to the propositions he judges optional for him' (Levi 2000: 394). DCOP implies that from an agent's point of view, a contemplated action must be regarded as probabilistically independent of anything to which she does assign an unconditional credence, even if *other people* (or she herself *at other times*) could legitimately take something of that kind as evidence about her choice, or vice versa. This independence *from the agent's point of view* is what Ramsey means by 'ultimate contingency', in my view.

For present purposes, the crucial point is that probabilities assessed from the first-person, present-tensed perspective of a deliberating agent, are legitimately *different* from those assessed from the standpoint of 'another (or...ourselves in the future)', as Ramsey himself puts it. In particular, this means that these agent-probabilities can ignore some of the correlation-based evidential dependencies that Cartwright rightly takes to play havoc with the distinction between effective and ineffective strategies.[12] *Pace* Cartwright, we get to this distinction not by *adding* causal laws to bare associations in the ontological realm, but by *taking something away* from the import of those associations in the epistemic realm. Ramsey's great insight is to see how deliberation does the subtraction for us.

So long as causal subjectivism is grounded on Ramsey's insight, then it can explain the distinction on which Cartwright's argument relies between effective and ineffective strategies, the former tracking probabilistic relevance *from the agent's point of view*. In a similar way, I think, it can draw a plausible line through the forest of Newcomb-like problems, avoiding the sins of which Evidentialists are normally accused. (See Price 1986, 1991, 2012, forthcoming: ch. 12; Price and Liu 2018.)

5.3 Explaining the Temporal Character of Causation and Chance

Closer to our current concerns, I have also argued (Price 1996, 2007; Price and Weslake 2010) that the neopragmatist approach provides the most satisfactory

---

[12] Ramsey's formulation of the point can be improved in two respects, I think. First, it is not only past events with respect to which deliberation breaks evidential dependencies. If I am deliberating about whether to move the needle of my barometer, I should not take my choice to provide evidence about present or future weather, or vice versa. Second, a minor point here, Ramsey has not given us a reason to be sure that *everything* in the past is off limits in this way. As I have argued elsewhere, the possibility that some of it is not turns out to be interesting in making sense of quantum theory (see Price 1996 and Price and Wharton 2015 for this 'retrocausal' proposal).

account of the *temporal* characteristics of the causal relation—in particular, the fact that the causal 'arrow' has such a striking temporal orientation. Here there are actually two things to be explained. The first is the difference between cause and effect—without such a difference, there could be no arrow in the first place. The second is the temporal component of the puzzle, the fact that causes typically *precede* their effects. Once again, the explanation follows Ramsey. Roughly speaking, causes are variables thought of as under the control of an (often highly idealized) deliberating agent, and effects are variables correlated with these controlled variables in such a way the correlation survives, when the other variable is brought about by an agent in this way.

If we imagine a simple example, it will be easy to see how the typical temporal orientation of the cause-effect relation reflects that of the agents concerned, for an approach of this sort. Let's begin with an observed Humean regularity of a familiar kind, say between dropped plates (DP) and mess on the floor (MF) soon afterwards, in our campus cafeteria. Does DP cause MF, does MF cause DP, or does neither relation obtain?

To settle the issue, Ramsey's approach requires us to consider the cases in which a deliberating agent *chooses* to produce DP, and *chooses* to produce MF. Given our temporal orientation as agents, this involves putting ourselves into the picture *before* the variable in question, in each case. Keep a close eye on this fact, because it, and nowhere else, is where the time asymmetry gets into the account. When we put ourselves into the picture before DP—i.e., as we would ordinarily, say, when we choose to drop a plate—a mess on the floor soon afterwards is a reliable co-occurrence. So the DP-MF correlation continues to hold, in this case, and we conclude that dropping plates does *cause* messy floors (at least in the circumstances that normally obtain in our campus cafeteria).

What about when we choose to produce MF directly? In this case, we are considering instances in which what lies in the immediate *past* of MF—again, it has to be the past, given our own temporal orientation as agents—is our own action, messing the floor in some way. (We might throw down a handful of peas and some broken china, for example.) In these cases, there is no guarantee whatsoever that MF is preceded by DP. Our *intervention* breaks the normal DP-MF correlation.[13] So making the floor messy is not a cause of just-dropped plates, despite the observed correlation between these things in normal circumstances.[14]

---

[13] I use the term 'intervention' deliberately here, though it is given a somewhat more precise sense in so-called interventionist approaches to causation (e.g., that of Woodward 2003). My view is that such approaches cannot account for the ordinary time orientation of causation unless they retain this link to our *de facto* temporal orientation as agents; see Price (2017) for discussion.

[14] Things become more complicated when the correlations in question involve features of ourselves, as in the so-called medical Newcomb problems. See Price (1986, 1991) for my proposed treatment of those cases.

This is a textbook example of the neopragmatist direction of explanation. The character of the manifest image reflects the contingencies of our own nature and viewpoint. In particular, the temporal character of the causal relation reflects the temporal orientation of agents like us, not the other way round.

Similar temporal questions arise in the case of chance. Typically a theory of chance is taken to tell us the chance of a *future* event, given a past history. Where does that temporal direction come from? A pragmatist will say that it reflects our own epistemic orientation. In crucial respects, we often have less information about the future than the past, and yet we care about the future. As we would ordinarily put it, our welfare often depends on what happens to us in the future.[15] A time-directed theory of chance is a rule book for an ideal agent of this kind, who knows everything about the past but nothing, except via such a theory, about the future. (Similar remarks apply to the apparent direction of causality, only here the temporal orientation of agency is also relevant. Indeed, one of the reasons we often know little about highly relevant bits of the future is that we haven't yet decided what to do![16])

5.4 Confronting Objectivism

This asymmetry of epistemic and agentive perspective can be deeply embedded in a theoretical description, and it takes work to dig it out. When a pragmatist does dig it out, they are liable to be accused of denying the reality of something obviously real, such as objective chance and objective causation. They should persist, of course, and press home two advantages. As we have seen, one advantage stems from the Practical Relevance Constraint. The neopragmatist is uniquely well placed to explain why probability and causation *matter* in the way that they do—why they properly play a characteristic role in rational decisions. This is where neopragmatism begins, in these cases.

The second advantage exploits the perspectival character of neopragmatism—its Copernican face. We can often highlight the perspectival character of a term or concept by pointing out that we can make sense of creatures who, in virtue of having a different perspective from ours, would apply the term differently, or not have a use for it at all. In this way, neopragmatism can undermine the assumption that categories such as probability and causation are simply part of the furniture, to be studied like mass or charge.

The most dramatic of these alternative perspectives are those that imagine creatures with the opposite temporal orientation to ours. I have in mind the

---

[15] I put this seemingly obvious point in this careful way in order to return (in section 9) to the point that this is something that a pragmatist should not merely take for granted, but rather highlight it as the contingent pragmatic grounds of much of our thought and linguistic practice.

[16] Choice is an epistemic 'wild card', as Ismael (2011: 161) puts it.

Boltzmann-Schuetz proposal, and its contemporary cousins: in other words, cosmological proposals that allow regions of the universe in which the gradient associated with the second law of thermodynamics is reversed relative to that in our own region. As we noted in section 4, it is plausible that intelligent creatures in such regions would have the opposite view to us as to which temporal direction is past and which future. We are now extending that thought to their notions of chance and causation.[17]

In debates of this kind a neopragmatist's opponents will often include philosophers who regard themselves as committed realists about science (especially physics), and who regard realism about probability and causation as part of the same package. But there are allies of pragmatism within philosophy of science, and even within philosophy of physics. For the benefit of neopragmatist readers I am pleased to call attention to recent work on avowedly pragmatist philosophies of quantum theory. I'm thinking particularly of the work of Healey (2017), though the so-called QBist or Quantum Bayesian approach (Timpson 2008) also acknowledges its inspiration from pragmatism and probabilistic subjectivism. Motivated by the puzzles of quantum theory, these views have come from a very different direction than neopragmatism to the conclusion that some fundamental physics is not to be understood as offering bare representations of independent reality. Instead, these views take quantum theory to embody the perspective of idealized observers and experimenters—idealized versions of contingent creatures like us.

Welcome as these allies are for a neopragmatist, they need to be embraced with a caveat. It is possible to read these views as *contrasting* quantum theory with other parts of science, and with the descriptions we employ in ordinary life. On such a contrastive view, pragmatism would be a local view in science, applicable where ordinary modes of description fail us. Pushing back against that localism leads us to our next step.

6. A World of Dispositions

It has often been proposed that many, if not all, of the fundamental properties ascribed in physics—charge, mass, and the like—are *dispositions*. What is a disposition? Here is Maier (2020):

---

[17] See Price (1996, 2007); Price and Weslake (2010) for discussion. For both probability and causation, it is also possible to find much more familiar variations in the standpoints of different speakers, sometimes within the same conversation. In the case of probability, two speakers may have access to different bodies of evidence. In the case of causation, they may be treating different things as 'background conditions', and hence drawing different conclusions as to what should be counted as the cause of a given event. A further advantage of neopragmatism is that it accommodates such cases smoothly, and doesn't require an abrupt discontinuity between these cases and talk of 'real', 'objective', probability, and causation.

> Dispositions are, at first pass, those properties picked out by predicates like 'is fragile' or 'is soluble', or alternatively by sentences of the form 'x is disposed to break when struck' or 'x is disposed to dissolve when placed in water.' Dispositions so understood have figured centrally in the metaphysics and philosophy of science of the last century (Carnap 1936 & 1937, Goodman 1954), and also in influential accounts of the mind.   (Ryle 1949)

The term 'disposition' is to some extent a piece of philosophers' jargon, aiming to nail down a meaning shared (at least in part) by many other ordinary and philosophical terms:

> Many terms have been used to describe what we mean by dispositions: 'power' (Locke's term), 'dunamis' (Aristotle's term), 'ability', 'potency', 'capability', 'tendency', 'potentiality', 'proclivity', 'capacity', and so forth. In a very general sense, they mean disposition, or otherwise something close by.   Choi and Fara (2021)

The claim that the fundamental properties of physics are dispositions is closely linked to empiricism. The thought is that we have no direct access to the intrinsic nature of the physical world, but know it only indirectly, via its tendencies to affect our measuring devices. This thought in itself is easy to give a pragmatist flavor: we know the world through its practical effects. But my interest lies a step further back.

In asserting a dispositional property of an object—whether in physics or in more familiar domains—we commit ourselves to an *expectation* about how the object would behave, in certain circumstances. Expectation is a psychological notion. Where should we look for an account of the psychological relevance of dispositional properties? This is simply another case of the Practical Relevance issue, discussed above with respect to probability and causation.

As in those cases, we can distinguish two approaches, linked to the two possible answers to the *Euthyphro* question. The metaphysical approach takes on board the task of explaining the psychological relevance in terms of the nature of dispositions. The pragmatist approach begins at the other end, saying that we develop these descriptions because they are the kind we need, as epistemically limited creatures, acting for the sake of our future welfare. The expectational character of the manifest image is grounded in our own psychology and temporal character.

For present purposes, the point I want to emphasize is that neopragmatism about dispositions greatly broadens the relevance of the human temporal perspective. The previous step took us to its relevance to particular concepts, such as probability and causation. This step takes us to a very broad class of properties indeed—arguably, in fact, all of them. We need to move quickly, so I want simply to mark four philosophical waypoints that I think can be seen to be in the spirit of this sort of neopragmatist perspective on dispositions. Together, they will take us much further in the direction of globalism.

6.1 Hume on Causal Necessity

The first and most obvious waypoint is Hume. This talk of expectation calls to mind the interpretation of Hume according to which he takes talk of causation to be a 'projection' of the expectations to which observed regularities give rise.

> Hume locates the source of the idea of necessary connection *in us*, not in the objects themselves or even in our ideas of those objects we regard as causes and effects. In doing so, he completely changes the course of the causation debate, reversing what everyone else thought about the idea of necessary connection.
> Morris and Brown (2021)

If we read Hume as a proto-neopragmatist about causation, then the points we have just made can be put by saying that the same expectation-grounded neo-pragmatism seems to fit our talk of dispositions, not just our talk of causation.

6.2 Wittgenstein on the Hypothetical Character of Language

For a second waypoint I'll turn to some little-known remarks of Wittgenstein, delivered in a lecture in Cambridge in January 1930. Anna Boncompagni (2017) has noted the relevance of these remarks to the question of pragmatist influences on Wittgenstein.

> When I say 'There is a chair over there', this sentence refers to a series of expectations. I believe I could go there, perceive the chair and sit on it, I believe it is made of wood and I expect it to have a certain hardness, inflammability etc. If some of these expectations are mistaken, I will see it as proof for retaining that there was no chair there. Wittgenstein (1930)

These remarks occur in a context in which Wittgenstein is interested in a contrast between the language of ordinary life and the (supposed) primary language of immediate perceptions. They link to reasons Wittgenstein offers for being skeptical of the possibility of such a primary language.

> Every sentence we utter in everyday life appears to have the character of a hypothesis.
> A hypothesis is a logical structure. That is, a symbol for which certain rules of representation hold.
> The point of talking of sense data and immediate experience is that we are looking for a non-hypothetical representation.

> But now it seems that the representation loses all its value if the hypothetical element is dropped, because then the proposition does not point to the future any more, but it is, as it were, self-satisfied and hence without any value.
>
> Wittgenstein (1930)

As Boncompagni points out, it is very likely that Wittgenstein was influenced by Ramsey at these points. It is easy to link these remarks to the themes of GPC, written just a few months previously. In GPC, as we saw, Ramsey's initial concern is with the status of lawlike and unrestricted generalizations, such as 'All men are mortal'—what Ramsey calls 'variable hypotheticals'. Contrary to his previous view that these should be construed as infinite conjunctions, Ramsey now argues that they are not propositions at all. As Ramsey puts it, such a generalization is 'not a judgment but a rule for judging'. Rules like this 'form the system with which the speaker meets the future'.

Wittgenstein's remarks can be seen as extending such a perspective to ordinary notions such as chair, an extension to which Ramsey would surely have been sympathetic. Again, the pragmatist view is that such property ascriptions support expectations *because expectations are built in from the very beginning.*

Mathieu Marion (2012) puts the point like this, introducing some terminology I want to appropriate for our present purposes:

> Ramsey introduced his notion of 'variable hypothetical' as a rule, not a proposition, on pragmatist grounds and...Wittgenstein picked this up in 1929, along with a more 'dynamic' view of meaning than the 'static' view of the *Tractatus*, and...this explains in part Wittgenstein's turn to his 'later philosophy'.
>
> Marion (2012: 26)

A large part of my message in this chapter is that the dynamic, temporal quality of human thought goes at the center of everything (and that this is a profoundly pragmatist message).

6.3 Ryle on Inference Tickets

Our third waypoint takes us to Oxford, twenty years later. It is Ryle's view of conditionals and dispositions. As Alexander Bird describes Ryle's view:

> [T]he sentence "this lump of sugar would dissolve if placed in water" does not assert some factual truth, such as the attribution of a property to a thing. Rather, along with law-statements, such assertions must be understood as inference-tickets: one is entitled to infer from "this lump of sugar is in water" to "this lump of sugar is dissolving." In effect the modal feature of dispositions is located in the

inference ticket. Ryle does not tell us what features of the world entitles us to employ such an inference ticket. Bird (2012: 733)

Against the background of the Ramsey-Wittgenstein view above, Bird's last remark here invites the thought that, by Cambridge lights, it might be inference tickets all the way down. All belief is a matter of dynamic habit, not static picturing. This doesn't seem very far from global inference tickets.[18]

Bird notes that both Ryle and Thomas Storer make the link between dispositions and counterfactuals:

> Ryle (1949: 123) asserts that, "To say that this lump of sugar is soluble is to say that it would dissolve, if submerged anywhere, at any time and in any parcel of water." Storer (1951: 134) says concerning definitions of dispositional concepts (such as colour predicates):
>
>> The peculiarity of all such definitions is the occurrence of sentences of the type: "If so and so were to happen, then such and such would be the case". In a current phrase, all definitions of dispositional predicates involve the use of contrary to fact conditionals.
>
> So both Ryle and Storer recognize the connection between dispositions and counterfactuals, but retreat from making much of this connection when giving further detail, primarily because of empiricist concerns at the metaphysical implications of taking counterfactuals at face value. Bird (2012: 732–3)

Bird also mentions the view of Sellars (1958), in our terms another proto-neopragmatist, on whom more in a moment. Bird then summarizes the mid-century landscape:

> The position in the 1950s was that philosophers recognized that dispositional and counterfactual assertions are related and that both of these have connections with statements concerning laws and causes. Goodman (1954) distinguished the analysis of counterfactuals from analyzing the meaning of law statements. On the other hand, by his own admission, Goodman was unable to articulate the details of their relationship. Furthermore, he remained committed to a Humean view of laws that distinguishes them from other regularities only in virtue of our propensity to use them in inferences and predictions (cf. the Rylean inference ticket view of dispositions and laws mentioned above). 2012: 734

---

[18] It is a familiar idea that Ryle might owe some unacknowledged debt to Wittgenstein. In recent work, Cheryl Misak makes a strong case that this gets both the source and the path of the influence wrong. Ryle's biggest unacknowledged debt is to the work of his friend Margaret Macdonald in the 1930s, and through her work to Ramsey and to Peirce. As Misak puts it, 'Ryle owes his central ideas to pragmatism. He helped himself to the underappreciated Margaret MacDonald's reading of Peirce and Ramsey—to the distinction between knowing how and knowing that and the idea that laws are inference tickets' (Misak forthcoming: 1).

As Bird goes on to say, however, the field took a very different turn in the decades that followed:

> The discussion of the analysis of dispositions was given a major impetus by the development of a semantics for counterfactuals by Stalnaker (1968) and Lewis (1973), following earlier work by Kripke on semantics for modal logic. The semantics provided for counterfactuals made them philosophically respectable, while also articulating their problematic relationship with laws. Lewis also provided an account of causation in terms of counterfactuals, allowing a further dissociation of counterfactuals, laws, and causes. 2012: 734

It is fair to say that with this shift, the neopragmatist perspective on dispositions becomes very deeply submerged. To bring it to the surface we need to tackle a bigger opponent. In my view the appropriate way to do this is to press the Practical Relevance challenge against talk of possible worlds, whether in Lewis's form or otherwise—to argue that unless an account of *them* begins with the epistemic and agential perspective of creatures like ourselves, it will find itself unable to put them in later, except by fiat.[19]

I have explored some aspects of this challenge in work mentioned in the previous section, concerning the practical utility and temporal orientation of causation. Similar remarks will apply to the time asymmetry of counterfactuals, in terms of which Lewis seeks to explain that of causation. Another aspect of this challenge—presently rather underexplored, so far as I know (though see Blackburn 1984: 213–17)—might build on Kripke's famous challenge to Lewis's account of transworld personal identity. Why should Hubert Humphrey care that his counterpart in some other possible world—according to Lewis's view an entirely different person, in a region of reality entirely disconnected from ours—won the presidential election?[20] Again, neopragmatism seems likely to have the upper hand.

6.4 The Kant-Sellars-Brandom Thesis

Interesting as those issues are from a neopragmatist perspective, I want to keep our focus on the broader message: the dynamic, temporal character of (at least much of)

---

[19] The same kind of fiat as is involved in treating the relation between chance and rational credence as a primitive fact, requiring no explanation—a move to which, as we saw, Lewis himself is opposed.

[20] Varzi (2020) describes Kripke's point like this:
> Someone other than Humphrey enters into the story of how it is that Humphrey might have won the election. Saul Kripke famously complained that this is bizarre: "Probably, Humphrey could not care less whether someone *else*, no matter how much resembling him, would have been victorious in another possible world." 1972: 344, n.13

conceptual thought. Our final waypoint is Brandom's Sellarsian inferentialism. Here is Brandom on the history of these ideas.

> Kant was struck by the fact that the essence of the Newtonian concept of mass is of something that, by law, *force* is both necessary and sufficient to *accelerate*. And he saw that all empirical concepts are like their refined descendants in the mathematized natural sciences in this respect: their application implicitly involves counterfactual-supporting dispositional commitments to what *would* happen *if*. Kant's claim, put in more contemporary terms, is that an integral part of what one is committed to in applying any determinate concept in empirical circumstances is drawing a distinction between counterfactual differences in circumstances that *would* and those that *would not* affect the truth of the judgment one is making. One has not grasped the concept cat unless one knows that it would still be possible for the cat to be on the mat if the lighting had been slightly different, but not if all life on earth had been extinguished by an asteroid-strike.
>
> In an autobiographical sketch, Sellars dates his break with traditional empiricism to his Oxford days in the 1930s. It was, he says, prompted by concern with the sort of content that ought to be associated with logical, causal, and deontological modalities. Already at that point he had the idea that
>
>> what was needed was a functional theory of concepts which would make their role in reasoning, rather than supposed origin in experience, their primary feature. [Sellars 1975: 285]
>
> Somewhat more specifically, he sees modal locutions as tools used in the enterprise of making explicit the rules we have adopted for thought and action
>
>> ...I shall be interpreting our judgments to the effect that A causally necessitates B as the expression of a rule governing our use of the terms 'A' and 'B'.
>> [Sellars 1949: 136, fn. 2]
>
> In fact, following Ryle, he takes modal expressions to function as *inference licenses,* expressing our commitment to the goodness of counterfactually robust inferences from necessitating to necessitated conditions. If and insofar as it could be established that their involvement in such counterfactually robust inferences is essential to the *contents* of ordinary empirical concepts, then what is made explicit by modal vocabulary is implicit in the use of any such concepts. That is the claim I am calling the "Kant-Sellars thesis." Brandom (2008: 97–8)

For the present, what matters about this is two things. First, the Kant-Sellars thesis puts the dynamical character of dispositional concepts at the core of all empirical concepts without exception. Second, it replaces the bare Humean *habitual* conception of the dynamical relations involved with a *normative* one. Concepts are to be understood in terms of their role in the dynamic behavior of norm-governed inference engines.

6.5 Summary

We have been moving at pace through a landscape with one central theme. A major part (at least) of the category of properties we ascribe to the world, and of our system of empirical concepts as a whole, have a strong claim to reflect the dynamic, serial character of human thought—in particular, our striving to prepare for an uncertain future. In this way our own temporal character is reflected not only in the nature of conceptual thought itself, but in our image of the world we inhabit, both in science and in everyday life. Once again, I want to urge that these are pragmatist lessons. Specifically, they are pragmatist lessons that require that we reflect, as pragmatists, on our own (contingent?) natures as physical entities of a particular kind—processes embodied in time.

I qualify the claim about contingency here because in this case it isn't easy to make the move, so useful elsewhere in the neopragmatist program, of imagining ourselves otherwise, and asking how things would seem from that alternative perspective. It is far from clear that we can imagine an intelligence that isn't temporal in a similar way. More on this in section 8 below. But I don't think this imaginative roadblock is an obstacle to the pragmatist conclusion I want to extend to this point. Here, as in easier, more local cases, we need to understand what we *are*, in order to understand what we think, what we say, and how we describe our world.

Before we move on, I want to address a concern that will have occurred to sharp-eyed readers. In section 4, I associated neopragmatism with the view that many of the apparent differences between time and space are manifestations of the human perspective. This viewpoint is often linked to so-called 'static' or 'block universe' conceptions of time, conceptions opposed to 'dynamic' views of time, that take time to be more radically different from space.[21] So I may seem to have put myself in a difficult position. On the one hand, I am opposing the dynamic conception of time. On the other hand, I am giving a central role to the dynamic, serial character of human thought. Isn't there a tension here?[22]

It is a reasonable concern, but the answer we need is in D. C. Williams' classic manifesto for the block universe picture, 'The Myth of Passage' (1951). Williams calls the block universe the *manifold*, and here he is responding to the challenge that such a picture cannot make sense of change:

---

[21] As every proponent of the view is well aware, the term 'static' is merely a metaphor. There is not thought to be some external time, outside the block, in which the block itself is unchanging.

[22] A different challenge at this point would be that I seem to be favoring one *metaphysical* view of time over another; and as a neopragmatist, what business do I have in messing with such metaphysical questions, let alone in picking sides? My answer is that by my lights, the issue here isn't metaphysics, but simply physics. What do we need in the physics of time, to explain the appearances? I say we just need the block. Remember Copernicus—he's doing physics, and what we might call phenomenology, but not metaphysics. Cf. section 9.

Let us hug to us as closely as we like that there is real succession, that rivers flow and winds blow, that things burn and burst, that men strive and guess and die. All this is the concrete stuff of the manifold, the reality of serial happening, one event after another, in exactly the time spread which we have been at pains to diagram. What does the theory allege except what we find, and what do we find that is not accepted and asserted by the theory?   Williams (1951: 467)

The message of this section, indeed of the chapter as a whole, is that neopragmatists need to pay close attention to the fact that we humans 'strive and guess and die', and related aspects of the kinds of beings that we are, stretched out across the manifold. This is what I have been calling our dynamic, serial character. I cannot put more eloquently than Williams the conclusion that this doesn't require that we burden ourselves with some additional metaphysics of change or passage, in addition to the 'reality of serial happening'.

7. Signs and Dispositional Triggers

In the previous section, we considered dispositional properties, and empirical concepts on the Kant-Sellars-Brandom model, as tools adapted for temporal creatures like us. I now want to observe that a similar point can be made about any symbolic language. Language 'points to the future', in Wittgenstein's phrase, not merely in the sense Wittgenstein has in mind here: 'When I say "There is a chair over there", this sentence refers to a series of expectations.' It also points to the future in the sense in which any linguistic sign is a gift to the future—a nut added to a store for the winter. Such a practice is only possible because language users can take each other to be disposed to use and respond to signs in similar and predictable ways.

It is worth pulling apart two aspects of this. Signs are both effects and causes, *triggered by* one set of dispositions, or habits, and *triggering* another. We take each other, and indeed ourselves, to *apply* the term in the same way on different occasions, and to *respond* to the term over time with the same consistency. There would be no point in writing 'Don't forget to buy milk' on the palm of one's hand, unless one could rely on one's own habit of interpreting those marks in a certain way when one gets to the supermarket. Most of the time, we can rely on the constancy of the relation between us and the signs, at both ends of the transaction.

For present purposes, we can again skate over very large issues about the nature of such habits. One important divide, like the one we encountered above, will be between Kantian and Humean conceptions, normative and non-normative, respectively. For present, what matters is simply that this is another place at which our own temporality is immediately important to understanding what we do.

In this case, our own contingency can easily be made salient, and doing so is at the heart of some well-known philosophical points. The so-called rule-following considerations turn on the observation that no finite set of shared experiences can guarantee that different language users will form the *same* expectations for what counts as 'going on in the same way', in new applications. (This point is usually made in terms of classification of a new instance, but it applies equally to the interpretation of yesterday's sign—it is the same issue.) So here is a particular place at which, thanks to the temporal, open ended, nature of language—the way it 'points to the future'—the contingencies of our own dispositions to recognize patterns provide a universal source of the trail of the human serpent. (We can't imagine non-temporal language users, but we can imagine users who, though mostly like us, project into the future in different ways.)

Elsewhere I have argued that the rule-following considerations provide a direct path to global neopragmatism. In the forthcoming second, expanded, edition of *Facts and the Function of Truth* (Price forthcoming) I put the point in terms of the recipe for neopragmatism summarized above.

> Two of the ingredients in the recipe are a use-first approach to meaning, and the identification of pragmatic grounds. Once we have these ingredients in view, there's an obvious path to globalisation. We simply need to argue that any kind of declarative cake needs a handful of pragmatic grounds, blended into a use-first account of some aspect of its meaning.
>
> Where to find such an argument? In effect, [the first edition of *Facts and the Function of Truth* (Price 1988)] claimed to do so in the rule-following considerations, and what they reveal about the way in which meaning depends on what are at base simply contingent dispositions to treat one thing as like another. Communication is possible because, most of the time, we are disposed to 'go on in the same way' *in the same way*—but divergence is always possible, leading, in principle, to [No Fault Disagreements]. These dispositions are themselves pragmatic grounds, in the terminology we have been using, and they are absolutely global. Anything that counts as language depends on them.
>
> These dispositions are thus an essential ingredient, without which no linguistic cake can possibly stand up. In fact, we have more than we need. It would have been enough to show that any assertoric language game needs some sort of use-first component—perhaps a different one in different games. We have shown that there is *a particular kind of use-first component* that is needed in all such games.   Price (forthcoming: ch. 12)

Again, the message I want to emphasize here is that these are lessons that depend on the dynamic, serial, temporal character of language and thought.

8. Great Expectations: Thought as a Predictive Engine

We might summarize the previous two sections by saying that at all three corners of the Mind-Language-Manifest World triangle—in *concepts, terms,* and *properties,* respectively—we have found the marks of the kind of temporal creatures that we are. I have argued that these are deeply neopragmatist conclusions. As the sixth and final step on our stairway, I want to describe some recent developments in the science of the mind that seem to push this viewpoint even further, with further implications for pragmatism.

By way of introduction, let's revisit a prominent theme in twentieth-century pragmatism, one that has already played a role in our story. We touched in section 6 on Ramsey's conception of the hypothetical, *future-facing* character of human thought. As Ramsey puts it, '[v]ariable hypotheticals or causal laws form the system with which the speaker meets the future' (1929a: 137). Elsewhere in GPC, as Misak (2016: 189–200) notes, Ramsey characterizes beliefs in general as future-facing habits: 'all belief involves habit' (1929a: 138), and 'it belongs to the essence of any belief that we deduce from it, and act on it in a certain way' (1929a: 147). Ramsey makes similar remarks about concepts, definitions of which 'show how we intend to use them in the future', as he puts it (Ramsey 1929b: 1; quoted by Misak forthcoming: 2).

As I noted, Misak (2016) shows us how Ramsey got these ideas from Peirce, and bestowed them in turn on Wittgenstein. The remarks we quoted from Wittgenstein in 1930—'Every sentence we utter in everyday life appears to have the character of a hypothesis', and 'the representation loses all its value if the hypothetical element is dropped, because then the proposition does not point to the future any more'—may thus be regarded the intellectual grandchildren, via Ramsey, of remarks like this from Peirce: 'The rational meaning of every proposition lies in the future' (Peirce 1905: 174). As Misak glosses Peirce's view, '[p]art of a proposition's meaning is how action and experience will play out' (Misak, forthcoming: 4).

I have emphasized this future-facing theme in early pragmatism in order to make the point that in our own time, the so-called *Predictive Processing Framework* (PPF) puts a stance recognizably related to it at the core of the study of the brain itself. 'Brains, it has recently been argued, are essentially prediction machines' (Clark 2013). Jakob Hohwy introduces PPF like this:

> A new theory is taking hold in neuroscience. The theory is increasingly being used to interpret and drive experimental and theoretical studies, and it is finding its way into many other domains of research on the mind. It is the theory that the brain is a sophisticated hypothesis-testing mechanism, which is constantly involved in minimizing the error of its predictions of the sensory input it

receives from the world. This mechanism is meant to explain perception and action and everything mental in between. It is an attractive theory because powerful theoretical arguments support it. It is also attractive because more and more empirical evidence is beginning to point in its favour. It has enormous unifying power and yet it can explain in detail too.   Hohwy (2013: 1)

Similarly from Andy Clark:

The key idea, one that seems to be turning up in very many guises in contemporary cognitive science, is that we also *learn* about the world by attempting to generate the incoming sensory data for ourselves, from the top-down, using the massed recurrent connectivity distinctive of advanced biological brains. This works because good models make better predictions, and we can improve our models by slowly amending them (using well-understood learning routines) so as to incrementally improve their predictive grip upon the sensory stream.

The core idea, as it emerges for the simple...case of passive perception, can now be summarized. To perceive the world is to meet the sensory signal with an apt stream of multilevel predictions. Those predictions aim to construct the incoming sensory signal 'from the top down' using stored knowledge about interacting distal causes. To accommodate the incoming sensory signal in this way is already to understand quite a lot about the world. Creatures deploying this kind of strategy learn to become knowledgeable consumers of their own sensory stimulations. They come to know about their world, and about the kinds of entity and event that populate it. Creatures deploying this strategy, when they see the grass twitch in just that certain way, are *already expecting* to see the tasty prey emerge, and *already expecting* to feel the sensations of their own muscles tensing to pounce. An animal, or machine, that has that kind of grip on its world is already deep into the business of understanding that world.   Clark (2016: 6)

I hope that these introductory remarks, by two of the leading philosophers writing about PPF, are enough to convey a sense of alignment between the dynamic view achieved by the route described in the previous sections—pragmatists ascending a stairway without venturing very far from their armchairs—and PPF. I hope that they provide grounds for confidence that the ascent was worth it, and that the viewpoint achieved will turn out to have respectable empirical foundations. The main message, once again, is that the temporality of our own natural condition—in many ways, like that of all our animal ancestors and cousins—is central to an understanding of who and what we are.

But is this really a pragmatist lesson? As Daniel Williams (2018) has pointed out, this is controversial. Some writers, including Hohwy, draw lessons from PPF that seem deeply in tension with core tenets of pragmatism. For example, they take it to support a Cartesian, representational conception of the brain:

The prediction of the generative model of the world maintained in the brain is an internal *mirror of nature*, it recapitulates the causal structure of the world and prediction error is minimized relative to the model's expected states
Hohwy (2013: 220; emphasis added)

Having approached this shared predictive ground by our own route, it is immediately clear how we might resist this conclusion. By neopragmatist lights, the 'causal structure of the world' is not brutally *there*, waiting to be recapitulated by passing brains. On the contrary, a causal model is in an essential respect a tool for a brain of a certain sort (one with the capacity to intervene in its environment). This is not to deny that there are better and worse such models, and hence room for improvement by the error-correcting techniques at the core of PPF.[23] But it is to deny that the upshot of such techniques is usefully compared simply to a more accurate mirror.

Daniel Williams describes several apparent tensions between pragmatism and PPF, but concludes that they are superficial:

> These considerations, then, suggest that the initial appearance of a deep conflict between pragmatism and predictive processing is illusory. Far from an image of minds as passive spectators on the world, recovering the objective structure of the environment like an idealised scientist, predictive processing advances a fundamentally pragmatic brain, striving to maintain the viability of the organism under hostile conditions and in so doing actively *generating* an affective niche—an experienced world structured by the idiosyncratic practical interests of the organism. What emerges is something much closer to Price's (2011a) metaphor of a "holographic data projector"...than a passive reflection of an independently identifiable world.[24] As Clark (2015: 4) puts it, it is a vision of experience that is "maximally distant from a passive ("mirrors of nature") story." Williams (2018: 848)

Whilst less central to Peirce's work, this commitment to the constructive nature of experience lay at the core of James's pragmatist vision, underlying his famous remark that "the trail of the human serpent is...over everything"

---

[23] Throughout GPC, Ramsey is sensitive to the question of what improvement looks like, for mental states that have this habitual, expectational character.

[24] This is the passage from Price (2011a) that Williams has in mind:

> [I]f language is not a [representational] telescope, then what is it? As Brandom points out, a traditional expressivist option is the lamp. I think that modern technology allows us to make this a little more precise. Think of a data projector, projecting internal images onto an external screen. Even better, helping ourselves to one of tomorrow's metaphors, think of a holographic data projector, projecting three-dimensional images in thin air. This isn't projection *onto* an external, unembellished world. On the contrary, the entire image is free-standing, being simply the sum of all we take to be the case: a world of states of affairs, in all the ways that we take states of affairs to be.   2011a: 28

[James 1907: 64]. For James, our status as a certain kind of creature inextricably colours our commerce with the world. Likewise, Dewey's famous interactive conception of knowledge holds that knowledge of the world is formed as an adaptive response to environmental circumstances given the agent's needs and purposes, an ongoing process in which the subject moulds and constructs the very environments it inhabits (Dewey 1925; Godfrey-Smith 2013). For this reason, Dewey was a central influence on Gibson and the tradition of ecological psychology, where the idea that an organism's perceived environment is fundamentally a world of "affordances"—roughly, opportunities for environmental intervention (Chemero 2009)—highlights the functional importance of its practical interests, abilities and morphology in bringing forth its experienced world Gibson (1979). Williams (2018: 839–40)

These passages give some sense of the richness of the question of the relation of PPF to pragmatism, or traditions on which pragmatism builds. Hohwy (2013) also gives a brief account of its origins in Helmholtz's response to Kant. If PPF fulfills its present promise this history will become well known. But to wrap up here, I want to close with a different kind of historical connection. Here is Dennett, proposing that PPF offers an insight into the metaphor at the heart of Hume's neopragmatism:

> It is everybody's job—but particularly the philosophers' job—to negotiate the chasm between what Wilfrid Sellars (1962) called the *manifest image* and the *scientific image*. The manifest image is the everyday world of folk psychology, furnished with people and their experiences of all the middle-sized things that matter. The scientific image is the world of quarks, atoms, and molecules, but also (in this context particularly) sub-personal neural structures with particular roles to play in guiding a living body safely through life. The two images do not readily fall into registration...
>
> Consider what I will call Hume's Strange Inversion (cf. Dennett 2009). One of the things in our world is causation, and we think we see causation because the causation in the world directly causes us to see it—the same way round things in daylight cause us to see round things, and tigers in moonlight cause us to see tigers. When we *see* the thrown ball causing the window to break, the causation itself is somehow perceptible "out there." Not so, says Hume. This is a special case of the mind's "great propensity to spread itself on external objects" (*Treatise of Human Nature*, Hume 1739/1888/1964, I, p. xiv). In fact, he insisted, what we do is misinterpret an inner "*feeling*," an anticipation, as an external property. The "customary transition" in our minds is the *source* of our sense of causation, a quality of "perceptions, not of objects," but we mis-attribute it to the objects, a sort of benign user-illusion, to speak anachronistically. As Hume notes, "the contrary notion is so riveted in the mind" (p. 167) that it is hard to dislodge.

It survives to this day in the typically unexamined assumption that all perceptual representations must be flowing inbound from outside...

If we use the shorthand term "projection" to try to talk, metaphorically, about the mismatch between manifest and scientific image here, what is the true long story? What is literally going on in the scientific image? A large part of the answer emerges, I propose, from the predictive coding perspective.

Every organism, whether a bacterium or a member of *Homo sapiens*, has a set of things in the world that matter to it and which it (therefore) needs to discriminate and anticipate as best it can. Call this the ontology of the organism, or the organism's *Umwelt*... An animal's *Umwelt* consists in the first place of *affordances* (Gibson 1979), things to eat or mate with, openings to walk through or look out of, holes to hide in, things to stand on, and so forth...

But among the things in our *Umwelt* that matter to our well-being are *ourselves*! We ought to have good Bayesian expectations about what we will do next, what we will think next, and what we will *expect* next! And we do. Here's an example:

Think of the cuteness of babies. It is not, of course, an "intrinsic" property of babies, though it seems to be. What you "project" out onto the baby is in fact your manifold of "felt" dispositions to cuddle, protect, nurture, kiss, coo over,... that little cutie-pie. It's not just that when your cuteness detector (based on facial proportions, etc.) fires, you have urges to nurture and protect; you expect to have those very urges, and that manifold of expectations just is the "projection" onto the baby of the property of cuteness. When we expect to see a baby in the crib, we also expect to "find it cute"—that is, we *expect* to *expect* to feel the urge to cuddle it and so forth. When our expectations are fulfilled, the absence of prediction error signals is interpreted as confirmation that, indeed, the thing in the world we are interacting with has the properties we expected it to have. Cuteness as a property passes the Bayesian test for being an objective structural part of the world we live in, and that is all that needs to happen. Any further "projection" process would be redundant. What is special about properties like sweetness and cuteness is that their perception depends on particularities of the nervous systems that have evolved to make much of them. The same is of course also true of colors. This is what is left of Locke's (and Boyle's) distinction between primary and secondary qualities.   Dennett (2013: 209–10)

9. Neopragmatism, Natural Science, and the Physics of Time

Those remarks from Dennett began with Sellars' distinction between the scientific and manifest images, and closed with the distinction between primary and secondary qualities. This is thus an apt point to return to a question I raised but postponed in section 1. In what sense can a *global* neopragmatist really allow either distinction? Doesn't a global version of the view necessarily put science itself on the manifest or secondary side? This is one of two issues I want briefly to discuss in this section. The other is in a sense a more specific form of the same question. What is the relation between temporal neopragmatism of the kind advocated above and the science, or more specifically the physics, of time itself?

9.1 Making Science Manifest?

Hilary Putnam once proposed that Kant is someone who thinks that everything is a secondary quality (Putnam 1981: 60–1). Putnam interprets this as a kind of global pragmatism. This is a convenient taster for global neopragmatism in my sense, though as I have noted elsewhere (Price forthcoming: ch. 11), we need to understand the proposal in the right way. Putnam himself describes the view like this: 'If *all properties are secondary,* what follows? It follows that everything we say about an object is of the form: it is such as to affect us in such-and-such a way' (1981: 61). My kind of neopragmatism will not put things this way, because it wants to put the human element in the background, in *use conditions,* rather than in the foreground, in the content or truth conditions of *what is said*. Neopragmatism does not tell us *what our words say,* but *how our words are used.*[25]

With that important qualification, I think that a global neopragmatist should endorse the view that Putnam attributes to Kant, and see it as on all fours (so to speak) with James' remark about the human serpent. And as for the secondary/primary distinction, so for the manifest/scientific distinction: there is a sense in which global neopragmatism (rightly) implies that the manifest image goes all the way down. Science doesn't take us anywhere else.

But how then to square this with my neopragmatist endorsement of subject naturalism, naturalism in the sense of Hume? Doesn't that require that we see the scientific standpoint as privileged, in some sense? My answer is yes—but not in a sense that conflicts with the point just made.

To make this work, we need to distinguish two senses in which science might be held to be privileged. The first sense relies on the observation that the neopragmatists investigations are conducted *within* natural science. First and foremost, neopragmatists are interested in first-order scientific questions about natural creatures such as ourselves: why do these creatures think and talk in these terms? Call this the *home-turf* sense of privilege. In the neopragmatist's inquiry, science is indeed privileged in this home-turf sense—the inquiry is taking place on science's own territory. But it is not privileged in the sense that its own activities and practices are somehow excluded from the domain of investigation. There is no *ring-fence,* preventing the same scientific gaze being turned on the language and

---

[25] Compare my remarks about the notion of response-dependent properties in section 2.3. This distinction is central to my early piece 'Two Paths to Pragmatism' (Price 1993).

conceptual categories of science itself. So home-turf privilege for natural science, yes; ring-fence privilege, no. That's the combination that global neopragmatism recommends and requires.[26]

Two notes about how this relates to our discussion above. First, home-turf privilege is quite sufficient for the work of section 4, where we were distinguishing the human view of time—what Callender (2017) calls manifest time—from the view of time that emerges from physics. Second, a neopragmatist will already take the work of sections 5 and 6, let alone sections 7 and 8, to count against ring-fence privilege. The temporal modalities (section 5) and dispositions (section 6) are likely to prove essential to natural science, so neopragmatism there is already neopragmatism that breaches any plausible fence that might be erected around scientific practice.

9.2 Neopragmatism and the Physics of Time

Neopragmatism is an inquiry within natural science, although not primarily within physics. On the contrary, its main focus is on aspects of the behavior and psychology of creatures such as ourselves (mainly, our use of various words and concepts). However, it is certainly interested in explaining these aspects of behavior in terms of the natural character and situation of these creatures, and here physics soon becomes relevant. Whatever else these creatures are, they are creatures of physical form, within a physical environment. More specifically, the kind of neopragmatism described at each of our steps above has tried to tie aspects of what these creatures say and think to *temporal* features of their natural condition. Describing and explaining these temporal features seems likely to lead us quickly to the physics of time, although perhaps not necessarily at its most fundamental level.[27]

In practice, some of the required connections seem to be quite direct. We already have a hint of this in the Boltzmann-Schuetz hypothesis (section 4), which postulates that the kind of entropy gradient we observe in our region of the universe is responsible for our perception of the difference between past and future. Boltzmann proposes that this perception would reverse in regions in which the gradient sloped in the other direction, and would be wholly absent in regions without such a gradient at all (because creatures like us could not exist there). As he puts the former point, 'a living being in a particular time interval of

---

[26] This combination is familiar in other contexts, of course. Theoretical linguists do not exempt their own language from their subject's domain of inquiry. A well-constituted law enforcement agency has a duty and the means to enforce the law within its own ranks.
[27] In principle, really fundamental issues in the physics of time might turn out to have little to do with biology and psychology. In principle, indeed, time itself might not be fundamental; see Barbour (1999) for a view of this kind.

such a single world'—in other words, a single region in which entropy is, by chance, very low—will 'distinguish the direction of time toward the less probable state from the opposite direction (the former toward the past, the latter toward the future)' (Boltzmann 1964: 447).[28]

It has been a century and a quarter since Boltzmann and Schuetz discussed these issues, and there has been considerable progress in filling some of the details.[29] Beginning with the physics that makes the emergence of life possible, two things seem especially crucial. The first is the fact that entropy is very low at some point in (what we evolved intelligences think of as) our distant past. Now often known as the Past Hypothesis, this is widely assumed to be some sort of characteristic of the very early universe, and hence a matter for cosmology.[30] Its precise explanation, and indeed the question whether it calls for explanation at all, are still matters for debate.[31]

The second crucial requirement is that some of the processes that take the universe from this low entropy starting point toward thermodynamic equilibrium are extremely slow. It is a familiar feature of many everyday cases that equilibration takes different amounts of time in different physical systems. Milk mixes into coffee very quickly, but the coffee cools to room temperature much more slowly, especially in an insulated container. In the cosmological case the relevant processes take billions of years, in some cases. Luckily for us, these processes create two things: vast metastable reservoirs of low entropy, in the form of diffuse clouds of hydrogen; and many local 'furnaces'—what we know as stars—that tap into those reservoirs, allowing some of the energy trapped within them to escape. Both the reservoirs and the furnaces are comparatively stable, in many cases, over these cosmological time scales. In the regions surrounding the furnaces, if other conditions are suitable, life may arise and evolve, feeding on the hot photons provided by the nearby star.

From a very early stage, apparently, such life forms will find it useful to monitor their environments, and to modify their behavior accordingly. This is likely to be

---

[28] For an excellent recent discussion of the Boltzmann-Schuetz proposal, including the question how much belongs to Schuetz and how much is added by Boltzmann, see Barbour (2020b).

[29] To be clear, later scientists have not endorsed the Boltzmann-Schuetz hypothesis about the origin of low entropy in our region; see Penrose (1989), Price (1996, 2010), Carroll (2010), Barbour (2020a), Rovelli (2022a) for discussion. What has proved more durable is the associated postulate about the relationship between the entropy gradient and other matters, such as the human perception of time.

[30] So far as I know, the first writer to suggest this link is Eddington, who says: 'We are thus driven to admit anti-chance; and apparently the best thing we can do with it is to sweep it up into a heap at the beginning of time' (1931: 452). One of the notable things about this suggestion is that Eddington was writing only a few years after Hubble's discovery of the expansion of the universe, which gave new reason to suspect that it might have a beginning. See Price (2010) for further discussion. The terminology 'Past Hypothesis' is due to Albert (2000), who credits the idea to Feynman.

[31] See Penrose (1989), Price (1996, 2010), Carroll (2010), Barbour (2020a), and Rovelli (2022a) for discussions of various explanations; and Callender (2004) and Price (2004b) for discussion about whether such an explanation is needed.

advantageous as soon as they become capable of doing more than one thing, say by becoming capable of influencing their own motion. Once one can do that, it is useful to be able to detect a nutrient gradient, and to proceed to climb it. Notice that these are already time-asymmetric processes. We are imagining such creatures acquiring information from one temporal direction (the one their intelligent descendants think of as the past), and then modifying their behavior in the other direction.

Is this essential, or are we anthropomorphizing these simple creatures, in imagining them restricted in this way? It would be even more advantageous, presumably, if they could also obtain information directly from the other direction—i.e., about the *future* locations of nutrients, predators, and potential mates. But that's a much harder trick. In a universe (or a region of a universe, in the Boltzmann-Schuetz sense) such as ours, physics seems to permit the acquisition and storage of information from one temporal direction but not from the other—from the past but not the future, in ordinary parlance. This is known as the temporal asymmetry of *records,* or *traces.* Its precise explanation is not yet agreed,[32] but it seems clear that it is another point at which physics of time, especially thermodynamics, connects very directly to factors of relevance to the neopragmatist project.

Some recent writers have investigated the temporal characteristics of information-exploiting creatures in terms of simple formal models. In particular, the physicist James Hartle (2005) proposed to do so in terms of what he calls an IGUS—an *information gathering and utilizing system.* Philosophers such as Ismael (2016) and Callender (2017) have extended this idea, aiming to throw light on various features of the human psychology of time.

9.3 Boundary Disputes

Clearly, this kind of project calls for sharp attention to the questions of what goes into the manifest image, as something to be explained; and what is retained in the underlying science, whether in the physics of time or temporal aspects of biology. Not all of these demarcation lines are presently clear, in my view, and this remains true even if we set aside attempts by authors such as Maudlin (2007), Smolin (2013), and Dowker (2022) to resurrect a richer physics of time—a physics that finds a place for a distinguished present moment or for temporal passage, for example.

One particularly interesting case is that of causation. In section 5, I recommended a neopragmatist account of causation, including a neopragmatist explanation of

---

[32] See Reichenbach (1956), Albert (2000), Fernandes (2022), and Rovelli (2022a, 2022b) for discussion.

the time asymmetry of causation. But this is a strikingly less popular view than neopragmatism about some or all of the features of manifest time. Many writers are very happy to venture as far as the second step on our neopragmatist stairway, in other words, but balk at—or simply miss—the possibility of going further. Callender (2017) is an interesting case in point. While he doesn't take an explicit stand on the status of causation, he feels comfortable in appealing to the asymmetry of counterfactual dependence—itself closely related to the causal asymmetry, apparently—in explaining why we care more about the future than the past (Callender 2017: ch. 12). My kind of neopragmatist thinks that we need to dig a bit deeper, and to look for a package that *explains* our practice of counterfactual reasoning, including its temporal aspects.[33]

What is the alternative to a neopragmatist approach to the time asymmetry of causation and counterfactuals? Its main rivals attempt to account for these asymmetries directly in terms of the thermodynamic asymmetry (rather than indirectly, as the neopragmatist prefers, by appealing to the perspective of creatures whose own existence relies on the thermodynamic asymmetry).[34] The issues at stake here are subtle, and the main lesson I want to stress here is that we need to pay very close attention to what we take the question to be. Are we interested in saying what causation *is*, or in *explaining causal thinking?* These are very different projects, and unless all sides appreciate the difference, they are liable to find themselves arguing with imaginary opponents.

9.4 Memory versus Agency

Among the various aspects of manifest time, the apparent distinction between fixed past and open future seems particularly closely linked to the causal asymmetry. In my transition from sections 4 to 5 above, I took advantage of the fact that Ramsey treats them as one package, both to be explained in terms of the epistemic standpoint of a deliberating agent. It is worth stressing the difference between this approach and another common strategy for putting the former distinction on the manifest side, a strategy that appeals not to agency but to *memory*.

Here Russell provides an example. In the famous 1912 lecture in which he dismisses causation altogether—arguing that modern time-symmetric physics leaves no place for it—Russell says the following about the apparent difference between past and future:

---

[33] I recommend such an extension of Callender's project in (Price 2019b).
[34] See Albert (2000, 2015), Loewer (2007, 2012), and Rovelli (2022a) for versions of this proposal; and Frisch (2007, 2010, 2014) and Price and Weslake (2010) for criticism of it from various perspectives. Beebee (2015) makes the point that at least in the case of the Loewer-Albert version of the proposal, there is considerable convergence in the direction of the neopragmatist view, in the sense that counterfactuals involving (the supposed neural correlates of) human decisions play a crucial role.

> We all regard the past as determined simply by the fact that it has happened; but for the accident that memory works backward and not forward, we should regard the future as equally determined by the fact that it will happen.
>
> Russell (1913: 20–1)[35]

Contra Russell, it now seems plausible that this fact about memory is no mere accident, but is a reflection—a special case, evolved in the biological realm—of the asymmetry of records and traces, and hence of the entropy gradient. Intelligent creatures will always find that 'memory works backward and not forward', from their own points of view—even though *which direction that is*, from the universe's point of view, will depend on the orientation of the particular entropy gradient on which they find themselves.[36]

This point about 'mere accidents' aside, is Russell right that the apparent difference between fixed past and open future stems from a feature of our own memories? If so, we would have a pleasingly direct connection between temporal physics and this aspect of manifest time. But in section 4 we encountered Ramsey's alternative proposal. For Ramsey, the apparent openness of the future is associated with our perspective as *agents,* not as mere *observers* and *memorizers.* This is also a neopragmatist proposal, but a different one, for it ties the feature to be explained to a different aspect of the kind of creatures that we are. (For Ramsey, as we saw, it is a package deal with his agent-based neopragmatist account of causation.)

If we invoke agency in one or both of these ways, then again we should ask the scientific questions about the notions on which the account relies. What is it, in general terms, to be an agent? And how does the existence of agents relate to the physics of time? These questions, too, have been the focus of much recent work, from various perspectives.[37] Once again, it is common ground that the entropic environment is crucial for the physical existence of agents. As in the case of memory, it is no accident that we act for goals in one temporal direction only, in this case the direction in which entropy is increasing.

10. Demarcation Issues

In closing, let me list again the three demarcation issues touched on above. I do so because I take all of them to offer interesting live issues for further discussion,

---

[35] Presumably Russell knew of Lewis Carroll's White Queen, whose memory worked in both directions: 'It's a poor sort of memory that only works backwards', as the Queen says to Alice. So it is notable that this is the same lecture in which Russell famously dismisses the monarchy, along with causation, as 'a relic of a bygone age'. Moreover, the lecture was written at the period in which, as Norbert Wiener would later write of Russell, it was 'impossible to describe [him] except by saying that he looks like the Mad Hatter' (Wiener 1964: 194). So it would be a missed opportunity, to say the least, if Russell did not have the White Queen in mind!

[36] The White Queen is thermodynamically impossible, in other words.

[37] See, for example, Ismael (2011, 2016); Evans, Milburn, and Shrapnel (2021); and Rovelli (2021, 2022a, 2022b).

and because I want to emphasize again an important general lesson: in discussing neopragmatism and its rivals, it is crucial to keep in mind what questions we take ourselves to be addressing.

Two of these demarcation issues concern boundaries between neopragmatism and rival approaches, and involve questions that even an enthusiastic neopragmatist might fairly regard as still up for debate. The first concerns the split between manifest time and time as properly studied by physics;[38] the second, the split between neopragmatist and rival approaches to probability and causation. If we think of these two issues as active fault-lines, the key point I want to stress is that in each case, the materials on either side of the fault have very different compositions: on one side, the igneous bedrock of physics or metaphysics; on the other, the sedimentary strata of pragmatism, built like corals reefs from the activity of diverse creatures, human and otherwise.[39] These fault-lines are discontinuities, in the geological sense. They involve physics or metaphysics on one side, but psychology, broadly construed, on the other. To fail to notice that difference is a recipe for continued confusion.

The third demarcation issue is different. As I put it above, it is a question of whether we appeal to memory or to agency in accounting for the difference between fixed past and open future, or for the causal asymmetry. In this case we have a disagreement *within* the neopragmatist camp, between two rival explanations of the observed geological data. Both sides agree that the geology displays the trail of the human serpent, and no doubt of many pre-human ancestor serpents, in a way that igneous bedrock would not. They disagree about which characteristic of the serpent has left its mark.[40]

References

Ahmed, A. (ed.) (2018). *Newcomb's Problem*, Cambridge University Press.

Albert, D. (2000). *Time and Chance*, Harvard University Press.

Albert, D. (2015). *After Physics*, Harvard University Press.

Anscombe, G. E. M. (1975). 'The First Person', in Guttenplan 1975: 45–64.

Barbour, J. (1999). *The End of Time*, Weidenfeld and Nicholson.

---

[38] As I noted above, recent advocates of a richer physics of time—a physics including 'passage', for example—include Maudlin (2007); Smolin (2013); and Dowker (2022).

[39] Pragmatists will recognize 'coral reefs' as a hat-tip to Rorty. 'Davidson lets us think of the history of language, and thus of culture, as Darwin taught us to think of the history of a coral reef', as Rorty puts it (1989: 16).

[40] I am very grateful to Helen Beebee, Josh Gert, Cheryl Misak, Carlo Rovelli, and Dan Williams for comments on earlier versions of this chapter, and also to audiences at Cambridge, Berkeley, Munich, Helsinki, Dublin, and the Dewey Center, Fudan University, for much discussion at talks based on this material.

Barbour, J. (2020a). *Janus Point: A New Theory of Time*, Basic Books.

Barbour, J. (2020b). *A History of Thermodynamics*, typescript, accessed September 14, 2022: <http://www.platonia.com/A_History_of_Thermodynamics.pdf>.

Bardon, A. (ed.) (2011). *The Future of the Philosophy of Time*, Routledge.

Beebee, H. (2015). 'Causation, Projection, Inference, and Agency', in Johnson, and Smith 2015: 25–48.

Beebee, H., Hitchcock, C., and Price, H. (eds.) (2010). *The Oxford Handbook of Causation*, Oxford University Press.

Beebee, H., Hitchcock, C., and Price, H. (eds.) (2017). *Making a Difference*, Oxford University Press.

Bird, A. (2012). 'Dispositional Expressions', in Russell and Fara 2012: 729–40.

Blackburn, S. (1984). *Spreading the Word: Groundings in the Philosophy of Language*, Oxford University Press.

Boltzmann, L. (1964). *Lectures on Gas Theory, 1896–1898*, trans. S. Brush, University of California Press.

Boncompagni, A. (2017). 'The "Middle" Wittgenstein (and the "Later" Ramsey) on the Pragmatist Conception of Truth', in Misak and Price 2017: 29–44.

Braddon-Mitchell, D. (2004). 'How Do We Know It Is Now Now?', *Analysis* 64: 199–203.

Brandom, R. (2008). *Between Saying and Doing: Towards an Analytic Pragmatism*, Oxford University Press.

Brandom, R. (2013). 'Global Anti-Representationalism?', in Price et al. 2013: 85–111.

Braun, David (2017). 'Indexicals', *The Stanford Encyclopedia of Philosophy* (Summer edn), ed. Edward N. Zalta, <https://plato.stanford.edu/archives/sum2017/entries/indexicals/>.

Callender, C. (2004). 'There Is No Puzzle about the Low Entropy Past', in Hitchcock 2004: 240–55.

Callender, C. (ed.) (2011). *The Oxford Handbook of Time*, Oxford University Press.

Callender, C. (2017). *What Makes Time Special?*, Oxford University Press.

Calosi, C., Graziani, P., Pietrini, D., and Tarozzi, G. (eds.) (2021). *Experience, Abstraction and the Scientific Image of the World: Festschrift for Vincenzo Fano*, ed. Franco Angeli, accessed September 3, 2022: <arXiv:2007.05300>.

Carnap, R. (1936 and 1937). 'Testability and Meaning', *Philosophy of Science* 3: 419–71; 4: 1–40.

Carroll, S. (2010). *From Eternity to Here: The Quest for the Ultimate Theory of Time*, Dutton.

Cartwright, N. (1979). 'Causal Laws and Effective Strategies', *Noûs* 13(4): 419–37.

Castañeda, H.-N. (ed.) (1975). *Action, Knowledge, and Reality: Studies in Honor of Wilfrid Sellars*, Bobbs-Merrill.

Chemero, A. (2009). *Stage Setting: A BIT of Radical Embodied Cognitive Science*, MIT Pres

Choi, S. and Fara, M. (2021). 'Dispositions', *The Stanford Encyclopedia of Philosophy* (Spring edn), ed. Edward N. Zalta, <https://plato.stanford.edu/archives/spr2021/entries/dispositions/>.

Clark, A. (2013). 'Whatever Next? Predictive Brains, Situated Agents, and the Future of Cognitive Science', *Behavioral and Brain Sciences* 36(3): 181–204.

Clark, A. (2015). 'Predicting Peace: The End of the Representation Wars—A Reply to Michael Madary', in Metzinger and Windt 2015.

Clark, A. (2016). *Surfing Uncertainty*, Oxford University Press.

Colodny, R. G. (ed.) (1962). *Frontiers of Science and Philosophy*, University of Pittsburgh Press.

Davidson, D. and Harman, G. (eds.) (1972). *Semantics of Natural Language*, Reidel.

Dennett, D. (2009). 'Darwin's "Strange Inversion of Reasoning"', *Proceedings of the National Academy of Sciences* USA 106 (Suppl. 1): 10061–5.

Dennett, D. (2013). 'Expecting Ourselves to Expect: The Bayesian Brain as a Projector', *Behavioral and Brain Sciences* 36(3): 209–10.

Dewey, J. (1925). *Experience and Nature*, Open Court.

Dowker, F. (2022). 'Causal Set Quantum Gravity and the Hard Problem of Consciousness', arXiv preprint arXiv:2209.07653.

Earman, J. (1974). 'An Attempt to Add a Little Direction to "The Problem of the Direction of Time"', *Philosophy of Science* 41: 15–47.

Eddington, A. (1928). *The Nature of the Physical World*, Cambridge University Press.

Eddington, A. (1931). 'The End of the World: From the Standpoint of Mathematical Physics', *Nature* 127: 447–53.

Ernst, G. and Huttemann, A. (eds.) (2010). *Time, Chance and Reduction: Philosophical Aspects of Statistical Mechanics*, Cambridge University Press.

Evans, P., Milburn, G., and Shrapnel, S. (2021). 'Causal Asymmetry from the Perspective of a Causal Agent', preprint, accessed August, 25, 2022: <http://philsci-archive.pitt.edu/18844/>.

Feigl, H. and Scriven, M. (eds.) (1958). *Minnesota Studies in the Philosophy of Science*, Vol. 2, University of Minnesota Press.

Fernandes, A. (2022). 'How to Explain the Direction of Time', *Synthese* 200: 389.

Frisch, M. (2007). 'Causation, Counterfactuals and Entropy', in Price and Corry 2007: 351–95.

Frisch, M. (2010). 'Does a Low-Entropy Constraint Prevent Us from Influencing the Past?', in Ernst and Huttemann 2010: 13–33.

Frisch, M. (2014). *Causal Reasoning in Physics*, Cambridge University Press.

Gibson, J. (1979). *The Ecological Approach to Visual Perception*, Houghton-Mifflin.

Godfrey-Smith, P. (2013). 'John Dewey's Experience and Nature', *Topoi* 33(1): 285–91.

Goodman, N. (1954). *Fact, Fiction, and Forecast*, Athlone Press.

Guttenplan, S. (ed.) (1975). *Mind and Language: Wolfson College Lectures 1974*, Clarendon Press.

Haldane, J. and Wright, C. (eds.) (1993). *Reality, Representation, and Projection*, Oxford University Press.

Harper, W. L., Stalnaker, R., and Pearce, G. (eds.) (1981). *Ifs: Conditionals, Belief, Decision, Chance, and Time*, The University of Western Ontario Series in Philosophy of Science, Vol. 15, Springer.

Hartle, J. (2005). 'The Physics of Now', *American Journal of Physics* 73: 101–9.

Healey R. (2017). *The Quantum Revolution in Philosophy*, Oxford University Press.

Hitchcock, Christopher (ed.) (2004). *Contemporary Debates in Philosophy of Science*, Blackwell.

Hohwy, J. (2013). *The Predictive Mind*, Oxford University Press.

Ismael, J. (2007). *The Situated Self*, Oxford University Press.

Ismael, J. (2011). 'Decision and the Open Future', in Bardon 2011: 149–68.

Ismael, J. (2016). *How Physics Makes Us Free*, Oxford University Press.

James, W. (1907). *Pragmatism: A New Name for Some Old Ways of Thinking*, Longmans, Green, and Company.

Johnson, R. and Smith, M. (eds.) (2015). *Passions and Projections: Themes from the Philosophy of Simon Blackburn*, Oxford University Press.

Johnston, M. (1993). 'Objectivity Refigured: Pragmatism without Verificationism', in Haldane and Wright 1993: 85–130.

Klagge, J. and Nordmann, A. (eds.) (1993). *Ludwig Wittgenstein: Philosophical Occasions 1912–1951*, Hackett.

Kneale, W. (1949). *Probability and Induction*, Clarendon Press.

Knowles, J. and Rydenfelt, H. (eds.) (2011). *Pragmatism, Science and Naturalism*, Peter Lang.

Kripke, S. (1972). 'Naming and Necessity', in Davidson and Harman 1972: 253–355, 763–9.

Levi, I. (2000). 'The Foundations of Causal Decision Theory', *Journal of Philosophy* 97: 387–402.

Lewis, D. (1973). *Counterfactuals*, Blackwell.

Lewis, D. (1979). 'Attitudes De Dicto and De Se', *The Philosophical Review* 88: 513–43; reprinted in his *Philosophical Papers*, Vol. I, Oxford University Press, 133–55.

Lewis, D. (1980). 'A Subjectivist's Guide to Objective Chance', in Harper et al. 1981: 267–97; reprinted in Lewis's *Philosophical Papers*, Vol. II, Oxford University Press, 83–132.

Lewis, D. (1994). 'Humean Supervenience Debugged', *Mind* 103(412): 473–90.

Loewer, B. (2007). 'Counterfactuals and the Second Law', in Price and Corry 2007: 293–326.

Loewer, B. (2012). 'Two Accounts of Laws and Time', *Philosophical Studies* 160(1): 115–37.

Macarthur, D. and de Caro, M. (eds.) (2004). *Naturalism in Question*, Harvard University Press.

Maier, J. (2020). 'Abilities', *The Stanford Encyclopedia of Philosophy* (Winter edn), ed. Edward N. Zalta, <https://plato.stanford.edu/archives/win2020/entries/abilities/>.

Marion, M. (2012). 'Wittgenstein, Ramsey and British Pragmatism', *European Journal of Pragmatism and American Philosophy* 4(2): 54–80.

Maudlin, T. (2007). *The Metaphysics within Physics*, Oxford University Press.

Mellor, D. H. (1971). *The Matter of Chance*, Cambridge University Press.

Mellor, D. H. (ed.) (1978). *Foundations: Essays in Philosophy, Logic, Mathematics and Economics*, Routledge and Kegan Paul.

Mellor, D. H. (1982). 'Chances and Degrees of Belief: In What? Why? Where? When?', ed. R. B. McLaughlin, Reidel, 49–68; reprinted in his *Matters of Metaphysics*, Cambridge University Press, 1991, 235–53.

Mellor, D. H. (ed.) (1990). *Philosophical Papers*, Cambridge University Press.

Menzies, P. (ed.) (1993). *Response-Dependent Concepts*, Philosophy Program, RSSS, ANU.

Metzinger, T. and Windt, J. M. (eds.) (2015). *Open MIND: 7(R)*, MIND Group.

Misak, C. (2016). *Cambridge Pragmatism: From Peirce and James to Ramsey and Wittgenstein*, Oxford University Press.

Misak, C. (2020). *Frank Ramsey: A Sheer Excess of Powers*, Oxford University Press.

Misak, C. (Forthcoming). 'Ryle's Debt: Ramsey and MacDonald on Hypotheses and Laws'.

Misak, C. and Price, H. (eds.) (2017). 'The Practical Turn: Pragmatism in the British Long Twentieth Century', *Proceedings of the British Academy* 210, Oxford University Press.

Morris, W. E. and C. R. Brown (2021). 'David Hume', *The Stanford Encyclopedia of Philosophy* (Spring edn), ed. Edward N. Zalta, <https://plato.stanford.edu/archives/spr2021/entries/hume/>.

Nozick, R. (1969). 'Newcomb's Problem and Two Principles of Choice', in Rescher 1969: 114–46.

Pearl, J. (2000). *Causality: Models, Reasoning and Inference*, Cambridge University Press.

Peirce, C. S. (1905). 'What Pragmatism Is', *The Monist* 15: 161–81.

Penrose, R. (1989). *The Emperor's New Mind*, Oxford University Press.

Perry, J. (1979). 'The Problem of the Essential Indexical', *Noûs* 13: 3–21.

Price, H. (1981). *The Problem of the Single Case*, PhD thesis, Cambridge University, accessed August 13, 2022: <https://philarchive.org/rec/PRITPO-47>.

Price, H. (1986). 'Against Causal Decision Theory', *Synthese* 67: 195–212.

Price, H. (1988). *Facts and the Function of Truth*, Basil Blackwell.

Price, H. (1991). 'Agency and Probabilistic Causality', *British Journal for the Philosophy of Science* 42: 157–76.

Price, H. (1993). 'Two Paths to Pragmatism', in Menzies 1993: 46–82; reprinted in Price 2011a.

Price, H. (1996). *Time's Arrow and Archimedes' Point: New Directions for the Physics of Time*, Oxford University Press.

Price, H. (2004a). 'Naturalism without Representationalism', in Macarthur and de Caro 2004: 71–88; reprinted in Price 2011a: 184–99.

Price, H. (2004b). 'On the Origins of the Arrow of Time: Why There Is Still a Puzzle about the Low Entropy Past', in Hitchcock 2004: 219–39.

Price, H. (2007). 'Causal Perspectivalism', in Price and Corry 2007: 250–92.

Price, H. (2010). 'Time's Arrow and Eddington's Challenge', *Séminaire Poincaré*, Vol. XV, Le Temps, 115–40, <http://www.bourbaphy.fr/price.pdf>.

Price, H. (2011a). *Naturalism without Mirrors*, Oxford University Press.

Price, H. (2011b). 'The Flow of Time', in Callender 2011: 276–311.

Price, H. (2011c). 'Expressivism for Two Voices', in Knowles and Rydenfelt 2011: 87–113.

Price, H. (2012). 'Causation, Chance, and the Rational Significance of Supernatural Evidence', *Philosophical Review* 121: 483–538.

Price, H. (2017). 'Causation, Intervention and Agency—Woodward on Menzies and Price', in Beebee et al. 2017: 73–98.

Price, H. (2019a). 'Global Expressivism by the Method of Differences', *Royal Institute of Philosophy Supplements* 86: 133–54.

Price, H. (2019b). 'What Makes Time Special?', *Philosophical Review* 128: 250–4.

Price, H. (2022a). 'Cheryl Misak, Frank Ramsey: A Sheer Excess of Powers', *Society* 59: 52–5.

Price, H. (2022b). 'Family Feuds? Relativism, Expressivism, and Disagreements about Disagreement', *Philosophical Topics* 50: 293–344.

Price, H. (2022c). 'Causation and the Open Future; Russell, Eddington and Ramsey', presentation at a Blue Sky Thinking Workshop, University of Surrey, July 7, 2022, accessed August 25, 2022: <https://www.youtube.com/watch?v=eJhvF9MUcis>.

Price, H. (2022d). 'Global Expressivism and Alethic Pluralism', *Synthese* 200: 386.

Price, H. (Forthcoming). *Facts and the Function of Truth: New Expanded Edition*, Oxford University Press.

Price, H., with Blackburn, S., Brandom, R., Horwich, P., and Williams, M. (2013). *Expressivism, Pragmatism and Representationalism*, Cambridge University Press.

Price, H. and Corry, R. (eds.) (2007). *Causation, Physics, and the Constitution of Reality Russell's Republic Revisited*, Clarendon Press.

Price, H. and Liu, Y. (2018). '"Click!" Bait for Causalists', in Ahmed 2018: 160–79.

Price, H. and Weslake, B. (2010). 'The Time-Asymmetry of Causation', in Beebee et al. 2010: 414–43.

Price, H. and Wharton, K. (2015). 'Disentangling the Quantum World', *Entropy* 17(11): 7752–67.

Putnam, H. (1981). *Reason, Truth and History*, Cambridge University Press.

Ramsey, F. P. (1929a). 'General Propositions and Causality', in Mellor 1978: 133–51.

Ramsey, F. P. (1929b). 'Philosophy', in Mellor 1990: 1–8.

Reichenbach, H. (1956). *The Direction of Time*, University of California Press.

Rescher, N. (ed.) (1969). *Essays in honor of Carl G. Hempel*, Springer.

Rorty, R. (1989). *Contingency, Irony and Solidarity*, Cambridge University Press.

Rovelli, C. (2021). 'Agency in Physics', in Calosi et al. 2021.

Rovelli, C. (2022a). 'Back to Reichenbach', preprint, accessed September 3, 2022: <http://philsci-archive.pitt.edu/20148/>.

Rovelli, C. (2022b). 'Memory and Entropy', *Entropy* 24: 1022, accessed September 3, 2022: <arXiv:2003.06687>.

Russell, B. (1913). 'On the Notion of Cause', *Proceedings of the Aristotelian Society*, New Series 13: 1–26.

Russell, G. and Fara, D. G. (eds.) (2012). *Routledge Companion to the Philosophy of Language*, Routledge.

Ryle, G. (1949). *The Concept of Mind*, Hutchinson.

Schroeder, M. (2015). *Expressing Our Attitudes: Explanation and Expression in Ethics, Volume 2,* Oxford University Press.

Sellars, W. (1949). 'Language, Rules, and Behavior', in Sicha 1980.

Sellars, W. (1958). 'Counterfactuals, Dispositions, and the Causal Modalities', in Feigl and Scriven 1958: 225–308.

Sellars, W. (1962). 'Philosophy and the Scientific Image of Man', in Colodny 1962: 35–78; reprinted in W. Sellars, *Science, Perception and Reality*, Routledge & Kegan Paul, 1963.

Sellars, W. (1975). 'Autobiographical Reflections', in Castañeda 1975: 277–93.

Sicha, J. (ed.) (1980). *Pure Pragmatics and Possible Worlds—The Early Essays of Wilfrid Sellars*, Ridgeview Publishing Co.

Smolin, L. (2013). *Time Reborn: From the Crisis in Physics to the Future of the Universe*, Houghton Mifflin Harcourt.

Stalnaker, R. (1968). 'A Theory of Conditionals', in Harper et al. 1981: 41–55.

Storer, T. (1951). 'On Defining "Soluble"', *Analysis* 11: 134–37.

Timpson, C. (2008). 'Quantum Bayesianism: A Study', *Studies in History and Philosophy of Science Part B: Studies in History and Philosophy of Modern Physics* 39(3): 579–609.

Toulmin, S. (1950). 'Probability', *Proceedings of the Aristotelian Society* 24 (Suppl.): 27–62.

Varzi, A. C. (2020). 'Counterpart Theories for Everyone', *Synthese* 197: 4691–715.

von Wright, G. H. (1993). 'The Wittgenstein Papers', in Klagge and Nordmann 1993: 480–510.

Wiener, N. (1964). *Ex-Prodigy: My Childhood and Youth*, MIT Press.

Williams, D. C. (1951). 'The Myth of Passage', *Journal of Philosophy* 48(15): 457–71.

Williams, D. (2018). 'Pragmatism and the Predictive Mind', *Phenomenology and the Cognitive Sciences* 17: 835–59.

Williams, M. (2010). 'Pragmatism, Minimalism, Expressivism', *International Journal of Philosophical Studies* 18: 317–30.

Williams, M. (2013). 'How Pragmatists can be Local Expressivists', in Price et al. 2013: 128–44.

Wittgenstein, L. (1930). 'MS107', as catalogued in von Wright 1993.

Woodward, J. (2003). *Making Things Happen: A Theory of Causal Explanation*, Oxford University Press.

3
A Neopragmatist Approach to Modality

Amie L. Thomasson

Modality has long presented a range of philosophical problems and puzzles. For example, are there (really) modal properties, modal facts, or possible worlds? If there are modal properties, how could they be related to non-modal properties or relations? If there are modal facts, properties, or possible worlds, how could we come to know about them, given that modal features of the world seem not to be empirically detectable, and that possible worlds seem to be, in principle, causally disconnected from us?

I will argue that we can make a better approach to the problems of modality if we start a step back. That is, I will suggest that we should begin not with metaphysical questions about what modal properties or possible worlds *are* (or whether there are any), or with epistemological questions about how we could know them. Instead, I will argue, we should begin by asking what *functions* modal discourse serves, and what *rules* it follows. This, of course, is to take a broadly neopragmatist approach to the problems of modality.[1] For as neopragmatists such as David MacArthur and Huw Price have put it, "pragmatism begins with questions about the functions and genealogy of certain *linguistic* items...It begins with linguistic behaviour, and asks broadly anthropological questions: How are we to understand the roles and functions of the behaviour in question, in the lives of the creatures concerned?" (2007: 95). One overarching theme is that a better understanding of the language in question can lead us to reevaluate many traditional philosophical problems. But the proof is in the pudding. Here I will aim to demonstrate the plausibility and usefulness of the neopragmatist approach with some modal pudding.

The neopragmatist approach faces two central challenges. First, since neopragmatists want to begin from questions about the functions of forms of language, they need to give a clear and systematic story about what linguistic functions *are*, and how we may identify them. Without that, neopragmatists are subject to suspicions that the proffered functional analyses are just *ad hoc* suggestions designed to avoid philosophical problems. Second, the approach faces the challenge of showing clearly why the pragmatic analyses of the discourse (its functions and

---

[1] The neopragmatist approach has been developed, for example, in work by Brandom (2008); Price (2011, 2013); and Williams (2011).

Amie L. Thomasson, *A Neopragmatist Approach to Modality* In: *Neopragmatism: Interventions in First-Order Philosophy.* Edited by: Joshua Gert, Oxford University Press. © Amie L. Thomasson 2023. DOI: 10.1093/oso/9780192894809.003.0003

rules) are *relevant* to the old philosophical problems. For the standard response from metaphysicians is to insist that the pragmatist's questions are just different (linguistic) questions, whereas they (metaphysicians) are concerned with *worldly* questions to which the linguistic questions are just irrelevant.

In this chapter, I will try to show how to respond to both of these challenges, using modal discourse as the case in point. I will begin in section 1 by laying out some of the difficulties in understanding modal discourse, given the complexity and variety of forms that modal discourse can take. In section 2, I will review the general approach to understanding linguistic functions which I have developed elsewhere (2022), building on work from systemic functional linguistics. After considering some developmental questions in section 3, I will go on in sections 4-6 to apply the general approach to linguistic functions to analyse the range of functions different forms of modal discourse serve, in a way that enables us to systematically answer questions about the functions and rules of various forms of modal discourse. In sections 7 and 8, I turn to the second challenge, aiming to show that this work on the functions and rules governing modal discourse *is* relevant to traditional problems about modality—in part by suggesting that many of the traditional problems arise out of misunderstandings about the discourse. By addressing the challenges of developing a general approach to understanding linguistic function, and showing its potential relevance, I hope that this work on modality can serve as a case in point to exhibit the usefulness of a neopragmatist approach, and to show how to develop it in promising ways.

1. Initial Problems: Complexity and Methodology

Most of those who have taken a broadly neopragmatist approach to modal discourse have taken the question to be simply: 'what is the function of modal discourse?' and have offered a *unified* answer—at least for the sort of modality they are concerned with. So, for example, A. J. Ayer says that analytic statements "*illustrate* the rules which govern our usage" (1936/1952: 80); Simon Blackburn (1993) suggests that the function of modal discourse is to express the limits of our imaginative capacities—to say that something is necessary is to express the inconceivability of its denial (1993: 70); Robert Brandom argues that alethic modal vocabulary "make[s] explicit semantic or conceptual connections that are already implicit in the use of ordinary (apparently) non-modal empirical vocabulary" (2008: 99); and I argued that "modal language serves the function[s] of mandating, conveying, or renegotiating rules or norms in particularly advantageous ways" (2020: 15). But there is such a wide range of ways of expressing modality in language that it is questionable whether we should look for a straightforward, single answer to the question "What is the function of modal discourse?" at all.

Modal discourse is importantly varied across at least three dimensions. First, there are differences in what are sometimes called the *flavors* of modality. These include deontic and ability modals; physical, metaphysical, and logical modalities; and epistemic modals.[2] A complete account of modality should make clear what these varieties have in common, while also clarifying the differences among them. These distinctions *have* often been noted and respected in the neopragmatist literature to date. Many theorists have focused on just one 'flavor' of modal discourse—as Ryle (1949: 121) and Sellars (1958) focus on statements of scientific laws, Yalcin (2011) develops an expressivist approach to epistemic modal discourse, and I have focused on claims of *metaphysical* necessity and possibility (2020). Of course, that doesn't mean that we can't hope to find some unity across these stories that address particular flavors of modality. In earlier work (2020), I suggested that the *unity* behind various forms of modal discourse was that all serve to convey, mandate, or renegotiate rules or norms in useful ways,[3] while the *variety* can be captured in terms of the different *sorts* of rule or norm that are in question. Metaphysical modals, as I have argued (2020), are concerned with conveying, enforcing, and renegotiating *semantic* rules ('squares must have four sides of equal length'), which also regulate what sorts of *material* inferences we are entitled to or prohibited from making. Logical necessities regulate what logical *forms* of inference we are permitted and required to make, across different suppositions, as Greg Restall (2012) argues. *Deontic* modals (you *should* or *ought to* or *must* do *X*) can be seen as serving to regulate behavior according to *authoritative*, *prudential*, or *moral* rules or norms. Other root modals can be understood as having parallel regulative functions, where the relevant rules or norms vary. Ability modals can be understood as giving something like Rylean 'inference tickets': to say "I can reach that shelf" or "I can skate" is to not describe something one is doing at the moment, but to license the interlocutor to make certain (empirically grounded) inferences about what the speaker would do, in certain circumstances: it is to say what we *may* infer, and may not infer (don't infer that I won't be able to get to the cake if you put it on that shelf!). Here I will leave largely to the side these questions of how to respect and account for the unity and diversity across differences in 'flavor' of modality. For here I wish to consider instead, and show the relevance of, a dimension of variation that is less often acknowledged in the philosophical literature, but that is particularly relevant to philosophical problems: grammatical distinctions in our ways of speaking modally.

---

[2] Linguists classify deontic and ability modals as 'root' modals (and though they have been of less interest in linguistics, it seems physical, metaphysical, and logical modalities would be categorized as 'root', too), and contrast these with 'epistemic' modals (Cournane 2020: 3).

[3] Namely, by enabling us to express rules or norms in the indicative mood, in ways that enable us to better reason with and from them, while making the regulative status explicit, making our ways of reasoning with them explicit, and enabling us to express permissions as well as requirements (Thomasson 2020: 63).

Grammatical distinctions in how modal claims are expressed are orthogonal to distinctions of flavor. For whether we are making deontic, physical, metaphysical, logical, or epistemic modal claims, there are various grammatical options for *how* we express them. One way is to use auxiliary verbs (asking if Sarah *should* lie to avoid upsetting her sister; if penguins *can* fly; if that *might* be Josie at the door; etc.) or semi-auxiliary verbs (asking if Sarah *has* to lie; or if it's *supposed* to rain). But we can also introduce 'lexical' modal terms, including modal adverbs ('maybe', 'probably'), modal adjectives ('is possible', 'is obligatory'), and nouns ('possibility', 'necessity') (Cournane 2020: 6). Using those modal terms, we can ask if it is *morally necessary* to always tell the truth, if it is *possible* for penguins to fly, or if there is a *possibility* that Josie is the one at the door (see Cournane 2020: 5). From there, we can even go on to introduce talk of possible worlds, asking, say, if there are possible worlds in which a creature has the same physical properties as I do but lacks mental properties.

Beyond these two axes of distinctions, of course, is a third dimension capturing differences in the *strength* or *force* of the modal claim; for example, whether we are saying something *might* or *must* happen, whether it is *possible* or *necessary*, etc. (Cournane 2020: 2). These differences in *strength* are of course expressible in various *grammatical forms* for every *flavor* of modality.

Given all the complexity, it is hard to know where to begin in investigating the functions of various forms of modal discourse. I will suggest that we start at the *developmental* beginning, as this enables us to see, at each stage, what functions are added in developing progressively more sophisticated forms of modal discourse. Given the many variations, we also should not assume at the outset that we can simply ask 'What is the function of modal discourse?' For that seems to presuppose that all forms of modal discourse may be treated together, as having a unified function. However, we should not presuppose that all modal discourse serves just *one* function, nor that all forms of modal discourse serve the same *range* of functions. I will turn next to discuss how we can make use of work in systemic functional linguistics to help us identify the *plurality* of functions served by various forms of discourse—including modal discourse of various forms.

2. The General Challenge: Identifying Linguistic Functions

Central to the neopragmatist approach is the idea that we should begin with questions about the functions of the relevant forms of language, not with metaphysical questions, say, about the existence or nature of possible worlds. But how, in general, can we determine what the functions of a form of discourse are? While neopragmatists have long emphasized the importance of giving functional analyses, they also face recurring skepticism that anything helpful can be said about linguistic functions. Herman Cappelen, for example, has recently raised doubts that anything more can be said about linguistic functions than the representationalist mantra that "the function of 'F' is to refer to the Fs" (2018: 187), adding, "If the goal is to find functions that are more substantive and informative than the disquotationally specified functions, then it will be unsuccessful" (2018: 187). This echoes concerns raised long ago that language is *used* in so many ways that it's hard to find anything *systematic* to be said about linguistic functions (Austin 1961: 234). It also echoes frequent suspicions that neopragmatist proposals about the function of, say, moral, modal, or mathematical discourse are *ad hoc* suggestions to serve a philosophical purpose. Elsewhere I have addressed the general question about how to determine linguistic functions (2022). I will begin with a brief sketch of the approach to functional questions that I recommend there.

In addressing questions about the functions of (parts of) language, a common theme across neopragmatist literature is that we can begin by asking what the relevant linguistic forms enable (at least) some speakers to do that they could not do, or could not do so well or so efficiently, otherwise. One point to emphasize here is that there should be no requirement that fulfilling the function benefits *everyone*, nor that the linguistic form be absolutely *indispensable*. There is no similar requirement that, if archeologists or other outsiders (travelers, children) aim to identify the functions of concrete artifacts, the functions should be universally beneficial (think of weapons or fences), or that there is no *alternative* way to fulfill the relevant functions (think of a butter knife or ice cream scoop). Moreover, whether or how well an entity fulfills a function always must be judged in a total context of other available equipment; a total set of purposes; local human capabilities and practices; etc.

Another common theme, prominent in the work of Huw Price (2011, 2013), is to insist that these functional questions about language are basically *empirical* questions, about the roles these forms of language serve in human life. Other functional questions are certainly addressed by empirical sciences, as (for example) biologists address questions of biological function, and archeologists address questions about the functions of the historical artifacts they discover.[4] Accordingly, functional questions about language might be best addressed in what Price refers to as 'subject naturalist' mode (2013: 5), by work in anthropology and/or linguistics.

Fortunately, there is relevant work to draw on. Work in systemic functional linguistics, which has drawn from and has been highly influential in anthropology,[5] addresses exactly these functional questions about language. It begins from the idea that "language has evolved in the service of certain

---

[4] Naturalistic ways of addressing questions about function, whether for biological entities or artifacts, are famously developed by Ruth Millikan (1987).

[5] The anthropologist Bronisław Malinowski was particularly influential on the development of systemic functional linguistics (Eggins 2004: 88–9), especially through his influence on linguist J. R. Firth, who in turn taught Michael Halliday.

functions" (Halliday 1973: 14) and asks about the ways in which the functions of language in human life are reflected in the way language is structured (Malmkjaer 1991: 159). I have argued elsewhere (2022) that we may make use of the framework and central results from systemic functional linguistics to address questions about the functions served by various elements of the linguistic system, in ways that shed light on various old philosophical problems.

As Michael Halliday's work in developmental linguistics emphasizes, children (typically between ages 1 and 3) use a proto-language to serve a variety of functions—including instrumental (used to get goods or services), regulatory (used to control the behavior of others), interactional (used in greetings, partings...), personal (to express feelings of interest, pleasure, disgust...), heuristic (used to investigate the environment), imaginative (used in pretending), and (a little later) informational or representational (Halliday 2009: 101, 1975: 20-1). Notably, early childhood language is functionally simple, with each utterance typically serving a single function (Halliday 2009: 85).

What changes when children reach mature language is that, in mature language, *each utterance typically serves more than one function at a time*[6] (Halliday 1975: 26). This distinctive feature of mature language helps explain the ways language is grammatically structured. For it is the variability in grammatical forms that enables different functions to be served simultaneously. As Halliday puts it, grammar "allows for meanings which derive from different functions to be encoded together, as integrated structures, so that every expression becomes, in principle, functionally complex. Grammar makes it possible to mean more than one thing at a time" (1975: 48).

But what functions are these? Halliday categorizes them into three "macro-functions," where (typically) each clause simultaneously serves functions in all three of the macro-functional categories (Halliday 1973: 34). These macro-functions are:

Ideational: This is a matter of encoding and communicating a content (Halliday 2009: 110). It is often glossed as encoding a content *about the world or the speaker's experience*. But ideational content can also be given in highly abstract terms, far distanced from anything like direct experience (Halliday 2014: 712-20).[7] So, for example, we can also speak of the ideational content carried by "The

---

[6] Indeed each clause—with a few exceptions, such as 'How do you do?' and "No wonder!" (Halliday 2009: 99).

[7] Thus, ideational content need not be *congruent*; it can involve all sorts of *grammatical metaphors* (for more on congruence and grammatical metaphors, see below). As Halliday puts it, "the model of experience construed in the congruent mode is reconstructed in the metaphorical mode, creating a model that is further removed from our everyday experience—but which has made modern science possible" (2014: 718). This also shows that a form of discourse may possess ideational content without *tracking* certain features in the world (with which we are in causal contact) or being used to inform others about them—in Price's terms (2011: 20-1), it need not be e-representational.

perception of an inadequate retirement program consistently surfaces as a primary cause of our recruiting and retention problems" (Halliday 2014: 713), though this is far removed from anything anyone ever saw with their eyes. In later work, Halliday distinguishes two sub-components of ideational content: experiential (broadly construed) and logical (concerned with 'the expression of logical relations') (2009: 111, 2014: 361-2).[8] From a philosophical standpoint we can see the import of this meta-function roughly as carrying a *propositional content*,[9] which we can use in communicating information (broadly construed), or formulating proposals, and which (given its propositional form) can be used in *reasoning*.[10] This macro-function has been the primary focus of philosophical attention.

Interpersonal: These cover the broadly social functions of language—enabling speakers to take up or show their relation or roles with respect to their interlocutors (as questioner, respondent, commander, polite or impolite...), to express their attitudes toward the subject matter, to show their level of certainty, and points of view, and to (attempt to) regulate the behavior of others (Eggins 2004: 11-12). In English, the mood and modal systems support these interpersonal functions—they are ways language is structured to enable *interaction*. (Eggins 2004: 184).[11]

Textual: The textual macro-functions enable us to organize a text as an extended piece of writing or speech, making evident the relations among ideas, the central theme, etc. These textual functions are carried (for example) by terms such as 'since', 'therefore', 'although', and 'so'. They are also carried by the ability to engage in transformations from one grammatical category to another, forming what Halliday calls 'grammatical metaphors' (2009: 116-38). Such changes enable us to, for example, change word order and grammatical structure to better identify the topic and show what the important or new parts of information are, and to add expressive power to the language in ways that are crucial for developing scientific theories and bureaucracies.

This framework can enable us to address the first challenge, of how to systematically identify linguistic functions. In the case of modal discourse, as I will argue below, this framework can enable us to make progress in understanding how functions may vary systematically across different *grammatical formulations* of modal discourse.

---

[8] Where 'logical' is construed informally and broadly, to include causal relationships.
[9] Halliday uses 'proposition' to refer to a clause used to 'exchange information'; contrasted with a 'proposal': a clause used to "enable the exchange of goods and services" (Eggins 2004: 148-9).
[10] Talk of the ideational content as 'representing' the world or our experience, or communicating 'information' here should clearly be understood in a deflated sense—not one in which it is tied to a philosophical form of Representationalism, a correspondence theory of truth, etc.
[11] As Eggins puts it, "when we ask, 'how is language structured to enable interaction?' we find the answer lies (principally) in the systems of Mood and Modality" (2004: 184)—so it seems that these are the *principal* ways interpersonal functions are carried, but perhaps not the only ways.

This framework should also lead us to suspect that the pragmatist's query 'What is the function of modal discourse?' (or of '*X*'-discourse, where *X* is any topic: moral, modal, causal, mathematical...) may be not quite the right way to pose the question. For there may be typically more than one type of function served at a time, and the cluster of functions served may vary across different grammatical formulations of what has been treated as the same 'kind of' discourse (modal, moral, mathematical...).

3. Where to Begin? The Developmental Progression

Given all the complexities of modal discourse and different dimensions of variation identified in section 1, it can be hard to know where to begin in analyzing modal language. I propose that we start at the *developmental* beginning. If we can develop our account along these lines, we can do better in asking at each stage, what *additional* functions might be served by adding additional modal formulations to one's linguistic repertoire. So, a brief look at how and when children learn different forms of modal language will be useful in suggesting how to proceed.

In terms of variations in 'flavor', there is consistent evidence that the 'root' modals, including ability modals and deontic modals, are acquired before epistemic modals. Root modal verbs enter language at around age 2, starting with ability verbs ('can') and then progressing to deontic modal terms (Cournane 2020: 7). Epistemic uses of modals begin later, around age 3.[12] (As far as I know, linguists have not specifically addressed questions about metaphysical or logical modalities.) In terms of force, claims of *necessity* also come later than claims of *possibility* (Cournane 2020: 11-12), and children don't learn the strength of different modal claims until around age 7 (Papafragou 1998: 8-14).

But it is *grammatical* variations that I will focus on here, since less has been said about them in the philosophical literature, and yet (as I will argue) they are particularly relevant to understanding the emergence and persistence of philosophical problems about modality. Grammatically, modal expressions enter language in the form of auxiliary (and semi-auxiliary) verbs. 'Objectified' modal expressions such as 'it is possible that' and 'there is a possibility that' are acquired later, between ages 6 and 12. (Papafragou 1998: 22). This is confirmed by work in systemic functional linguistics, which classifies such objectified modal expressions as 'grammatical metaphors', and notes that children typically begin to process grammatical metaphors only around ages 8 or 9 (Halliday 2009: 46). (More on this below.) Possible worlds talk is so distinctively philosophical that, to my

---

[12] There is an interesting debate about the reasons for this 'epistemic gap'. See Papafragou (1998: 4) and Cournane (2020).

knowledge, there has been no linguistic study of it at all. But clearly if it is acquired at all, it is acquired quite late in life, in specialized academic contexts.

Given this developmental history, it is striking to note that many philosophical investigations *begin* at the *end* of the story, asking what possible worlds are, if there are any, or what possibilities or modal properties are. Indeed the standard metaphysical approach to these problems is to take talk of possibilities, possible worlds, or modal properties as what is *primarily* of interest, and to ask whether there are such objects, what they are like, how they can be known, and perhaps even how the relevant *objects referred to* can explain, justify, or serve as truth-makers for our modal discourse—including the basic discourse expressed using modal auxiliary verbs (e.g. 'it might rain tomorrow' is thought of as *about* and *made true by* a possibility of rain, or a possible world in which it rains tomorrow...).

In taking a step back to ask first about the functions of the discourse, we reverse direction. For if we want to understand the functions originally served by introducing basic modal discourse, we have reason to begin our inquiries instead with modal verbs, and ask what functions it serves for a child to add these to their linguistic repertoire—as that marks the beginning of acquiring a modal system. What can a child do, in acquiring modal verbs, that they couldn't otherwise do (or couldn't do so effectively, in the context)? Of course, the child doesn't stop there—so we can go on to ask, at later stages, what functions it serves to *add* modal adjectives and nouns to the child's linguistic resources, and perhaps even eventually ask what it adds to add talk of possible worlds. We can also ask how these new adjectival, adverbial, and nominative terms come to enter language: what introduction rules entitle us to add them to our language? Once we have better understood this progressive development and the functions progressively introduced, it may no longer seem so 'natural' to begin with the metaphysical questions.

4. Functions of Basic Modal Discourse

I have suggested that, in pursuing our functional question, we should begin at the developmental beginning. We have also seen that, grammatically, the most basic form of modal discourse is expressed with modal auxiliary verbs. What new functions are introduced with a modal system?

A first thing to note is that (in English) both mood and modal systems primarily carry 'interpersonal' functions (Halliday 1973: 33; cf. Eggins 2004: 172-84). So, if we ask, "Why would we have a language with a mood or modal system?," the fundamental answer is: it enables us to establish and make evident social roles and relationships, show our attitudes, get people to behave in certain ways, and so forth. Modality is "a complex area of English grammar which has to do with different ways a language user can intrude on her message, expressing attitudes and judgments of various kinds" (Eggins 2004: 172).

The mood system emerges early in language learning (before the modal system), and mastery of it enables the child to speak in various grammatical moods—uttering declaratives, interrogatives, imperatives, etc. A proto-mood system can be observed in early language development, around 19 months (Halliday 2009: 14).[13] In a mature language, mood options enable speakers to take up a range of social relationships to their interlocutors, including questioner/respondent (with interrogative form), commander/commanded (with imperative form), etc. Among other things, a *mood* system enables speakers to use language to take on the task of regulating behavior, by uttering imperatives.

Use of a *modal* system, as we have seen, emerges somewhat later (around ages 2 to 3), even in its initial form. What does a modal system give speakers that they would lack if they had only a mood system at their disposal? We can identify at least four further advantages gained by using a modal system (rather than just a mood system). A first is that it enables us to fulfill regulative functions without overtly taking on the role of commander. So, as a professor, I can utter the imperative to my students: "Read Kant's *Groundwork*." But I could also use a modal verb instead, saying, "All students of Philosophy 1 *must* read Kant's *Groundwork*." This has the advantage not only of being more polite (I am now not barking orders but impersonally laying out the requirements), but also of being explicitly *generalized*, making it clear that the regulation applies to any *students of the class, given their role*, not just to whoever happens to be hearing my command. Shifting to a modal formulation also enables speakers to present their regulations *impersonally*, as not "not 'just their own' but [as having] some objective status" (Eggins 2004: 175).

A second advantage gained by using modal verbs in regulating behavior is that it introduces variability in *force*, enabling us to 'temper' what we say. Modal terminology introduces *degrees* by the processes of 'modalization' (moving from "Henry James wrote 'The Bostonians'," to "Henry James *might have written* 'The Bostonians'" (Eggins 2004: 173)); and 'modulation' (moving from 'Clean your room' to 'You *should* clean your room'). Both modalization and modulation are "grammatical resources for tempering what we say" (Eggins 2004: 181). Modalization introduces attitudes toward propositions, so that we aren't limited to: it *is* or it *isn't*. Instead, we can more subtly say: it *might* be, it *could* be, it *must* be...Modalization enables the speaker not just to assert or deny, but to express their judgment of the certainty, likelihood, or frequency of something (Eggins 2004: 174). So, by shifting from "Henry James wrote 'The Bostonians'", to "Henry

---

[13] As Halliday puts it, the child who was studied distinguished utterances with a 'pragmatic' 'doing' function, from those with a 'mathetic' or learning function, by use of a rising and falling tone respectively (2009: 14).

James *might have written* 'The Bostonians'," I *show* my uncertainty while still *talking about* the author and text (Eggins 2004: 173).[14] Modulation, by contrast, enables speakers to express degrees of *obligation* and *requirement* (Eggins 2004: 179). Modulation enables us to attempt to direct behavior in more subtle and graded ways than we can manage using imperatives. So, rather than commanding "Clean your room," we can stringently insist "You *must* clean your room," or more mildly suggest, "You *should* clean your room." (Eggins 2004: 179). Like modalization, modulation introduces degrees; in this case, degrees of attitudes toward *proposals*, so we aren't limited to the: 'do x' or 'don't do x' of imperatives. Instead, we can say: you *may* do it, you *should* do it, you *must* do it...(Eggins 2004: 180).

A third advantage of introducing modal formulations (rather than using the imperative mood) is that we can aim to regulate behavior while using the *declarative* mood. And that in turn enables us to reason with and from these expressions in ways that are not available with imperatives. We can say, for example, 'If students *must* read Kant's *Groundwork*, then this is going to be a hard class'; whereas it isn't even grammatical to say: 'If: Read Kant's *Groundwork*, then...'. By making this shift, to using the declarative mood, statements with modal verbs express their propositional content in a grammatical form that enables us to reason with them and from them in all the ways characteristic of declaratives, enables us to categorize them as true or false, etc.—thereby fulfilling additional *ideational* functions alongside their *interpersonal* functions.

A fourth advantage of introducing modal (rather than just mood) terminology is that, as Ryle observed, while we can issue *commands* (using the imperative mood) without modal terms, having modal terms also enables us to give *permissions* (1950: 244).[15] These last two features bring advantages in enabling us to lay out generalized systems of rules and permissions: rules that apply to *everyone* (who meets certain stated conditions), from which we can reason about what follows from these requirements, and where *permissions* may also be expressly given or revoked. This may even play a key role in enabling us to move from the 'rule of man' (where a recognized ruler or rulers issue commands to those present) to the 'rule of law', where there are *generalized principles*, supposed to apply to *everyone* (meeting certain conditions), imposing certain general requirements or permissions.

An interesting upshot of this analysis is that it shows that early prescriptivists, who took moral language to share important features with imperatives, were *onto*

---

[14] This way of thinking about epistemic modal language is cohesive with Yalcin's (2011) interesting arguments that we should not (with descriptivists) take these to be *describing* the epistemic states of agents or some body of evidence.
[15] With perhaps this exception, suggested to me by Jamie Dreier: "Go ahead and do X (if you want to)" is a way of giving permission without a modal verb. But this, being still in the imperative form, doesn't enable all the same sorts of reasoning as the modalized "You may X"—for example, the former cannot be embedded in the antecedent of a conditional ('If go ahead and do X...' isn't grammatical), while the latter can.

something, and yet it also makes it clear why more was needed to fully understand moral discourse. Carnap wrote, "a value statement is nothing else than a command in a misleading grammatical form" (1935: 24). Stevenson suggested that ethical judgments are "social instruments" (1937: 31) and have "a quasi-imperative force" (1937: 19), and their "major use" is "not to indicate facts, but to *create an influence*" (1937: 18), though unlike an imperative "it enables one to make changes in a much more subtle, less fully conscious way... [for] the ethical sentence centres the hearer's attention not on his interests, but on the object of interest" (1937: 26). Hare famously argues that "the language of morals is one sort of prescriptive language" (1952: 1). These prescriptivists were onto something (if the above analysis is correct) since modal language (of which moral *shoulds*, *musts*, and *mays* are one distinctive species) can be seen as a more sophisticated way of taking over some of the interpersonal functions of the mood system (especially of imperatives). But we can also see why saying that alone is insufficient, given the developments of modal language that enable it to fulfill a range of other functions that imperatives cannot reach—including functions in reasoning, even in embedded contexts (this difference can be seen to lie behind the infamous Frege-Geach problem (Geach 1965)). I only have space to gesture toward these implications here; fuller discussion will have to be left for elsewhere.

5. Functions of Sophisticated Modal Discourse

As we have seen above, modal discourse enters language in the form of auxiliary and semi-auxiliary modal verbs, which are introduced primarily to serve interpersonal functions, but also enable us to form expressions that serve additional *ideational* functions, since they can be expressed in indicative form, enabling us to reason with and from these claims.

Other modal expressions come as grammatical innovations that the child learns later, between ages 6 and 12, adding 'objectified' modal expressions such as 'it is possible that' and 'there is a possibility that' (Papafragou 1998: 22). What functions are added here? Why go on to learn other modal formulations, using not just modal auxiliary verbs but introducing modal adjectives ('is possible', 'is obligatory') and nouns ('a possibility' 'a necessity', 'an obligation')?

These late developments in modal language, into modal adjectives and nominalizations, play a central role in prompting metaphysical perplexities. It is only with this sort of modal vocabulary that we can even ask questions such as: what are modal properties? How are the modal properties of an object related to its non-modal/categorical properties? How can two objects (the statue and the clay) have all the same *non-modal* properties, and yet have different modal properties (one being incapable, the other capable, of surviving dramatic changes in shape)?[16] What are possibilities, or chances? What are possible worlds? Are there any? So, if we have interest in these philosophical problems, it is particularly useful to be able to understand these forms of modal discourse, their functions, and the ways they enter language.

Modal predicates and nouns enter language via grammatical transformations from more basic modal statements that use modal auxiliary verbs. So, for example, we can make a trivial inference from 'It *might* rain' (using a modal auxiliary verb) to 'Rain *is possible* tomorrow' (introducing a modal predicate) or to 'There is *a possibility of* rain' (introducing a modal nominalization).[17] In the parlance of systemic functional linguistics, making such grammatical shifts involve introducing what Michael Halliday calls 'grammatical metaphors' (2009: 116-38), so it is worth pausing for a little background on grammatical metaphors.

The first terms we learn in early language—across languages—are 'congruent' terms: nouns for things, verbs for processes, adjectives for qualities... (Halliday 2009: 117). (Or, more neutrally, we can say nouns are used for what is *perceived* as a thing, verbs for what is *perceived* as a process, etc.)[18] An early subject-verb-object utterance like 'man clean car' is congruent. Congruent terms are "evolutionarily and developmentally prior" (Halliday 2009: 117). In early language development, these more basic 'congruent' nouns such as 'stick', 'car', and 'ball' are acquired in response to observations of interest in the environment: "In contexts of observation, recall, and prediction" (Halliday 1975: 27). As Halliday puts it, these terms function to contribute to the child's learning about the environment (1975: 27-8).

These congruent terms seem to be representational in what Huw Price identifies as the 'e-representational' sense: as having the job "to *co-vary* with something else—typically, some *external* factor or environmental condition" (Price 2011: 20). Congruent, observationally acquired terms can then be used in declaratives in ways that carry ideational content and are used to track features of the world (and, of course, can also be used in requests, commands, etc.). So understood, there are two important features of congruent language: (1) it introduces terms of different grammatical categories corresponding to the *perceived categories of entities experienced* (object, process, property...); (2) it is introduced *observationally*, in response to observed features of the environment.

---

[16] This, of course, is the so-called 'grounding problem' (for discussion, see Bennett 2004).

[17] Talk of 'potential' and 'potentialities' similarly involves a grammatical metaphor, introduced from more basic talk using modal auxiliary verbs like 'can'. For example, 'The student could become a great painter' becomes 'the student has the potential to become a great painter' (Halliday 2009: 45).

[18] That is, to understand and make use of this way of understanding 'congruence' we need not interpret these as making any deep metaphysical claims about the 'real natures' of the things perceived, or the basic metaphysical categories of the world. Instead, we can easily see this initial form of language as connected to basic categories we use in *experiencing* and *navigating* the world as we perceive it—perhaps in ways that are pre-linguistic and shared with many non-human animals. (For interesting work on psychologically basic categories of 'core cognition' shared with cottontop tamarins and Rhesus macaques, see Susan Carey (2009).) Here we can see questions of developmental psychology interact with those of developmental linguistics.

Later in language development, the child learns to go beyond congruent language, to understand and utter grammatical metaphors. 'Metaphor' derives from the Greek *metaphora*, a transfer or carrying-over.[19] While familiar (lexical) metaphors carry over one *semantic meaning*, transferring it for another (if we shift from speaking of a 'sharp knife' to 'sharp words'), in *grammatical* metaphors we carry over a term from one *grammatical category* to another (if we shift from saying 'he has a knife' to 'he knifed someone', or from 'the barn is red' to 'the property of redness is possessed by the barn').[20] The ability to make such grammatical shifts is common across languages, although there may be variations in which kinds of shift are permitted and which kinds are common. Children typically do not acquire the ability to process grammatical metaphors until around ages 8 to 9 (Halliday 2009: 46). Grammatical metaphors introduce new terminology to the language, by means of trivial inferences. The rules that enable us to introduce grammatical metaphors are the same as those supporting what I have elsewhere (2015) called 'easy ontological inferences'.

But now the functional question arises: why would we want a language that permits such trivial inferences, enabling us to introduce new terms like these?[21] Here again we get an interesting answer from systemic functional linguistics: the capacity to form grammatical metaphors enables our language to serve new, *textual* functions (on top of those *ideational* and *interpersonal* functions it already served). Such textual functions in general include showing the connections among ideas in a longer piece of text and enabling us to construct scientific theories and bureaucracies (Halliday 2009: 119-38; see also discussion in my 2022: 19-23).

Modal grammatical metaphors add some useful additional textual functions, beyond the interpersonal (and ideational) functions introduced by auxiliary modal verbs. With modal auxiliary verbs, we can say 'It might rain' or 'It might snow'. But by introducing modal adjectives and nouns, we can introduce graded comparisons, saying, 'Snow *is more possible* than rain tomorrow' or '*The possibility of snow* is greater than *the possibility of rain*'—introducing what Carnap (1962: 9) called 'comparative concepts'.[22] We can even go on from there to introduce what Carnap called 'quantified concepts', saying for example, "the possibility of snow is 70 percent; but the possibility of rain is only 20%" (1962: 8-15).[23] As Carnap

---

[19] Thanks to Manuel Gustavo Isaac for pointing this out in conversation.

[20] The terminology, thus, should not be taken to suggest that the resulting statements are anything less than literally true, and should not be confused with 'fictionalist' proposals about how to understand discourse about properties, numbers, etc.

[21] This is a question I did not consider in my (2015) *Ontology Made Easy*. I have since found that systemic functional linguistics provides an extremely interesting and helpful answer to this question, making clear why we would want a language that allows for trivial inferences.

[22] Carnap noted that these comparative concepts are more useful for scientific inquiry than merely 'classificatory concepts', though not as desirable as quantitative concepts.

[23] Of course, more should be said about what it takes to *successfully* introduce such quantitative concepts. Carnap held that to do so, we must not just nominalize, but give *rules* for assigning the relevant numerical values, defined by "exact rules of measurement" (1962: 14). In the case of 'temperature',

emphasizes, quantitative concepts are particularly useful in developing precise scientific theories, enabling us to formulate precise general laws. So, for example, we might have classificatory concepts of 'warm' and 'cold', but we can only formulate the ideal gas laws if we have introduced a *quantitative* concept of *temperature*, defined in ways that make it measurable (Carnap 1962: 13). Similarly, we can only get precise probabilistic meteorological, physical, or medical theories if we introduce quantified modal concepts. Only then can we say not just "Taking the drug *might* help you avoid pulmonary complications" but rather "Taking the drug reduces *the possibility* of pulmonary complications by 42%."[24]

Talk of possible worlds, similarly, is a matter of introducing a new grammatical metaphor, by making trivial inferences from talk of what's possible. David Lewis himself originally suggested this (long before he presented his famous Inference to the Best Explanation arguments for possible worlds), writing:

> I believe there are possible worlds other than the one we happen to inhabit. If an argument is wanted, it is this. It is uncontroversially true that some things might have been otherwise than they are... But what does this mean? Ordinary language permits the paraphrase: there are many ways things could have been besides the way they actually are... I believe things could have been different in countless ways; I believe permissible paraphrases of what I believe; taking the paraphrase at its face value, I therefore believe in the existence of entities that might be called 'ways things could have been'. I prefer to call them 'possible worlds'.   1973: 84

As Lewis also showed, adding talk of possible worlds (beyond sentential modal operators) adds expressive power to a language, for example, enabling us to formulate global supervenience claims (1986: 12-17). That is, introducing talk of possible worlds, like introducing modal adjectives and nominalizations, can be done via trivial inferences from more basic forms of modal speech, and is useful because it adds additional *textual* functions to the language.

The advantages of being able to make these grammatical shifts work similarly for deontic modal vocabulary. We can say 'You *should* keep your promises' or 'You *mustn't* kill', using auxiliary modal verbs. But we can do more sophisticated

---

for example, this was initially given in terms of the volume of mercury in a thermometer (Carnap 1962: 13); in the case of probability, Carnap linked this with long-term relative frequency (1962: 19). Moreover, Carnap suggests that such quantitative concepts would only be *retained* if they turn out to figure fruitfully in general laws (some quantitative concepts of psychology, for example, have turned out not to do so) (1962: 14). In any case, the point here is simply that the ability to introduce grammatical metaphors is a necessary precondition for introducing such quantitative concepts at all—not to lay out the conditions needed to successfully introduce quantitative concepts.

[24] Such precise probabilistic theories then of course can be better confirmed, figure in more precise scientific theories, and also can be better used in making decisions (whether to take the medication) and bureaucratic evaluations (whether the drug should be approved, covered by insurance, etc.).

things by introducing moral adjectives and nouns—enabling us to say that it is *more* obligatory to refrain from killing than it is to keep your promises; or that the former *obligation* is more stringent. Nominative talk of obligations and permissions enables us to formulate complex bureaucratic systems, saying not simply (in imperative mode) "Pay taxes," or with modal auxiliaries, "You must pay your taxes," but rather to speak of the ways in which property owners in the state of Vermont incur a range of tax *obligations* and as well as *permissions* for modifications to their land, subject to *requirements* for planning *permission* and environmental stewardship.[25] We can also quantify and qualify obligations and requirements, saying that students must satisfy *five* requirements to pass Philosophy 80, and that these requirements are *more onerous* than those for Philosophy 1.

All in all, then, sophisticated modal discourse enables speakers to fulfill all three types of meta-function at the same time. Mood and modal systems enter originally to contribute interpersonal functions.[26] But they simultaneously serve *ideational* functions, carrying propositional content that we can go on to reason with and from in useful ways. Introducing grammatical metaphors to our modal discourse, in turn, brings about new *textual* functions that enable such expressions to play key roles in developing sophisticated scientific theories and bureaucracies.

6. Lessons So Far

At the outset I mentioned two challenges for developing a neopragmatist approach to modal discourse. One was showing how we can, in general, develop a clear and systematic approach to determining the functions of a type of discourse. The other was showing the relevance of that analysis to reevaluating old philosophical problems.

So far, I have focused on the first challenge, and I hope to have pointed the way to a sophisticated and multifaceted neopragmatist approach to modal discourse.[27] One lesson we can take from this is that we can draw on work in linguistics

---

[25] Notice also the other grammatical metaphors involved in this text, and the density of grammatical metaphors in a typical piece of bureaucratic prose.

[26] In my prior work (2020), I have been particularly interested in the *regulative* functions, but do not mean to limit them to that.

[27] More sophisticated, at any rate, than anything *I* had offered before. When I wrote *Norms and Necessity* (2020), I was attuned to the functional differences that different parts of language could serve, and I developed the idea that metaphysical modal discourse serves regulative functions of conveying, endorsing, or renegotiating semantic rules. But I had not yet discovered the work in systemic functional linguistics, and the ways it provides of getting a more fine-grained understanding of the functions served by different parts and aspects of language, including those that are introduced via grammatical variations in modal discourse.

(especially systemic functional linguistics) to help us address questions about the functions of various areas of discourse.[28]

Another lesson we can draw so far is that the neopragmatist's question, if we formulate it as 'What is the function of modal discourse?' may be too broad, given the variations modal discourse may take. This variety doesn't mean, however, that our analysis of the functions of modal discourse must be a hopeless mish-mash. Instead, we can see how the different functions are layered up as modal language develops into more sophisticated grammatical forms.

As we progress developmentally and come to master the entry rules for new expressions, different grammatical forms for modal discourse enable us to introduce modal terminology that adds new functions to the old, including ideational functions and textual functions, so that different forms of modal discourse may come to serve different *ranges of* functions. As we have seen, adding modal auxiliary verbs to a language enables us to serve *interpersonal* functions in useful ways, while also serving those *ideational* functions that come with being stateable in propositional form. Transforming modal auxiliary statements into forms that include modal adjectives and nominalizations adds additional *textual* functions, crucial in forming structured theories and bureaucracies.

Turning to work in developmental and functional linguistics thus enables us to develop both a more *justified* and a more *fine-grained* neopragmatist theory. It is more *justified* because it gives us empirical ways of determining which forms of modal language are more basic (developmentally), and what sorts of functions are added to language by adding a basic modal system, and by licensing grammatical transformations to introduce more sophisticated forms of modal expression. It is more *fine-grained* because it enables us to give a more detailed accounting of the range of functions added to language by these grammatically different forms of modal expression. At the same time, it also enables us to understand the entry rules that entitle us to introduce more sophisticated forms of modal expression (modal adjectives and nouns) by trivial inferences from more basic forms of modal expression.

This is, no doubt, just the start of a more complete neopragmatist account of the diverse forms of modal discourse, the functions they serve, and the rules governing their introduction and use. Nonetheless, now that we have taken a step back to address questions about the rules and functions of various forms of modal

---

[28] What I have focused on so far, one might call the 'formal', grammatical dimensions of function. We can still ask further questions about what we might call the 'material' dimension of function. That is, for example, we can identify talk of *numbers* and of *truth* as both involving grammatical metaphors, where grammatical metaphors typically add *textual* functions. But we can go on from there to also ask about the *differences* between the textual functions added by nominative number talk versus truth talk. On this material dimension of function, an approach such as that developed by Matthieu Queloz (2021) may provide a helpful complement.

discourse, let us turn to see what relevance this might have for the traditional philosophical problems about modality with which we began.

7. What Does All of This Have to Do with Metaphysics?

At this stage, I can hear an army of impatient metaphysicians saying: "Interesting linguistic story. *But what does any of this have to do with metaphysics?*"

The burden on the neopragmatist is to show how the story about linguistic functions and rules can enable us to dissolve, avoid, or undermine alleged metaphysical (or other philosophical) problems. If we can show how this works for the modal case, this may also provide a model for other neopragmatist projects.

At the outset I mentioned several characteristic philosophical puzzles about modality:

1. Are there (really) modal properties, modal facts, or possible worlds?
2. If there are modal properties, how are they related to non-modal properties or relations?
3. If there are modal facts, properties, or possible worlds, how could we come to know about them, given that modal features of the world seem not to be empirically detectable, and that possible worlds seem to be, in principle, causally disconnected from us?

What new light can a subtle neopragmatist story shed on these old problems? Given the above linguistic story, we can see that all of these diverse problems arise, at least in their most troubling or worrying form, by treating talk about modal properties, possible worlds, etc., *on analogy to congruent, observationally acquired discourse*—discourse that has the function of tracking features of the world as we perceive it, and that enters language via observations of the environment.[29] By making clear the very different *functions* of modal discourse and the different *rules* by which modal discourse (of various forms) enters language, we can undermine the idea that there is a valid analogy here. We can thereby also challenge the idea that these are major problems that should lead us to deny that there are modal facts or properties, or to deny that we could know them.

Congruent language comes early in language development, through observation of the environment. Children begin by learning congruent nouns ('goat', 'tree', 'ball'), verbs ('run', 'jump', 'wash'), and adjectives ('brown', 'tall'), used to track and learn about features of their environment. This early congruent,

---

[29] Roughly, what Price (2013: 36) calls discourse that is representational in the 'e-representational' sense. Other problems, as we will see, arise from taking it as analogous to discourse about unobserved explanatory 'posits'.

observationally acquired language tends to become our paradigm of how *all* language functions.

But it is crucial to notice that not all terms are congruent, and that not all terms enter (or are even *supposed* to enter) language observationally or via causal relations. Moreover, while basic declaratives using congruent terms may serve to describe the world in the sense of aiming to track and co-vary with features of the world, not all declaratives do that. For example, as we have seen, we might begin with imperatives that serve an interpersonal, regulative function ('Read Kant'), and transform them into declaratives with modal verbs ('Students *must* read Kant'). The latter serve additional ideational functions, carrying propositional content that we can reason with in all the ways characteristic of declaratives. But that does *not* mean that these terms should function (like congruent terms for sticks and cars) to track special (modal) features of our environment. Let us see why this should lead us to reconsider some central philosophical problems about modality.

Are there (really) modal properties, modal facts, or possible worlds? If so, how are they related to non-modal properties or relations?

First, consider debates about whether there (really) are modal properties, facts, or possible worlds. Doubts are often raised about the existence of such things because it is thought that they would be problematic, as they would seem to be entities that are not observable. But given the above story about the functions and introduction rules for modal predicates and nouns, we can begin to see why such debates are otiose, and we can better support the idea that such questions can be answered easily—without need for any deep ontological debates.

True enough, many (congruent) predicates are observationally introduced, and are used to refer to trackable, perceptible features of the world. We can introduce a predicate like 'is red' in the presence of a red ball, and we can track the presence of redness perceptually (as we can ask whether the redness has spread across the patient's face).

But as we have seen, modal predicates such as '*is possible*' are not introduced via observation to track perceptible features of the world. The fact that modal properties and facts are not directly perceptible is a reflection of the way these terms are introduced, and the functions they serve. Terms such as 'is possible' enter language not through direct observation, but rather via grammatical shifts that take us from modal verbs, which primarily serve interpersonal functions (as in 'It might rain'), to say instead 'Rain is possible'. And this grammatical shift does not aim to track new features of the world, but rather it adds new *textual* functions to our linguistic repertoire (so that we can, for example, go on to ask whether rain is *more possible* than snow). Since the discourse does not aim to track worldly features, it needn't be a problem if we can't introduce it via observation, and can't think of it as describing observable features of the world.

While more must be said to fully address all the arguments that have been given against there being modal properties, the point here is that once we have the linguistic back-story, the burden of proof shifts. For why should we think that it's a general rule that 'to exist is to have causal powers', that we should accept the existence only of *observable* properties, or accept any similar constraints? Once we have the pragmatic linguistic story in hand, we can see that such principles arose and looked natural by considering only the paradigm of *congruent* discourse. We can then place the challenge on the skeptic to say why these are good principles to apply *across the board*, even once we understand how other (non-congruent) forms of discourse are introduced to language, what functions they serve (often serving them perfectly well), and why these functions are useful.

Much the same goes for modal nouns. Congruent nouns like 'goat' are introduced observationally, in the presence of visible creatures, and enable us to track and investigate goats. Here, it makes sense to say: if no one has ever actually had causal commerce with a goat, the term may be problematic; there may be a 'block' in the chain of reference (to use a phrase of Donnellan's (1974: 23-4)), and we should perhaps say that it turns out that goats, like unicorns, don't exist. But while terms like 'a possibility' and 'a chance' are *grammatically* parallel to 'a goat', they are introduced via a completely different route, via different rules, to serve completely different sets of functions. Modal nouns are not even supposed to track a new 'kind of thing' that we could observe and investigate in the ways we investigate goats. Instead, introducing these nouns adds new *textual* functions to the interpersonal and ideational functions served by other forms of modal discourse—not new perceptual connections to previously unnoticed or unnamed things in the world.

Debates about whether there are possible worlds typically proceed by asking whether our best overall theory quantifies over possible worlds, whether the theoretical benefits of 'positing' possible worlds outweigh the costs. David Lewis explicitly develops his argument for possible worlds in these terms, writing "The benefits [in theoretical unity and economy] are worth their ontological cost. Modal realism is fruitful; that gives us good reason to believe that it is true" (Lewis 1986: 4). Now it is easy to see, in the case of black holes, say, why one might ask whether positing black holes provides a better overall physical theory or not, what the posit explains, etc. The function of introducing a term such as 'black holes' presumably is to enable us to refer to and track entities that can play a causally explanatory role in our cosmological theories.[30] But if the above

---

[30] I suspect that the introduction rules and functional roles of terms for unobserved entities to serve as explanatory 'posits' in empirical theories are importantly different from those governing

linguistic story about the functions of possible worlds talk and the rules for introducing it is correct, then it is misguided to attack or defend the existence of possible worlds on these grounds. For on this model, talk of possible worlds does not aim to posit some entities that should explain our observations.

Once we understand the functions and introduction rules for these forms of modal discourse, we can also get new support for the idea that the relevant existence questions are 'easy' to answer, in the sense given by 'easy ontology' (Thomasson 2015). We are entitled to make a trivial inference from 'It might rain' to 'There is a possibility of rain', and that inference is guaranteed to succeed, provided the initial statement is true.[31] We can similarly, given the rules for introducing modal nouns such as 'possibility' and 'chance', give an 'easy' answer to the questions, 'Are there possibilities?' and 'Are there chances?'—yes, of course there are. Talk of possible worlds, in turn, is licensed via trivial inferences (grammatical transformations) from more basic forms of modal speech. If we can legitimately say that there could have been talking donkeys, then we are licensed to infer that there is a possible world in which there are talking donkeys. There is no need to make an 'inference to the best explanation' argument for 'positing' these things, or to enter protracted arguments about whether they add 'explanatory power' to our 'theories'. The entry rules alone license us to introduce terms for possible worlds, and to say that there are such things—and these terms don't fall short in fulfilling their *actual* functions (adding textual functions, including expressive power) even if they don't themselves serve as *explainers* in our theories.

In short, better appreciating the different functions and entry rules of different forms of discourse gives us reason to think that the earnest ontological debates are misplaced, and that we can use an easy ontological approach to answer the question 'Are there possible worlds?'[32] Of course, many objections have been raised to the idea that such 'easy' arguments are valid—I can't go into those here, but have responded to many of them at length elsewhere (2015). The point here is simply to say that, once we understand the functions of the relevant forms of discourse,[33] and the rules that enable us to introduce such discourse to fulfill these functions, the idea that we can make harmless 'easy' inferences to their existence should seem far more natural, and less problematic. And the burden of proof shifts to those who think there is some big problem if these 'entities' can't be

---

congruent terms for observable parts of our world. Both of these kinds of discourse are again importantly different from discourse introduced via trivial inferences to refer to numbers, properties, etc.

[31] I realize of course that this leaves a remaining question of how we should understand the truth of basic modal statements. I have elsewhere given a story for the case of metaphysical modal discourse (2020) but will have to leave the rest for another occasion. Those who have doubts that such trivial inferences succeed are referred to my (2015), where I respond to many common objections to the claim that they do.

[32] For a technical development of a pleonastic account of possible worlds, including showing what is needed to introduce talk of possible worlds as complete and maximal, see Steinberg (2013).

[33] Which I had not yet identified in my (2015).

observed or lack explanatory powers. For the skeptics must say why that should matter, once we can see the bigger linguistic picture, and why that isn't simply based on a false generalization.

The pragmatic linguistic story can also help us see ontological 'placement problems'[34] in a new light. These 'placement problems' ask what sorts of things modal properties could be, how they could 'fit into' the natural world, and how they would be related to non-modal (say, physical) properties. For at least some kinds of modal properties (e.g. *metaphysical* modal properties) this is thought to raise particularly troubling questions, since it seems we can't even say that metaphysical modal properties *supervene* on natural properties. For the statue and the clay (for example) have all the same physical properties, and yet different metaphysical modal properties—as the clay could survive radical changes in shape while the statue could not.[35] Such ontological puzzles arise when we think of modal adjectives and nouns on the model of congruent adjectives and nouns and wonder what 'features of reality' we could be responding to or tracking with these terms, and how those features relate to supposedly less problematic 'natural' properties.

But once we have the functional story in place, we can come to realize that modal talk enters language not with a world-tracking function, but rather with *interpersonal* functions. And we can come to see that the rules that introduce modal adjectives and nouns differ from those for congruent terms as well. As we have seen, sophisticated modal terminology (including modal adjectives and nouns) is introduced on the back of more basic modal terminology, via trivial inferences that leave no room to wonder if there *really* are modal properties, possibilities, or possible worlds (for we can derive claims that there *are* from trivial inferences from undisputed truths). These new adjectives and nouns (unlike their congruent counterparts) are not even *supposed* to pick out or track ostended features of the environment. Instead, they add ideational and textual functions to the interpersonal functions carried by more basic modal language.

---

[34] The terminology of 'placement problems' comes from a discussion in Price (2011: 6); these sorts of problems were identified earlier by Frank Jackson, who called them 'location problems' (1998: 3).

[35] Why should supervenience hold for one kind of modal property (say, physical or nomological modal properties or dispositions, which do seem to supervene on the 'categorical' non-modal properties of the world), yet not for another (say, metaphysical modal properties)? I will have to leave full discussion of this for elsewhere. Here I can only suggest that this has to do with different introduction rules for different sorts of modal claims, given differences in their functions. Suppose, say (with Carnap 1962: 19), that talk of probabilities is introduced via observations of long-term relative frequencies, in order to enable us to better predict future observations, adjust our credences and behaviors, etc. Then it makes sense to have rules that allow no variation in the probabilities attributed without variation in past observations. But if, by contrast, claims of metaphysical modality reflect rules of use *for our terms*, then we are not constrained to assign 'possibly survives a crushing' in the same way to a statue versus a lump of clay, even if all the physical properties instantiated in a given region remain the same.

Thinking that such terms must 'refer to' odd features of the world, so that it's surprising that these modal features wouldn't supervene on physical features (in the way the observable macro-level properties of water supervene on its micro-level properties), results from thinking of these terms on analogy with observationally acquired congruent adjectives like 'liquid' or 'transparent', where it makes sense to ask how these observed features arise from underlying microphysical features. But modal adjectives and nouns aren't introduced to track observable properties. Understanding the functions and introduction rules of these non-congruent modal adjectives and nouns should help dispel objections to thinking that there 'really are' such things, and dispel mysteries about how they could 'fit' into a physical world.

If there are modal facts, properties, or possible worlds, how could we come to know about them, given that modal features of the world seem not to be empirically detectable, and that possible worlds seem to be, in principle, causally disconnected from us?

The puzzles of modal epistemology might be thought to arise from a similar source. If metaphysical modal properties don't supervene on physical, or observable, properties, then it makes sense to think that we can't come to know them through ordinary observation or other empirical methods.[36] But then modal skepticism seems to threaten. For example, Robert Nozick argues that to have justified beliefs in a given domain, we must have a reliable faculty for forming beliefs of that sort, the existence of which is best explained in terms of natural selection. But, he argues, where metaphysical modal beliefs are concerned, "we do not appear to have such a faculty, and it is implausible that evolutionary processes would instill that within us" (2001: 122). He argues that we have no good explanation of why we should have developed a reliable faculty for detecting metaphysical necessity, and that as a result we should be skeptical about claims that we have such knowledge—and even about the claim that there are such necessities (2001, 125). Nozick concludes that "there are no interesting and important metaphysical necessities" (2001: 120-1).

These doubts about metaphysical modal knowledge rely on a generalized picture according to which knowledge of things of any kind *K* requires a good explanation of why we should have a 'reliable faculty for *detecting*' *K*s. This

---

[36] There has been a recent surge in the development of empiricist approaches to modal epistemology (for example, see Williamson (2007); Bueno and Shalkowski (2015); Vetter (2015); Leon (2017); and Roca-Royes (2017)). As I argue elsewhere, however (2020: 150–65), such approaches hold promise for explaining our knowledge of *empirical* modalities (empirically grounded counterfactuals, dispositions, etc.)—but not for explaining our knowledge of specifically *metaphysical* necessities and possibilities (which include many modal claims of *philosophical* interest), since these are cases in which we might have the very same empirical information, and yet ascribe different modal properties (say, to the statue and the clay).

demand is plausible for knowledge of *K*s, where '*K*' is a congruent noun, observationally acquired (we have a reliable faculty for detecting wolves but not auras). But once again we should not expect it to generalize to a requirement for acquiring knowledge about *any* *K*s *whatsoever* (where '*K*' is *any* noun term). Terms for metaphysical modal properties and possible worlds are unlike congruent adjectives and nouns that are introduced to detect and track features of our environment. For, as we have seen, these are forms of language introduced to add textual functions to the interpersonal and ideational functions already served by more basic forms of modal expression. We have no need for a good evolutionary story about why we should have evolved to have a reliable faculty for 'detecting' the relevant features or worlds. What we can get instead is a good naturalistic story about why such forms of vocabulary would have evolved as they did, and why they would have stuck around in our language.[37] And we can tell that story by identifying what uses they might have for us, where these *needn't* always be uses in detecting or tracking features of our environment—as our language serves a wide range of other functions as well.

This, of course, is not to deny that we need a good story of some sort about how we *can* come to have modal knowledge of various sorts (acknowledging that somewhat different stories might be required for knowledge of modal claims of different sorts—of metaphysical necessity versus physical necessity, for example). I have myself tried to develop one such story—for knowledge of metaphysical modalities—elsewhere (2020: ch. 7), arguing that we can come to know basic *metaphysical* modal truths by *mastering* the rules of use for applying and refusing expressions, and learning how to explicitly *convey* those rules and what follows from them in object-language indicatives (2020: 163-4). (Other, derivative, metaphysical modal truths may also require empirical knowledge.) Accounts for other forms of modal discourse will have to be developed and assessed separately.

There has, of course, been a great deal of discussion about whether past pragmatist approaches to various areas of discourse enable us to circumvent old epistemological problems—for example, about whether (broadly) expressivist approaches to understanding *moral* discourse can or cannot avoid problems of moral epistemology.[38] There is not space here to assess those debates or how they would fare, given the new neopragmatist proposal at hand.[39] The goal here is not to settle those old debates, but rather to begin to construct a linguistic platform that can enable us to climb out of the weeds to get a good overview of the

---

[37] I begin to develop this story in my (2020: ch. 7).
[38] See, for example, Blackburn (1984, 1993, ms); Gibbard (1990, 2003); Street (2006, 2011); Dreier (2012); Berker (2014); Vavova (2015); Schechter (2018); and many more. Of course, it would require considerable discussion to examine whether the problems outlined for expressivist theories of morality would carry over to other forms of pragmatist approach to modality. I made a start (for the normativist approach I defended there) in my (2020: ch. 7).
[39] I provide more detailed discussion of these past debates, and their relevance to my earlier normativist view of metaphysical modality, in my (2020: ch. 7).

territory. Once we do that, and can see the diversity of functional roles and introduction rules, it begins to seem misguided to think that there is a major *barrier* to giving an account of modal knowledge—a barrier that might appropriately lead us to a form of modal skepticism. The misguided thought that there is an insuperable barrier arises by illegitimately generalizing thoughts about how we can come to know the things tracked by our congruent, observationally acquired, terms, and applying that model to *all discourse whatsoever*. Once the pragmatist's linguistic story is on the table, the challenge for the skeptic is to show that their reservations are not just built on a faulty overgeneralization that arises from failing to appreciate the variety of linguistic rules and functions.

8. General Lessons

I hope that the work done here may prove valuable across a variety of neopragmatist projects. The challenges faced by neopragmatists are, first, to give a clear, systematic story about how we can identify linguistic functions; and, second, to show why this work on linguistic functions and rules is relevant to traditional philosophical problems (for the metaphysician always wants to say that the pragmatist's analyses just ignore the 'real metaphysical problems' by taking up linguistic questions instead).

I hope to have made progress on both of those challenges here. On the first, I have shown how we can build on work in linguistics to develop a clear and systematic approach to understanding linguistic functions. I have also shown how applying this to the case of modal language enables us to address questions about the functions of, and rules governing, modal discourse in a fine-grained way. This then enables us to restructure the classic neopragmatist question about the 'function of modal discourse' by noting the differences in functions served across different modal terms with different grammatical roles and origins.[40] On the second challenge, I have aimed to show why starting a step back, and addressing questions about the functions of the various forms of modal language, and the rules by which they are introduced, *is* relevant to classic philosophical problems about modality. I have argued that understanding how the relevant puzzling forms of language work enables us to reconsider certain classic (alleged) ontological problems and epistemological problems. For we can come to see some of these as arising from mistaken overgeneralizations we are prone to make when we take congruent terms, introduced observationally, as our only model; and others we can see as easily answerable, given the rules of the discourse.

---

[40] One might similarly ask what differences it would make to address questions about the functions of moral discourse, causal discourse, number discourse, etc., in this way. (For a start on moral discourse, see Warren and Thomasson forthcoming.)

I hope that this case study has suggested how we can develop a neopragmatist approach systematically. I hope it has also shown that a neopragmatist approach that begins a step back, by examining the functions parts of language serve and the rules they follow, can lead us to reassess various old philosophical problems. For it can give us new ways of seeing why many traditional puzzles may arise from mistakes, requiring not earnest debates but the kind of dissolution (or easy solution) that can come from properly understanding how these puzzling forms of language work.[41]

References

Austin, J. L. (1961). 'Performative Utterances', in Urmson and Warnock 1961.

Ayer, A. J. (1936/1952). *Language, Truth and Logic*. New York: Dover.

Bennett, K. (2004). 'Spatio-Temporal Coincidence and the Grounding Problem', *Philosophical Studies* 118: 331–71.

Berker, S. (2014). 'Does Evolutionary Psychology Show that Normativity Is Mind-Dependent?', in D'Arms and Jacobson 2014: 215–52.

Blackburn, S. (1984). *Spreading the Word*. Clarendon Press: Oxford.

Blackburn, S. (1993). *Essays in Quasi-Realism*. New York: Oxford University Press.

Blackburn, S. (ms). "Sharon Street on the Independent Normative Truth *as Such*," <https://swb24.user.srcf.net/PAPERS/Meanstreet.htm>.

Brandom, R. (2008). *Between Saying and Doing: Towards an Analytic Pragmatism*. Oxford: Oxford University Press.

Bueno, O. and Shalkowski S. (2015). 'Modalism and Theoretical Virtues: Toward an Epistemology of Modality', *Philosophical Studies* 172: 671–89.

Cappelen, H. (2018). *Fixing Language: An Essay on Conceptual Engineering*. Oxford: Oxford University Press.

Carey, S. (2009). *The Origin of Concepts*. Oxford: Oxford University Press.

Carnap, R. (1935). *Philosophy and Logical Syntax*. London: Kegan Paul.

Carnap, R. (1962). *Logical Foundations of Probability*. Chicago: University of Chicago Press.

Copp, D. and Bloomfield, P. (eds.) (Forthcoming). *Oxford Handbook of Moral Realism*. Oxford: Oxford University Press.

Cournane, A. (2020). 'Learning Modals: A Grammatical Perspective', *Language and Linguistics Compass* 14/10: 1–22.

---

[41] Many thanks to Joshua Gert, David Plunkett, Samia Hesni, and Justin Khoo for extremely helpful comments on an earlier version of this chapter.

D'Arms, J. and Jacobson, D. (eds.) (2014). *Moral Psychology and Human Agency: Philosophical Essays on the Science of Ethics*. Oxford: Oxford University Press.

Donnellan, K. S. (1974). 'Speaking of Nothing', *Philosophical Review* 83/1: 3–31.

Dreier, J. (2012). 'Quasi-Realism and the Problem of Unexplained Coincidence', *Analytic Philosophy* 53/3: 269–87.

Egan, A. and Weatherson, B. (eds.) (2011). *Epistemic Modality*. Oxford: Oxford University Press.

Eggins, S. (2004). *An Introduction to Systemic Functional Linguistics*, 2nd edn. London: Continuum.

Feigl, H., Scriven, M., and Maxwell, G. (eds.) (1958). *Minnesota Studies in Philosophy of Science*, Vol. 2: *Concepts, Theories and the Mind-Body Problem*. Minneapolis: University of Minnesota Press.

Fischer, B. and Leon F. (eds.) (2017). *Modal Epistemology after Rationalism*. Cham: Springer.

Geach, P. (1965). 'Assertion', *Philosophical Review* 74: 449–65.

Gibbard, A. (1990). *Wise Choices, Apt Feelings*. Cambridge, MA: Harvard University Press.

Gibbard, A. (2003). *Thinking How to Live*. Cambridge, MA: Harvard University Press.

Halliday, M. (1973). *Explorations in the Functions of Language*. New York: Elsevier.

Halliday, M. (1975). *Learning How to Mean: Explorations in the Development of Language*. New York: Elsevier.

Halliday, M. (2009). *The Essential Halliday*, ed. Jonathan Webster. London: Continuum.

Halliday, M. (2014). *Halliday's Introduction to Functional Grammar*, revised by Christian M. I. M. Matthiessen. New York: Routledge.

Hare, R. M. (1952). *The Language of Morals*. Oxford: Clarendon Press.

Jackson, F. (1998). *From Metaphysics to Ethics*. Oxford: Oxford University Press.

Leon, F. (2017). 'From Modal Skepticism to Modal Empiricism', in Fischer and Leon 2017.

Lewis, D. K. (1973). *Counterfactuals*. Oxford: Blackwell.

Lewis, D. K. (1986). *On the Plurality of Worlds*. Oxford: Blackwell.

Macarthur, D. and Price, H. (2007). 'Pragmatism, Quasi-Realism, and the Global Challenge', in Misak 2007: 91–121.

Malmkjaer, K. (ed.) (1991). *The Linguistics Encyclopedia*. London: Routledge.

McPherson, T. and Plunkett, D. (eds.) (2018). *Routledge Handbook of Metaethics*. London: Routledge.

Millikan, R. (1987). *Language, Thought and Other Biological Categories*. Cambridge, MA: MIT Press.

Misak, C. (ed.) (2007). *New Pragmatists*. Oxford: Oxford University Press.

Nozick, R. (2001). *Invariances: The Structure of the Objective World*. Cambridge, MA: Harvard University Press.

Papafragou, A. (1998). 'The Acquisition of Modality: Implications for Theories of Semantic Representation', *Mind and Language* 13/3: 370–99.

Price, H. (2011). *Naturalism without Mirrors*. New York: Oxford University Press.

Price, H. (2013). *Expressivism, Pragmatism and Representationalism*. Cambridge: Cambridge University Press.

Queloz, M. (2021). *The Practical Origins of Ideas*. Oxford: Oxford University Press.

Restall, G. (2012). 'A Cut-Free Sequent System for Two-Dimensional Modal Logic, and Why It Matters', *Annals of Pure and Applied Logic* 163: 11, 1611–23.

Roca-Royes, S. (2017). 'Similarity and Possibility: An Epistemology of *De Re* Possibility for Concrete Entities', in Fischer and Leon 2017.

Ryle, G. (1949). *The Concept of Mind*. London: Hutchinson.

Ryle, G. (1950). '"If," "So," and "Because"', *Collected Papers*, Vol. 2. London: Hutchison, 1971.

Schechter, J. (2018). 'Explanatory Challenges in Metaethics', in McPherson and Plunkett 2018: 443–59.

Sellars, W. (1958). 'Counterfactuals, Dispositions and the Causal Modalities', in Feigl, Scriven, and Maxwell 1958: 225–308.

Steinberg, A. (2013). 'Pleonastic Possible Worlds', *Philosophical Studies* 164: 767–89.

Stevenson, C. L. (1937). 'The Emotive Meaning of Ethical Terms', *Mind* 46/181: 14–31.

Street, S. (2006). 'A Darwinian Dilemma for Realist Theories of Value', *Philosophical Studies* 127: 109–66.

Street, S. (2011). 'Mind-Independence without the Mystery: Why Quasi-Realists Can't Have it Both Ways', *Oxford Studies in Metaethics* 6: 1–32.

Thomasson, A. L. (2015). *Ontology Made Easy*. New York: Oxford University Press.

Thomasson, A. L. (2020). *Norms and Necessity*. New York: Oxford University Press.

Thomasson, A. L. (2022). 'How Should We Think about Linguistic Function?', *Inquiry*. DOI: 10.1080/0020174X.2022.2074886

Urmson, J. O. and Warnock, G. J. (eds.) (1961). *Philosophical Papers*. Oxford: Clarendon Press.

Vavova, K. (2015). 'Evolutionary Debunking of Moral Realism', *Philosophy Compass* 10/2: 104–16.

Vetter, B. (2015). *Potentiality: From Dispositions to Modality*. Oxford: Oxford University Press.

Warren, M. and Thomasson A. L. (Forthcoming). 'Prospects for a Quietest Moral Realism', in Copp and Bloomfield forthcoming.

Williams, M. (2011). 'Pragmatism, Minimalism, Expressivism', *International Journal of Philosophical Studies* 18/3: 317–30.

Williamson, T. (2007). *The Philosophy of Philosophy*. Oxford: Blackwell.

Yalcin, S. (2011). 'Nonfactualism about Epistemic Modality', in Egan and Weatherson 2011: 295–332.

4
Neopragmatism in the Philosophy of Perception? The Case of Primitive Color

Mazviita Chirimuuta

1. Introduction: Discarding the "Mirror" and Querying "Nature"

A guiding maxim for neopragmatism has been the setting aside of the conception of language as mirror. There has been less effort paid to interrogating what language is allegedly a mirror of—nature.[1] In this chapter, I argue that neglect of the preconception of nature as mind- and human-independent reality—the core preconception of metaphysical realism[2]—sometimes leads neopragmatism to underperform in its metaphysical quietism. Contrary to expectations, a little foray into metaphysics is needed as an inoculation against the more troubling metaphysical questions. I focus in particular on the primitivist and realist theory of color developed by Joshua Gert (2017b), which has many attractions and is one of the most compelling examples of applied neopragmatism to date. My claim is that the realism in Gert's theory undermines the primitivist insight that colors are *sui generis*, objective properties that lack hidden essences, such that we can gain full knowledge of them through ordinary perceptual experiences, guided by members of our linguistic community. The aim of my excursion into the metaphysical notions of nature and reality is to ensure that a primitivist like Gert can finally and conclusively reject the question, "but are there colors, REALLY?"

In order to give a rough sense of my agenda, I will first remark on a couple of points that led me to it, also indulging in some intellectual autobiography.

---

[1] An exception is Price (2013: ch. 3).

[2] This is how I am framing metaphysical realism for the purposes of this chapter. This characterization is the mainstream one, but there are important exceptions. A view that rejects the notion of reality as what is absolutely human- and mind-independent can still claim to be a "realism," as in Charles Taylor's (2013) project of "retrieving realism" from the notion of mind-independence. Within philosophy of science, Hasok Chang (2018) proposes a "realism for realistic people" which consciously rejects previous versions of scientific realism that, "took 'reality' as mind-independent nature." Of particular relevance to this chapter is the study John McDowell (1985) makes in which the weakness of projectivist anti-realism about values and colors is attributed to its "thin conception of reality" supported by a "contentiously substantial version of the correspondence theory of truth, with the associated picture of genuinely true judgment as something to which the judger makes no contribution at all" (1985: 122). On rejecting that conception of reality, one is entitled to say that colors are both real and human-related properties.

The original inspiration for the view I have called "perceptual pragmatism" (Chirimuuta 2015: ch. 5, 2017a) came not from neopragmatism, which was not familiar to me at the time of writing, but the work of Charles Taylor. He suggests that one of the consequences of the success of science is that we tend to measure all ways of making sense of the world in comparison with the methods and standards of the empirical sciences (Taylor 2007: 285). For example, if one interprets the Book of Genesis as if it is aiming to be an account of historical, archaeological, or geological facts, one is implicitly measuring it against the standard of those empirical disciplines and assuming that there is just the one relevant aim, whether one is a scientist or author of a biblical narrative—namely, the representation of said facts. This observation led me to the idea that a fundamental mistake in the philosophy of color has been the implicit comparison between scientific instruments—which have been designed to measure and detect, as precisely as possible, the properties and entities featuring in physical theory—and ordinary sensory systems that serve the purpose of guiding animals' behavior and need not aim at physical precision in order to do this. On acknowledgment of the distinct aims of sensory systems, one realizes that the subjectivity or "narcissism" (Akins 1996) of sensory systems should not be held against them.

The point inspired by Taylor is that all our sense-making and action-guiding activities, which appear to be straightforwardly representational, do not have the *same job*—that of representing the unalloyed facts. There is a parallel here with the neopragmatist observation that various forms of language do not uniformly perform the task of representation, if at all.[3] However, an opinion entertained by Taylor, that I have not seen articulated in the neopragmatist literature, is that this notion of the one job, to be performed uniformly across our various practices, happens to be the task that natural science, perhaps disingenuously, declares itself to be undertaking—that of plainly representing how things stand in the world.[4] This is what Taylor (2013) calls the "disengaged" view. The implication is that the philosophical malaise whose symptoms the neopragmatist seeks to treat by applying a sophisticated account of language, should be diagnosed, more profoundly, as a spreading of scientific attitudes and presumptions into areas of philosophy that would be healthier without them.

In this chapter, I follow through on the implications of this diagnosis for understanding the "nature" side of the mirror/nature dyad. This is what prompts my criticism of realism. Again, Taylor serves as a starting point (e.g. Taylor 2007: ch. 7). It is a presumption of a scientific account of the origin of the universe—a physical

---

[3] Here I mean representation in a robust sense. Price (2011) and Gert (2018) dispense with a robust notion of representation (*Representation*, capital R) which requires a substantial notion reference relation (*Reference,* capital R), but retain a deflated one.

[4] I give reasons to say this is disingenuous elsewhere (Chirimuuta forthcoming: ch. 8). Briefly, modern science has always been linked with the instrumental aims of manipulating and controlling phenomena, and so should not be read as disinterested fact seeking. Science is not as disengaged as it seems.

cosmology—that its explanations are conceptually independent of the existence of humans. This nature has been, for most of its duration, void of humans and thus its explanations of it may only proceed in human and mind-independent terms. The Book of Genesis, need we be reminded, is not a physical cosmology. Its task is not the recovery of physical facts but is, more plausibly, the offering of an account of the world that helps see people through the quandaries of human existence. Thus the world of Genesis cannot be one that is conceptually independent of the existence of humans.

Fundamentalist interpretations of the Bible err both in the *same-job* assumption, and the *same-nature* one. Scientific knowledge can only be taken as a rival to the Bible, and vice versa, if it is assumed that in both cases the one task (factual Representation), with the same target (the World, conceived as human- and mind-independent nature) is being pursued. As Taylor, and others such as Karen Armstrong (2001) have shown, religious fundamentalism is a modern phenomenon that appears against the background of a generalized, scientific worldview. I propose—provocatively—that the naïve perceptual realism which is usually paired with color primitivism is the philosophical analogue of religious fundamentalism. That is, it assumes that science and the senses have the same job, carried out in the same kind of world—the task of detecting mind-independent properties of physical objects.[5]

Gert's version of primitivism makes an important advance in that it explicitly rejects the same-job assumption for color discourse. To go further and reject the assumption that the activities of science and ordinary perceiving occur within the "same kind of world" may strike you as bizarre. But let me state things differently. The natural world *as conceived by science* is one whose basic constituents are human- and mind-independent entities, properties and processes. The world *as we encounter it in perception* necessarily includes constituents that are human-related since the act of perception presupposes us human perceivers. Put this way, what is bizarre is the assumption that there should be an alignment between the scientific world (whose presumed ontology is human-independent) and the perceptual world (whose default ontology is, I argue elsewhere, human-relative[6]—the things that *we* perceive).[7]

---

[5] See e.g. Brewer (2011) and Allen (2016).

[6] The mainstream view in today's analytic philosophy of perception is that perceptual phenomenology presents the world as a collection of mind-independent objects and properties. See Chirimuuta (2015: ch. 8) for arguments that perceptual phenomenology is indecisive on this point. Having put aside the argument from phenomenology, the idea that the default ontology is human-relative is simply the idea that the most obvious way to characterize the perceptual world of the human is to demarcate all that appears via human sensory systems (as opposed to the senses of goldfish or the mechanisms of thermometers). It is a further question (the problem of "placement") whether all that appears to humans can be fully characterized in the human-independent terms of the physical sciences. Thus the default perceptual ontology, prior to attempts at physical reduction, is human-relative.

[7] For the purposes of this chapter, I only discuss the relation to human perception (in particular color vision) and dependence on human minds. However, the realist notion of mind-independence means independence from any human or animal minds.

However, what renders this obvious point hard to articulate and acknowledge is the background of metaphysical realism. I characterize this as the view that there is a way the world is, independently of human minds and conceptions. This one world (the *World*, capital *W*) is treated as both the target of scientific conceptions, and the ultimate ground of perceptual encounters, such that both science and perception can be thought of as getting things more or less right regarding this one reality. Through my study of color primitivism, I will argue that for neopragmatism to achieve its philosophical goals it should be *methodologically non-realist*. This means that the neopragmatist should disallow overt and tacit appeals to the World in her theorizing. Non-realism is not necessarily a denial of the existence of a mind-independent world. It is consistent with a Kantianism in which there are unspoken-of things-in-themselves. It is also in line with a Hegelianism which treats the notion of the World in itself as an abstraction from the *de facto* world in which there are ineliminable mutual dependencies between the human and non-human, ignored for the purposes of doing natural science.

In fact, the latter Hegelian view is one that synergizes with my argument that realism about the World is not a default or common-sense view, but is a metaphysical posit of science which, we will see by the end of the chapter, serves as an idealization or simplifying assumption.[8] This idea will sit oddly with anyone influenced by logical empiricist philosophy of science who takes metaphysical posits to be superfluous (at best), or impediments to the scientific method. For example, Carnap (1950: 21) asserts (without evidence or argument, I note) that, "the external question of the reality of the thing world itself...is raised neither by the man in the street nor by scientists, but only by philosophers." Pace Carnap, my point in the second part of section 2 is that precisely through its trading in explanations whose terms are mind-independent entities and properties, it is the scientific attitude that prompts the asking of external questions about the existence of colors.

Jenann Ismael is one neopragmatist who does remark that the notion of the real, perspective-independent World is part of the shared heritage of philosophy and science:

> there is a good tradition stemming from Aristotle according to which metaphysics is inquiry directed at the study of Being qua Being, which is to say, the study of what there is in the most general sense, not from a particular perspective in space and time, or as it appears to a particular class of creatures, but as it is *in itself*. Physics aims for such a conception...   Ismael (2014: 89)

In contrast, positivists from Comte to Carnap acknowledged that science was historically related to metaphysics, but took it to be on an upward trajectory in

---

[8] Also argued in Chirimuuta (forthcoming: ch. 10), "Cartesian Idealisation."

which metaphysics would be overcome and abolished. This approach to science, fostered by Carnap and others in the early to mid-20th century sought to disconnect science from metaphysics by rejecting any characterization of science as the description of mind-independent reality beyond the empirical appearances, denying ontological commitment to unobservable entities and forces through which the appearances are *explained*.

It is telling that in its classic phase, logical empiricism excluded the topic of explanation from the philosophy of science. Hempel (1966) brought explanation into the fold by equating it with bare prediction, and dissociating explanation from the notion of science's making the observable world intelligible to us through the discovery of the operations of unobservable processes. A theme of my discussion is that the realist metaphysical commitments of science crystallize precisely when science presents explanations (in terms of a reality behind the appearances), and that primitivism, developed as a true quietist doctrine, is precisely the denial that, for colors (as perceived and discussed by humans) there is anything for science to explain, in terms of an unobservable reality.

In the next section, I offer my exposition of primitivism and show that as currently formulated it cannot avoid external questions about the Reality of color in the World, because of its residual commitment to realism. Section 3 argues that the primitivist can say everything she wants to about the objectivity of color—e.g. that color judgments are evaluable as true or false—even when realism is abandoned. Section 4 offers some bigger picture observations about the relationship between non-realism, idealism, and global pragmatism.

2. What Primitivism Is and Why Realism Causes It Trouble

2.1 The Primitivist Insight: Colors Have No Hidden Essence

Primitivism is characterized by Gert (2017b: 9) as,

> the view that colors are irreducible, mind-independent, *sui generis* properties of objects, and that any normal eight-year-old in the developed world knows which objects in their environment have which ones.

That colors are "irreducible" and "sui generis" sets primitivism apart from the physicalist realism which solves placement problems by identifying colors with complexes of standard physical properties. Furthermore, it is stated that knowledge of the colors of things is revealed in ordinary visual perception, unlike knowledge of an object's micro-physical and chemical properties. In the context of the debate over color ontology, the assertion of color realism—that colors are mind-independent properties—serves to mark a distinction from anti-realism

(Hardin 1993) and relationism (e.g. Cohen 2009; Chirimuuta 2015), to make the point that rubies and garnets *are* red (*simpliciter*). Yet, as I will now argue, this notion of mind-independence works to undermine the core insight of Gert's primitivism.

This core insight is the point that, "[t]he central truths about color do not need to be explained in terms of anything outside the domain of color" (Gert 2017b: 12). It follows from the irreducible and *sui generis* nature of colors that they form an autonomous domain. Like the numbers, but unlike natural kind terms, colors do not have a "hidden essence" awaiting revelation via scientific investigation (Gert 2017b: 21). Instead, mastery of color concepts requires ordinary perceptual experiences and induction into a linguistic community which employs color terms. The thesis that Gert (2017b: 23) calls "Modest Revelation" is that,

> A complete understanding of what dark blue is can be given by showing someone something that is dark blue, if that person has normal vision and has already acquired color concepts.

What I like about the primitivism (in spite of my having defended a rival relationist theory) is that it gives full weight to a very intriguing fact about color facts: that we treat them as impervious to scientific correction. No scientist could convince me that blackcurrant cordial is green and not purple; I would defer to the expert as to the chemical composition of the liquid.

Gert's primitivism has an advantage, in comparison with versions more closely aligned with naïve perceptual realism, in that the revelation thesis does not come across as strange or mysterious. It is not some apprehension of a realm of color facts but a result of the pragmatics of color terms. With natural kinds, as Gert (2017b: 49) puts it, "we have an interest in differentiating *genuine* instances of the kind from other instances that merely share a superficial appearance." In contrast, appearances (not the production of the appearances, or the "essences" behind them) are what matter to us for the uses to which we put our color vocabulary. Furthermore, it is useful in this domain to uphold standards of truth and falsity for color judgments, and this makes sense of our community enforced standards here, in the absence of scientific arbitration of color truths. Gert's neopragmatism allows him to avoid questions about what the color terms are (*Really*) referring to, because he rejects an account of language whose mode of operation is Representation of mind-independent facts via a robust notion of Reference.[9]

---

[9] "The neopragmatist alternative [to robust representation relation] is to say that when talk of truth and falsity in a domain is pragmatically useful—for reasons that do not appeal to the notion of reference, and that can vary from domain to domain—then we have a truth-apt domain. And the same thing goes for reference talk and representation talk" (Gert 2018: 11). See Teller (2021: S5029) for the argument that "referential realism" (cf. the notions of Reference and Representation rejected by global pragmatism) is a prerequisite for scientific realism—which is the kind of realism that I criticize in this chapter.

104 NEOPRAGMATISM

The aimed-for position is a metaphysical quietism which treats color discourse as non-Representational, by analogy with traditional forms of expressivism. Because the "global pragmatist" (Price 2013: 29–31; Gert 2017b) rejects the notion of a truly Representational discourse against which the expressive one can be invidiously compared, there turns out to be no difference between quasi-realism and realism (Gert 2017b: 50).[10]

2.2 Metaphysics Sneaks Back

The neopragmatist anti-metaphysical trick works by taking away the linguistic tools needed in order to raise the metaphysical questions, such as the "external question" of whether there *really are* the colorful things that we so happily and conveniently talk about. What I have not seen brought into consideration is whether there are non-linguistic ways for metaphysical problems to be posed. Let me have a go:

The point of these cartoons is to prompt, in a non-linguistic manner, concern about the difference between quasi-real and Real properties. The idea here is that philosophical worries begin with some root intuition, some picture of how things stand, which is then articulated in language. Without addressing the root intuition,

Figure 4.1 The Case of Color.

---

[10] Although Gert does not describe himself as a "quietist," I employ this term just to refer to Gert's stated disavowal of a difference between color realism and quasi-realism. This fits with a standard definition of quietism as the denial, "that there can be such a thing as substantial metaphysical debate between realists and their non-realist opponents" (Miller 2019).

Figure 4.2 The Case of Sound.

or picture, a superficial reform of language will not unsettle the philosophical worry. Properties depicted on the left hand side may be Real or quasi-real, and the neopragmatist can deny a meaningful difference here; properties remaining on the right hand side can only be the Real in a metaphysically robust sense (i.e. human- and mind-independent), because human perceivers and linguistic practices have been obliterated from those pictures. I contend that nothing in the neopragmatist account of color stops us from picturing these scenarios to ourselves and hence being bothered about the difference in the instantiation of chromatic properties across worlds containing, and not containing, perceiving, speaking humans. This prises the Real apart from the quasi-real, undermining the neopragmatist strategy. What's significant is that these imaginaries of the world emptied of humans carry philosophical weight for us—we deem them relevant for our theorizing of a world which necessarily (since we are here doing the theorizing) contains us. Non-realism, which I propose as a methodological supplement to neopragmatism, is just the doctrine that the notion of the human- and mind-independent world (the World) should not play a role in our philosophical theorizing. Without an explicit caution against questions about how things stand in the World, metaphysical worries will always sneak back.

By calling colors "mind-independent" properties, it is not clear whether Gert is committing himself to the metaphysical claim that in a world in which there were no human minds there would nonetheless be colors, or whether the terminology of "mind-independence" serves only to distinguish Gert's primitivism from antirealist and relationist theories. Gert (2017b: 91) does specify that objective colors (the referents of ordinary color ascriptions) are "monadic properties of physical objects." In line with the intended metaphysical silence about the nature of the objective colors restated on the same page, are we supposed to take this not as a metaphysical claim (despite the vocabulary of "monadic" and "physical object") but as an observation about how color words operate within ordinary discourse?

Whatever the answer to this question, Gert's realist commitments are on display in his discussion of explanation. As noted in section 1, the logical empiricists before Hempel rejected the idea that science explains anything as being too metaphysically loaded. To see where this reaction is coming from, note that one canonical form of explanation is a statement of how empirical appearances (e.g. meter readings, perceived material changes) are the results of goings on in Reality (activities of unobservable entities posited in physical science). These denizens of Reality are mind-independent and are by definition never manifest to human observation, such that our knowledge of them would seem, especially to an empiricist, to raise more questions than it answers. It has been the practice of scientific realism to brush such empiricist scruples under the carpet and to welcome ontological commitment to the posits of scientific explanations.[11]

Gert's deployment of an appearance/Reality distinction is central to his theory of color—there are the "objective colors" that ordinary objects have, and the fine-grained "color appearances" that are perceiver- and perspective-relative.[12] Ascription of objective color terms is truth evaluable and consistent across most individuals, whereas faultless disagreements are the norm for color appearances. While in the next section, I endorse a version of his "Hybrid" view, I believe it is a mistake to equate objective colors, with Real colors—the ones that explain color appearances. Following a longstanding realist tradition, Gert takes seriously the comparison between color and shape, a paradigmatically Real property. He writes that, "[n]either colors nor shapes are to be *analysed* in terms of their effects, although both sorts of properties help to *explain* those effects" (Gert 2017b: 104). Shape is also an archetypal primary quality, and one way to characterize the primary/secondary distinction is as between those qualities that participate in physical explanations, and those that do not. Gert, it seems, wishes to grant primary-like status to the objective colors by showing that they figure in explanations, even if restricted only to explaining color appearances and nothing else—e.g. that blood has a red appearance because it is red (Gert 2017b: 109). Colors, like shapes, are said to have "causal powers"; it is just that shapes, in contrast to colors, do more than just produce appearances (Gert 2017b: 90).

The core primitivist insight about color was that the correctness or falsity of ordinary color ascriptions needs no scientific explanation. The problem with drawing the comparison between colors and shapes is it takes you back into the game of explaining the correctness/falsity of color ascriptions in terms of the

---

[11] Alastair Wilson's (2018) review of Healey's pragmatist interpretation of quantum mechanics is a nice illustration of the realist outlook. Wilson's main criticism is that Healey's approach cannot explain the empirical success of quantum theory. It strikes me that only the realist must feel an explanatory burden here—at least for explanations in terms of facts about unobservable reality.

[12] Note that on Gert's view, the real, objective colors are not hidden behind the appearances but available to visual perception. However, as I object in section 3.1, the manifestness of chromatic properties is problematic because it cannot be given any naturalistic explanation, even though Gert has invoked a naturalistic picture in which mind-independent properties with causal powers elicit responses in human perceivers.

instantiation of a property that causally explains the appearances, and is conceptually and ontologically distinct from those appearances. Now Gert can point out here that his view, more precisely, is that the *objective colors* have no hidden essence (e.g. that a strawberry is red needs no physical explanation), and that it is *these* which explain color appearances. But this takes us into the difficult territory of naïve realist theories of perception, which posit that we are somehow acquainted with a range of mind-independent properties that are instantiated in physical objects but figure nowhere in a scientifically informed ontology. To apply the diagnosis introduced in section 1, this is a kind of fundamentalism that harps after the success of scientific explanation. Here, the objective colors take on a role modeled by physical/chemical unobservables in order to explain the appearances for color. It is an instance of the same-job assumption.

In the course of an argument against dispositionalism which proceeds by drawing an analogy between colors and shapes, Gert (2017b: 94–6) asserts that there is more to an object's having a purple color than its reliably and without exception being disposed to appear purple. I think this is the most telling evidence that we cannot be dealing here with a metaphysically quietist view. For we have an assertion that, yes, colors are human- and mind-independent properties, conceptually and ontologically distinct from their appearances; such properties could possibly (if not actually) be instantiated in worlds in which there are no humans. It strikes me that quietism has been quietly abandoned because of the immense gravitational pull of the Real World, the habit of theorizing in terms of what is "out there." As soon as one buys into the language of "mind-independent properties," takes shapes to be examples of these, and argues that colors are like shapes, one is committed to colors being Real in a metaphysically loaded sense, something more than quasi-real. Most color realists have no wish to be metaphysical quietists,[13] and so would see no difficulty here. But it is a problem for Gert, whose stated aim is to avoid recognition of a difference between real and quasi-real colors. In the next section, I argue that there is life after realism, and that a meaningful distinction between objective and non-objective colors can be upheld without a foundation in the idea of a mind-independent reality.

3. Abandoning Realism: Objective and Subjective Colors

3.1 Agreement Is Enough

Objectivity without realism means that community practices of agreement ensure that there are standards for truth of predication. Following the non-realist maxim, there can be no appeal to facts about how things are in the human-independent World. However, Gert (2017b: 99) calls this a "silly" view:

---

[13] See Allen's (2016: ch. 8) arguments against quietism.

> I do not mean... To suggest the obviously false view that agreement in the use of a predicate to describe a particular object ensures the truth of that predication... That is, it can admit that there were canonical methods in the past for determining whether or not someone was a witch, and that these often yielded virtually unanimous positive verdicts despite the fact that there were no witches.[14]

Gert's argument is that to be a witch (as with being Gold), one must have "certain essential causal powers," and as a matter of fact no person ever did possess them. Even though Gert has told us at the outset that colors, unlike natural kinds such as Gold, do not have *hidden* essences, it turns out that the validity of color judgments does turn on an alignment between ordinary color perception ("the canonical method"), and their essential causal powers. It is just that coincidentally, in the case of colors, their essential causal powers are the ones latched onto in ordinary perception, and so they are not hidden ones.

> Unlike the property of being a witch, the property of being yellow involves only causal powers that really do belong to the things identified by the canonical methods.   Gert (2017b: 99)

Lest we find ourselves having to resort to the metaphysics of pre-established harmony, in order to explain this lucky coincidence, let me argue that the "silly" view is actually the one truer to the primitivist insight—that colors are not the kinds of properties that *could* have hidden essences.

This last point merits some clarification. For Gert, the properties of being Gold, being a witch, or yellowness all have essential causal powers. Whereas the essential causal powers of the first two properties are hidden to ordinary human observation—one cannot tell just by looking whether something or someone has the essence of Gold or Witch—this is not so with the colors. The sticking point is that essential causal powers are normally hidden. Colors are unusual in this respect, and Gert leaves it open that the essential causal powers of colors *could have been* hidden (e.g. if our visual systems had evolved differently). And so it is strange that the causal essence of color happens to be recoverable in ordinary perception. This has to be left as an *inexplicable* fact on Gert's view, because colors have no causal powers other than their capacity to produce color appearances for us; this means that they cannot figure into physical explanations of perceptual stimulation analogous to those for our perception of primary qualities, such as for shape where we can formulate explanations in terms of the causal process of casting projections on to surfaces, like the retina, which accounts for why we are able to recover objective shapes. Objective colors are said to explain color

---

[14] In the literature on scientific realism witches and phlogiston are extremely popular examples of non-referring terms. Chosen, no doubt, for their intuition-pumping causal powers.

appearances in the same way that objective shapes can explain shape appearances, and yet there is literally nothing to be said about the kind of explanation to be had in the color case. This difficulty is a symptom of the same-nature assumption: the entities and properties are treated in the quasi-scientific manner of having essential causal powers that are usually hidden to human observation, and figure in explanations of appearances. Gert makes an important partial break with the same-nature assumption in denying that colors *actually have* hidden causal essences. But he should go further by insisting that colors *could not have had* hidden causal essences. In other words, that is to reject the picture in which objective colors are conceptually and ontologically distinct from their appearance to human perception.

To see how we might work toward a view in which colors are not the kinds of properties that could have hidden essences, we may think of the property of "being a monarch" as an analogous case. Consider someone asserting that there never was a British monarch. What this person means is that there never was an individual appointed by God to rule over that island, the embodiment of political will of the nation. All those kings and queens buried in Westminster Abbey were identified as monarchs by the canonical methods of society; there was near universal agreement on it, and yet—our contrarian tells us—the widespread opinion was mistaken. The error made here by the contrarian is a failure to see that being a monarch is a human-instituted condition, one not grounded on the having of essences that ordinary, canonical methods for determining kingship can be mistaken about, such potentially hidden essences as divine appointment and embodying of the nation. Whatever the monarchist propaganda might allege, being a monarch is a state grounded in socially manifest recognition, not hidden essences.

The core primitivist insight about colors was that they do not have a hidden essence, and therefore no scientist could persuade me that blackcurrant juice is actually green. Gert's remarks about the insufficiency of group agreement for truth has back-tracked on this insight. In fact, these two opinions seem inconsistent. On the one hand, Gert asserts that there is nothing more required for knowledge that blackcurrant juice is purple than to be a person with normal vision, inducted into English color discourse. On the other hand, he draws up a comparison with witches (defined as persons with certain causal powers), and thereby opens up the possibility that all English speakers might turn out to be mistaken on this fact— that scientists might one day discover that colors have causal powers at variance with their manifest appearance to us.

The neopragmatist primitivist should stick to her first instincts and assert that agreement in the use of color predicates underwrites their truth, even if in the use of color terms we are not referring to agreement. "[C]olor talk," as Gert (2017b: 100) observes, "is not talk about responses." Nor is king talk about a subject's ingrained feeling of deference in response to the person at the summit of a social hierarchy. That truth of predication comes about via social agreement does not mean that it is cheaply acquired. How many of us can demonstrate the genealogical connections dating back to the Norman Conquest required for acceptance as a British aristocrat, let alone monarch? Socially enforced standards can be as stringent as you like. Hence it is appropriate to say that blood being red, or a person's being blue-blooded are objective facts (even while rejecting any beliefs in aristocrats having causal essences, such as inherited traits that make them a breed superior to common stock). While the social forces that drive agreement over class and regal status do mutate with history, the shared visual faculties which underlie peoples' convergence on color judgments are fixed in the timescale appreciable to a linguistic community, and the minority of "abnormal" color perceivers are taught to conform to majority practice as best they can. Thus convergent color perceptions serve as an extremely stable basis for evaluation of color judgments, within linguistic communities.

3.2 Between Mind-Dependence and Mind-Independence

A valuable contribution to the philosophy of color is made by Gert's proposal of the "separability thesis":

> there could be facts of the matter about the rough colors of objects [e.g. green and yellow] even if there were none with regard to the precise colors of objects [e.g. unique green and unique yellow]. Gert (2017b: 57)

Up until this proposal, the rough colors that are referred to using ordinary color names, with consistent judgments across normal color perceivers, had been theorized in the same fashion as the precise shades which are only named in the technical contexts of colorimetry and psychophysics, and which show variation across normal perceivers.[15] As follows from the discussion above, I dispute Gert's construal of the distinction between precise and rough colors as the difference between mind-dependent appearance and mind-independent reality.[16] At the same time, it is important to hold on to the objectivity of the rough colors, even though (following non-realist practice) we have ruled out appeals to mind- and human-independent facts. In this section, I show how the objectivity of rough

---

[15] The fact that precise colors can only be defined and measured in laboratory conditions is highly significant. According to Daston and Galison (2010: 273–83), the precise, subjective colors, and even the condition of dichromacy (color blindness) were not noticed before the development of color psychology in the 19th century. It is appropriate to say that precise colors, such as unique green, are as much scientific properties as charge or acidity, even though they cannot be defined without a human visual system being used as part of the apparatus for detection. Furthermore, a curious thing about chromatic properties is that the more precisely they are measured, the more they lose their objectivity (their ability to support inter-subjective agreement). This probably is the reason why colors never made it into the scientifically respectable ontology of primary properties, such as length and speed.

[16] Note that for Gert the difference with the standard appearance/reality distinction is that with chromatic properties the reality (the objective, rough colors) are not hidden to an accomplished perceiver, even though they can sometimes be mistaken for appearances. When a perceiver correctly sees an objective color, that color is "apparent" to her (Gert 2017b: 90).

colors—grounded in the notion of inter-subjective agreement—comes into sharper relief when contrasted with the mind-dependence and subjectivity of the precise colors.

The central idea here is that the denial that colors are mind-dependent properties (i.e. dependent on the mental state of any *one* perceiving subject) is not the same thing as the assertion that colors are mind-independent properties (i.e. in no way human-dependent). The space between the mind-dependent and the mind-independent has been passed over because of neglect of the ways that communal practice and inter-subjective comparison take us beyond the merely subjective, such that we do not have to start theorizing about the human-independent World in order to account for the objectivity of color.[17]

Discussions of the subjectivity of perceived properties have tended to focus on characteristics that a perceiver could note in a situation of social isolation: whether a property seems to come and go as I shift my line of sight, or change my mental state, whether or not it has perceptual constancy. The important observation made by Gert about the precise colors is that even though they often have constancy, and are not in any sense imaginary, the fact that they are not targets of inter-subjective agreement means that they do not figure in truth-evaluable discourse.[18] Thus inter-subjective convergence can serve as a test of whether a property is not merely subjective. This reliance on inter-subjective convergence removes the need to employ a further condition—that of instantiation in the mind-independent World—for the objectivity of color properties. The lesson of the neopragmatist, community-based notion of objectivity is that one can go beyond mere subjectivity and mind-dependence without having to make the extra step of supposing that the objective properties are the ones instantiated in the perceiver-independent World. Thus one can agree that common claims such as "daffodils are yellow" are true, and that their truth is not relative to any one perceiver, while at the same time avoiding the metaphysical trouble that comes with color realism—the problem of locating colors in a physical World.

4. Non-Realism, Idealism, and Global Pragmatism

4.1 Realism and Science

Non-realism is the methodological policy of avoiding appeals to states of affairs in human- and mind-independent Reality. I have argued that in order to live up

---

[17] Neopragmatism has been a valuable corrective to this neglect, as I acknowledge in my (2017b) response to Gert (2017a).

[18] Of course, his is currently a minority view. Realists who do not accept the separability thesis, and hold that there is a fact of the matter about which precise colors an object has, are committed to saying that there are unknowable color facts (Byrne and Hilbert 2003) or to claiming that each object instantiates an indefinite number of monadic color properties (Kalderon 2007).

to the aim of metaphysical quietism, the neopragmatist must follow the guidance of non-realism. In the case of color, this means that primitivists like Gert can only avoid the placement problem by uprooting realism. The promise of avoidance of metaphysical challenges might be enough to incline some toward non-realism. However, for the majority of philosophers realism is unmovable ground, the most non-negotiable common-sense—no prize would persuade them to relinquish realism.

For such adherents of realism I now offer a few reasons to give it up. My proposal is that the realist notion of the ready-made world, the way things just are independently of all human conception, discourse, and existence, is not the basic, common-sense worldview but a piece of conceptual artifice which has practical benefits within science, while its usefulness is doubtful in other areas of enquiry. Before this strikes you as too odd, I recall the point introduced at the outset that the perceptual world, the world we inhabit and discuss with others, is a world with humans in it. Common-sense, like the author of Genesis, has no use for the notion of a world absolutely void and independent of humans in order to underwrite the kinds of claims that are made in our everyday practices. As argued in section 3, the objectivity of claims about color (and claims to royal succession) are underwritten by observations accessible in this shared human world and need make no appeal to a realm of absolutely human-independent facts.

However, in the practice of modern physical science it is requisite to describe the world in terms of properties that are, near as possible, independent of the sensory systems and social norms of human beings. The idea of "nature as an objective and independent existent" seems to have been a novelty of the "new science" (Hesse 1962: 75). The idea that the Real World, human- and mind-independent, is a construct or posit of mathematized science is actually the received view amongst the phenomenologists—Heidegger, Merleau-Ponty, and especially Husserl (Moran 2012). For example, Merleau-Ponty (1961/2001: 288) writes,

> Science manipulates things and gives up living in them...Science is and always has been that admirably active, ingenious, and bold way of thinking whose fundamental bias is to treat everything as though it were an object-in-general—as though it meant nothing to us and yet was predestined for our own use.

The notion of the willful detachment of science is crucial. In order to do science effectively, the World is cast as a causal order of non-human nature against which the human conceptual and mental order is juxtaposed. This is a departure from the common-sense attitude with which we ordinarily engage with things.[19]

---

[19] Cf. Taylor (2013: 85) on Heidegger: "The aim is to show that grasping things as neutral objects is one of our possibilities only against the background of a way of being in the world in which things are disclosed as ready to hand. Grasping things neutrally requires modifying our stance to them which primitively has to be one of involvement."

Cassirer makes a related point. On his account, progress in the exact sciences comes about with the removal from scientific systems of representation (symbols, concepts, etc.), the relation to human subjective experience, and any intent to express how the world appears to our senses.[20] As Cassirer describes, in physical science, "all particularities resulting from consideration of the apprehending subject are effaced...And it is this transition that opens up the realm of genuine, strict 'science'" (Cassirer 1929/1957: 399). In different ways, these philosophers emphasize the validity and irreplaceability of a default, non-technical way of apprehending the world—the engaged stance depicted by the phenomenologists, and the "expressive" and "representative" functions in Cassirer's philosophy of symbolic forms.

These views about the nature of scientific thought probably bear the influence of Hegel, in particular the notion of the *understanding* as achieving clarity of thought by positing self-sufficient (and therefore human- and mind-independent) external items. As Beiser (2005: 167) relates:

> The understanding postulates something unconditioned or something absolute, which it attempts to conceive in itself, as if it were independent and self-sufficient. This is the moment of the understanding whose specific virtue is to make sharp and fast distinctions between things, each of which it regards as self-sufficient and independent. But, in insisting upon its hard and fast distinctions, the understanding is in fact making a *metaphysical* claim: it holds that something exists in itself, that it can exist on its own without other things.[21]

I have no doubt that readers with strong realist inclinations prefer to take David Lewis as their philosophical authority, and not Husserl or Hegel. I bring up these figures not as an argument from authority but simply to show that there is a tradition traceable back through the 19th century and well represented in 20th-century thought, in which it is commonplace to characterize the notion of mind- and human-independence as a conceptual tool of the sciences, rather than as a non-negotiable item of common-sense.

---

[20] Cassirer's narrative is influenced by Max Planck. Other philosophers have questioned whether this worldview is as de-anthropomorphized as physicists like Planck would have us believe (Arendt 1958: 288; Canguilhem 1965/2008).

[21] See also Taylor's interpretation of Hegel's notion of conscious subjectivity as negativity: "For man as a conscious, knowing, rational being aims...at a clarity and self-sufficiency of rational thought which he only attains by separating himself from nature, not only without but also within...We can think of the movement which posits and holds other being or external reality as something independent as negativity" (Taylor 1975: 84, 110). Again we see that the notions of mind-independent Reality, separate from human existence, is a posit of the exact manner of thought demanded by science.

4.2 Global Pragmatist Quietism as an Idealism

I close the chapter by presenting an analogy which, if taken to heart, has the implication that the scientific image is just another manifest image. The refusal to be captivated, in one's philosophy, by the idea of anything in principle beyond the manifest is the point of connection between idealism and the neopragmatist's quietism—her rejection of external questions. Thus, I conclude that global pragmatism is best understood as a kind of idealism.[22]

Imagine a human child raised by a pack of wild dogs—creatures with minimal color vision and with a superior sense of smell in comparison with the human. This family of human and non-human animals finds its meals by hunting at night, a task for which color vision is of little use. The girl follows the pack, as the dogs are guided by their nose, toward food. To the sole human, without a community of people around her picking out objects by their colors, her world of color might seem to her (if only she had the language to describe it) as subjective as a dream; the unsmelt smells that lead her to her meals would in comparison seem to be a reality hidden to her senses. As we become ever more reliant on scientific instruments and theories to guide us to our goals, we are a little like the child running with dogs. We question the world as it appears to our senses because the machines capable of detecting hidden clues are more reliable guides in actions toward ever more technically ambitious goals. The difference is that we are not alone with our human senses—we have a community of other similarly equipped perceivers around us such that we still collectively treat the manifest world as having its own validity, one that sits oddly besides the supposed hidden Reality of science.

However—we would say to the wild girl if we could ever teach her our language—the hidden Reality she takes to be revealed to her companions, the dogs, is only another manifest world but one different from the world manifest to human senses. So—we can say to the scientific realist—the hidden Reality revealed to science should really be thought of as another manifest world, but one apparent to non-human and non-animal modes of "perceiving." There is no pressure to classify as resident in transcendent Reality those items that happen not to appear to human senses, but only to our instruments. The scientific image is not a revelation of Reality, but a different kind of manifest image.[23]

There is an idealist flavor to much of what I have said in this chapter, but at the same time the stated aim has been metaphysical quietism. This might seem odd because idealism has come to be associated with metaphysical excess. Yet Hegel

---

[22] See Redding (2010) for a different argument toward a similar conclusion. Lest confusion arise, the idealism in question is the German kind, not the "immaterialism" of Berkeley (Redding 2010: 274–5).

[23] This was Kant's position, according to the interpretation of transcendental idealism given by Lucy Allais:
 e.g. "causal explanation in science neither requires postulating hidden essences, nor...involves insight into intrinsic properties of things in virtue of which they have their powers." (2015: 220)

claimed not to be a metaphysician precisely because he refused to speculate about transcendent entities (Beiser 2005: 55). Likewise, the non-realist refuses to speculate about how things are in the mind- and human-independent World, and thereby avoids external questions and the division between the Real and quasi-real properties. The link between non-realist quietism and idealism comes down to this similarity in approach, and not any notion of everything being human- and mind-dependent. An idealist turn would also constitute a return of neopragmatism to its historical roots in American pragmatism, a movement originally shaped by German idealism (Good 2005).

Price (2013: 54–5) implies that idealism is a kind of idiocy that global pragmatism cleverly avoids:

> We can't speak about the facts in question until we play the relevant game, and within the game, very special cases aside, it certainly won't be appropriate to say that we *created* the facts. (There's no soapbox here for the village idealist.)

However, the kind of idealism that the non-realist mandate leads us to is not one that claims that humans construct the world or create the facts, *tout court*; rather, it is one that denies a clean enough separation between the human-dependent and the human-independent for the notion of human-independent Reality to play a reliable role in our philosophizing. That said, we are to give full acknowledgment to the fact that scientific practice operates on the assumption of a clean separation between the human and natural orders of things, and that modern science would be unrecognizable without such an assumption. But as with other posits such as point masses and infinite populations, the notion of the absolutely human-independent should be treated as an idealization whose indispensability for science does not entail that it is non-optional for philosophy.

Acknowledgments

I send warm thanks to Joshua Gert and John McDowell for their comments on this chapter, to members of the Pittsburgh Philosophy of Perception reading group for their discussion, and to the audience at the William & Mary Applied Neopragmatism conference in 2018 for another lively debate.

References

Akins, K. (1996). 'Of Sensory Systems and the "Aboutness" of Mental States', *Journal of Philosophy* 93: 337–72.

Allais, L. (2015). *Manifest Reality: Kant's Idealism and His Realism*, Oxford: Oxford University Press.

Allen, K. (2016). *A Naïve Realist Theory of Color*, Oxford: Oxford University Press.

Arendt, H. (1958). *The Human Condition*, Chicago: Chicago University Press.

Armstrong, K. (2001). *The Battle for God*, New York: Ballantine Books.

Beiser, Frederick. 2005. *Hegel*, Routledge: London.

Brewer, B. (2011). *Perception and Its Objects*, Oxford: Oxford University Press.

Byrne, A. and Hilbert D. (2003). 'Color Realism and Color Science', *Behavioral and Brain Sciences* 26: 3–64.

Canguilhem, G. (1965/2008). 'Machine and Organism', in P. Marrati and T. Meyers (eds.), *Knowledge of Life*, New York: Fordham University Press.

Carnap, R. (1950). 'Empiricism, Semantics, and Ontology', *Revue Internationale de Philosophie* 4: 20–40.

Cassirer, E. (1929/1957). *The Philosophy of Symbolic Forms*, Volume 3: *The Phenomenology of Knowledge*, New Haven: Yale University Press.

Chang, H. (2018). 'Realism for Realistic People', *Spontaneous Generations* 9: 31–3.

Chirimuuta, M. (2015). *Outside Color: Perceptual Science and the Puzzle of Color in Philosophy*, Cambridge, MA: MIT Press.

Chirimuuta, M. (2017a). 'Perceptual Pragmatism and the Naturalized Ontology of Color', *Topics in Cognitive Science* 9: 151–71.

Chirimuuta, M. (2017b). 'Replies', *Philosophy and Phenomenological Research* 45: 244–55.

Chirimuuta, M. (forthcoming). *The Brain Abstracted: Simplification in the History and Philosophy of Neuroscience*, Cambridge, MA: MIT Press.

Cohen, J. (2009). *The Red and the Real*, Oxford: Oxford University Press.

Daston, L. and Galison, P. (2010). *Objectivity*, New York: Zone Books.

Gert, J. (2017a). '*Outside Color* from Just Outside', *Philosophy and Phenomenological Research* 95: 223–8.

Gert, J. (2017b). *Primitive Colors: A Case Study in Neopragmatist Metaphysics and Philosophy of Perception* (Oxford: Oxford University Press).

Gert, J. (2018). 'Neopragmatism, Representationalism and the Emotions', *Philosophy and Phenomenological Research* 97: 454–78.

Good, J. A. (2005). *A Search for Unity in Diversity: The Permanent Hegelian Deposit in the Philosophy of John Dewey*, Lanham, MD: Lexington Books.

Hardin, C. L. (1993). *Color for Philosophers*, Indianapolis, IN: Hackett.

Hempel, C. G. (1966). *Philosophy of Natural Science*, Upper Saddle River, NJ: Prentice Hall.

Hesse, M. B. (1962). *Force and Fields: A Study of Action at a Distance in the History of Physics*, New York: Philosophical Library.

Ismael, J. (2014). 'Naturalism on the Sydney Plan', in M. C. Haug (ed.), *Philosophical Methodology: The Armchair or the Laboratory*, London: Routledge.

Kalderon, M. E. (2007). 'Color Pluralism', *Philosophical Review* 116: 563–601.

McDowell, J. (1985). 'Values and Secondary Qualities', in T. Honderich (ed.), *Morality and Objectivity*, London: Routledge.

Merleau-Ponty, M. (1961/2001). 'Eye and Mind', in R. Kearney and D. Rasmussen (eds.), *Continental Aesthetics: An Anthology*, Oxford: Blackwell.

Miller, A. (2019). 'Realism', *The Stanford Encyclopedia of Philosophy* (Winter 2021 Edition), ed. Edward N. Zalta, <https://plato.stanford.edu/archives/win2021/entries/realism/>.

Moran, D. (2012). *Husserl's Crisis of the European Sciences and Transcendental Phenomenology: An Introduction*, Cambridge: Cambridge University Press.

Price, H. (2011). *Naturalism without Mirrors*, Oxford: Oxford University Press.

Price, H. (2013). *Expressivism, Pragmatism and Representationalism*, Cambridge: Cambridge University Press.

Redding, P. (2010). 'Two Directions for Analytic Kantianism: Naturalism and Idealism', in M. De Caro and D. MacArthur (eds.), *Naturalism and Normativity*, New York: Columbia University Press.

Taylor, C. (1975). *Hegel*, Cambridge: Cambridge University Press.

Taylor, C. (2007). *A Secular Age*, Cambridge, MA: Harvard University Press.

Taylor, C. (2013). 'Retrieving Realism', in J. K. Schear (ed.), *Mind, Reason, and Being-in-the-World*, Routledge: London.

Teller, P. (2021). 'Making worlds with symbols', *Synthese* 198, 5015–36.

Wilson, A. (2018). 'Review of Richard Healey, *The Quantum Revolution in Philosophy*', *Notre Dame Philosophical Reviews*. https://ndpr.nd.edu/reviews/the-quantum-revolution-in-philosophy/

5
A Neopragmatist Treatment of Causation and Laws of Nature

John T. Roberts

> The Bible...tells us that just a few hours after tasting from the tree of knowledge, Adam is already an expert in causal arguments.
>
> When God asks, 'Did you eat from that tree?'
>
> This is what Adam replies: 'The woman whom you gave to be with me. She handed me the fruit from the tree, and I ate.'
>
> Eve is just as skillful: 'The serpent deceived me, and I ate.'
>
> The thing to notice about this story is that God did not ask for explanation, only for the facts—it was Adam who felt the need to explain. The message is clear: causal explanation is a man-made concept.
>
> Another interesting point about the story: *explanations are used exclusively for passing responsibilities.*
>
> Pearl (2009: 402; emphasis added)

1. Introduction

One of the central tasks of the metaphysics of science is to find an acceptable theory of what it is to be a law of nature.[1] Another is to find an acceptable theory of causation; but that is actually two separate tasks, because causation is really two different relations: general causation, exemplified by the fact that ice storms cause power outages, and singular causation, exemplified by the fact that the ice storm in Durham North Carolina on January 1, 2002, caused the power outage on a certain street that same day. A fourth task is to find a good theory of what makes

---

[1] I am grateful to the following people, plus everyone I forgot, for helpful discussion and advice regarding this material: Joshua Gert, Philip Pettit, Ram Neta, Christian Loew, Laura Townsend, Mike Hicks, Siggi Jaag, Chris Dorst, Nina Emery, Al Wilson, Heather Gert, Luc Bovens, and audiences at the William and Mary 'Workshop on Applied Neopragmatism' (2019), the Birmingham 'Workshop on Laws and Grounding' (2019), the UNC-KCL 'Joint Graduate Workshop on Explanation' (2019), and the FramePHYS 'Workshop on Humeanism' (2021), and the students in my graduate seminar at UNC-Chapel Hill in 2014.

John T. Roberts, *A Neopragmatist Treatment of Causation and Laws of Nature* In: *Neopragmatism: Interventions in First-Order Philosophy*. Edited by: Joshua Gert, Oxford University Press. © John T. Roberts 2023.
DOI: 10.1093/oso/9780192894809.003.0005

counterfactual conditionals true or false. Obviously, these tasks are not unrelated: causal relations (of both kinds) and laws of nature and counterfactuals are bound up together, with each other and with other things like dispositions and objective chance. All these items form a family that I will call *the natural modals*.

What binds the natural modals into a family is many things, including the ways their extensions evidently depend on one another, the important roles they all play in scientific explanation, and the fact that they all plainly have something to do with the kind of "necessary connexions between distinct existences" that David Hume worried about. For this reason, it seems that it would be a clear mistake to try to theorize about one of the natural modals, say lawhood, in abstraction from all the others. It seems that we will only really understand any one of the natural modals when we understand them all—and when we understand why there even are such things as natural modals at all.

My medium-term goal is to develop a unified neopragmatist theory of all the natural modals. In this chapter, though, I will only treat laws, singular causation, and general causation. Philosophers have already given some very promising accounts of particular natural modals that arguably count as neopragmatist: for instance, Menzies and Price (1993) on causation: Ward (2002) on laws of nature; and Brandom (2008: ch. 5) on laws and counterfactuals. The theory I present here will be very different from all of these. In this chapter, I will try to make the case for my own theory, without trying to argue against any of these other promising theories.

Here's how the theory I propose will be structured: I will not try directly to give a non-representationalist semantics for statements about laws and causation. Instead, I will offer a non-representationalist, neopragmatist semantics for something else—namely, discourse about the *effectiveness of methods*—and then I will offer old-fashioned conceptual analyses (with necessary and sufficient conditions) of lawhood and causation in terms of *it* (viz., effectiveness of methods). With these analyses in hand, we can take any statement to the effect that something is or is not a law, or that there is or is not a certain causal relation, and replace it with a semantically equivalent statement that does not mention lawhood or causation, but only effectiveness of methods. The resulting statement, since it is only about effectiveness of methods, is handled by my neopragmatist account of such statements. Thus, the non-representationalist character of my theory of effectiveness "trickles up" to statements about laws and causation. The neopragmatist character of the theory attaches *directly* to the account of effectiveness, and only indirectly to the account of laws and causation.[2]

---

[2] For this reason, a representationalist could accept my analyses of laws and causation in terms of effectiveness of methods, but then reject my neopragmatist account of effectiveness in favor of some representationalist account of it. Such a view might be perfectly coherent. I suspect it would not be very attractive to many representationalist philosophers, however.

Incidentally, I think that the same kind of treatment can be given to all the other natural modals (counterfactuals, objective chance, dispositions and powers, and maybe other things). That is, I think each of them can be analyzed in terms of effectiveness of methods. What all the natural-modal concepts have in common, on this theory, is that they are all devices we have for putting a complex batch of information about the set of all effective methods into convenient bite-sized packages. The explanation for why we have such a family of concepts at all is that in all departments of life, we frequently need to handle such complex batches of information about which methods are the effective ones, and it is very hard to do that directly, just because of their complexity. (Again, though, in this chapter, I only treat laws and causation.)

2. Some Clarification of the Explicata: Responsibility and Effectiveness

As it happens, I think that the concept of an *effective method* is inextricably tied up with the concept of an agent's being responsible for an outcome. So the nonrepresentationalist semantics for effectiveness that I offer will really be a semantics for both effectiveness talk and responsibility talk, as a package deal. Let me start with some remarks about effectiveness and responsibility.

In my view, the key to understanding effectiveness of methods is to see how it is tied to attributions of responsibility. There is more than one kind of responsibility—e.g. causal responsibility, moral responsibility, legal responsibility—so I need to clarify what kind I mean.

Philosophers of action sometimes speak of an agent's being "causally responsible" for some outcome. Roughly, "agent A is causally responsible for outcome O" is defined to be true just in case some action of A's is among the causes of O (or is identical with O). I think the kind of responsibility I am talking about has the same extension as this "causal responsibility." But I don't accept this definition, since I think this sort of responsibility is conceptually prior to causation and therefore should not be defined in terms of it. Since the name "causal responsibility" so readily prompts one to think of this standard definition which I reject, I won't use it; instead, I will call the sort of responsibility I am talking about "basic responsibility" or "*b*-responsibility." Whenever we characterize some outcome as the work of some agent—as due to the activity of some agent—then we thereby attribute *b*-responsibility, regardless of whether we say that the agent meant to do it or is blameworthy (or worthy of some other reactive attitude) for it. *B*-responsibility for a given outcome is a necessary condition for moral responsibility for that outcome, but not sufficient.

I should also clarify what I mean by an "effective method." First off, what is a "method" (effective or not)? I assume that a particular method can be picked out by an ordered triple of propositional functions:

$$\langle M(x), K(x), E(x) \rangle$$

where the variable x is some kind of index, typically a spatiotemporal location. The propositional function M is called the *means*, E the *effect*, and K the *condition* of the method. Informally, the idea is that this is a method for getting $E(x)$ to be so by means of getting $M(x)$ to be so, and $K(x)$ is the background condition that must be in place in order for this method to be used. For example, if:

$M(p, t)$ = the proposition that the match at place p at time t is vigorously struck at t

$K(p, t)$ = the proposition that there exists a unique match at place p at time t, and at time t this match is dry, surrounded by oxygen, and not already struck

$E(p, t)$ = the proposition that the match at place p at time t begins to burn just after t

then <$M(p, t)$, $K(p, t)$, $E(p, t)$> is the familiar method of getting a match to ignite by seeing to it that the match is struck.

Importantly, $M(x)$ & $K(x)$ can be true even if no agent actually uses $M(x)$ as a means to promoting the goal $E(x)$. $M(x)$ might be made so by an agent whose conscious goal is something totally different from $E(x)$ (for example, I might strike a match for the purpose of demonstrating to you that there is no oxygen around, only to see the match begin to burn). Or it might be that $M(x)$ occurs as a wholly natural phenomenon.

A method is *effective* if implementing it is a potentially successful way of promoting its end. This doesn't mean that there actually is anyone in the universe who has the potential or the ability to use the method. What it does mean is that any agent who did have the ability to implement this method would thereby have the ability to promote its end: getting it to be true that $M(x)$, while it is already true that $K(x)$, for the purpose of getting $E(x)$ to be true, is a gambit that just might succeed. Call this *the end-promoting characterization* of effectiveness of methods.

My aim is to analyze causation (among other things) by reducing it to effectiveness; this might seem a misguided and hopeless task, given what I've just said. For it looks as if what makes a method count as "effective" is precisely that its means can be used to promote its end—and what can "promote" mean here except "help to cause"? Is this a fatal circularity?

No, it isn't. The end-promoting characterization of effectiveness is, I think, a very good informal way of specifying the *extension* (and even the *intension*) of effectiveness, but it is not my official definition. For my official purposes, I need a way of saying what effectiveness is otherwise than by characterizing it in terms of causation. And I think there is such a way. Effectiveness can be characterized in terms of b-*responsibility*, understood as a kind of normative status an agent can have. In particular: A method <M, K, E> is effective just in case you can come to be b-responsible for the outcome $E(x)$, via coming to be b-responsible for $M(x)$— so long as $K(x)$ is true. In other words, the effective methods are the ones in which b-responsibility transfers across from the M to the E, in any case where M, K, and E are all realized. Call this *the responsibility-transferring characterization* of effectiveness. Though the end-promoting and responsibility-transferring characterizations are distinct, I take it to be highly plausible that they both pick out the same set of methods. (If you're not convinced of this, I'll return to the question below in section 4.)

It is tempting, and mostly harmless, to think of effectiveness as the property that a method has when it can *potentially* be used to successfully promote its end. But we must be careful about how exactly we understand this. In particular, in order for a method to qualify as effective, it is not necessary for there actually to be any agent who has the ability to implement it. In fact, it doesn't even have to be *nomically possible* for there to be such an agent. For example, method <$M(x)$, $K(x)$, $E(x)$>, where:

$M(x)$ = there are three non-conductive copper cubes
$K(x)$ = (some tautology)
$E(x)$ = there is at least one cube that is not conductive

should count as effective. Nobody can make there be three non-conductive copper cubes, but even if (*per impossibile*) someone *did*, they would *thereby* earn b-responsibility for there being at least one cube that was non-conductive. This is obviously so, even if it is a law that all copper is conductive. Similarly, if we let:

$M(p, t)$ = the planet at location p at time t collides (at t) with a supermassive black hole

$K(p, t)$ = a global pandemic is raging on the planet at place p at time t

$E(p, t)$ = the global pandemic on the planet at p at time t comes to an end at t

Then the method <M, K, E> is, again, effective; one effective way of ending a global pandemic is to steer the planet right into a supermassive black hole. This method is neither cost-effective nor remotely feasible, but it is effective because, if only you were able to use it, you could thereby end a pandemic. And this is so even if the laws of nature make it nomically impossible to steer a planet into a black hole. If anyone did such a thing, they would thereby earn responsibility for the end of the pandemic (and for the end of many other things as well)—this is a counterfactual conditional, and it might even be a counternomic conditional, but it is evidently true nonetheless.[3]

This fact about effectiveness preempts one obvious objection to my whole program here: there are presumably laws of nature and causal relations pertaining to events that no existing agent could manipulate as a means to anything; since no agent can manipulate those events, they cannot figure in any effective methods; doesn't this mean that there are laws and causal relations that have nothing to do with any effective methods? Moreover, it seems that there might have been no agents at all, in which case perhaps there would have been no effective methods at all, but surely there could still have been laws and causes in that case? The reason why there is not really a problem here for me is that what I call the "effective methods" are just the ones that always do and always would transfer b-responsibility from means to ends, even if there are no agents that can come to have b-responsibility for the means in the first place.

3. Neopragmatist Semantics for Responsibility and Effectiveness

Now let's consider statements of this form:

(1) Agent A bears b-responsibility for outcome O

Of course, we are not likely to find anyone uttering a statement of form (1) outside of a philosophy seminar. But many more ordinary statements are equivalent (in an obvious sense) to ones of form (1), e.g.:

Heather made me happy
That is your mess in the kitchen
You didn't receive a call back, and that's on me

I suggest that to assert (1) is to endorse a policy of treating A in a certain way.[4] Which way? Roughly: rendering unto A all the rights, privileges, duties, and

---

[3] I have been using counterfactuals to characterize effectiveness of methods. Yet, I have said that I want to give a theory of counterfactuals that reduces them to effectiveness of methods (though not in this chapter). There is no circularity here, though, because in the present section, I am merely clarifying my explicata; the aim here is to make it clear to the reader just what property of a method I aim to pick out with my word "effectiveness," not to give an analysis of it. (For similar reasons, it's okay for me to speak of nomic possibility and impossibility here, though ultimately I want to analyze those in terms of effectiveness.)

[4] We neopragmatists disagree amongst ourselves on the details of the technical machinery that is needed to make neopragmatism work—what kind of thing the non-representational content of an assertion can be, how to solve the Frege-Geach problem, and so forth. In this essay, I do my best to leave those issues to the side, to make my theory an attractive one for any brand of neopragmatist. Toward this end, I use the informal phrase "endorsing a policy" here. Different neopragmatists can

penalties associated with b-responsibility for O. These rights, etc., will differ depending on what O is, and they may vary with the social context. But mature, competent speakers can be expected to know what they are, more or less, or at least to know how to find out. For example, whoever bears b-responsibility for the existence and aesthetically relevant properties of a work of art owns the copyright thereto,[5] and deserves whatever praise or disparagement is appropriate for the work. Moreover, the finding that driver D was at fault in a certain traffic accident is essentially the finding that they bear b-responsibility for the accident, and it has certain implications involving fines and insurance policies. You might worry that it is really *moral* responsibility rather than b-responsibility that comes with attendant rights, penalties, and so forth, but these two examples both show that (mere) b-responsibility comes with its own attendant rights, etc., too;[6] a driver can be 'at fault' for an accident even if she did nothing blameworthy—if, for example, she was distracted at the crucial moment by a rowdy passenger—and it is not at all clear whether moral responsibility is involved when an artist can claim a work as her own. A further illustration of this is the case of the mess in the kitchen. Under some household arrangements, at least, the fact that it is *my* mess in the kitchen means that I am the one who must clean it up, even if I've done nothing *morally* blameworthy in making that mess.[7]

Again, to assert (1) is to endorse a policy, namely a policy of rendering certain rights, etc., associated with O. What do we do, then, when we deny (1), i.e. assert its negation? We endorse *not* having that policy in effect. This is different from endorsing a policy of *not* rendering unto A all the rights, etc., associated with b-responsibility for O. The body of policy that one recommends might simply leave it open whether to render unto A one or more of these rights and so on. Thus, denying (1) is a different act from simply declining to assert it. Anyone who both asserts and denies (1) thereby endorses a logically impossible set of policies—that is, it is logically impossible to put into effect a body of policy that

---

understand this phrase in different ways—for example, as expressing a pro-attitude toward actions that conform to the policy and a con-attitude toward those that don't; as expressing one's Being-For behaviors that conform to the policy, or Being-For the policy itself (in the sense of Schroeder 2008); or as not expressing *anything* so much as constituting a certain definite move in some kind of social scorekeeping game; or in some other way. Incidentally: because I take the last-mentioned possibility seriously, I reject the common identification of "neopragmatism" with "global expressivism." The heart of neopragmatism is *non-representational* semantics; representing and expressing are not the only two things you can do with language.

[5] Unless and until she voluntarily transfers it to someone else.

[6] Moral responsibility entails b-responsibility, but not vice versa, so the rights, etc., that attend moral responsibility for a given outcome are a superset of the ones that attend b-responsibility for the same outcome.

[7] True, the duty I now have to clean up the kitchen might well be a *moral* duty. More generally, the duties and rights associated with b-responsibility for an outcome might be moral rights and duties. But the point here is that these rights and duties come into play when someone has *basic* responsibility for the outcome.

agrees with all of such a person's endorsements. This explains the inconsistency of both asserting and denying (1).

Policies like (1) cannot just be adopted or not at will, however you like; we have certain meta-policies in effect, which govern the adoption of ground-level policies like (1).[8] In particular, in some situations, b-responsibility for one outcome automatically transfers to another outcome—for as we saw, b-responsibility transfers from the means $M(x)$ to the end $E(x)$ of an effective method $<M, K, E>$, whenever $M(x)$, $K(x)$, and $E(x)$ are all true. Thus, to assert a proposition of the form (2):

(2) Method $<M(x), K(x), E(x)>$ is effective

is to endorse the following meta-policy:

For any x, if $M(x)\&K(x)\&E(x)$ is true, then do not attribute b-responsibility for $M(x)$ to any agent without also attributing b-responsibility for $E(x)$ to that same agent.

In other words, it is to take the stance that wherever K holds, b-responsibility carries over from M to E. To call a method "effective" is to say it is one of the methods in which b-responsibility transfers from means to end.

To assert that $<M, K, E>$ is *not* effective should be different from merely refraining from asserting that it *is* effective. And it is different. To see why, we need to consider another meta-policy that governs our attributions of b-responsibility. Unlike the meta-policy endorsed by (2), this one seems to be more-or-less permanently in place. Intuitively, the idea behind this meta-policy is that whenever you attribute b-responsibility for some outcome O to some agent A, you must make sure that one of two conditions holds: either (i) making it so that O is something A is able to do "just like that," simply by deciding to—the way that most people are able to raise their arms or blink their eyes simply by deciding to; in other words, A can make it so that O as a *basic action*; or (ii) A has promoted the outcome O by using an effective method for doing so—that is, there is some effective method $<M, K, E>$ and some location x such that $K(x)$ is true, $E(x) = O$, and A has b-responsibility for $M(x)$.

But what does it mean to say that agent A is capable of making it so that O simply as a basic action? On the theory I'm proposing, this is another thing such that to assert it is to endorse a policy. Note that whether an agent is capable of doing something as a basic action itself depends on background conditions: I can

---

[8] Though perhaps (1) is itself really a meta-policy—rendering unto A one of the rights, duties, privileges, duties, or liabilities associated with b-responsibility for O might itself be a matter of putting some policy into effect.

raise my arm as a basic action most of the time, but not when I am tied up or paralyzed. With this in mind, we can understand an assertion of (3):

(3) Under conditions $K(x)$, agent A is in direct control over whether outcome $E(x)$ obtains

as the endorsement of a (meta-)policy something like this: Whenever $K(x)$ holds and $E(x)$ obtains, attribute b-responsibility for $E(x)$ to A.

The principle that agent A can have b-responsibility for outcome O only as a basic action or via some effective method puts a strong restriction on us, but it is not as strong as it might seem at first. For example, it doesn't mean that in order to pin the mess in the kitchen on Joe, I must already know whether he made the mess as a basic action or via some effective method, and it doesn't mean that I must have any notion of which effective method Joe used; in fact, it is possible that I am in a position to pin the mess on Joe even though he actually made that mess via a method that I myself do not even know to be effective. What it does require is that I must not attribute the outcome of the mess to Joe while also closing off every possible way in which Joe could have made the mess. Thus, the meta-policy in question here is formulated like this:

(4) Thou shalt not attribute b-responsibility for outcome O to agent A unless O actually does occur and one of the following conditions holds:

(i) There is some K, E, and r such that $K(r)$ is true, $E(r) = O$, and you do not deny[9] that for all x, under condition $K(x)$, A is in control of whether $E(x)$;

(ii) There is some M, K, E and r such that $K(r)$ is true, $E(r) = O$, you do not deny that $<M, K, E>$ is effective, and you do not deny that A is responsible for $M(r)$

(4) captures the idea that you can only be responsible for an outcome in two ways: either directly, when the outcome is something you have control over; or indirectly, when you earn responsibility for the outcome via being responsible for another outcome which is a means to it, via some effective method.

With the meta-policy (4) in the background, we can see that to deny one of (2) or (3) is not at all the same thing as simply declining to assert it. To decline to assert (2) is to decline to endorse one policy, and need not involve endorsing anything at all; but to *deny* (2) does involve endorsing a change in policy—in particular, a change that narrows down the range of possible cases in which we can

---

[9] The requirement here (and in clause (ii)) is that *you do not deny* this rather than that you *assert* or *agree* to it. This is because if I say Joe is responsible for outcome O, I need not know of (or believe in) any particular way in which he may have promoted O; consistency demands only that I not rule out every possible pathway from Joe to O.

permissibly attribute responsibility for $E(x)$ to some agent. Similarly with (3). To disavow it is not to endorse anything, but to deny it is to endorse a policy-change that narrows down the conditions in which agent A (in particular) can be permissibly credited with responsibility for O.

The account on the table so far thus gives a non-representational semantics for assertions of statements of the forms (1), (2), and (3), as well as for denials of them—i.e. for assertions of their negations. It remains to show how to extend the account to cover logically complex sentences that contain statements of forms (1), (2), and (3) as components. (In other words, it remains to show how to solve the Frege-Geach problem.) I don't have space to enter into this issue in this chapter; let me just say that I am hopeful that the technical machinery that Gibbard uses in his (2008) can be adapted here, with my "policies" playing a role analogous to his "plans."[10]

4. An Objection Considered

I initially characterized an *effective* method as one whereby an agent might successfully promote a practical end. But later, I characterized the effective methods as the ones in which, in any implementation for which the end is realized, b-responsibility transfers from the means to the end. Are these characterizations equivalent? If not, then it seems that sometimes I mean one thing by "effective" and sometimes another.

But I claim that they are equivalent. I think it is pretty obvious that whatever satisfies the second (responsibility-transferring) characterization must also satisfy the first (end-promoting) one. The interesting question is whether a method could satisfy the first without satisfying the second.

It might seem as if this must be possible. After all, a method can be effective without being sure-fire: I might vigorously strike a previously unused match while it is dry and surrounded by oxygen, only to see the match fail to light. Obviously, in such a case, the usual pathway from striking to lighting has been blocked. But even if so, the match might still ignite for some unrelated reason; for instance, it might be struck by lightning a fraction of a second after I struck it. In such a case, I will have employed a method whereby an agent might successfully promote the end of getting this match to light, whose background condition will have been satisfied, and the match will have lit—but we would not want to say that I am now b-responsible for the lighting of the match. This appears to be a case where a method satisfies the possibly successful end-promotion definition of an effective method, without satisfying the responsibility-transferring definition.

---

[10] Failing that, Gert (2023) and Shapiro (Chapter 10, this volume) provide distinct suggestions for dealing with this issue.

We can block this kind of counterexample by being careful about what must be included in the background condition K of an effective method. In the match case just described, there must be some event that usually occurs between the striking and the lighting, and which is essential to the way in which striking promotes lighting, which failed to occur in the present case. The failure of this event to occur is thus a defeating condition of the method. I say that the background condition of an effective method must include or entail the absence of every possible defeating condition. Thus, when I first presented the match-striking method, I was a bit sloppy in my formulation; I should have defined the method as $<M(p, t), K(p, t), E(p, t)>$, where:

$M(p, t)$ = the proposition that the match located at place p at time t is vigorously struck at t

$K(p, t)$ = the proposition that there exists a unique match at place p at time t, and at time t this match is dry, surrounded by oxygen, and not already struck, and none of the following conditions holds: ...

$E(p, t)$ = the proposition that the match at place p at time t begins to burn just after t

Now the counterexample ceases to be a counterexample, since $K(p, t)$ is no longer true in the actual world.[11]

I confess that I do not know how to fill in the "..." in the definition of $K(p, t)$. And this might not just be a matter of my personal ignorance; it might be that no one can fill it in, either because there are infinitely many possible defeating conditions or because some of them are unknown to present-day science, or both.

This might seem like a problem for my theory. But it isn't. It would be a problem if people sometimes needed, and were able, to fully specify the background condition in some effective method. But in practice, we never need to do this. If I want to light this match, and I wonder whether striking it will get that done, it is good enough if I can reasonably believe that *there exists some* K such that $<M(p, t), K(p, t), E(p, t)>$ is effective, and $K(p, t)$ is true (where $M(p, t)$ and $E(p, t)$ are still defined as they were before, but now $K(p, t)$ is allowed to vary). And I can indeed reasonably believe this—I would go so far as to say that I know that there is some such K, even though I cannot specify it. For I have a great deal of empirical evidence that inductively justifies the conclusion that almost all of the time,

---

[11] This solution works in general only if there will always be some such defeating condition, in every case where it appears that a method is end promoting but not necessarily responsibility transferring. I think there will always be one, but I won't try to defend this claim here. For an able defense of what is in effect the contrary view, see Carroll (1994: 134–40). What Carroll introduces as "the key case" on page 137 is a model for constructing putative counterexamples to my claim. I think these are *merely* putative counterexamples, but I can't defend that claim here.

in the sorts of situations in which someone is apt to try to light a match by striking it, and in which the match is previously unstruck, dry, and surrounded by oxygen, there is *some* such K.[12]

Thus, for practical purposes, we never really need to know *of some particular* K that <M, K, E> is effective and K(x) is true. Instead, what we need to know is that *there exists some* K such that <M, K, E> is effective and K(x) is true. And we can know this, even if every such K is far too long and complex for us ever to spell it out explicitly. Since what we need to know here is somewhat logically complicated, it wouldn't be surprising if we had developed some linguistic device for stating it in a syntactically simpler form. I think that we have indeed such a device, namely the sentence schema:

Under prevailing circumstances, $M(x)$ is a potentially effective means to $E(x)$

This omits all reference to the Ks and manages to avoid quantifying over methods, making it much easier for us to process in real time. (We will encounter this schema again in section 7, when we turn to the topic of singular causation.)

This illustrates an important point that we will meet again before we are done: it often happens that a kind of fact we all need to know on a daily basis has a somewhat complicated logical form and involves quantifying over the set of all effective methods—but we turn out to have a device in our ordinary language that lets us state that fact without explicitly representing its complex logical form. I think the other examples of this phenomenon include the words and phrases we use to express many of the natural modals. Let's turn to them now.

5. General Causation

Cartwright (1979) showed us that the general causal relation is importantly connected to the idea of an effective method whereby we might promote a practical goal. To promote one of my practical ends, I must manipulate one of the causes of that end; it will not suffice to manipulate something that raises the probability of my end without causing it. For example, there might be a strong positive correlation between having stained teeth and developing lung cancer, since smoking is a cause of each, even though neither is a cause of the other; even so, if I smoke, getting my teeth whitened is not a potentially effective way for me to promote my goal of avoiding lung cancer. If I want to promote this goal, then I need to make something happen that is a cause of avoiding lung cancer.

---

[12] In my (2014), I defend a similar suggestion about *ceteris paribus* laws.

Cartwright's view (in Cartwright 1979) is that general causal relations—which she calls *causal laws*—provide the grounds for the effectiveness of the effective strategies we may use to promote our ends. I propose to reverse the order of explanation here, and theorize that the general causal relations are as they are in virtue of which methods are the effective ones.

This leaves me in agreement with Cartwright that in any effective method <M, K, E>, the kind of state of affairs that can be a value of $M(x)$ must be among the causes of the kind of state of affairs that can be a value of $E(x)$, when the background condition $K(x)$ is in place—at least in the kinds of cases that Cartwright was interested in. There is an important exception, though: in some cases, the means in an effective method helps to ground the end, rather than to cause it. For example, consider the method <$M(t)$, $K(t)$, $E(t)$> where:

$M(t)$ = the proposition that Bert believes at t that it is raining at t
$K(t)$ = the proposition that it is not raining at t
$E(t)$ = the proposition that Bert has a false belief about the weather at t

This is a clear case of an effective method. You can indeed get Bert to have a false belief about the weather by means of getting him to think it's raining when it's really not. But in a successful implementation of this method, the means does not *cause* Bert to have a false belief about the weather—it simply *is* Bert's false belief about the weather. In a case like this, $M(x)\&K(x)$ entails $E(x)$, in the sense that there is no (broadly) logically possible world in which $M(x)\&K(x)$ is true while $E(x)$ is not. One of the things that Hume got right about causation is that there can be no such entailment of an effect by its cause. Causal connections are not logical connections.[13]

So, here are three plausible principles relating general causation to effectiveness of methods:

(5a) If $M(x)\&K(x)$ entails $E(x)$ for some value of x, then $M(x)$ is not a cause of $E(x)$ in conditions $K(x)$.

(5b) If <M, K, E> is effective, and $M(x)\&K(x)$ does not entail $E(x)$ for any value of x, then $M(x)$ is a cause of $E(x)$ in conditions $K(x)$.

(5c) If M is a cause of E in conditions K, then <M, K, E> is effective.

We might call (5a) "Hume's principle" and (5b) "Cartwright's principle." Here is the rationale for (5c): suppose I do bring about a cause of my end, under conditions in which that cause does indeed act as a cause, and suppose my end is then realized—don't I bear *b*-responsibility for the realization of my end, then?

---

[13] I am grateful to Philip Pettit for discussion on this point.

(Of course, I might not be the only agent who is b-responsible for this outcome, but I am surely one of them.) So, when M is a cause of E in K, the method <M, K, E> would seem to be automatically responsibility transferring—which makes it an effective method.

The conjunction of (5a), (5b), and (5c) is logically equivalent to:

(5) C-type states of affairs cause E-type states of affairs under conditions of type K just in case:
(i) <C, K, E> is an effective method, and
(ii) for no value of x does $C(x)\&K(x)$ entail $E(x)$.

(5) has the right form to be an analysis of general causal relations that reduces them to effective methods. It seems to be true, and what makes it seem true is (broadly) *a priori* reflection, and seems not to depend on contingent details of the actual world (such as what actually causes what, and which methods are actually the effective ones). So it's plausible that (5) is necessarily true. You might agree that (5) is necessarily true while disputing my suggestion that it is a good *analysis* of general causation; for example, you might think (5) is necessarily true because which methods are effective depends on what general causal relations hold. The best case that (5) *does* provide an analysis that reduces general causation to effectiveness is that this hypothesis is part of a larger theory that sheds light in many directions. So let's get on with sketching that theory.

6. Lawhood

What distinguishes the laws of nature from the accidental regularities?[14] The obvious and easy answer is: "The accidental regularities are true, but they could have been false, whereas the laws of nature are inevitably true; there is no way for them to fail, and there never has been." But what are we to make of this modal talk? The laws of nature are not logically necessary. A case can be made that at least some of the laws are not metaphysically necessary either (see Roberts 2010). So what kind of necessity do the laws have? One familiar answer is that the laws have *nomic necessity*, defined as follows:

(6) It is nomically necessary that P iff the laws of nature collectively logically entail that P

---

[14] Readers who know Marc Lange's work on laws of nature, necessity, and counterfactuals will find the following paragraphs familiar. Though the proposal I am about to make is quite different from the one Lange makes, the form that my account takes, and the strategy for discovering it and defending it, are directly borrowed from him. See Lange 2009.

But if this is all there is to the necessity of laws, then it fails to set them apart from just any old bundle of truths. For any set S of true propositions—such as the truths about the colors of the fur of the cats who live in my house—we can define "S-necessity" by saying that it is S-necessary that P just in case S logically entails that P. So it is cats-at-my-house-necessary that no cat at my house is orange, but merely cats-at-my-house-contingent that water boils at 100 degrees Celsius. In the light of this, "nomic necessity," as (6) defines it, does not seem to be a special property at all—because there is an analogous kind of "necessity" for any other set of truths you pick. So the fact that the laws have nomic necessity cannot justify, validate, or explain our belief that the laws "could not have failed to be true" though the accidental regularities could have.

So then, *is* there any genuine sense in which the laws could not have failed to be true though the accidental regularities could have? Perhaps this: there are available means that could be effective for ends that would violate the accidental regularities, but there are no effective means for ends that would violate the laws. More formally:

(7a)　It is a law of nature that P iff there is no M, K, E, r such that $<M, K, E>$ is effective and $E(r)$ is inconsistent with P.

This is too strong, though. Suppose that:

P = [there are no magnetic monopoles] (and this is a law)
$M(x)$ = the proposition that there is a spherical magnetic monopole at locus x
$K(x)$ = (some tautology)
$E(x)$ = the proposition that there is an ellipsoidal magnetic monopole at locus x

Then the method $<M, K, E>$ certainly seems to count as effective: Since a sphere is one kind of ellipsoid, putting a spherical dingus at x is one way of putting an ellipsoidal dingus at x, for any sort of dingus; moreover, anyone who bears b-responsibility for there being a sphere at x certainly seems thereby to earn b-responsibility for there being an ellipsoid there. But $K(x)$ is true, and $E(x)$ is inconsistent with the law that P. So this case is a counterexample to (7a).

It is obvious what the problem is here. The motivating thought behind (7a) could be better expressed like this: *If an end is ruled out by the laws of nature, then there is no effective means to it.* This is a natural thought to have. In order for it to be remotely plausible, though, it needs to be slightly weakened. When it quantifies over effective means, we must take this quantification to be implicitly further restricted. Of course, a means that is *itself "already"* in violation of the laws might promote (via an effective method) an end that is in violation of the laws, too. (That's what's going on in the case we just looked at.) Fortunately, the fix is easy:

(7) It is a law of nature that P iff: For any M, K, E and r, if <M, K, E> is effective and E(r) is inconsistent with P, then M(r)&K(r) is inconsistent with some law of nature.

In other words: a method for promoting a nomically impossible outcome cannot be effective, unless it is also nomically impossible to implement it.

(7) is logically equivalent to:

For any M, K, E, and r: if <M, K, E> is effective and (M(r)&K(r)) is consistent with the laws of nature, then so is E(r).

This attributes a certain property to the set of propositions that are laws of nature in the actual world. Let's call this property "unbreakability." We can define it like this:

A set S of true propositions is *unbreakable* $=_{def}$ for every M, K, E, and r: if <M, K, E> is effective and M(r)&K(r) is consistent with S, then E(r) is consistent with S.

When a set of true propositions has this property, there is no way to render any of its members false, unless one of its members is already false. Thus, all of its members being actually true, its members have a special, protected status: there is no unactualized but potentially effective means of rendering any of them false. They are all true, and—things being as they are—there is no way to change that.[15] This justifies the label "unbreakability," and it also shows that such a set of true propositions is, in at least one important sense, *necessary*. Unlike the sort of "nomic necessity" that we were just considering, unbreakability does set apart the sets of truths that have it. For unbreakability is a very rare property among sets of truths.

To see why it is such a rare property, consider the set:

{The sky is blue; Grass is green; On June 1, 2021, John T. Roberts weighs over 90 kg}

I have it on good authority that there do exist effective methods that might have been employed to bring it about that my weight was under 90 kg on June 1, 2021; the employment of these methods is consistent with the sky's blueness, grass's

---

[15] The point here is not that since they are all true now, there is nothing we can do that will render any of them untrue in the future. Rather, the point is that, all of these propositions being eternally true in the actual world, there is nothing that qualifies as an unused means that would have been potentially effective as a way of producing violations of any of them. Not only do they lack any counterexamples anywhere in spacetime—there is not even a missed opportunity to produce a counterexample anywhere in spacetime.

greenness, and my weighing over 90 kg on June 1, 2021. (The employment of such a method *had the power to get* my weight below 90 kg, but it doesn't *logically entail that* my weight be that low; methods can be effective without being foolproof.) Hence, the set in question is not unbreakable. For similar reasons, most any random list of true propositions you can come up with will fail to be unbreakable in the same way.

But the laws of nature are not the only unbreakable set of true propositions. The set of all (narrowly) logical truths is another one: for no method with logically consistent means and background condition could possibly be an effective method for promoting a logically inconsistent end. (You cannot effectively boost the chances of the logically impossible by doing the logically possible under logically possible conditions.) And the logical truths, of course, also enjoy a species of necessity (though we don't need to appeal to the notion of unbreakability to explain why it does). The set of all metaphysically necessary truths (if there are such things) is presumably another unbreakable set. But we can count logical truths and metaphysically necessary truths as laws of nature, 'by courtesy.' At any event, logical truths are logically entailed by the laws, and metaphysical necessities are metaphysically entailed by the laws (as they are by everything else), so we may legitimately count them as nomically necessary, i.e. as enjoying at least the same grade of necessity as the laws of nature.[16] But these other unbreakable sets of truths are themselves proper subsets of the set of laws of nature. It seems clear that the propositions in any such set should count as necessary in the same way that laws do—which means that they should qualify as laws themselves. Thus, we may plausibly conjecture that:

(8) It is a law of nature that $P =_{def} P$ is a member of at least one unbreakable set.

Or, equivalently:

(8eq) It is a law of nature that $P =_{def}$ there exists a set S of true propositions such that P is in S and for every M, K, E, and r: if $<M, K, E>$ is effective and $M(r)\&K(r)$ is consistent with S, then $E(r)$ is consistent with S.

The only non-logical concept used in the right-hand side of (8eq) is that of an effective method. Hence, according to (8eq), the predicate "is a law of nature" is a device for abbreviating a complex, multiply quantified statement about the effective methods.

---

[16] In effect, I am here deciding to use "law of nature" and "nomically necessary truth" interchangeably. A different terminological option would be to treat (7) and (8) as definitions of nomic necessity instead of definitions of laws of nature, and then to define a "law of nature" as a nomic necessity that has some further property—perhaps logical or metaphysical contingency. As far as I can see, this is a merely terminological question; nothing substantive seems to turn on it.

7. Singular Causation

Singular causation is a relation among token events. A little notation for talking about events: if $P(x)$ is a propositional function, and r is a possible value of its index such that $P(r)$ is the proposition that a certain event—call it $p(r)$—occurred, then we may write $[p(r)]$ for $P(r)$; more generally, where e is a token event, $[e]$ is the proposition that e actually does (did, will) occur.

Now suppose that m and e are both actual token events. Suppose there is an effective method $<M(x), K(x), E(x)>$, and an index-value r, such that $M(r) = [m]$, $E(r) = [e]$ (thus, $M(r)$ and $E(r)$ are both true), and $K(r)$ is true. Now recall the principle that in effective methods, (basic) responsibility transfers from means to end in any successful implementation of an effective method. This principle implies that in this case, any agent who is responsible for $[m]$ is also responsible for $[e]$.[17]

Of course, it might be true for any number of different reasons that any agent who is responsible for $[m]$ is also responsible for $[e]$. For example, this might be vacuously true, simply because no agent is responsible for $[m]$. Or it might be a coincidence that Joe is responsible for both $[m]$ and $[e]$, while no one other than Joe is responsible for $[m]$. But in the case in hand, something more interesting is true: $[m]$ and $[e]$ stand in the relation that whoever is responsible for the former is also responsible for the latter, and they do so because the events m and e are linked by an effective method with a satisfied background condition. In this case, any agent who is responsible for $[m]$ is *thereby* responsible for $[e]$, because responsibility for $[m]$ automatically transfers across to responsibility for $[e]$. In this case, the network of effective methods, together with the actual history of the world, connect the events m and e in such a way that to have helped bring it about that $[m]$ is to have helped bring it about that $[e]$.

I suggest that this is precisely the situation in which we are willing to judge that m is a (singular) cause of e. Of course, not every cause is the work of any agent. But in every case where we judge that some event e_1 is a cause of some other event e_2, I think we also have the following conditional commitment: should we now learn that some agent A is in fact responsible for the occurrence of e_1, and our new information does not lead us to change our minds about e_1 having caused e_2, then we should judge that that agent is also responsible for e_2.

It is a truism that making one event happen which then causes a second event is a way of making that second event happen. Reverse side of this coin is: for one event to cause a second event is for making the first event happen to be one way

---

[17] This "e" always denotes an event, while "$[e]$" denotes a proposition. In the text, I always write as if it is propositions rather than events that an agent can be b-responsible for. But I doubt that anything of substance depends on this; think of it as my notational convention.

of making the second event happen. Thus, c is a cause of e iff b-responsibility for $[c]$ automatically transmits to $[e]$. More formally:

(9) Where c and e are events, c is a cause of e iff: c occurs, e occurs, and there is an effective method $<M, K, E>$ and an index-value r such that $M(r) = [c]$, $E(r) = [e]$, and $K(r)$ is true.

Of course, the task of theorizing about singular causation is a minefield full of tricky counterexamples involving such things as overdetermination, pre-emption, prevention of preventers, and the fact that HRH Elizabeth II did not have to water anybody's plants. In the space I have left, there is no way to survey this field and see whether (9) emerges from it unscathed. But here is a reason for hope. It is plausible that in the difficult cases, our intuitions about what event causes what closely track our intuitions about who we think would deserve blame/credit for what. For example, Suzy's parents owe compensation for the broken window, not Billy's; Backup Assassin is the murderer of Victim, and Assassin is at most guilty of attempted murder; anyone who prevented Her Royal Highness from watering my plants while I was out of town was not thereby to blame for the plants' demise. By hooking up the singular causal relation to the notion of an effective method, and thereby to questions of which agents are responsible for which outcomes, (9) proactively defends itself against all present and forthcoming attempts to counterexample it.[18]

8. Conclusion

I have sketched a neopragmatist theory of effective methods, and I have shown how to reduce general and singular causation as well as laws of nature to the effectiveness of methods, thereby producing a neopragmatist theory of all three. Official statements of these reductions are in propositions (5), (8eq), and (9). I believe this account can be smoothly extended to cover counterfactual conditionals, dispositions, powers, and objective chance—but that is work for a later occasion.

In the theory I have presented, simple statements about these natural modals, as well as their negations, are neat and closed syntactic devices we have for packaging more complex batches of information about which methods are the effective ones. The complicated batches are sometimes just the parcel of information we need for some practical purpose—such as knowing whom to pin the blame on for an accident. Thus, it is to be expected that we should have developed some

---

[18] In this connection, compare Sartorio (2007: 749): "Causation is the vehicle of transmission of moral responsibility."

convenient way of packaging and conveying such information, without explicitly getting into the quantificational structure of the propositions that contain the information. If I am right, then we have indeed developed such convenient ways—and they are the various natural modals. This accounts for the contents of our concepts of the various natural modals, as well as for why there should be any such things as natural modals at all. If they did not exist, it would behoove us to invent them.

References

Brandom, R. (2008). *Between Saying and Doing*. Harvard University Press.

Carroll, J. (1994). *Laws of Nature*. Cambridge University Press.

Cartwright, N. (1979). 'Causal Laws and Effective Strategies', *Noûs* 13, 419–37.

Gert, J. (2023). 'Neopragmatist Semantics', *Philosophy and Phenomenological Research*, 106 (1), 107–135.

Gibbard, A. (2008). *Thinking How to Live*. Harvard University Press.

Lange, M. (2009). *Laws and Lawmakers*. Oxford University Press.

Menzies, P. and Price, H. (1993). 'Causation as Secondary Quality', *British Journal for the Philosophy of Science* 44 (2), 187–203.

Pearl, J. (2009). *Causality*, second edition. Oxford University Press.

Roberts, J. T. (2010). 'Some Laws of Nature are Metaphysically Contingent', *Australasian Journal of Philosophy* 88 (3), 445–57.

Roberts, J. T. (2014). 'CP-Law Statements as Vague, Statistical, Self-Locating, Self-Referential and Perfectly in Order', *Erkenntnis* 79 (10), 1775–86.

Sartorio, C. (2007). 'Causation and Responsibility', *Philosophy Compass* 2 (5), 749–65.

Schroeder, M. (2008). *Being For: Evaluating the Semantic Program of Expressivism*, Oxford University Press.

Ward, B. (2002). 'Humeanism without Humean Supervenience: A Projectivist Account of Laws and Possibilities', *Philosophical Studies* 107 (3), 191–218.

PART III
LANGUAGE, TRUTH, AND LOGIC

6
A Pragmatic Genealogy of Rule-Following

Philip Pettit

1. Introduction

How to make sense of our ability to follow rules, especially those basic rules for doing things that we may not be able to define? How, for example, to make sense of the rules we presumably follow in judging properly that something is a tool or a game, or is smooth or crimson, or regular or irregular in shape, where we have no other words in which to analyze those properties? Or if it seems that we might be able to define those rules and employ the definitions as formulae to guide us, how to make sense of the basic rules we presumably follow in making judgments about the properties—on pain of regress, there must be some—that we cannot define in that way? This I take to be the main rule-following problem highlighted in Wittgenstein's (1958) classic discussion, in the well-known commentary provided by Saul Kripke (1982), and in various other sources.[1]

I approach the problem here in a novel fashion, asking about how creatures otherwise like us in make-up, might develop the ability to follow basic rules—and so rules in general—beginning from a point where that capacity hasn't yet materialized. I argue that some features that they have in common with us, going on accepted psychological theories, would make certain practices more or less inevitable and that those practices would give rise to a skill that answers to our notion of rule-following. Those practices and that skill would emerge with robust probability, so the proposal goes: the likelihood of their emergence would be independent of fortuitous events.[2]

The thought experiment I propose is an example of the sort of counterfactual genealogy—by a recent account a 'pragmatic genealogy' (Queloz 2021)—that

---

[1] For an overview of other approaches to the problem, and attempted resolutions, see (Miller 2018: chs. 5–6). I concentrate generally on properties, although the rule-following problem arises for other entities too such as the plus-function on which Kripke (1982) focuses.

[2] The genealogy provided builds on my earlier work but reworks and develops it in novel ways. Much of the earlier work is in part I of (Pettit 2002). I do use the word 'genealogy' in that work to describe my approach but do not spell it out in the way I do here. This essay might be seen as a response to Miller (2018: ch. 6.2), who suggests that the genealogy I offer may be circular, presupposing rule-following in the course of explaining it.

Bernard Williams (2002) hails as a novel approach to philosophical problems. It was used explicitly by Edward Craig (1990) in his account of knowledge, as it was used by Williams in his explanation of the importance of truth and truthfulness, and as I myself used it in a recent reconstruction of the nature of ethics (Pettit 2018). But it was also employed, without being named, in Wilfred Sellars's (1997) explanation of psychology, originally published in 1956, in Herbert Hart's (2012) account of law in 1961, and in David Lewis's (1969) theory of convention.[3]

Lewis offers a particularly clear example of a counterfactual or pragmatic genealogy. He begins with creatures otherwise like us but lacking conventions or the idea of conventions; argues that they would face various coordination predicaments, as in deciding what side of the road to take in meeting one another; shows that they would individually adjust to such problems on the basis of precedence or salience; and maintains that such adjustments would aggregate into recognized social regularities, serving a purpose that conventions typically serve. His suggestion, then, is that the regularities that would appear amongst our counterfactual counterparts can serve as models for conventions, providing a good sense of what they involve and what pragmatic purpose they serve.

I think that a genealogical account of broadly the same sort can help to illuminate even something as cognitively fundamental to our species as rule-following. I take two well-documented, evolutionarily explicable features of human beings as given: the disposition to act jointly for shared, otherwise unattainable goals, and a form of teaching the young that does not just rely on their tendency to copy their elders. And I try to show that with features like these, our counterparts in the thought experiment—for short, humanoids—would be robustly likely to follow rules, including the basic rules where analyses run out.

My hope is that the humanoid practice of rule-following that would appear under those imagined conditions can serve as a model of rule-following amongst our own kind, illuminating its nature and demystifying its existence. Insofar as our account of rule-following traces it to the pressures and opportunities opened up by independently sourced practices, it has a distinctively pragmatist character, although it is realist rather than skeptical about rules and the following of rules.

The chapter is in six sections. In section 2, I offer an account of rule-following, explaining why it has seemed so problematic to many. In the following three (sections 3–5), I look respectively at three developments we can expect among the humanoids—sensitization to patterns, identification of patterns, and triangulation on patterns—arguing that together they would lead the humanoids into following rules. I argue in a brief conclusion (section 6) that rule-following among humanoids offers a model of what rule-following amongst human beings involves

---

[3] Huw Price (1988) also gestures at something close to a genealogy in this sense but unlike the examples given, his book is often cast, fairly or unfairly, as debunking in character: it represents truth as something less important or real than it is commonly taken to be. For a general account of the genealogy approach, see Queloz (2021).

as well. On this model, there really are rules, even basic rules, that we humans can be said to follow, but the rules present to us as important and discernible realities only within the perspective of practices that have an independent appeal.

2. Rule-Following and the Problem It Raises

2.1 Following Rules, Basic and Otherwise

A distinctive feature of our species is that we ask one another questions, we even ask ourselves questions, and try when the evidence is available to generate answers. Among the questions raised, we ask about whether properties that we cannot analyze or define—for short, basic properties—are realized in this case or not. And without having personal access to definitions, we try to provide answers. Is that a *tool* in your hands? Is that a *game* that they are playing? Is this number the *sum* of those? Is that coat *red* in color? Is that a *regular* shape or not? That we lack personal access to definitions in such cases does not mean that the properties are indefinable; they may be basic for us without being basic for experts. But some properties—some suitably determinate properties—must be basic for us, on pain of regress, as indeed some must be basic for experts. And we may assume that the cases given illustrate that category.[4]

When we try to answer a question of this kind, the manifest assumption is that we understand the property involved, being aware of the sorts of conditions determining whether it is present, and that the aim of the exercise is to check on whether they are realized according to the evidence at our disposal. We think of that exercise as one in which we may fail but, at the same time, as one in which a greater effort on our part—paying closer attention to the property and to the evidence at hand—can reduce the likelihood of failure.

That there are stable conditions linked with the property, determining whether it is present or not, means that there is a regularity in that linkage. That regularity will serve intuitively as a rule governing judgments about its presence, insofar as we have the ability to consciously try to conform to it—equivalently, to try to track the property—expecting that the attempt may raise our chances of success, but without ensuring it. We cannot try to conform to it by consulting a formula that lays out the realization conditions of the property, since such a formula would require the sort of analysis or definition that we are taking to be absent. We can only try to conform to it by seeking to track the property directly, looking for evidence of its realization in this or that situation.

---

[4] It may be, for all we assume, that what is basic for us or basic for experts are inter-defined packages of properties, not properties in isolation: this, in the way a line is defined, roughly, as the shortest distance between two points and a point as the intersection of two lines. We ignore that possibility here for reasons of convenience.

2.2 Modes of Rule-Following

When a regularity serves as a rule in this sense, then we control for conforming to it in a conscious and intentional manner; we manifestly try to ensure conformity. That the control is conscious follows from the part that the property plays as an object we take to be a target to track; that it is intentional is implied by the need for effort in this tracking. The fact that control is necessary to make conformity to the rule likely means that besides being conscious and intentional, rule-following has the further feature of being defeasible, indeed defeasible in a way that must be salient to the agent. Despite our best efforts, we may fail to conform: the control may be unsuccessful.

The notion of control invoked here is quite straightforward, being relevant in the case of mechanisms as well as agents. The air-conditioning system controls for the ambient temperature in a room, keeping it within certain limits. It ensures that the temperature will remain within the pre-set limits, robustly across a range of variations in circumstances—say, an influx of hot or cold air—although success is not guaranteed; after all, a mechanical glitch is always going to remain a possibility. In following a rule, we control in a similarly robust, if defeasible, fashion for conformity with the rule, adjusting the judgments we make on the questions before us as circumstance and evidence require. And we do that consciously, of course, and by acting out of an intention to get the correct answer.

Or at least we do this consciously and intentionally when rule-following has an active character that requires conscious effort and an explicit intention to conform. But consistently with being a form of control, rule-following may have a virtual or standby character instead. In that form it would not involve consciousness or intention but, as we shall see, it would still represent a form of agential control.

Think of how the cowboy in the classic western controls for the direction the cattle will take when he lets them follow their noses and rides herd from the rear. Riding herd may just involve strolling along singing a song, as in the kitsch image, provided the cowboy is poised to notice any animal going off track, thereby raising a red flag, and provided he is ready to intervene in such a case and put it back on the desired route. The cowboy exercises virtual or standby control over the cattle and, even if he is never required to intervene, he will still expect to be remunerated for the job he has done.

We may follow rules, including basic rules, in the same standby sense. Suppose we let habits dictate the judgments we make, and the words we utter, in response to various questions about the instantiation of this or that property; suppose, in other words, that we let habits take over as the cowboy lets the cattle follow their noses. We will still be in control of the judgments made if the fact that the habits prompt an implausible judgment—a judgment that conflicts with standing assumptions—is likely to raise a red flag, and if that in turn is likely to prompt us to intervene as the errant animal would prompt the intervention of the cowboy. Habit might lead us to mistake a pepper for a tomato but biting into it would certainly raise a red flag. And such a flag would prompt us to resort to conscious, intentional effort in determining what it is we put in our mouth.

This possibility is worth noting, because otherwise it might seem that our earlier description of what rule-following involves is excessively reflective and intellectual. It is likely that on most of the occasions when we follow a basic rule, we do so without thinking, as we naturally say: we let habit take over. Even when we do this, however, we will remain in control to the extent that we are disposed to notice a red flag—'Is this really a tomato?'—and to let that force us to think reflectively about the case. We will enjoy the virtual or standby control involved in riding herd on our habitual responses.

Although the possibility and prevalence of standby control is worth noting, however, the focus of our discussion will be on active rule-following only. By definition, standby rule-following is possible only if active rule-following is possible, for it can occupy the stage only when the active mode is in the wings. In any case, it is the active mode that makes the problem of rule-following salient.

2.3 The Rule-Following Problem

The problem is this. How do we manage to directly track a property that is basic for us in the sense explained: a property or indeed any similar entity, such as the plus-function implied in the property of being a sum? Rule-following in familiar cases involves explicit or implicit definitions or formulae and, while it too may raise some problems, we shall concentrate here, following Wittgenstein, on the basic case where definitions are lacking.[5] In the definitional case, the resources that enable us to control appropriately for conformity are provided by the formula available. The problem in the case of following basic rules, specifically the active version of this case, is to explain what the resources are that enable us to track a property directly rather than definitionally.

The idea that certain rules are basic connects with the idea of basic acts. That an act is basic means that while we perform it intentionally, we do not perform it by performing any other acts intentionally (Hornsby 1980). I may fasten my shoes intentionally by tying my shoelaces intentionally. But if I am proficient in doing so, I will tie my shoelaces intentionally without relying on doing anything else intentionally. The child may have to learn to move their fingers, now in this way, now in that, to tie their shoelaces, so that the act of tying is not basic for them. But when the child becomes proficient, they will tie the laces intentionally without

---

[5] Paul Boghossian (2012) focuses on a more general problem, which we shall ignore here. For a response, see Pettit (2024: ch. 2).

any awareness of what they do with their fingers, and so without intentionally moving those fingers in any independently characterized way. They will tie their shoelaces intentionally; and they will tie them without relying on intentionally taking a distinct step as a means to that end.

Actively following basic rules is not only an intentional act but a basic intentional act. Following a rule that is defined for us in other terms means intentionally conforming to the rule in suitable situations by means of intentionally applying the relevant definition or formula. Following a basic rule means intentionally conforming to it in response to appropriate evidence but not by means of doing anything else intentionally—anything more basic—such as applying a definition.

With plausible examples of basic rule-following, such as those given above, it may be hard to imagine that any creature, human or otherwise, could try to track a property without having a word to refer to that property or, equivalently, a word to express the concept under which it is viewed. Trying to track the property may consist as a matter of practice in trying to use a relevant word only in the presence of the appropriate property. But even if the effort to track a property is essentially connected with having a word for it—or at least being able to use words to identify it—this should not be taken to indicate that the problem primarily concerns how we learn to use that word. The main problem is how we can identify a basic property, or any such basic entity, as something to guide us in judging that it is present in certain cases and absent in others.

2.4 The Problem in Wittgenstein

The rule-following issue, as we have described it here, is at the center of Wittgenstein's discussion, and indeed Kripke's commentary. Kripke (1982: 24) puts the problem nicely when he formulates the requirement for the direct tracking of a property or other basic entity. The requirement is normative, and manifestly normative, in character: it requires that the property involved 'should *tell* me what I ought to do in each new instance'. If it didn't speak to me in some such sense, he suggests, then to judge that the property is present in this or that case would be to 'make an unjustified leap in the dark' (Kripke 1982: 10).

Wittgenstein's (1958: §175) discussion highlights the challenge of explaining basic rule-following in much the same way, arguing that the target involved—the property tracked—should *guide* me, as he puts it. It may seem that, in following a rule, I was just moved to go one way rather than another. But that seems wrong, he writes: 'I feel as if there must have been something else'. '"For surely," I tell myself, "I was being *guided*"'. The problem, then, is to say how a basic property could *guide* me across cases: how, in Kripke's phrase, it could *tell* me which cases are instances of the property, which not.

It would be unilluminating, according to Wittgenstein, to say in the sort of example he has in mind that I just grasp the nature of the property, the sense of the concept or word that ascribes it (see too Kripke 1982: 54). "It's as if we could grasp the whole use of a word in a flash," so I may think (Wittgenstein 1958: §197). But how is that grasp, that intuition, to guide me? An 'inner voice' tells me, someone may suggest. But 'how do I know *how* I am to obey it? And how do I know that it doesn't mislead me? For if it can guide me right, it can also guide me wrong' (Wittgenstein 1958: §213).

Putting intuition aside, Wittgenstein asks whether I might grasp a basic property by surveying a set or series of instances and then extrapolating from those to other instances. Might I cotton on to the property by looking at instances, for example, of 'the same colours, the same lengths, the same shapes' and thereby learn to 'continue' the 'pattern uniformly' (Wittgenstein 1958: §208)? No, he claims. For how am I to know how 'to continue a pattern' (Wittgenstein 1958: §211)? Might I find reasons to go this way rather than that? No, for 'my reasons will soon give out' and then I can only 'act, without reasons'. The problem is that there is nothing about a finite series of any items that gives me reason to think of extrapolating to further items as following a rule. 'Whatever I do is, on some interpretation, in accord with the rule' (Wittgenstein 1958: §198).

It is plausible with any series of items, of course—say, examples of addition which illustrate numbers as the sum of others—that we develop a disposition to continue in one way rather than others; that is part of what happens when we learn to add. So perhaps rule-following just consists in forming such a disposition and then acting as it prompts me in extrapolating to further instances? Perhaps to follow the rule for detecting sums, for example, is just 'to be disposed, when asked for any sum "x + y" to give the sum of x and y as the answer' (Kripke 1982: 23). In a plausible interpretation of Wittgenstein, Kripke (1982: 24) argues that this won't work either, principally for the reason that to be subject to a disposition in proceeding is not to be guided toward what one ought to do or is justified in doing; it conflicts with the assumption in such a case that 'whatever in fact I (am disposed to) do, there is a unique thing that I should do'.

On the face of it, Wittgenstein holds a realist view of rule-following, never doubting that we do follow rules even in the basic cases on which he focuses. But he defends that view in a somewhat aphoristic and opaque manner. Thus, he argues that when you follow a sign-post, in his own analogue, you will not only 'have been trained to react to this sign in a particular way', you will go 'by a sign-post only in so far as there exists a regular use of sign-posts, a custom' (Wittgenstein 1958: §198). He suggests that we will each have learned those customs—those uses or institutions, as he also says—insofar as we teach them to one another. And he thinks that such teaching will proceed 'by means of examples and by practice', 'by expressions of agreement, rejection, expectation, encouragement', and by the sort of 'gesture that means "go on like this" ' (Wittgenstein 1958: §208).

In Kripke's (1982: ch. 3) interpretation, however, Wittgenstein assumes a very different profile, conceding in an anti-realist or skeptical spirit that no explanation of rule-following can save the phenomenon. I can be said to give the right answers in different cases, so the idea goes, but that is just to say that I give the sorts of answers most others in the community would give. And if I am described in such a case as following a rule, that only has the force of an honorific: it may imply approval for my conformity with established habits—I properly belong to the community—but it does not imply that in any literal sense I am actually following a rule: I am controlling my responses with a view to conforming to the rule.

3. Being Sensitized to Patterns

In this section we begin to go through three practices and capacities that human beings generally display and that, by a range of accepted accounts, have been features of the human make-up well back into the history of the species. These capacities will belong to humanoids as well and the question is whether their exercise would engage them in following basic rules, by our account of what that involves. If it would, then the capacity of humanoids to follow rules would be explicable in naturalistically unproblematic terms. And if it could be explained in that way amongst the humanoids, it may lend itself to a similar explanation in our own kind.

The capacities we explore enable human beings, and would enable the humanoids, first, to be sensitized to basic patterns; second, to identify those patterns as such; and, third, to triangulate on the patterns, making them objects of purportedly common attention. We discuss sensitization in this section, identification in section 4, and triangulation in section 5. Except when context implies otherwise, the patterns we have in mind throughout the discussion are all basic patterns that we cannot analyze in other terms.

3.1 Patterns Unlocked by a Key

The notion of a pattern invoked here is best introduced by contrast with a random set. A set of items will be patterned as distinct from random insofar as it is possible to present them more compactly than just by listing the members (Chaitin 1975, 1988). Thus, given one or another proper subset of the members, it should be possible to determine other members in the patterned set without having to list them one by one; in any case, listing members would be impossible with an unbounded set (Dennett 1991; Jackson, Pettit, and Smith 1999).

That which makes it possible to grasp the extension or membership of a patterned set, without having to list all the members, may be an independently identifiable key to the pattern, in which case the pattern will be analyzable. Take the Fibonacci series of numbers, 0, 1, 1, 2, 3, 5, 8, 13… This is a patterned rather than random set, as is probably intuitively obvious. But we can confirm that appearance insofar as there is an explicit key to unlock the pattern, so to speak. The key is that the series begins with 0 and 1 and that later members are each the sum of the two preceding numbers: the value of x_n, a member of the series at the nth position, is given by the formula, $x_n = x_{n-1} + x_{n-2}$.

This way of unlocking or reading a pattern is special because the possibility of applying the key depends on the independent possibility of seeing a pattern in applications of the key: seeing them as applications of the same key. In the example, this would require an ability to see a pattern in the notion of summing, in the notion of two, and in the notion of preceding. And, of course, there may be no key available for doing that: no key to unlock the key itself. If patterns are to be detected, therefore, including a pattern as simple as that in the Fibonacci series, then there must be some patterns that can be unlocked without reliance on an explicit key; there must be some basic patterns.[6]

3.2 Patterns Unlocked without a Key

Happily, this is not a problem, since there is a host of patterns that natural creatures engage with, and effectively unlock, without applying such a key. The dog that learns to expect an outing on hearing the word 'Walk' engages with a pattern in that manner. And so does the pigeon that is conditioned to peck for food at doors that have a triangular shape. In such cases, as in a variety of cases that involve human beings and humanoids, the key to the pattern, if we can speak of a key, is presumably implemented in the brain of the creature involved as distinct from being applied in the manner of the key to the Fibonacci series. It works to unlock the pattern insofar as it means that, having been exposed to just a few instances of the pattern, the subject becomes sensitized to an open range of other instances, including instances that may vary in all sorts of other ways.

Thus, when the dog or the pigeon is sensitized to a pattern in this engaged sense, instances of that pattern—instances of a 'walk' call in the dog's case, a triangular door in the pigeon's—will present to it as belonging to a single similarity class, despite varying in other ways. That the animal is sensitized to that class or property means that instances will prompt the same response robustly over

---

[6] The idea is reminiscent of the lesson taught by Lewis Carroll's (1895) classic paper on Achilles and the tortoise: viz. that if someone is to be moved by any explicit deductive argument, they must subscribe to a rule of inference that does not appear as a premise in the argument.

variations in other features: variations of the voice and accent in which the call is made, for example, variations in the color and shape that a triangular door may assume.

3.3 Back to Rule-Following

Any agential creature that engages in the designated sense with a given pattern will form beliefs, on a functionalist account of belief, that that pattern—in our standard case, that property—is present in this or that situation and will be led on that basis to act accordingly for the satisfaction of its desire (Stalnaker 1984).[7] Thus, in recognizing triangular doors, the pigeon will form beliefs, now in this case, now in that, that a door is triangular—or that it has some equivalent property—and will be prompted to act as such a door would make sense for it to act, given its other beliefs and desires; it will peck at the door and receive its reward.

This should not be in any way surprising. After all, we might construct a simple robot to emulate the performance of the pigeon, identifying triangular doors and doing something that corresponds to the pigeon's pecking. That robot will also merit the ascription of beliefs, on the functionalist conception of belief that I favor, since it will operate as an agent that aims at the achievement of a goal—pecking on regular doors—and adjusts its behavior for achieving that goal in light of how it represents the situation: it pecks on a door just when it believes that it is triangular in shape.

As this is true of the simple pigeon and robot, so something similar will be true of the humanoids—as it is true of humans—across a much wider domain. They will be engaged in the relevant sense by patterns on any front where they learn to form beliefs and select means for satisfying their desires. Thus, for example, they will recognize the foods that nourish and the foods that don't; the animals on which they can prey, and the animals that prey on them; the areas that provide a safe refuge and those that don't; the materials that can be used to make tools and those that can't. In each category they will respond to the similarity that binds things together, the pattern that they display, and form corresponding beliefs that the associated property is present here, absent there, and so on.

Might this capacity enable the humanoids to track the properties that they thereby engage with in a rule-following manner? Might they be able to control in a conscious and intentional way for making judgments, given the evidence available in any situation, on whether the relevant property is present or not? Might they be able, for example, to control for making a judgment—and forming a judgment-based belief—that this activity is indeed a game, this artifact a tool?

---

[7] For simplicity, I ignore various complexities in the functionalist account of belief such as its connection with desire and the fact that beliefs and desires come in degrees.

No, for reasons similar to those emphasized by Kripke's Wittgenstein. He argues that while the humanoids might become disposed to track certain properties, such a disposition, however reliable it may be by our lights, would not enable them to identify something that might guide them on how they ought to proceed, telling them what to do in each new case; it would not play the required normative role. Their sensitization might lead the humanoids in the right direction, by our lights, in ascribing a certain property in this instance or that: it might constitute a suitable extrapolative disposition. But it would not give them the ability to identify that property as such—that is, in abstraction from its instances—and to try consciously and intentionally to track it in judgment.

That ability would require the humanoids to view the property tracked as an object of attention and awareness distinct from its instances. And sensitization to patterns, on its own, will not do the job. It will make it possible for them to form beliefs and desires about the concrete objects available for perceptual attention; if something is a game, for example, they may form the belief that it is a game or form the desire to take part. But this sensitization to particulars will not deliver sensitization to properties. It will not enable them, abstracting from particulars, to pay attention to the properties as such—say, the property of being a game or a tool—and to form a conscious controlling intention to look out for instances of that property and to make judgments about its presence or absence only when that is appropriate.

Putting this point in another way, sensitization ensures that a property will be represented *in* any humanoid who is suitably sensitized but not ensure that it is represented *for* them: that is, as a representation they can consult (Cummins 1989). A representation in an agent may figure in explaining their performance, as when it plays a causal role in triggering certain beliefs and desires and generating actions. But the representation in the agent may play do this without playing the distinct role of enabling the agent to pay attention to the property itself and to form beliefs or desires about that abstract entity.

4. Identifying Patterns

The capacity to be sensitized to patterns that the humanoids enjoy is replicated in a range of creatures, human and non-human. But while such a species-general capacity would not involve the humanoids in following rules, in particular basic rules, perhaps some species-specific practices and abilities would have this effect. We begin to explore that idea in this section, focusing on the capacity for joint action that human beings, and perhaps only human beings—the issue is debated in the empirical literature—display.

The problem that sensitization to patterns leaves in place is that it may materialize in the humanoids, as in many other creatures, without giving them the ability to view any patterns or properties as objects of awareness, forming beliefs and other attitudes about them. And that means, of course, that they cannot aspire to track basic patterns, following them as rules. We shall now see that the pressure to act jointly explains why the humanoids will come to treat certain patterns as objects of awareness, thereby overcoming at least this particular obstacle to rule-following.

4.1 Joint Activities

Human beings, and hence the humanoids of our narrative, are creatures who spontaneously act together for various common goals, going beyond the sort of action that mere sensitization would support. They have a distinctive capacity and inclination to combine their efforts to advance any goal where it is manifest, first, that they each desire its realization; and, second, that they can only or best achieve this in tandem, with each playing their part in a salient plan. Thus, if they are on the beach and they observe that a swimmer is in difficulty, they will be likely to get together to save the swimmer when it is manifest that this is a goal they share, that there is a salient plan under which they can realize it together, and that anyone who begins to enact the plan will be joined by others. They may save the swimmer under such conditions, for example, by getting together to form a chain of people into the water; this may be the salient thing to do, perhaps because someone suggests it.[8]

Michael Tomasello (2016) argues that this predisposition toward jointly intentional action is one of the most distinctive features of human beings, and is indeed exclusive to human beings. We may go along with him, if only for reasons of convenience, in thinking that it is exclusive to human and humanoid subjects, but our argument at this point does not depend on that extra claim. The main point is that human and humanoid agents may be taken to be capable of joint activity.

Tomasello relies on two sources of evidence to support the claim that joint action is a characteristic of human beings. The first source of evidence is that in a crucial period of human evolution, between about 400,000 and 150,000 years ago, the environment was such that our human forebears would have been forced to forage and hunt together—this, or die alone—and that this would have created a selectional pressure in favor of a natural disposition to act jointly. They would have had to be able to distinguish edible from poisonous plants, and to collaborate in picking the edible and avoiding the poisonous. And equally they would have had to be able to recognize potential prey and potential predators and to

---

[8] This is a very stark statement of what is involved in joint action, broadly in line with Bratman (2014); see Pettit (2017, 2023: ch. 4). For other approaches to the analysis of this notion, any one of which would work for our purposes here, see Tuomela (2007); Searle (2010(; Gilbert (2015).

combine in hunting the animals of the one sort and in defending against animals of the other.

The second source of evidence on which Tomasello draws is that the disposition to act jointly with others is displayed by children between the ages of 1 and 3, although it is generally not displayed by other primates. 'These young children coordinate on a joint goal', Tomasello (2014: 41) says,

> commit themselves to that joint goal until all get their reward, expect others to be similarly committed to the joint goal, divide the common spoils of a collaboration equally, take leave when breaking a commitment, understand their own and the partner's role in the joint activity, and even help the partner in her role when necessary.

As examples of such collaboration among very young children—a form of cooperation in which they hold one another to their expectations and protest at non-compliance—he mentions 'giving and taking objects, rolling a ball back and forth, building a block tower together, putting away toys together, and "reading" books together' (Tomasello 2014: 44).[9]

4.2 Why Patterns Will Become Salient

In order for any agents to practice jointly intentional activity of this kind, they must not only be sensitized to the pattern in this or that particular, be it an activity or an object, they must also be able to direct their attention to the pattern or class itself. They will have to do this when they form a belief that a partner is seeking a joint action in a certain class: say, that of playing some sort of game. And they will have to do it when they seek with others to find an object in a certain class: say, a plant of such and such a kind. They must be attuned to the property that unites instances of that activity and instances of that object. And, more than that, they must assume that their partners in the enterprise are also attuned to the property and that the partners assume the same thing about them.[10]

If agents did not have this extra capacity, then they could hardly plan to pursue a certain class of animals with others, or search out a certain class of plants. Indeed they could not plan to engage with others in any class of activity, even

---

[9] See too Tomasello (2008, 2009, 2016).
[10] This consideration may also support the stronger claim that the assumption has to be manifest or a matter that is public between them. Such manifestness may be interpreted for current purposes as involving common awareness in the sense of David Lewis (1969): that is, a hierarchy of assumptions involving the assumption by each, not only that they all assume a commonality, but that they all assume that they all assume the commonality, and so on. On the case for rival interpretations, see Lederman (2018).

something as simple as playing a game together. Thus, without that capacity, to return to Tomasello's case, no child could expect collaboration on the part of another in rolling a ball or building a tower or reading a book. And no child would have grounds to remonstrate with another, as is apparently common among children, about their not enacting the pattern properly: not adding to the tower, not rolling back the ball, not joining in looking at a book, and so on.

These observations show that in order to pursue joint activities as we human beings do, the humanoids will have to be able to classify the items they seek in gathering or hunting, as well as the sorts of activity involved in that exercise, seeing them as belonging to a class with which they are familiar. And, furthermore, the observations show that the humanoids will have to ascribe the same classificatory practice to others—the same practice of assigning particulars to one or another familiar class—and, more generally, must take it to be a practice that others ascribe to them.

Sensitization would enable the humanoids to have beliefs about the particular objects they confront, in the way it would enable the pigeon to believe in one or another case that that object is a triangular door. And it would enable them individually to pursue specific goals, with a goal of a general form of behavior—say, the search for food—crystallizing only under a suitable stimulus into the goal of gathering those plants or pursuing those prey. But the capacity for joint action would require the extra ability to have beliefs about classes of objects or activities: in effect, about properties. The humanoids would have to be able to form beliefs that others want to take part in a certain kind of activity like hunting or gathering, that they want to catch this or that sort of animal or find this or that variety of plant. They would have to be acquainted with the kinds or sorts or varieties involved in such cases.

The shift required by joint action might be cast as one of intentional or semantical ascent. Previously, the humanoids, like other animals, would have been able to form beliefs that predicate certain properties of particular objects or assign the objects to certain classes. But now they must be able to form beliefs that take those properties or classes as items of which they can predicate other properties, as in thinking that this is the sort of thing others propose that they seek together, or this is the sort of activity that they intend to undertake jointly. Where particulars were previously the only items that served as objects of attention, now properties or classes can also enjoy that status.

4.3 Salient Patterns and Signs

It may be that, under the pressure of acting together, the humanoids will find certain patterns salient without having signs or words for them. The pattern associated with a certain game may be salient to them, for example, insofar as they can see any instance, or perhaps the simulacrum of an instance, as exemplifying the class of game in question (Goodman 1969). But whether not that is the case, their capacity for joint activity would certainly be much improved if they had signs, gestural or sounded, to denote the objects on which they act or the pursuits they conduct. Such signs would enhance their capacity to initiate joint practices, and might even be essential for their success and spread.

But can we assume that the humanoids will be able to support their joint activities with the development of suitable signs? Two pieces of evidence from non-human animals suggest that we can. The first is evidence of the use of standardized calls or signs to register this or that scenario and the other is evidence of a capacity to use a sign—in this case, a simple gesture—intentionally for a communicative effect.

Taking up the first, we know that various animals utter cries that serve as signs, prompting in others the sorts of activity that they would perform if they had witnessed the situation eliciting the cry in the first place. The clearest example is from the vervet monkeys in Kenya studied by Dorothy Cheney and Robert Seyfarth (1990). These animals regularly warn one another of dangers by making appropriate calls: one call for an approaching leopard, another for a hovering eagle, another for a snake in the grass. Those hearing such a call generally come to believe that the relevant danger is present, taking the action that is appropriate, depending on whether they are on the ground or in a tree, for example.

The calls emitted by the vervet monkeys may be more or less automatic, not intentional, but to turn to the second piece of evidence, there are also examples among non-human animals of intentional, communicative signing, this time by means of gestures. The outstanding example here is the way chimpanzees communicate in situations of targeted help, as they are called.

In one oft cited study, for example, a first chimp needs a stick to reach food outside its enclosure and notices a stick that would do the job lying in an adjoining enclosure occupied by a second chimp (Yamamoto, Humle, and Tanaka 2009, 2012). The first chimp draws the attention of the second to the stick, and to its desire for that stick, by reaching toward it as if it were within its grasp, which it clearly is not. In taking that action the first chimp reveals, not just a desire to get the stick, but a desire to get it by means of having the second chimp recognize its desire—see the significance of the futile reaching—and to respond appropriately. The first chimp acts in a broadly communicative manner and generally succeeds in conveying the message and winning the cooperation of the second (Grice 1957; Neale 1992; Moore 2016).

Given such capacities among non-human animals, and given the utility that signs would have for the humanoids in conducting joint action, it is plausible to think that they will come to intentionally use different sounds as names, as we might say, for the objects on which they do or might act together and for the activities they might jointly perform. And with such a naming capacity at their disposal, they will surely extend the names they use to just about any pattern that becomes salient to them, whether in the world around them, or in their own individual or collective efforts.

The development envisaged here among the humanoids can be highlighted by returning to the contrast with our simple, sensitized pigeon. Even the pigeon might be trained to make a sound, say 'troor', on forming the perceptual belief that a door is triangular, where the belief is a disposition to act on its desire as it is appropriate for it to act in the presence of such a door. But while the pigeon might be trained in this way, there would be no reason to think that it uses the sound 'troor' intentionally to mark the presence of the property assigned in its belief. That property does not exist for it as an object of attention and so the sign cannot function in its mind—though it might function in ours—as giving information about the property: viz. that it is instantiated here or there.

Things are going to be very different for the humanoids, given the use of signs that we are positing among them. Suppose that they come to use 'tigroo' of animals in a certain class. Since they will be attuned to that class as such, and the property common to members of the class, the sound 'tigroo' will presumably function for them as a marker of the property; it will not require any great cognitive insight for them to link the sound with the property. And that means in turn that an utterance like 'tigroo' amongst them will naturally be taken by them and by others—assuming no incompetence or insincerity—as an expression of the belief that there is a tigroo present. That utterance on the part of an individual humanoid will publicly assign the animal perceived to the kind to which their belief assigns it in their own mind.

Again, suppose that the humanoids have a sound like 'ganting' that they use to identify instances of a certain sort of activity. As they learn to use 'ganting' of a kind of activity presented here or there, they will take the utterance of that sound to correspond to a belief they form, assigning to the activity on display the sort of property assigned in the belief. And likewise in a suitable context—say, in the absence of any evidence of ganting—they will naturally take and use the call to propose a joint ganting venture.

In the foregoing discussion, we have assumed that joint activity will require certain classes or patterns to become salient objects of attention and that the humanoids will naturally develop signs to facilitate such activity. For all we need assume, however, it may be that joint activities and signing practices would evolve in tandem, with each being enabled or at least facilitated by the other. For all we need assume, indeed, it may even be that signing is a pre-requisite for making classes or patterns into objects of attention; this is close to a view maintained by Thomas Hobbes (Pettit 2008: ch. 2).

4.4 Back to Rule-Following

We saw in the last section that just being sensitized to a basic pattern or property, being able to detect it instance by instance, will not enable the humanoids to have that pattern as an object of awareness, forming beliefs or other attitudes about it. That means that it cannot explain why or how they might come to track such a property consciously and intentionally. The discussion in this section shows why and how patterns might become objects of awareness for the humanoids, thereby getting over that particular obstacle. The humanoids will be able to identify the pattern that binds any items together, and they will be able to form beliefs and desires about such a kind. Where the pigeon of the last section can only form the belief about a particular object that it, as we would say, is triangular, the humanoids will be able to form this or that belief about the class of triangles or about triangularity itself.

Will the capacity to identify and name patterns, as distinct from being merely sensitized to those patterns, enable the humanoids to follow basic rules? No, it will not.

The appearance of signs might seem to make it possible for any one of the humanoids to use a relevant name—say, 'tigroo' for an animal or 'ganting' for an activity—with the intention of using it just when the name is appropriate: to assert the presence of a tigroo only when such an animal is present or to use 'ganting' only of an activity where the name applies. But there are two problems that stand in the way of that possibility.

The first problem is that the humanoids may form the intention, now in this case, now in that, to use 'tigroo' in response to the presence of such an animal—say, to use it to communicate with others—and yet have no general intention, however tacit, to use the word only when there is a tigroo present: only when the sign is appropriate. But even if we put aside that difficulty, there is a second problem to notice. This is that if we ascribe such a general intention about sign usage to the humanoids, there will be no suitable criterion of appropriate usage available to them, and so no basis for taking them to be following a rule.

While each of the humanoids in joint action will identify one or another pattern that they expect others to identify too, they will always identify it as a class or kind or property corresponding to their own sensitization. Suppose, then, that two humanoids diverge from one another in a given case, with one using 'tigroo' to signal the presence of that sort of animal, while the other refuses to do so and, more generally, refuses to go along with the first by acting as the presence of a tigroo would make it appropriate for them to act. There is no reason in the story so far why either of them might balk at the divergence, as they would presumably do if they could be cast as intentionally and consciously seeking to follow a common rule. For all that we have assumed, they may simply turn away from such a conflict in their signaling and in their beliefs; they may just give up on the joint activity that convergence would likely have triggered.

The fact that the humanoids generally succeed in marshalling joint activities, and in converging on the use of the corresponding sounds, means that they are more or less commonly disposed to perceive and respond to a common world.

But consistently with that being the case, they may each act as appropriate to a given activity, and use corresponding signs appropriately, only to the extent that their own sensitization to the patterns in question prompts those responses. Thus, they may be surprised or perplexed by the divergence envisaged. But there is no reason to think that they will not just walk away from the episode rather than reacting as would be appropriate if they were each seeking to follow a shared rule.

If there is room for rule-following among the humanoids, by all that the account so far has suggested, it can only involve an attempt on the part of each to follow a solipsistic rule, as we might call it. This would be the rule each might follow of tracking a pattern—say, the tigroo pattern—across different instances by using the tigroo sign only when their sensitization supports that response: only when they are prompted independently to believe that an animal is a tigroo.

Might this make sense? Might an individual humanoid intentionally and consciously seek to conform in their usage of a term like 'tigroo' to a pattern in the world: the pattern displayed by all and only tigroos? Might they do that, in particular, if their basis for using the term in a given case is provided by their own disposition, grounded in sensitization, to believe that this or that is or is not a tigroo?

Not if it is the case, as we have assumed, that the idea of intentionally conforming to a pattern—that is, trying to conform to it—implies that manifestly the effort may not be successful: manifestly, the subject may fail to get the rule right. For on the picture presented, the disposition that prompts a humanoid to say 'tigroo' of a certain animal is just going to be the disposition that determines that that animal is indeed a tigroo. The diagnostic of success will itself be a guarantor of success, ruling out the possibility that they might get things wrong. They might claim to be following a rule, of course, but they could hardly claim to follow an elusive rule: a rule that they might miss or mistake.[11]

5. Triangulating on Patterns

Sensitization to a pattern or property, as we saw in section 3, can enable the humanoids to form beliefs about concrete items to the effect that they instantiate the property or not. And, as we saw in section 4, the awareness of a pattern that is required in creatures capable of joint action, can enable the humanoids to go one better and form beliefs and other attitudes about the property relevant in such a

---

[11] It is conceivable in principle, but hardly robustly likely, that an individual humanoid might recognize over time that their responses vary, might identify obstructing factors that occasionally affect them, and might try to track the property—still, of course, a potentially idiosyncratic property—that shows up only in the absence of obstruction (on the idea of obstruction, see the discussion of restriction and distortion in the next section). For defenses of rule-following that is private in this sense, see Blackburn (1984) and Azzouni (2017).

case. But as we have just noted, even with this awareness of patterns, the humanoids may be unable to track a basic pattern or property in the manifestly defeasible or fallible way that rule-following requires.

Apart from the general practice of joint action, however, there is a distinct practice of teaching and learning—a distinctive species of joint action—that is also characteristic of human beings and, by all accounts, exclusive to them. And this, as we shall see, can help us out of the defeasibility problem just raised; it can explain how humanoids might get to be able to intentionally and consciously track patterns that remain elusive: patterns that, as they recognize, they may miss or mistake in a given case.

5.1 Teaching and Learning

In its developed form, teaching and learning involve jointly intentional action in which one party plays the role of teacher, the other or others the role of learner, and the shared aim is to achieve the transfer of practical skills or of received pieces of knowledge (Sterelny 2012; Lalande 2017). It is a kind of apprentice learning in which the man or woman who occupies the position of master gets the learner up to speed, as they work with one another on the job. Each makes an appropriate effort, whether in teaching or in learning, with a view to achieving the transfer of expertise that is sought by each. This might be the ability to prepare food, build a home, or fashion a hunting tool; a form of know-how about the dangers and opportunities of their environment; or the skill of recognizing edible plants, sowing and harvesting a crop, raising or hunting various animals.

The evidence is that human beings have long interacted across generations, and indeed within generations too, to communicate how to perform the infinite variety of tasks on which human culture depends. Unlike other animals, or at least most other animals, they do not just rely on the young to copy what their elders do. They do not merely hope that the members of each generation will pick up skills in foraging for plants, hunting prey, or keeping clear of predators. Those in each generation teach those in the next generation how to do those things, eliciting the required pattern-reading dispositions in them.

In illustrating this practice, Kim Sterelny (2012: 37–8) maintains that 'a full apprentice model of expertise transmission' came on stream amongst our ancestors a few hundred thousand years ago, applying in activities like tool-making, child-minding, and foraging. In this version, the practice presumably represented a distinctive species of joint action. But Sterelny cites reasons for thinking that an earlier version was already present among early hominins—*homo erectus* rather than *homo sapiens*—a couple of million years ago. The young 'learned by doing, in environments that advantageously shaped individual trial-and-error learning' and that were 'structured advantageously by adults through the exercise of the adults' own expertise'; in these environments, for example, 'tools, partially completed tools, and raw materials were readily available as objects of play, experiment, and exploration'.

Assuming that humankind has long been involved in the practice of teaching and learning, we can also ascribe that practice to the humanoids of our narrative. Developed as a species of joint action, so we shall now see, the practice will enable them to consciously control for tracking patterns in such a way that they may manifestly fail in certain cases. It will enable them to bring the activity into line with our conception of rule-following.

5.2 Defeasible Tracking

For all that joint action in general guarantees, as we saw, the most salient response to divergence in the use of a sign like 'tigroo' may be for the parties to assume that they are tracking different patterns, albeit patterns that coincide in enough cases to make joint action possible. Will the presence of teaching and learning among the humanoids make a difference to the response they are likely to make? Suppose that one does not take something to instantiate a pattern that the other does take to be an instance, or takes something to be an instance that the other does not view in that way. How would we expect them to respond to that divergence?

The teaching-and-learning assumption means that they are unlikely to respond by concluding that they must not be targeting the same property. Or at least that will be so insofar as the case falls within the domain, as it surely will, where in principle teaching and learning is possible. Assuming that there is a common pattern targeted on both sides—a pattern-for-us, as they might cast it—and authorizing one another as generally capable of tracking that pattern, they will balk at the divergence. One of them, so it will seem to each, must fail in the tracking enterprise; they must miss an instance of the pattern that is there, or mistake another property for such an instance.

But why would either party fail? Why, in particular, would either fail if they are both competent participants in the practice, trained up to a passing degree in sensitivity to the pattern? The only possible answer for them to endorse is that the sensitization of one or the other is affected by a restriction in the evidence presented—the prompt for triggering their sensitivity—or by a distortion in their perception of that evidence: something that perturbs the triggering of that sensitivity. In the tigroo example, they must assume that one or the other cannot see the animal properly or that their perception is not working properly.[12]

---

[12] Both might be subject to a hindrance of some kind, while only one of them is lucky enough to get the pattern right. I put aside that possibility for ease of presentation.

What in theory might establish that such a difference or distortion—such an evidential hindrance—is present on one side of a dispute rather than on the other? The factor would have to differentiate the parties, for sure, and it ought to be the sort of thing that could conceivably have a restricting or distorting effect. It might be independently obvious that one or the other party is subject to such a hindering effect: that they are too far away, for example, to be sure of what they see or hear or smell. But again, it might not. So, which factor in that case will deserve to be indicted as the hindrance? The answer presumably is: that which would best explain the divergence, consistently with the assumption of a common pattern and shared sensitization.

But how might the humanoids identify such a culpable factor? The most salient method would be to see which of the competing judgments a majority of others would endorse and to defer to their view. If only one of the parties is out of step with most others, after all, that suggests that it is they who are evidentially hindered. The majority will necessarily be reliable if the disputed instance of the property at issue is in a domain where more or less arbitrary convention rules: say, in determining whether a telephone booth, as in some usages, counts as an instance of a box. And it will be reliable on empirical grounds in other cases: say, in determining the exact color of an object, where it is more likely that a single individual is color blind or impaired in some other way than that they alone see the color properly.

Whatever the reason why the majority view should be taken as correct in this way, it is important to note that when an individual defers to the majority, in the scenario imagined, they will not do so just for the sake of social ease: they will not coordinate just for coordination's sake. Rather, they will defer to others for the sake of triangulating reliably on a property they seek in common to track. Each individual will be guided by their own sensitization to the property they identify, but they will rely on that guidance only under the proviso that they are not subject to evidential restriction or distortion. If they defer to the majority, then, that will be for the sake of triangulating on the property they target—a pattern-for-us—not for the sake of coordinating, despite divergence, on how they publicly respond: say, on what word they use for that feature (Davidson 2001).

Thus, if one party to a dispute finds that they are in the minority, then other things being equal, they will self-correct and restore convergence with others. It may take some time for the parties involved to negotiate with one another and to reach such a resolution, but we can leave out such details here. We need only register that they will recognize the case for triangulating intersubjectively on one another to determine what is objectively so and that they will routinely do this to resolve their differences. Even the color-blind subject can be expected to treat the color that is there objectively to be one that they identify only very vaguely, due to their impaired vision: due to an impairment of which they will have become aware in the course of intersubjective triangulation.

This story does not require, of course, that negotiation will never fail and that every dispute will be resolved. One response to failure might be to ignore and insulate the problematic case, with each agreeing that there is no saying who is tracking the pattern, and who is not. Another might be for each to assume that they are tracking the pattern, others not, and that there is an unrecognized restriction or distortion that is putting others astray. And a third might be to deem cases where there is continual divergence as unimportant, taking the property tracked to be one that is not defined for that range: on this account, the property tracked would be cast as a vague or indeterminate target in the manner of baldness.

The use of something like the majoritarian method would presumably lead the humanoids to a position where, like folk epistemologists, they can track the properties of evidential restriction or distortion across different cases, and introduce words to name them. And that would facilitate triangulation as a means of distinguishing what is objectively so, by their intersubjective lights, from what merely seems to be so. It would mean that they could identify when they or others were likely to be going wrong, without explicit reference to majority judgment. They would do this on the basis of detecting the presence on one or another side of a recognized source of restriction or distortion.

The upshot of these considerations is that if the humanoids practice teaching and learning of the kind that has long distinguished human beings, then their tracking of basic properties is likely to be defeasible, and defeasible in a way that will be manifest to them. They will target properties that are revealed, not necessarily via their subjective sensitization, but via a corrected counterpart: their sensitization in the absence of factors that deserve to be identified as evidential restrictions and distortions.

5.3 Back to Rule-Following

On the picture developed so far, the humanoids will each be sensitized like any animals to certain basic patterns: in our paradigm case, properties; they will be able to attend to those properties, making them into candidates about which to form beliefs and other attitudes; and specifically, they will be able to attend to them as properties that they may occasionally miss or mistake.

To the extent that this picture fits, the humanoids will count as following basic rules. Each of them will be able to control consciously and intentionally for identifying instances of this or that basic property, making an effort to get things right but without a guarantee of success. They will realize that the patterns they track are those that show up for them only in the absence of the hindrances that are revealed in triangulation with others. And they will see that while their efforts can help to promote the chance of success, they will not make success inevitable.

The rule-following that we ascribe to the humanoids does not presuppose any great intellectual sophistication. The presentation given of the achievement is liable to be misleading in that regard, since it may suggest that the humanoids will reach the goal described in a series of insights and inferences. But the achievement is really the more or less inevitable precipitate of a network of assumptions that are encoded in the practice we have described.

Jointly acting as teachers and learners, the humanoids must assume that there are basic patterns in the shared world they inhabit—patterns-for-us—and that they in general are sensitized to such patterns; they could not reject those assumptions and continue with the practice. But they may make those two assumptions only in the sense of being disposed, perhaps unwittingly, to act in relevant contexts as their truth would require. The two assumptions, operating at this level, will force the humanoids to conclude in the case of divergence that something is amiss with the sensitization of those on one or another side: they are affected, as suggested, by a restriction of the evidence that triggers their sensitivity or a distortion of the effect of the evidence on their sensitivity. And the presumptive way of identifying and locating such a hindrance will be to check for how other individuals will respond in the relevant case.

Let working assumptions that register points like these be encoded in the practice and responses of the humanoids, and rule-following will materialize amongst them without the need for reflective thought. It will prompt them without hesitation to treat their dispositions, on the one side, as lenses in which basic patterns reveal themselves instance by instance; but, on the other, as lenses that are likely to require correction in light of the hindrances that may arise. In actively making a judgment on some basic case, then, they will naturally see themselves as trying to attend to the pattern or property targeted, conscious that effort is needed to avoid the danger of going astray. In other words, they will control consciously, intentionally and defeasibly for tracking that property. They will fit the bill for following basic rules.

How might a rule show up in the experience of the humanoids? Looking at an example of a tool or a game or a sum, to revert to earlier cases, how might they be able to see an abstract pattern there that they might try to track over further instances? Presumably the extrapolative disposition resulting from their sensitization, modulated by the disposition to interrogate that disposition for the presence of a hindering factor, would let that pattern become salient. It will not be a pattern with which they can be acquainted in the way a defining formula would allow but a pattern discerned proleptically in their anticipation of where those dispositions would lead.

For a model of what is likely to happen, think of how a group of friends might be said to know a route across a complex mountain park from points *A* to *B*. They might not be able to draw that route or describe it or give instructions to others about how to follow it. Yet, they can be said to know the route in virtue of knowing that they each have a generally reliable disposition to move correctly from the starting point to a particular landmark; that at each landmark short of the terminus they will have a similar disposition to move on correctly to another landmark; and that any failure on the side of one is likely to be corrected in negotiation about the discrepancy with others. They will know the route proleptically, by grace of the interacting dispositions on which they rely.

As that group of friends have this dispositional, intersubjectively dependent grasp of the route from A to B, so we may think of the humanoids as having such a grasp of the pattern associated with a basic rule. And as the friends can set out consciously and intentionally to follow the route across the mountains, knowing that despite their best efforts, they may fail, so something similar is going to be true of the humanoids as they control for following a basic rule.

6. Conclusion

The genealogy provided makes sense of how basic rule-following might emerge among humanoids and what it would constitute for them. But the practice described in the genealogy may also be the practice that allows us human beings to follow basic rules, as we clearly do, in our own thought and talk. If rule-following does not consist in the sort of practice described, so we might urge, what does it involve? If not this, what?

The model of rule-following proposed suggests that basic properties—and other basic items like the addition function—become salient for us and present as features of the world only in virtue of practices that we undertake for pragmatic reasons associated with joint action and with teaching and learning. They are not data revealed in the pure light of theoretical reason, but patterns summoned to view under the pressure of practical concerns. Does this pragmatist aspect of the model count against it? Surely not, for it allows us still to embrace an important form of realism—pragmatic realism, if you will—about the basic properties and about the properties they serve in turn to analyze.

The first point to make in support of this realism is that the model is consistent with holding that there is a fact of the matter about whether this or that basic property is instantiated in one or another case. It may be that we get to be able to access basic properties and take them as guides only to the extent that we are sensitized by nature to certain similarity classes and only to the extent that we operate with practices that allow in principle for the reconciliation of differences. But this still allows us to think that the properties that become visible by grace of those dispositions and practices are discovered by us, not invented or created.

This way of thinking about those properties is supported by the model insofar as it implies that when we negotiate about differences we do not seek to coordinate for coordination's sake; we do not look for convergence, at whatever cost to our sense of being subject to pressures from without. We seek the sort of convergence that our practices make important, to be sure, but this form of convergence is built around the assumption that there is something in principle available to all that may not inevitably be accessed in practice. We display that assumption insofar as we authorize one another as potential sources of correction and, seeking to identify and neutralize evidential hindrances, look for what is accessible on all sides.[13]

It may be said, however, that the model offends against realism on a second count. The charge is that while the basic patterns or properties acknowledged are sustained by how the world proves to be—they are not our invention—still they can only be patterns of species-specific interest, even perhaps of just culture-specific interest. They cannot constitute properties that have a wide cosmological role in making sense of the world as a whole (Wright 1992).

But that is not correct. The pattern that makes something tasty to human beings may be highly idiosyncratic and play no significant role in explaining anything other than our disposition to eat it. But a pattern like that of solidity may also be tracked in the manner of a basic property and enjoy much greater explanatory significance. It is capable of detection by more than one sensory modality, capable of detection by many other creatures as well, and capable of affecting how even non-sentient objects relate to one another. Thus, it can play a much wider role in explaining how the world operates than the tastiness of various foods to human beings.

Finally, the pragmatic character of the line defended here may seem to offend against realism in a third respect. On a realist image of the world, there is only a contingent connection between what there is in our view and what there is in fact, so that human ignorance and error remain a permanent possibility. But, it may be said, our model of rule-following suggests that this is not so: that a majority of individuals cannot be wrong about what holds and does not hold at the basic level. Conceiving of the world as revealed in our practices, so the idea would go, we fail in a characteristically pragmatist fashion to distinguish how the world appears within those practices and how it is in itself.

It is certainly true according to the model developed here that if someone operates in a normally competent manner and is free from the hindering effects of evidential restriction and distortion, then they are bound to be accurate in the identification of a basic property: their sensitization to the property will dispose

---

[13] The anti-realism of Kripke's (1982) Wittgenstein takes coordination to serve a coordinating purpose only. A realist account of rule-following, similar to that developed here, is present in the essays collected in (Pettit 2002: part 1). For pragmatic accounts that apparently look for a middle way between anti-realism and realism in those senses, see Price (1988) and Gert (2012).

them to ascribe it just when it is present. This means that basic properties must satisfy a biconditional like this: $(x)(x$ is an instance of a basic property F if and only if it is disposed to present as an instance of F to competent observers in ideal, unhindered conditions).

An example of such a biconditional might be: $(x)(x$ is red if and only it is disposed to look red to competent observers in ideal, unhindered conditions). Basic properties will satisfy this condition in virtue of the fact, not that observers think of F-ness as a disposition to evoke that effect—they will think of it as a categorical property, in the way they think of a color like red—but because mastering the concept of F requires being disposed to ascribe F-ness to anything under such conditions (Jackson and Pettit 2002). Reflection on how we use terms for basic properties—presumptively, a term like 'red'—ought to make that clear.

This observation does not reflect a failure endemic among pragmatists to distinguish the world in itself from the world as it appears in human practices. It is supported, rather, by a highly plausible assumption: that the conditions that explain why our basic words have certain denotata—why 'red' ascribes red—must reflect the conditions that we have to meet if we are to master those words. I would scarcely count as understanding 'red', giving it an appropriate referent, if I were not disposed to use it of things that looked red, at least when I had no reason to think that I was subject to some hindering factor.

But not only is the claim implied in our model independently plausible, it also does not seriously compromise realism. The truth of the biconditionals to which we are committed under the model of basic rule-following does not give us a title to claim any individual or collective infallibility. Any one human being, and any group or generation of human beings, may fail to recognize some of the hindrances that affect judgment—new hindrances are always likely to show up—and may fail to see that there is a hindrance present in a particular case. And so any individual or group, even a whole generation, may miss or mistake one or another basic property, being subject to a hindrance that only becomes obvious later. It has recently been suggested, for example, that continuing human evolution has increased sensitivity to violet, and that previous generations simply missed this color; that would explain why violet only began to appear in paintings from the 1860s on (Tager, Kirchner, and Fedorovskaya 2021).

The upshot is that qualms about betraying realist instincts need not inhibit us from endorsing the pragmatically oriented model of rule-following suggested by our genealogy. The model is decidedly different in that respect from the account of rule-following that Kripke ascribes to Wittgenstein. Wittgenstein's own remarks leave rule-following somewhat obscure, but it may be worth mentioning in conclusion that the model developed from the humanoid genealogy might be taken to make sense of those remarks.

Wittgenstein (1958: §201) insists that 'there is a way of grasping a rule which is *not* an *interpretation*, but which is exhibited in what we call "obeying the rule" and "going against it" in actual cases'.[14] Our model plausibly explains how that can be the case, with assumptions built into practices driving judgments that follow appropriate rules. Wittgenstein compares such non-interpretational rule-following to following a sign-post, as we saw, arguing that an individual will only be able to do this insofar as they 'have been trained to react to this sign in a particular way' and 'there exists a regular use of sign-posts, a custom' (Wittgenstein 1958: §198). Those remarks can be read in various ways, but they certainly make good sense on the model of rule-following recommended here.[15]

References

Azzouni, J. (2017). *The Rule-Following Paradox and Its Implications for Metaphysics.* New York, Springer.

Blackburn, S. (1984). "The Individual Strikes Back." *Synthese* 58: 281–301.

Boghossian, P. (2012). "What Is Inference?" *Philosophical Studies* 169: 1–18.

Bratman, M. (2014). *Shared Agency: A Planning Theory of Acting Together.* Oxford, Oxford University Press.

Carroll, L. (1895). "What the Tortoise Said to Achilles." *Mind* 4: 278–80.

Chaitin, G. J. (1975). "Randomness and Mathematical Proof." *Scientific American* 232, May: 47–52.

Chaitin, G. J. (1988). "Randomness in Arithmetic." *Scientific American* 259, July: 80–5.

Cheney, D. L. and R. M. Seyfarth (1990). *How Monkeys See the World: Inside the Mind of Another Species.* Chicago, Chicago University Press.

Craig, E. (1990). *Knowledge and the State of Nature.* Oxford, Oxford University Press.

Cummins, R. (1989). *Meaning and Mental Representation.* Cambridge, MA, MIT Press.

Davidson, D. (2001). *Subjective, Intersubjective, Objective.* Oxford, Oxford University Press.

Dennett, D. (1991). "Real Patterns." *Journal of Philosophy* 88: 27–51.

Gert, J. (2012). *Normative Bedrock: Response-dependence, Rationality, and Reasons.* Oxford, Oxford University Press.

Gilbert, M. (2015). *Joint Commitment: How We Make the Social World.* Oxford, Oxford University Press.

Goodman, N. (1969). *Languages of Art.* Oxford, Oxford University Press.

Grice, H. P. (1957). "Meaning." *Philosophical Review* 66: 377–88.

---

[14] For a fine account of Wittgenstein's rejection of the role of interpretation in basic rule-following, see Miller (2015); see also Swindlehurst (2020).
[15] My thanks for helpful comments on an earlier draft by Alex Miller and for detailed and insightful comments by Joshua Gert on the penultimate version of this chapter.

Hart, H. L. A. (2012). *The Concept of Law*, 3rd edn. Oxford, Oxford University Press.

Hornsby, J. (1980). *Actions*. London, Routledge.

Jackson, F. and P. Pettit (2002). "Response-Dependence without Tears." *Philosophical Issues* 12: 97–117.

Jackson, F., P. Pettit, and M. Smith (1999). "Ethical Particularism and Patterns." *Particularism*. London, B. Hooker and M. Little: 79–99; reprinted in F. Jackson, P. Pettit, and M. Smith (2004). *Mind, Morality and Explanation*, Oxford, Oxford University Press.

Kripke, S. A. (1982). *Wittgenstein on Rules and Private Language*. Oxford, Blackwell.

Lalande, K. L. (2017). *Darwin's Unfinished Symphony: How Culture Made the Human Mind*. Princeton, NJ, Princeton University Press.

Lederman, H. (2018). "Common Knowledge." *Handbook of Social Intentionality*, ed. M. Jankovic and K. Ludwig. London, Routledge.

Lewis, D. (1969). *Convention*. Cambridge, MA, Harvard University Press.

Miller, A. (2015). "Blind Rule-Folllowing and the 'Antinomy of Pure Reason'." *Philosophical Quarterly* 65: 396–416.

Miller, A. (2018). *The Philosophy of Language*. London, Routledge.

Moore, R. (2016). "Meaning and Ostension in Great Ape Gestural Communication." *Animal Cognition* 19: 223–31.

Neale, S. (1992). "Paul Grice and the Philosophy of Language." *Linguistics and Philosophy* 15: 509–59.

Pettit, P. (2002). *Rules, Reasons, and Norms: Selected Essays*. Oxford, Oxford University Press.

Pettit, P. (2008). *Made with Words: Hobbes on Language, Mind and Politics*. Princeton, NJ, Princeton University Press.

Pettit, P. (2017). "Corporate Agency—The Lesson of the Discursive Dilemma." *Routledge Companion to Collective Intentionality*, ed. M. Jankovic and K. Ludwig. London, Routledge.

Pettit, P. (2018). *The Birth of Ethics: Reconstructing the Role and Nature of Morality*. Oxford, Oxford University Press.

Pettit, P. (2023). *The State*. Princeton, NJ, Princeton University Press.

Pettit, P. (2024). *When Minds Speak: A Genealogy of Human Thought and Capacity*. Oxford, Oxford University Press.

Price, H. (1988). *Facts and the Function of Truth*. Oxford, Blackwell.

Queloz, M. (2021). *The Practical Origins of Ideas: Genealogy as Conceptual Reverse-Engineering*. Oxford, Oxford University Press.

Searle, J. (2010). *Making the Social World: The Structure of Human Civilization*. Oxford, Oxford University Press.

Sellars, W. (1997). *Empiricism and the Philosophy of Mind*. Cambridge, MA, Harvard University Press.

Stalnaker, R. C. (1984). *Inquiry*. Cambridge, MA, MIT Press.

Sterelny, K. (2012). *The Evolved Apprentice: How Evolution Made Humans Unique*. Cambridge, MA, MIT Press.

Swindlehurst, Z. M. (2020). "Blind Rule-Following and the Regress of Motivations." *Inquiry* 64: 1–14.

Tager, A., E. Kirchner, and E. Fedorovskaya (2021). "Computational Evidence of First Extensive Usage of Violet in the 1860's." *Color Research and Application* 46: 961–77.

Tomasello, M. (2008). *Origins of Human Communication*. Cambridge, MA, MIT Press.

Tomasello, M. (2009). *Why We Cooperate*. Cambridge, MA, MIT Press.

Tomasello, M. (2014). *A Natural History of Human Thinking*. Cambridge, MA, Harvard University Press.

Tomasello, M. (2016). *A Natural History of Human Morality*. Cambridge, MA, Harvard University Press.

Tuomela, R. (2007). *The Philosophy of Sociality: The Shared Point of View*. Oxford, Oxford University Press.

Williams, B. (2002). *Truth and Truthfulness*. Princeton, NJ, Princeton University Press.

Wittgenstein, L. (1958). *Philosophical Investigations*. Oxford, Blackwell.

Wright, C. (1992). *Truth and Objectivity*. Cambridge, MA, Harvard University Press.

Yamamoto, S., T. Humle, and M. Tanaka (2009). "Chimpanzees Help Each Other upon Request." *PLoS OnNE* 4: e7416.

Yamamoto, S., T. Humle, and M. Tanaka (2012). "Chimpanzees' Flexible Targeted Helping Based on an Understanding of Conspecifics' Goals." *Proceedings of the National Academy of Sciences* 109: 3588–92.

7
Neopragmatism and Reference Magnetism

Joshua Gert

Reference magnetism is a theoretical posit, meant to explain (or simply give a name to) the fact that some things are more eligible to be the referents of our words than others; blueness is more eligible than grueness, for example, and the element with atomic number 79 is more eligible than whatever impure mix of gold and other elements might have been ostended in the first uses of the ancestor of the English word 'gold'. It is easy to think of such a posit as the metasemantic reflection of a certain metaphysical picture of the world: one according to which it comes equipped with joints at which to carve it. Described in this way, it isn't hard to see why reference magnetism might be regarded as a conceptual tool designed to be of use to hard-core metaphysical realists, against their pragmatist opponents. And in line with this suspicion, the first sophisticated development of reference magnetism—though not under that name—was offered by David Lewis (1983, 1984), against Hilary Putnam (1980, 1981), who was arguing for a pragmatic conception of truth and reference on which truth could not outrun idealized human capacities.

I think it is fair to say that many semantic phenomena associated with reference magnetism are widely acknowledged by philosophers of language. That is, many popular theories of reference acknowledge that, unsupplemented, their central mechanism for binding words to worldly things leaves too much latitude, or too little. Either way, what is needed is something to correct matters. When a word might—for all the central mechanism says—refer to X, Y, or Z, we often have a strong intuition that it refers to X. And when two words in two different languages might—if the central mechanism were given the exclusive role—refer to two different properties, so that what seem like genuine disagreements turn out to be merely verbal, we nevertheless often have a strong intuition that the initial appearance of substantive disagreement is correct. Enter reference magnetism as a solution; if some potential referents are easier to refer to than others, our intuitions in both of these cases can be vindicated.

The central point of this chapter is to show that neopragmatism has the resources to capture the phenomena that reference magnetism is meant to explain. That is, the chapter provides a neopragmatist vindication of literal talk of certain

Joshua Gert, *Neopragmatism and Reference Magnetism* In: *Neopragmatism: Interventions in First-Order Philosophy*. Edited by: Joshua Gert, Oxford University Press. © Joshua Gert 2023. DOI: 10.1093/oso/9780192894809.003.0007

things being more eligible as referents than others. As it happens, the argument for this conclusion emerges from a response to a criticism of neopragmatism: that it makes a certain intelligible kind of skepticism unintelligible, because it makes truth too easy to come by. So a secondary point of the chapter is to address this particular criticism. But first let me say more about reference magnetism.

1. Reference Magnetism

In a pair of papers in the early 1980s, Hilary Putnam (1980, 1981) argued, using some model-theoretic machinery, that a certain kind of metasemantic theory radically underdetermined the reference of our words. Putnam's target was the combination of metaphysical realism and something we might call 'global descriptivism'. Simplifying somewhat, global descriptivism is the view that the referents of our words are whatever entities out there in the world do the best job, taken together, of making the sentences we hold true come out true. This statement of global descriptivism can be made more precise in various ways. For example, 'the sentences we hold true' might refer to a special set of platitudinous sentences, or to a much wider set, or to the set of sentences of an idealized theory of everything. In the context of Putnam's criticisms of global descriptivism, these subtleties don't matter. His arguments rely only on the fact that there are an infinite number of interpretations—that is, assignments of referents to our words—that do an equally good job of making the sentences we utter come out true. And virtually all of them assign referents that are wildly, obviously wrong. The problem is that the global descriptivist has no way of explaining why the wrong ones are wrong.

Most of the details of Putnam's argument do not matter for our purposes. Even David Lewis, who regarded those arguments as a failure, agreed that virtually any world can make virtually any (consistent) set of sentences true, if we are allowed complete freedom in assigning referents to words (Lewis 1983, 1984). Lewis' response was therefore to question Putnam's assumption that we have complete freedom. In particular, Lewis added something beyond the principle of truth-maximization, when selecting interpretations: the *naturalness* of the potential referents of the names and predicates of a language.[1] The more natural a referent— and naturalness is explicitly a metaphysical notion here—the more eligible it is to be the referent of a word in our language.[2] It is reference magnetism that helps

---

[1] For Lewis, as for many others, naturalness comes in degrees. Often it is a matter of the complexity of the simplest description of a property, when the basic predicates in the language in which that description is couched name *perfectly* natural properties. For Lewis, those were the basic properties of ideal physical theory. See Williams (2020: 151).

[2] In fact, naturalness has its magnetic effect, for Lewis, via the role it plays in the substantive rationality (what Lewis calls 'the humanity') of our beliefs and desires, and thence via the relation between beliefs and assertions. But this detour through rationality and the conventions governing language use doesn't matter for present purposes.

explain why our word 'gold' refers to the element with atomic number 79, even though there are other possible referents that might have made more of our past claims about gold come out true. The pure element is simply much more natural than any complex substance—mostly gold, but adulterated with various impurities—that might often be found where we identify gold. Likewise, it is naturalness and its reference magnetism that helps explain why our word 'blue' refers to blueness, rather than grueness.

For Lewis, it was crucial that something's degree of naturalness, and its consequence—its strength as a reference magnet—was a metaphysical notion. Unless we think of it in explicitly extra-linguistic terms, we will have to think of 'natural' simply as another term for our global descriptivism to interpret. And there will be interpretations of 'natural' that will classify all the bizarre and wildly wrong interpretations to which Putnam was referring as equally, and maximally, good. This point about the word 'natural' is the crux of Putnam's 'just more theory' criticism of attempts to patch the hole in global descriptivism by appeal to *any* additional machinery. For example, if one tries to add a causal constraint on reference to help narrow down the set of truth-maximizing interpretations, Putnam's (1981: 45–6) response will be that all one has done is to add a few sentences to one's total theory: sentences in which the words 'cause' and 'referent' figure. And there will remain an infinity of interpretations that make the resulting patched-up theory come out true.

Lewis was not persuaded by the "just more theory" objection. He was explicit that his claims about naturalness were about how the world *really is*. As he might have put it, the referents of our terms are not simply whatever makes our best theory, including the theory of naturalness and reference-determination, come out true. Rather, the referents are the most natural entities and kinds—the ones that are *really* most natural—that satisfy our best theory. The italics of '*really*' here signal that the notion Lewis was gesturing at is the elusive one that is meant to distinguish the *real* reality of the metaphysically committed representationalist from the reality of the neopragmatist. To make this contrast clearer, let me now describe the sort of neopragmatism I have in mind, and to which I will be appealing in the remainder of this chapter.

2. Neopragmatism

Neopragmatism is an approach to philosophical problems that have typically been handled by metaphysicians. That is, it is a strategy for dealing with our worries about the nature of such things as numbers, unrealized possibilities, moral properties, and so on. It stresses that human language is a naturalistic phenomenon, and that since the origin of many of our distinctly philosophical worries can be seen as linguistic, they can be addressed in a naturalistic way, even when they concern properties and entities that seem hard to accommodate naturalistically. For example, we talk about numbers, possibilities, and moral properties in ways that are truth-assessable, and we wonder how this can be. Isn't truth a matter of correspondence with reality, or of the obtaining of the relevant truth-makers? But what in the world corresponds to a number, or a possibility? What makes it true that eight divided by two is four? The neopragmatist sidesteps these questions by offering naturalistic explanations of our *talk* about such things, accompanied by deflationary accounts of truth, reference, property, belief, and so on.

Although neopragmatists can endorse the letter of a correspondence theory of truth, they cannot regard it as the most basic or illuminating theory.[3] They will regard the biconditional at the heart of a correspondence theory more as an explanation of how we use 'correspond' in certain contexts, than as an explanation of the nature of truth. As a result, most neopragmatists endorse some sort of deflationism about truth. But some versions of deflationism are more substantial than others, offering deeper explanations of the origin and function of truth-talk.[4] Huw Price has offered one of the most substantial deflationary accounts of truth, going well beyond a mere redundancy or disquotational account. Price argues that the terms 'true' and 'false' are useful primarily because they help push the psychological states of a community of speakers into a kind of harmony (see Price 1988, 2003). On his view the linguistic form of assertion—as distinct, for example, from the forms of command, question, or greeting—exists because, for some psychological states, such a harmony is both useful and feasible. To give one concrete example, it is useful if a community of speakers are disposed to count in the same way: to produce the counting words not only in a reliable order, but in the same reliable order. This coordination does not require the existence of any metaphysically heavyweight entities called 'the counting numbers', to which the counting words refer. Rather, it requires that people in the linguistic community be disposed to use such words as 'wrong' or 'false' when other speakers depart from the useful pattern—whether because those other speakers are just learning to count or have made a performance error, or for some other reason.

The neopragmatist's explanation of truth-talk in the realm of the counting numbers also applies to, for example, moral language. In particular, one plausible explanation of the existence and nature of moral talk is that it is useful to make public a reliable set of norms, the violation of which makes one liable to punishment. And the same sort of explanation—that is, a pragmatic one—is available for talk about the physical layout of the world. But, it is important to stress, there is nothing special about assertions about the physical world, for the neopragmatist. They are not to be taken as the only *genuinely* true assertions, with other

---

[3] Even old-style pragmatists realized this. See James (1907: 146–7), who puts the point in terms of *agreement* rather than *correspondence*.
[4] As emphasized in Misak (1998).

assertions being only *quasi-true*.[5] All true assertions are true in the very same sense for the neopragmatist, since the very same explanation is available for the applicability to them of the words 'true' and 'false'. That explanation does not rely on the existence of a property of truth. It relies only on the following two ideas: that for some psychological states, it is very useful for a community of speakers to get onto the same page, and that truth-assessments are crucial tools in applying the pressures that push them onto that page.

Admittedly, the existence of a causal/historical connection between token words and particular things helps explain the usefulness of the assertoric form, and of truth-assessments, *in the particular case of discourse about physical objects*. But calling that connection 'reference' adds absolutely nothing to the explanation, and misleadingly it suggests that semantic notions apply in other domains only in a derivative, metaphorical, or second-class way. Moreover, even in the case of physical objects and kinds, the typical reference-establishing causal connection can sometimes fail to do its job, and can be overridden by something that looks very much like the reference-magnetic power of a more eligible referent. This sort of reference magnetism—one that can pull a name off of the entity or kind at the end of a perfectly good causal/historical chain, and attach it to something to which it is causally unrelated—may seem too metaphysically robust even to those who have no problem with a substantive notion of reference (see Sundell 2016). But, I will argue, it can be nicely accommodated within a neopragmatist view. To begin to see how this works, let me now present an objection to neopragmatism, and a response that shows how neopragmatism is perfectly consistent with the sort of phenomena that—to a metaphysical realist—might seem to require an extremely powerful form of reference magnetism.

3. A Tempting Objection to Neopragmatism

It can look as if the neopragmatist must say that as long as the members of a group of speakers are using words as they have learned to use them—following the rules of a practice that is explained by appeal to its usefulness—then there is no sense to be made of the claim that, *as a group*, they are using those words wrongly, and making false claims. To fix ideas, let's consider a simple referring word, like 'banana', and a group of speakers who say such things as 'That's a banana' and 'There are four bananas in the bowl' when they have the sorts of experiences that would lead *us* to make the same sorts of claim. Virtually no one in such a group of speakers would deny such claims. And those who did would be regarded as blind, or crazy, or joking. So it looks as though the neopragmatist will

---

[5] The view the neopragmatist is rejecting here is what Robert Kraut (1990) calls 'bifurcationism', and it is characteristic of *local* expressivists.

have to say that the use of 'true', by these speakers, to classify these banana assertions, is correct. And this seems tantamount to saying that those banana assertions are as true as true gets.

So far so good. But now let us suppose—in standard philosophical fashion—that our hypothetical group of speakers are actually brains in vats, connected to a simulation of our world in which they walk around and interact with each other, go to university, get PhDs, and read and write philosophy papers. One such philosopher has a sneaking suspicion that he is a brain in a vat. Many of us would like to say that his suspicion isn't incoherent. Indeed, many of us would like to say that, as it turns out, he is correct. But it may seem that the neopragmatist can say neither of these things. This objection to neopragmatism has some obvious similarities to Putnam's objection to global descriptivism. Both objections stem from the claim that the criteria for truth, according to the theories that are their respective targets, are too easy to satisfy. Both theories also—according to the objection—rule out certain skeptical views as incoherent when they should not. One cannot rule out skepticism about the external world just by doing some philosophy of language.

Of course there may be an important distinction between what the envatted philosopher can *say* and what they can *suspect* or *think*, and appeal to this distinction might form the basis for some response to the objection. But I elide this distinction for two reasons. The first is that an attempt, by the neopragmatist, to evade the objection by appeal to the contents of thought would require an account of such content, which would—in my view—lead us right back to the account of the content of overt speech (see Corti 2022). And the second is that by eliding the distinction I am doing a favor to the objector, not the neopragmatist. That is, the objector is on firmer ground when talking about the neopragmatist's views of overt truth-assessments of public assertions than when talking about belief, since the objection is based on how truth-assessments are used to produce uniformity in the psychological states expressed in overt speech.

To see the force of the objection more clearly, it may help to consider a simpler case. Suppose the owner of one envatted brain gives the owner of another such brain directions to the local Whole Foods, and the owner of that other envatted brain follows those directions. They are using words as they have learned to use them, and the result is perfectly agreeable to everyone concerned. Moreover, it is the usefulness of the assertive form that explains why there are assertions about the location of Whole Foods (and other physical things)—and why there are truth-assessments of such claims. When one of these brain owners says to another "Whole Foods is at the intersection of Roosevelt and State," what they say is itself useful, and its usefulness is linked to the usefulness of location-talk more generally. In short: it is *perfectly in order*. So it looks as if we should say it is true. Certainly all competent and reasonably well-informed inhabitants of our envatted community will say that it is true, and they will be using 'true' in the same way that we do. And, for virtually the same reasons, it seems as if someone who responded to our worried skeptical envatted philosopher by saying 'You are not a brain in a vat. Your brain is right there, inside your skull; you can see it on this x-ray' should count as speaking the truth.

4. Some Clarifications of the Objection

I do not think the above objection to neopragmatism works. But before addressing it, it is important to get a little clearer on exactly what the objection is, and what the target is. One important error that can make the objection seem stronger than it is is to think that the neopragmatist is offering an account of the *property* of truth: a more sophisticated version of James' pragmatist definition of the true as the useful. But there is a much larger difference between (1) James' pragmatism and (2) the sort of neopragmatism I am defending than the difference between (1') an assertion being useful on its own, and (2') an assertion following from the rules of a linguistic practice that is useful as a complex whole. The difference between James and my sort of neopragmatist is the explicit refusal of the neopragmatist to think of truth as a property at all—not even one that is defined in pragmatic terms. Traditional pragmatists did offer accounts of truth in terms of usefulness or of what would ultimately be agreed upon at the end of ideal inquiry (Peirce 1878; James 1907). Those were certainly radical suggestions, and their appeal to considerations of usefulness justified the label 'pragmatist'. But the neopragmatist is trying to explain our use of the words 'true' and 'false', rather than the nature of the properties of truth or falsity.[6] That is, the appeal to usefulness comes into the neopragmatist's explanation not when 'truth' is being defined—which it isn't—but in a linguistic-anthropological explanation for the existence of words that function as 'true' and 'false' do. The role of usefulness is part of a *contingent historical explanation* of the emergence of truth-talk. Usefulness is not, in any way, *constitutive* of truth (since *nothing* is constitutive of truth). As a result, there is plenty of room to hold that the practices governing truth-talk in some domain will, in some situations, take us beyond what is useful. In this way usefulness is like fittingness in evolutionary explanations. Considerations of (historical) fittingness help explain the emergence of adaptations that, in certain environments, are not particularly fittingness-enhancing. Similarly, considerations of (historical) usefulness can help explain the emergence of the whole *linguistic practice* of making truth-assessments. But that certainly does not mean that what makes an utterance true is its usefulness!

---

[6] Compare Wittgenstein (1953: §241), in which agreement takes the place of usefulness, but the error being discussed is essentially the same in form.

I should also address some worries about the objection that might otherwise arise, given that I will be discussing whole populations of language users who are living in a virtual world. If these people acquired language before being envatted, this would complicate any discussion of the semantics of their terms, since there would be a real worry that the referents of their terms would be inherited from the language of the real-world engineers of their virtual world. Similarly, if the trees and cars and clouds and stars they experience were "put there" by real-world software engineers, this would complicate matters as well. There would be a temptation to think of virtual trees as representing real trees, or to think of experiences of virtual trees as indirectly representing real trees. So I will stipulate away all of these complications. The reader is free to make up whatever story seems most plausible, on which the envatted creatures developed language themselves, over many generations. Perhaps the simulated world, in its present form, was the result of an electronic analogue of biological evolution, so that its current inhabitants had non-linguistic primates as their ancestors. Perhaps, on the other hand, they are a community-sized, electronically linked version of a Boltzmann brain: the inevitable result of quantum randomness and infinite time, materializing without any other further explanation, in the deeps of space (see Kotzen 2020).

5. The Objection Answered

Suppose now that our envatted creatures are freed from virtuality and wake up, as Neo did in the Matrix. When they talk amongst themselves about the "new world" they have discovered, what sorts of things will they say? In particular, what sorts of things will they say about the truth of their former beliefs about such things as the existence and location of Whole Foods? Of course any answer to this question will necessarily be fairly speculative. But we can firm up our intuitions quite considerably by imagining that *we ourselves* are these creatures. We can ask ourselves what *we* would say if, one day, we underwent a traumatic process of emerging from a vat and, looking around, we saw a world quite different from the one in which we thought we had been living.

I think that many people, upon being decanted from their vats, would regard much of their former lives as an illusion. They would think, and say, such things as 'Whole Foods never really existed—the real world is a dystopian nightmare'. The objector will suggest that this makes trouble for the neopragmatist. But why is this? Presumably it is because the neopragmatist—according to the objector—is committed to two things. First, that earlier claims, by these envatted people, about the location of Whole Foods, and their own brains, were *true*. And, second, that unless we are going to distort the concept of truth beyond recognition, the past truth of those present-tense claims entails the present truth of claims about what was the case in the past. But the neopragmatist need not accept the first of these claims. If the neopragmatist account of truth-*talk* is correct, it is no surprise that we would, while envatted, have *assessed* a token utterance of the following as true: 'Whole Foods is at the intersection of Roosevelt and State'. Our assessment here is the result of mastery of physical location-talk and truth-talk. Recall, the rules for using 'true' and 'false' have nothing to do with a substantive property of truth, defined in terms of causal/historical relations between words and things. Rather, truth-assessments are used to influence other speakers when their assertions agree or conflict with what we ourselves are disposed to assert. So once we are "woken up," there is nothing in the neopragmatist view to suggest that the proper use of 'true' would mandate our continued assessment of *our initial claim about Whole Foods* as true. It is open to the neopragmatist to make the plausible claim that mastery of the use of physical object talk would spontaneously lead us to take the evidence of our senses to give no warrant to the claim that there is a physical object called 'Whole Foods' at a certain physical location. If this is right, the neopragmatist will predict that we will assess our earlier utterance as *having been* false, though they were *competently assessed* as true at the time.[7]

One idea that allows the neopragmatist to avoid the objection described above is that language use—even when we restrict our view to assertion—is a skill that allows for the generation of completely new claims under unforeseen circumstances. Mastering a certain assertoric practice is no more a matter of memorizing a fixed set of assertions than mastering basketball is a matter learning to execute a fixed set of movements. In the case of the recently decanted beings of our thought experiment, their mastery of physical object talk may well yield virtually uniform agreement on a set of claims that they would never have thought likely. The idea here isn't that this counterfactual agreement *constitutes* the truth, of course, since nothing does that. Rather, the point is that neopragmatism predicts and explains *the very same linguistic behavior* as would be regarded as correct from the perspective of someone who held substantive views about truth and reference, and who endorsed Lewisian views on naturalness and reference magnetism. For example, virtually all the recently decanted people may agree—according to the neopragmatist—that the real world is a dystopian one, and lacks a Whole Foods. They may also, by the by, agree that the life they had been living was perfectly real in other respects: the love was real, the fights were real, the personalities were real. Plausible neopragmatist explanations of these differences in what they regard as real are not hard to find. Most of what was of practical importance about the love, the friendships, or the fights continues to be of

---

[7] I think reflection on such cases will also lead us (non-envatted people) to assess the relevant beliefs of a group of envatted brains as false, even if we never witness their decanting. But it doesn't matter if there is disagreement about this. Neopragmatism is perfectly compatible with the existence of cases in which there is no determinate answer to certain true/false questions. In fact, this is one of the advantages of neopragmatism, since it allows it to sidestep paradoxes that plague views that treat truth as a substantive property.

practical importance after the "great decanting"—and in the same way. The fights will continue to simmer, the love will continue to give meaning to their lives, and through it all they will continue to rely on their friends.

Of course, some readers may disagree with my assertions about what recently decanted people would say about what is real and what is not. Some readers may also disagree with my claims about whether the envatted people were speaking truly when they uttered such claims as 'Whole Foods is located at the intersection of Roosevelt and State'. I disagree with those readers; that is, I would assess their claims as false. But such disagreements are not, at this point in the dialectic, at all relevant to the discussion. After all, the objection at issue is being raised by someone who holds (1) that the envatted people had systematically false beliefs about the external world, such that only one lone skeptical envatted philosopher had an inkling of the truth and (2) that the neopragmatist cannot accommodate this. The worries of readers who would deny (1)—who would, that is, say that the envatted speakers had *true* beliefs about Whole Foods—are not the present concern, though the neopragmatist can certainly deal with such worries. One way of doing so is by saying that the rules by which we assess the existence and location of physical objects are less determinate than we might have thought, given the possible existence of virtual worlds in which one might live one's entire life. This sort of indeterminacy in the meaning of assertions about physical objects is perfectly consistent with my response to the primary objection, since it still allows the neopragmatist to say that there is a perfectly good sense to be made of the worries of the envatted external-world skeptic.

6. Reference Magnetism as a Corollary of Neopragmatism

My response to the objection from the coherence (and possible truth) of external-world skepticism contains the materials for a general-purpose explanation of the sort of phenomena associated with reference magnetism. The central point is that mastery of the vocabularies that figure in assertions involves various open-ended dispositions and skills that are manifested when that vocabulary is used. Sometimes these dispositions and skills result in psychological states of the sort that find expression in assertions. And if they are so expressed, they are exposed to pressures that push them into harmony with those of other speakers. The words 'true' and 'false' play a crucial role in all of this. But the forces that push these states around, and mold them, typically operate in a restricted environment. Little children are corrected in their application of 'apple' when they apply it to real-world pears. They are not, by contrast, repeatedly envatted and decanted, and taught to use 'apple' only for the apples they see when decanted. Nevertheless, the whole set of dispositions they acquire when learning the language of physical objects, pictorial representation, dreams, and so on may result in a robust disposition to regard the world they come to see once decanted as the real one, and the world as they formerly experienced it as an illusion. This would explain why members of an envatted community whose banana-related experiences are sufficiently like ours can coherently be understood—by us—to be talking about external-world bananas even before they have any causal contact with bananas.[8] Reflection on what I myself would think, were I to be decanted, makes me quite sure that is precisely what would happen. And, more importantly, *the objector agrees with me*: the basis of the objection was that external-world skepticism, as voiced by an envatted philosopher, makes perfect sense, and might be true.

The account of reference magnetism I've offered will not be accepted by those who take reference to be a substantive relation. They will protest that it is only an account of what we might call the 'reference-magnetic phenomena'. That is, they will complain that I have only offered an explanation of the fact that we *talk in the way we would* if there really were a kind of 'semantic action at a distance' to which we were sensitive. My response to this is that it is correct, but that it is a mistake to want more. This is a characteristic neopragmatist response: if all of the phenomena have been explained, why ask for more? What work is being done by the addition of a substantive notion of reference, and a substantively metaphysical metasemantics in which reference magnetism plays a role? It cannot be that these additions are justified, as theoretical entities are in physics, because of their role in explanations of the relevant phenomena. After all, the objector here has granted that the neopragmatist has *already* provided a good explanation of the linguistic phenomena.

The question to which reference magnetism is offered as an answer is the following: given that an unsupplemented theory of reference—for example, global descriptivism—underdetermines the reference of a certain predicate, why it is that we ought to apply that predicate to *this*, rather than *that*? Theories of reference magnetism look for an answer by trying to identify some special property of the referent. But for the neopragmatist, the 'ought' in the phrase 'we ought to apply that predicate to *this*, rather than *that*' is not to be explained in terms of properties of the referent. Rather, what is to be explained is why speakers competent with the predicate would assess claims using those words as true or false. And similar claims go if we change our focus from predicates to names.

In addressing the objection to which reference magnetism is offered as the answer, the neopragmatist changes the focus from reference to linguistic practice. Understanding (let alone *accepting*) this change of focus is a process that involves

---

[8] Kripke (1980: 24) highlights that his view has the counterintuitive implications that even if we discovered some things that looked exactly like unicorns, they wouldn't be unicorns, and that it is not even possible that there were unicorns. In my view the counterintuitive nature of these claims is nicely explained by their simple falsehood. What is going on in such cases is that reference magnetism has overridden the verdicts of a purely causal/historical account, so that 'unicorn' refers—and referred—to the newly discovered creatures.

a significant risk of backsliding for those who are still in the representationalist camp. It is tempting to think that the appeal to linguistic practice just widens the basis on which a referent is assigned.[9] But the appeal to social linguistic practices is not meant to fix a reference. It is meant to explain and demystify linguistic phenomena. The dispositions we humans would have, having learned language while hooked up to a matrix, make it unsurprising that, having been freed from that matrix, we would say such things as 'All this time I've never seen a real banana, like this one here in my hand now' and 'All my former beliefs about my appearance were false; as it turns out, I am very tall'. What 'makes it true' that my earlier token claims about bananas were claims about these (actual) bananas is not a massive set of dispositional claims about the people in my linguistic community. That way of viewing things takes truth to be a property bestowed on a proposition by some state of affairs. But while 'true' and 'false' certainly function syntactically like predicates (and indeed, in a deflationary sense it is perfectly acceptable to think of them as naming properties) their practical function is to push around the psychological states of people in a linguistic community. So the reasons we ought to claim that my former assertions about bananas were false are to be found in the first-order reasons we would cite in defending that claim, and not in any metasemantic claims about how my word 'banana' got hooked up to certain fruits. For example, we might say, 'real bananas provide nourishment, whereas what I used to call bananas did nothing of the sort'.

7. Theories of Reference as Heuristics

One sort of complaint about neopragmatism comes—unsurprisingly—from those who have been persuaded of the truth of particular substantive theories of reference. For example, some people are persuaded by Kripke that the referents of proper names are the entities at the far end of a causal/historical chain of transmission, starting with an initial baptism. But if all we can look at in determining truth and reference is our *present linguistic practices*, how could the referent be determined by these causal/historical facts, especially since they are—in virtue of being in the past—irrelevant to how we now use the relevant names? Surely, that is, we could be using a name like 'Aristotle' *exactly* as we now are using it, whether or not a certain brilliant Greek philosopher lies at the end of the sort of causal chain at issue.

---

[9] The result may be something like Laura Schroeter's (2012) account of samesaying. Her sophisticated account bases facts about co-reference in the appearances of sameness of content among speakers in a linguistic community. In Gert (2018), I suggest that Schroeter is one easy step away from an attractive neopragmatist account of reference. Alternately, the result may be something like David Lewis' (1984) causal descriptivism.

The answer to this question is that acceptance of *something like* the causal/historical theory of reference characterizes our *present* use of names. That is, we *presently* accept a set of counterfactuals about, say, Aristotle claims. Here is one: if historians and archeologists were to discover that all of Aristotle's texts had been forged by an 8th-century monk, we would retract a great many of our Aristotle claims. And, in accord with the sort of deflationary views of truth and reference that emerges from neopragmatism, we could express this retraction by saying 'We thought "Aristotle" referred to an ancient Greek philosopher, but that was false'. On one such deflationary view, this simply amounts to the claim that we thought Aristotle was an ancient Greek philosopher, but he wasn't. More generally, for a certain class of words—including, most centrally, proper names—we endorse claims of the following sort:

> *N* is the person at the end of a long causal chain leading back to an initial baptism in which they received a name that either was, or gradually changed into, 'N'.

This claim can of course be expressed using—in a deflationary sense—'refers', as follows:

> 'N' refers to the person at the end of a long causal chain leading back to an initial baptism in which they received a name that either was, or gradually changed into, 'N'.

But, however it is expressed, it is basically an identity claim which *uses* (as well as mentions) the name 'N' (see Price 2013: 9). The neopragmatist will offer an explanation for the existence of a class of words that function like this. I don't have space to offer it here, but it is not particularly surprising that there will be a use for words linked, through time, to the very same past person (or city, or building). This explanation is not a vindication of the causal/historical theory of reference, though, since that theory is meant to tell us what *reference*—the substantive relation—is. The neopragmatist, on the other hand, is telling us what *the reference* of a certain class of words is.

Of course the causal/historical account has some drawbacks as an account of what reference *is*. Most conspicuously, it forces its advocates to deny that we really refer to, say, numbers, or, more generally, anything that lacks causal powers. For that reason one may prefer some form of global descriptivism. This would allow one to include some claims about the causal powers of, say, Aristotle, in the relevant description of Aristotle, thereby accounting for the same phenomena that the causal/historical account explains. But it would also allow one to provide descriptions of the counting numbers that don't mention anything about causal relations at all. The problems with all this, though, have already been mentioned. They were at the heart of Putnam's model-theoretic argument, and were what prompted Lewis to introduce reference magnetism as a solution. If we try to fix the reference of all our referring words by saying that they are the entities that make our ideal theory of everything come out true, it will turn out that we have done remarkably little reference fixing. There is a truth-maximizing assignment on which 'Aristotle' refers to the Eiffel tower, for example, and this remains the case even if the relevant description includes 'Was the student of Plato' and 'Was born in Stagira', since the referents of 'student', 'Plato', 'born', and 'Stagira' are also up for grabs. Again, one way of diagnosing the problem here is that the global descriptivist has confused *reference* with *the reference*. It is true that *the referent* of 'Aristotle' is the entity that satisfies the description 'The student of Plato who was born in Stagira and...' But this is not a substantive semantic claim. Rather, it is simply a rephrasing of the claim that Aristotle *is* the person who was the student of Plato who was born in Stagira and,...etc. More generally, no claims about *the referent* of 'Aristotle' can be taken to support any particular substantive account of *reference*.

Discussion of the two theories of reference just considered—the causal/historical theory and global descriptivism—illustrates a more general point. Plausible—but false—theories of reference offer us very useful heuristics for determining *the reference* of various sorts of names and predicates. In the case of the causal theory the heuristic is useful only in a restricted domain: names for physical entities and natural kinds. Global descriptivism is more generally applicable. But it can still be regarded as a heuristic: it tells us to come up with the right sort of description, and then look for the entity that satisfies it best. In calling these theories *heuristics for identifying the reference* I mean to indicate not only the difference between *picking out* the reference and being a substantive theory of what reference *is*. I also mean to indicate that, like heuristics in general, they cannot always be relied on to give the correct answer. That is, for example, even in cases to which the causal/historical theory is applicable—say, to the word 'banana'—it does not always give the right answer. Envatted shoppers at (what they take to be) Whole Foods may have had no causal contact with bananas—only with some sort of electronically realized data structures in the massive computer that is running the matrix in which they have been living their lives. Nevertheless, if *we* should turn out to be such people, and *we* were decanted, there is no reason to deny that, without a change in sense or reference, we might competently and truly say 'So this is what bananas *really* taste like', upon our first real-world encounter with a banana. This is an instance of reference-magnetic phenomena, and neopragmatism can explain it. The explanation is simply that the linguistic dispositions we acquired in the matrix, given a shared human sensibility concerning what is important, would make it very natural for us to talk in this way.

One might think that global descriptivism must be more than a mere heuristic, since the reference of a name is fixed by the *comprehensive* set of descriptions associated with that name. The problem is that—even bracketing Putnam's points about underdetermination—global descriptivism operates with a finite set of descriptions, since they are the descriptions that actual speakers actually hold. The referent is meant to be the entity that best satisfies that description. But it is impossible to foresee the developments that might influence how speakers will go on, spontaneously, to apply a predicate or name. No finite set of descriptions can possibly be expected to predict the results of these developments. And that means that on some occasions our considered judgments of what counts as, say, a banana, or a logical operator, or a virtue, will deviate from what the global descriptivist must say.

A similar problem arises even for forms of global descriptivism that do not base reference in what actual speakers actually hold, but that instead make reference to "ideal theory": our full theory of everything, at a point at which such a theory has achieved all the theoretical virtues. Certainly there are pretty good reasons to think—again bracketing Putnam's model-theoretic points—that such a theory would serve to pick out the referents of the terms of physics, chemistry, and biology. But unless we stipulate that nothing of relevance would arise after the appearance of an ideal theory—nothing that would put any pressure on linguistic practice—the niggling possibility remains that something might occur that would cause us to revise our overall theory. We do not want the determinacy our theory of reference achieves to be hostage to facts about the determinacy of the future! To give this doubt a little more bite, note that one of the terms that might respond in unexpected ways to unforeseeable circumstances is 'theoretical virtue'.

What I have been offering in this section and the last is what J. R. G. Williams calls a 'recapture' project (Williams 2020: 96). Williams uses an interesting variation on Lewis' interpretationism to explain why conceptual role semantics seems like a good theory of reference for, say, 'and', while descriptivism plus reference magnetism seems like a good theory for the concepts we use to explain physical phenomena. The details of his theory do not matter here, except to note one important difference between his project and mine: Williams is offering a *metaphysics* of linguistic representation, while for the neopragmatist linguistic representation is not a substantive relation, and does not have a metaphysical nature. What I am doing is trying to make it plausible that, if one accepts neopragmatism, then causal/historical theories of reference will be plausible heuristics for names and natural kind terms, while descriptivism might be a good heuristic for terms that refer to entities and properties that lack causal powers. And some other sort of heuristic might be generally useful for, say, normative terms. But I am not doing this by showing that these more local substantive theories of reference approximate the results of the correct general substantive theory of reference, in the way that Newton's physics approximates the results of Einstein's physics. For the neopragmatist, there is no substantive theory of reference.

8. Robust Reference and Reference Magnetism

Putnam's model-theoretic argument is not best viewed as an attack on global descriptivism in isolation. Rather, it was intended as an attack on that view as part of a more complex view: metaphysical realism, as Putnam conceived it.[10] One mark of metaphysical realism, for him, was that truth was "radically non-epistemic." That is, if the metaphysical realist is right, 'we might be "brains in a vat" and so the theory that is "ideal" from the point of view of operational utility, inner beauty and elegance, "plausibility", simplicity, "conservatism", etc., might be false'. What I have been arguing in the last three sections is that neopragmatism shares this mark with metaphysical realism—even though it sidesteps Putnam's model-theoretic arguments. That is, neopragmatism allows that even our best theories might turn out to be false. This coincidence between the implications of quite a radical realism on the one hand, and a view like neopragmatism on the other, can seem surprising. Neopragmatism can, after all, be viewed as something very close to linguistic anthropology. Wouldn't it therefore support a kind of relativity to human nature that would be rejected by metaphysical realists? Moreover, neopragmatism can seem, at first glance, to rule out the falsity of our very best theories in another way. After all, if *we* come up with the rules for the use of our language—if *we* determine what they mean—then isn't it impossible for *us* to end up going systematically wrong in what we say using that language? Wouldn't the neopragmatist agree with Putnam's point that '*we* interpret our languages or nothing does' (Putnam 1980: 482)?

The answers to all these questions is, I have been arguing, 'No'. There is nothing relativistic about the truth of the claim that $2+2=4$, or that the sun is mostly hydrogen, or indeed that pain is bad. Nor is it "up to us" in any important sense, what 'water' or 'gold' refer to. It is true that our dispositions to use language help explain why, when it was discovered that laboratory samples of water and gold had a certain microstructure, we then identified water and gold with whatever had that same microstructure. But—the crucial point—for the neopragmatist these linguistic dispositions are not truth-makers. Rather, they are explainers: they explain why the language took the form it did, and they explain why we have been making the truth-assessments we have been making *so far*. They leave it open that future discoveries, or other sorts of changes in circumstances, will lead us to assess our former claims as false. Someone who would like to make radically non-epistemic truth the unique property of the metaphysical realist might here say that this only shows that we cannot know whether our theories are *yet* best, but that *best* theories—by definition—would not be open to revision in this way. But this is a cheat, and in any case it backfires. It cheats because it builds truth

---

[10] Hale and Wright (2017) make it very clear that this is his target, rather than a more general thesis about determinacy of reference.

right into the notion of 'best theory'. And it backfires because on *that* understanding of 'best theory', even the metaphysical realist must hold that best theories cannot turn out to be false.

So far I've pointed out that Putnam's arguments cannot be taken to rule out a non-epistemic conception of truth. Neopragmatism can deliver such a conception without falling prey to Putnam's arguments. The force of Putnam's argument works against the metaphysical realist—to the degree that it does work—only because such a realist also endorses a robust form of reference. This is evident in the following rhetorical question:

> Suppose we...are and always were 'brains in a vat'. Then how does it come about that our word 'vat' refers to noumenal vats and not to vats in the image?
> Putnam (1981: 127)

What makes trouble for the metaphysical realist (about the physical world) in this question is not the explicit supposition about the location of our brains, and the fact that we do not have the right kind of causal contact with the vats in which they are located to be understood as referring to them with our word 'vat'. Rather, the source of the trouble is the implicit supposition in the phrase 'come about that'. What this phrase reveals is a conception of reference facts as substantive. On a deflationary view of reference it does not *come about* that 'Aristotle' refers to the person at the far end of a certain causal/historical chain, since that reference claim is not the obtaining of a reference-involving state of affairs. This is easiest to see on a disquotational view of reference claims, on which they are equivalent to identity claims of the form 'Aristotle *is* Aristotle' or 'Aristotle *is* the person at the end of a certain causal/historical chain'. But it is also true on more sophisticated deflationary views: for example, Båve (2009).

9. Robust Reference Magnetism

In 1974 Lewis made the following claim

> If ever you prove to me that all the constraints we have yet found could permit two perfect solutions...then you will have proved that we have not yet found all the constraints   343

By 'two perfect solutions' he was talking about two distinct assignments of beliefs and desires to someone who is being "radically interpreted." He was not at that point arguing for anything like reference magnetism, or the role of naturalness in determining reference. But in the face of Putnam's arguments, he maintained the same sort of attitude to reference-determination. As a result, he added naturalness as a constraint, both when assigning beliefs and desires to agents, and when assigning referents to words.

I agree with Lewis that we need to take some claims at face value even to begin theorizing, and we can take those "Moorean facts" to motivate the search for constraints. But surely it is better if these claims are the most obvious ones. And claims about primitive naturalness—or about determinate reference—do not seem to be Moorean facts in the way that certain claims about human beings do seem to be. Here I mean such claims as that there are lots of human beings, that they live in groups, make the noises we call 'language', and teach their children to use language. The neopragmatist is explaining the phenomena associated with reference magnetism beginning only with such facts: facts that I think are *more Moorean* than Lewisian.

Those who are skeptical of the neopragmatist position might question the right of anyone who denies the existence of a reference relation to speak of human beings, rocks, and trees—at least until some unobjectionable theory explains how such talk could be understood to be referring successfully to human beings, rocks, and trees. And of course the neopragmatist can only offer such a theory by talking about—among other things—human beings, rocks, and trees. This is the "no exit" problem (see Blackburn 2013; Kraut 2016). What Putnam's arguments seem to me to show is that it is as much a problem for metaphysical realists as it is for neopragmatists. How *much* of a problem it is is another question. My view is that any theorist willing to give up on the impossible task of answering a Cartesian skeptic should be equally willing to put the no exit problem on the same shelf. Lewis himself (1984: 226) makes this point on behalf of the metaphysical realist, acknowledging the unanswerability of the skeptic's semantic challenge, but holding that, for all that, the metaphysical realist could still be right. I think many readers would be sympathetic to Lewis' point here. The neopragmatist is asking only for the same degree of sympathy.[11]

References

Båve, A. (2009). 'A Deflationary Theory of Reference', *Synthese* 169, 51–73.

Blackburn, S. (2013). 'Pragmatism: All or Some?', in Price 2013, 67–84.

Blatti, S. and Lapointe, S. (eds.) (2016). *Ontology after Carnap*. Oxford: Oxford University Press.

Corti, L. (2022). 'Demystifying the Myth of Sensation: Wilfrid Sellars' Adverbialism Reconsidered', *Synthese* 200, 1–21.

---

[11] Many thanks to Victoria Costa, Daniel Callcut, and Preston Stovall for comments on an earlier version of this chapter.

Dasgupta, S. and Weslake, B. (eds.) (2020). *Current Controversies in Philosophy of Science*. Abingdon: Routledge.

Gert, J. (2018). 'Neo-Pragmatism, Morality, and the Specification Problem', *Canadian Journal of Philosophy* 48, 3-4, 447-67.

Goldberg, S. (ed.) (2016). *The Brain in a Vat*. Cambridge: Cambridge University Press.

Hale, B., and Wright, C. (2017). 'Putnam's Model-Theoretic Argument against Metaphysical Realism', in Wright and Hale 2017, 703-30.

Houser, N. and Kloesel, C. (eds.) (1992). *The Essential Peirce*, Vol. 1. Bloomington, IN: Indiana University Press.

James, W. (1907). 'Pragmatism's Conception of Truth', *The Journal of Philosophy, Psychology and Scientific Methods* 4, 6, 141-55.

Kotzen, M. (2020). 'What Follows from the Possibility of Boltzmann Brains?', in Dasgupta and Weslake 2020, 21-34.

Kraut, R. (1990). 'Varieties of Pragmatism', *Mind* 99, 394, 157-83.

Kraut, R. (2016). 'Three Carnaps on Ontology', in Blatti and Lapointe 2016, 31-58.

Kripke, S. (1980). *Naming and Necessity*. Cambridge, MA: Harvard University Press.

Lewis, D. (1974). 'Radical Interpretation', *Synthese* 27, 331-44.

Lewis, D. (1983). 'New Work for a Theory of Universals', *Australasian Journal of Philosophy* 61, 4, 343-77.

Lewis, D. (1984). 'Putnam's Paradox', *Australasian Journal of Philosophy* 62, 3, 221-36.

Misak, C. (1998). 'Deflating Truth: Pragmatism vs. Minimalism', *The Monist*, Reunifying Epistemology 81, 3, 407-25.

Peirce, C. S. (1878). 'How to Make Our Ideas Clear', in Houser and Kloesel 1992, 124-41.

Price, H. (1988). *Facts and the Function of Truth*. New York: Blackwell.

Price, H. (2003). 'Truth as Convenient Friction', *The Journal of Philosophy* 100, 167-90.

Price, H. (2013). *Expressivism, Pragmatism and Representationalism*. Cambridge: Cambridge University Press.

Putnam, H. (1980). 'Models and Reality', *The Journal of Symbolic Logic* 45, 3, 464-82.

Putnam, H. (1981). *Reason, Truth and History*. Cambridge: Cambridge University Press.

Schroeter, L. (2012). 'Bootstrapping Our Way to Samesaying', *Synthese* 189, 177-97.

Sundell, T. (2016). 'Eligibility and Ideology in the Vat', in Goldberg 2016, 226-50.

Williams, J. R. G. (2020). *The Metaphysics of Representation*. Oxford: Oxford University Press.

Wittgenstein, L. (1953). *Philosophical Investigations*, trans. G. E. M. Anscombe. New York: Macmillan.

Wright, C. and Hale, B. (eds.) (2017). *A Companion to the Philosophy of Language*. Oxford: Blackwell.

8
Realism Rehabilitated

Claudine Verheggen and Robert H. Myers

1

Philosophical accounts of the relation between thought and reality tend to gravitate toward two extreme and diametrically opposed positions regarding the concept of truth. On the one hand, classical (a.k.a. "metaphysical") realists, as we shall call them, insist on a concept of truth so radically non-epistemic that even perfectly reasoned sets of beliefs could be largely false.[1] On the other hand, antirealists of various sorts either make do with a purely epistemic concept of truth or dispense with the concept altogether, thereby making it impossible to allow that particular beliefs often are true or false, as the case may be, independently of whether anyone does—or in better epistemic circumstances would—deem them to be so. Inspired by the writings of Donald Davidson, our goal in this chapter is to demonstrate that neopragmatists can provide a superior account of this relation, an account which at once acknowledges the substantive independence of truth and falsity from our beliefs and epistemic practices while also guaranteeing that whatever beliefs we have must in fact be largely true.[2]

Davidson's relationship to traditional pragmatism was always fraught. He never hesitated to endorse the galvanizing claim that truth is not a goal of inquiry. At the same time, however, he invariably tempered pronouncements of this sort with proclamations concerning the importance of possessing the concept of truth. And accounts of the concept portraying it as being to any degree epistemic or less than fully objective never met with anything but his scorn.[3] Indeed, on more than one occasion, Davidson took pains to make it clear that his antipathy was only to realism as classically construed, sometimes maintaining he was a realist, just not of a "metaphysical" sort, sometimes preferring to describe his view as nothing more than anti-antirealism.[4] Either way, though, he manifestly was more

---

[1] René Descartes and Thomas Nagel, for example, are realists in this sense. Hilary Putnam (1978) refers to this position as "metaphysical" realism.

[2] Without meaning to take a stand on the history, we use 'traditional pragmatist' to refer to pragmatists who are prepared to accept antirealism, reserving 'neopragmatist' for pragmatists who are not.

[3] To be sure, he did once describe himself as holding a coherence theory of truth, but that mistake (made in Davidson 1983) was one he quickly corrected (in Davidson 1987).

[4] Three of the more notable instances are Davidson (1983: 140, 1988: 185, and 1997: 70).

neopragmatist than traditionally pragmatist—happy to throw over classical realism, but not willing to embrace antirealism.

On the other hand, when we consider what Davidson thought possessing the concept of truth enables people to do, the differences between his views and those of other neopragmatists can certainly appear to be quite significant. Our goal in sections 3-5 of this chapter will be to illustrate these differences by comparing Davidson's views with those of Huw Price. Like Davidson, Price insists on the importance of possessing an objective concept. In the final analysis, however, he seems not to grant its possession the same impact Davidson does. For Price, possessing it enables people to find certain disagreements troubling in ways that call for further inquiry. By contrast, for Davidson, possessing an objective concept of truth enables people to determine which of the many different causes of their beliefs are the ones ultimately endowing them with the specific propositional contents they possess. As we shall go on to demonstrate in sections 6-8, these differences bring in their train further differences over the status of realism, making it substantive for Davidson in a way it is not for Price. Our conclusion in section 8 will be that Davidson was right to see his arguments as rehabilitating realism, although in sections 9-10 we shall also note two questions about which he might have said more.

2

Before considering what Price and Davidson thought possessing an objective concept of truth can enable people to do, let us consider why it has been thought that objective truth cannot serve as a goal of inquiry. We need to be especially clear why Davidson agreed to this, since agreeing to it is often taken to be a problem for realists.

In "A Coherence Theory of Truth and Knowledge," Davidson endorsed Richard Rorty's claim that "nothing counts as justification unless by reference to what we already accept, and there is no way to get outside our beliefs and our language so as to find some test other than coherence" (Davidson 1983: 141, quoting from Rorty 1979: 178).[5] However, whereas Rorty meant this to discredit any realist concept of truth, Davidson saw it as challenging only our knowledge of such truths. Moreover, as we shall see, he hoped to overcome this challenge by showing that any coherent set of beliefs must be largely true. This raises the question why he did not regard truth as a goal of inquiry and increasing coherence as a means of achieving it. If this was not in fact the lesson Davidson drew from this, as it pretty clearly was not, we need to understand why not.

---

[5] Consider also in this connection Davidson's famous claim (on the same page) that "nothing can count as a reason for holding a belief except another belief."

The answer can be found in "Truth Rehabilitated," where Davidson noted that "truths do not come with a 'mark', like the date in the corner of some photographs, which distinguishes them from falsehoods" and then said "what we will never know for certain is which of the things we believe are true. Since it is neither visible as a target, nor recognizable when achieved, there is no point in calling truth a goal" (Davidson 2000: 6).[6] His thought appears to have been that, because we cannot get outside our beliefs to check, we have no way of determining what sorts of revisions to our beliefs would take them closer to the truth. He appears to have concluded from this that, even if it does turn out that any coherent set of beliefs must be largely true, this will not make coherence evidence of truth in any useful sense. For there will always be many different ways in which revising our beliefs would make them more coherent, and no reason to think all of them would increase the extent to which our beliefs are true. The assumption appears to have been that a goal of inquiry should provide more guidance on this score, and that truth cannot provide the requisite guidance because we do not have independent access to it.

For reasons that will emerge later in this chapter, we do not fully share Davidson's worries on this point. Truth may not be visible as a target, exactly, but on some occasions it is recognizable when achieved—not, indeed, because we can get outside our beliefs to check, but because some beliefs can be known to be true from within. However, we will not be in a position to explain our differences with Davidson on this point until we get clearer about what he thought possessing the concept of truth does enable people to do. For the time being, therefore, let us remain agnostic on the question whether truth is fit to serve as a goal of inquiry. What else does possessing the concept enable people to do, if not to aim their inquiries at truth? If that is not a difference possessing the concept makes, what other differences can it make instead? We need to get clearer on these questions before returning to consider whether truth actually can serve as a goal of inquiry after all.

3

Price explores these issues by asking what the concept of truth adds to concepts of various other sorts, such as the concept of sincerity, the concept of personal warranted assertibility, and concepts of broader warranted assertibility. We shall focus on his discussion in "Truth as Convenient Friction," where Rorty again figures both as an ally and as a foil.

---

[6] For two subsequent discussions, neither of which gets Davidson's understanding of realism quite right, see Stout (2007) and Levine (2008).

Rorty's position was that the concept of truth simply enables people to caution one another that assertions justifiable by the lights of their current audience may not be justifiable by the lights of some future audience.[7] But people do not need an objective concept of truth to do this; and doing this does not bring out the troubling nature of such differences. Price's (2003: 170ff) suggestion is that the concept of truth precisely enables its possessors to *censure* certain differences of opinion they believe ideally should be resolved.[8] If one person asserts p, while another asserts something different from p, the concept of truth enables its possessors to express unhappiness with this difference by remarking that at least one of them must be mistaken. Each may be justified by whatever lights bear on their own assertions, but they cannot both be right, so further inquiry is in order, at least in the sense that there is some reason to engage in it, even if there may be other reasons not to bother.

It might be asked, once again, whether an objective concept of truth is needed in order to censure differences of opinion in this way. Could the same work not be done by the concept of an assertion that would prove to be warrantedly assertible at the end of inquiry? If one person asserts p, while another asserts something different from p, could people not express unhappiness with this difference by remarking that at least one of them would prove to be unjustified at the end of inquiry? As Price notes, however, it is not clear that we have a concept of the end of inquiry that could actually sustain such claims. After all, inquiry could come to an end in all sorts of ways, many of which would be hospitable to such differences of opinion. Price's thought, therefore, is that people express unhappiness with such differences of opinion by invoking a *sui generis* concept of truth that cannot be informatively defined in terms of any epistemic notion like warranted assertibility (2003: 177ff).

Davidson of course agreed that the concept of truth is *sui generis*; but he nonetheless thought there are important connections to be traced between it and other concepts, including, notably, the concept of correspondence. Truth cannot be helpfully defined in terms of correspondence, since what true beliefs correspond to are the facts, and the facts cannot be understood independently of beliefs, as the parts of reality making true beliefs true (Davidson 1988: 183). But Davidson still thought there is much to be learned from the idea that truth-evaluable attitudes are answerable to the way things are. Indeed, on his view, it is because truth-evaluable attitudes are answerable to the way things are that incompatible truth-evaluable attitudes cannot both be right and compatible truth-evaluable attitudes could both be wrong. On Price's view, by contrast, the concept of truth

---

[7] Strictly speaking, the 'simply' here is too strong, as Rorty also allowed that the concept of truth has what he referred to as "endorsing" and "disquotational" uses. See, e.g., Rorty (1986: 127–8).

[8] Of course, good questions abound about which differences of opinion people believe ideally should be resolved, and why. As we shall see, however, Price's claim is going to be that we can answer questions like these without invoking a substantive concept of truth.

enables its possessors both to censure, in the case of the disagreements, and to caution, in the case of the agreements, without the need of such substance. It is often good for people to spur one another to inquiry and the concept of truth helps them to do that (Price 2003: 175ff). End of story.[9]

Now it might be objected that both Davidson's alleged differences with Price and Price's alleged differences with Rorty are much ado about nothing. This is certainly how Rorty responded to Davidson's arguments in "Truth Rehabilitated." He welcomed Davidson's concession that truth is not a goal of inquiry, before dismissing all his positive claims about the importance of the concept, as if they added nothing of note to the familiar point that the concept of truth enables its possessors to explain what someone asserts in asserting p by saying that their assertion is true iff p (Rorty 2000a).[10] Davidson of course did include "disquotation" of this sort among the many things he thought the concept of truth enabled its possessors to do. It may very well have been the most celebrated of those things. But it was very far from being the most important of them, as even a cursory examination of his theory of content makes clear. Whether in its earlier formulations, which focused on interpretation, or in its later formulations, which focused on triangulation, Davidson's theory of content reveals several more important things the concept of truth enables its possessors to do.

4

We see a vivid sign of Rorty's misunderstanding in passages like this (quoted by Price on the first page of "Truth as Convenient Friction"):

> The need to justify our beliefs to ourselves and our fellow agents subjects us to norms, and obedience to these norms produces a behavioral pattern that we must detect in others before confidently attributing beliefs to them. But there seems to be no occasion to look for obedience to an *additional* norm—the commandment to seek the truth. For—to return to the pragmatist doubt with which I began—obedience to that commandment will produce no behavior not produced by the need to offer justification.
>
> Price (2003: 163, quoting Rorty 1995: 26, emphasis in the original

The glaring mistake here is to suppose that in our endeavors to interpret one another we are bound only by what Davidson called norms of coherence and not

---

[9] Once again, there is obviously more to be said about when it is good for people to spur one another to inquiry, and why. The point is just that Price is not going to appeal to a substantive concept of truth to explain this.

[10] His response to Price's claims for the concept was different; he could not see how they even purported to go beyond his own. See his part of the exchange published as Rorty and Price (2010).

also by what he called norms of correspondence (see, e.g., Davidson 1991: 211). It is to forget that the principle of charity calls for interpreters to attribute *true* beliefs to their subjects so far as plausibly possible. Coherence among their beliefs is to be sought, where plausible, as well; but, as Davidson understood the process, it is no substitute for truth.

Why did Davidson hold that the principle of charity calls for interpreters to attribute true beliefs to their subjects so far as plausibly possible? Why could the requirement not instead be to attribute to their subjects, so far as plausibly possible, beliefs that are similar to their own? Davidson's simple worry here had to do with how such assessments of plausible possibility are to be made. As he saw things, they can only be made in light of facts about the subjects' causal histories. Interpreters can plausibly expect their subjects to possess beliefs similar to their own only insofar as their causal histories have been similar as well. And what this entails, Davidson concluded, is that interpreters must assume causal histories to play a significant role in determining the contents of beliefs. Interpreters cannot take facts about their subjects' causal histories to explain where they fall short of the standard by which interpretations are governed unless they also take such facts to be involved in setting the standard.[11]

Against this, Rorty might have reiterated his point about the inability of inquirers to get outside their beliefs to check for their truth. Are interpreters not in the same predicament? In a sense, of course, they are. This might be thought to speak in favor of a more modest norm, one calling for interpreters to attribute to their subjects, so far as plausibly possible, beliefs that they—the interpreters—take to be justified.[12] But interpreters have no reason to suppose that the contents of their subjects' beliefs are shaped by whatever makes their—the interpreters'—beliefs justified. What interpreters have reason to suppose is that the contents of their subjects' beliefs are shaped by whatever makes their—the interpreters'—beliefs true, viz., familiar objects and events in the environment they all share. Since beliefs taken to be justified are typically also taken to be true, there may rarely be much to choose between interpretations guided by a norm of justification and interpretations guided by the norm of truth. Still, it is only on the assumption that interpreters possess the concept of truth that good sense can be made of what they do.[13]

---

[11] It is surprising how often this point is missed. Commentators typically do appreciate why holism requires interpreters to start with some governing assumption about their subjects' beliefs but often fail to appreciate how the externalism necessarily presupposed in interpretation limits what the assumption can be. It is just not true that any assumption will do.

[12] It could not simply call for interpreters to attribute to their subjects, so far as plausibly possible, beliefs that they—*their subjects*—take to be justified without lapsing back into the norm of coherence. But interpreters must be guided by more than the norm of coherence if they are to overcome the challenges holism poses.

[13] See Verheggen (2021) for more detailed discussion of the reasons for which interpreters must assume externalism to be true.

What's more, as time went on, Davidson saw more clearly that this claim about interpretation does not get to the heart of the matter. It was never just that interpreters must proceed as if belief contents are largely determined by causal histories. There is no accounting for the contents of beliefs and other propositional attitudes without assuming externalism to be true. But externalism is not without challenges of its own, as beliefs will very often have many possible causes, each one of which will have many different aspects. What determines which causes endow beliefs with their contents? Davidson's answer was that "the contents of our thoughts and sayings are partly determined by the history of [our] causal interactions with the environment... What determines the content of... basic thoughts (and what we mean by the words we use to express them) *is what typically caused similar thoughts*" (Davidson 1991: 201, emphasis added). What we need to consider next, therefore, is how Davidson thought some causes come to be typical. This brings us to his triangulation argument, and to another job for the concept of truth to do.

5

Davidson's fundamental insight here was that we cannot hope to explain why people's beliefs and other propositional attitudes have the specific propositional contents they do without adverting to the linguistic activity of those people themselves. In the case especially of their earliest beliefs, this would have to involve their "triangulations" with other people and objects in their shared environment. Davidson defined triangulation as:

> the mutual and simultaneous responses of two or more creatures to common distal stimuli and to one another's responses   Davidson (2001a: xv)

But it is not enough that they have triangulated with other people in the "primitive" way we witness when, for example, two lionesses respond both to the movements of their prey and to one another's movements.[14] Davidson thought they have to have been in communication with other people, that is, they have to have been triangulating with other people *linguistically*, both querying other people and being queried by other people about the truth conditions of their utterances and the truth values of their claims. Davidson thought this sort of back and forth is needed in order for some causes of their beliefs to emerge as

---

[14] For the example of the lionesses, see Davidson (2001b, p. 7); for the notion of primitive triangulation, see Davidson (2001c, p. 292).

typical in the sense relevant to externalism and hence to become determinative of their contents.[15]

Now the crucial point for our purposes is that Davidson thought people need to possess the concept of truth in order to triangulate linguistically. He did not mean by this to deny that they also need to have triangulated linguistically in order to possess the concept of truth. His intention was not to assign priority to either engagement in the activity or possession of the concept but rather to trace the important connections between them and to show how each depends on the other.[16] He thought engagement in the activity of linguistic triangulation depends on possession of the concept of truth because of the nature of the activity, involving as it does querying other people and being queried by them about the truth conditions of utterances and the truth values of claims. And, again, he thought the querying has to concern truth because he thought this is the only way certain causes can emerge as the typical causes of people's beliefs and so as determinative of their contents.

Why did he think this is the only way certain causes can emerge as typical? Even if he was right in maintaining that external causes cannot settle this matter themselves, and hence that it must somehow be settled by the people actually acquiring the beliefs, why must this require people to query one another about truth conditions and truth values? Why would it not be just as good for them to query one another instead about, say, the assertibility conditions of their utterances and the actual warrant of their claims?[17] Simply put, Davidson's thought here was that the querying must concern matters related to truth because its point is precisely to make beliefs sensitive to the differences among possible causes. If the querying merely concerned assertibility and warrant, it would be doing something very different, making beliefs sensitive to the differences among other beliefs that might serve to justify them. Davidson would not have denied that some belief contents can be determined in this way, but only, he thought, because the contents of other beliefs are determined by their causes.[18]

For example, a child observes its caregivers using the word 'dog' and soon starts uttering the word herself, applying it at first to all manner of small furry things. Her caregivers prompt her with questions ("Where's the dog?," "Is Sylvester

---

[15] Insisting that the triangulation be linguistic prevents the account from being reductive, but it does not prevent it from being constructive. See Verheggen (2017b, 2021) for more discussion.

[16] For extensive discussion and references to Davidson, see Myers and Verheggen (2016: ch. 1).

[17] Another question that is often raised here, but which is less germane to our concerns in this chapter, is why it must be through interactions with other people that the contents of one's beliefs are determined. For discussion and references to Davidson, see Verheggen (1997, 2007) and Myers and Verheggen (2016: ch. 1).

[18] As explained in Myers and Verheggen (2016: ch. 1), internal causes or non-causal determinants of content are not serious options. Such items would also need disambiguating before they could be content determining. But they could not be disambiguated by people's linguistic interactions, since there is no way such interactions could triangulate on them.

[the cat] a dog?") and applaud or correct her answers ("Yes, there's the dog!," "No, Sylvester is a cat!"). Typically—but, importantly, not necessarily—her use of the word will eventually fall into line, so it will be dogs that are the typical causes of her beliefs about dogs.[19] In consequence, her beliefs about dogs will be, in this respect anyway, largely true; they will be, at least for the most part, about things that in fact are dogs. So too with many of her beliefs about the properties things such as dogs have, since she will have acquired many of those beliefs through similar processes of triangulation. Thus is forged the connection between truth, on the one hand, and meaning or content, on the other, that, as we shall see, was critical to Davidson's understanding of realism.

We are painting here very quickly, and with a very broad brush, but we hope at least to have said enough to illustrate just how important Davidson took possession of the concept of truth to be.[20] In his early work, he himself was not so clear about this. He always insisted that one could not have beliefs about, say, dogs, without understanding that any particular such belief could in fact be false. But he too often made it sound as if this was simply a stipulation about the sort of thing he took belief to be, leaving it unclear why one's understanding needed to concern truth and falsity rather than, say, warrant or unwarrant. His views here became clearer only when he turned his attention to questions about the determination of content. Only then did it become clearer that it is possession of the concept of truth that is needed, since nothing short of that would enable the activity required to determine belief contents in the first place.[21] Anyone who lacked the concept of truth would fail to be open to the world in the way required for causes to determine contents.

If, as we think, Davidson is the neopragmatist who most clearly escapes the orbit of traditional pragmatism, this is because he is the one who most rigorously pursues these questions about the determination of content. And if, as we also think, this fact about Davidson has not received the recognition it is due, this is because his later writings on triangulation are very often misunderstood, when they are not neglected altogether. Indeed, even his better-known writings on interpretation remain widely misunderstood, too often being read as advocating "interpretationism" rather than as developing externalism. As he eventually put the point himself (Davidson 2001c: 294), however, radical interpretation is just an instance of triangulation, and the externalist presuppositions of the triangulation

---

[19] If her use of the word does not fall into line, her beliefs about what she calls dogs will be typically caused by and hence about and largely true of something else—furry pets generally, perhaps. For discussion and references to Davidson, see Verheggen (2005, 2006) and Myers and Verheggen (2016: ch. 3).

[20] One absolutely critical issue glossed over here is the holistic nature of content determination.

[21] And, even then, Davidson himself was not always as clear about the role of the concept as he could have been. See Myers and Verheggen (2016: ch. 1).

argument were always at work in the interpretation argument as well.[22] Having seen now why he thought pragmatists should acknowledge that possession of the concept of truth is needed both for the interpretation of other people's propositional attitudes and for the possession of one's own propositional attitudes, let us return to the implications for the realism/antirealism debate. Was there really nothing more to Davidson's realism than anti-antirealism?

6

Let us begin by asking what Davidson meant in rejecting classical realism, before then asking what other sort of realism he might have accepted and how it might have differed from the realism accepted by Price.

In rejecting classical realism, Davidson meant to be rejecting only the claim that a person's beliefs could, at least in principle, be largely false. Given how he thought the contents of people's beliefs are typically determined, he thought beliefs are, as he put it, "in their nature" veridical (Davidson 1983: 146). But of course his idea was not that truth and belief are closely linked because what is true is determined by prevailing epistemic practices, which is, roughly speaking, what the antirealists would have us think. His idea was that truth and belief are closely linked because what is believed is determined, to a significant degree, by how things are. This is clearly anti-antirealism, but it is more than that; it is a commitment to a substantive sort of realism as well. It is a commitment to the existence of objects, events, and properties to which individual beliefs are answerable and which they can get wrong.[23] If this is not realism, it is not clear what would be.

In an exchange with Simon Blackburn, Price acknowledges that people often believe what they do because things are as they believe them to be. As he understands claims like this, however, they are not corollaries of philosophically defensible theories of content but simply further beliefs of ours—beliefs for which we can provide good reasons and to which we are firmly committed, to be sure, but perfectly ordinary beliefs on a par with any number of others that we hold, all the same. And, because of this, Price insists that we need to take a much more nuanced view about what such claims ultimately commit us to. They do commit us to the existence of objects, events, and properties to which individual beliefs are answerable and which they can get wrong. But Price maintains that this commitment to realism does not run deep, and that fuller analyses of the nature and

---

[22] For a more detailed discussion of the continuity of Davidson's earlier interpretation argument and later triangulation argument, see Verheggen (2017c, 2021).

[23] It is perhaps worth stressing once again that this does not mean truth can be *defined* as correspondence.

content of beliefs reveal that they are best understood in expressivist, rather than realist, terms (Price 2013: 158-60; see also Macarthur and Price 2007).[24]

At first, this might sound like straight antirealism, but that is not what Price intends, any more than Davidson intended his position to be identical with classical (or "metaphysical") realism. On the contrary, Price, like Davidson, is looking for an alternative to these polarized options, a way of accounting for the relation between thought and reality that evades such dichotomies. However, whereas Davidson thought the preferred alternative is a more modest version of realism, Price's view is that we should reject both sides of this debate in their entirety.[25] As we noted above, he does not believe the concept of truth is purely epistemic. He thinks it enables us to reach beyond our epistemic practices and initiate important change. But Price is not prepared to grant that there is anything of importance to be gleaned from the thought that truth-evaluable attitudes are answerable to the way things are. It is not surprising, therefore, that he is equally unimpressed by the claim that people often believe what they do because things are as they believe them to be.[26]

What are we doing in claiming that beliefs are in their nature veridical, or that people often believe what they do because things are as they believe them to be? An orthodox expressivist might insist that we are merely expressing our confidence in the prospect that other people's beliefs will always be found to cohere reasonably well with our own. In Price's view, however, this would be mistaken both as an everyday account of the import of such claims and as a fuller analysis of their nature and content. In refusing to analyze our talk of the causes and the objects of thought realistically, he does not mean to assert that it is merely expressive of our psychological states. That would be to assume that opposition to realism can only take the form of antirealism, whereas Price is hoping to steer clear of both sides of that interminable debate. As he says, his version of expressivism is best understood as a form of quietism. Thought is to be understood neither as representing something external nor as expressing something internal.[27]

Price puts considerable weight here on the example of evaluative beliefs, which, he thinks, likewise demand at first sight to be taken realistically, but not, on further analysis, in a manner incompatible with expressivism.[28] In fact, perhaps his

---

[24] Rorty (2000b) makes a similarly qualified concession in response to Ramberg (2000). (For more discussion of Rorty's concession, see Stout (2007) and Levine (2008).)

[25] Indeed, although Davidson was the one who liked to say that his view was nothing more than anti-antirealism, Price is the one whose position turns out to be more accurately described that way.

[26] Once again, he accepts claims like these as "the folk" understand them. His point is simply that nothing of philosophical importance turns on them. They are not acceptable, he insists, in the substantive sense realists intend.

[27] See Macarthur and Price (2007) for more detailed discussion. Given the depth of its differences with orthodox expressivism, calling Price's view expressivist is potentially a bit misleading, but it does highlight his opposition to realism.

[28] As he makes clear, the form of metaethical expressivism he favors is modelled closely on Blackburn's quasi-realism.

favorite reason for suggesting that we look past our realist commitments and embrace global expressivism is that he thinks we clearly should be looking past our realist commitments and embracing metaethical expressivism. It is therefore extremely important at this juncture that we be clear about why Price is so confident in the truth of metaethical expressivism. Given that he thinks we cannot get outside our beliefs to check, he can hardly be claiming that it is by getting outside them that we learn the evaluative ones are especially amenable to expressivist analyses. The claim must rather be that this is something we learn from within, by working out the implications of our whole set of beliefs, and particularly of scientifically informed beliefs about our capacities as human beings. Price maintains that these beliefs speak strongly in favor of metaethical expressivism, and that this in turn points the way toward fully global expressivism.[29]

In response, Blackburn has argued that expressivism cannot possibly go fully global. He of course is also of the view that scientifically informed beliefs about our capacities as human beings speak strongly in favor of metaethical expressivism. But the way they do this, he thinks, is by suggesting explanations of evaluative thought that do not commit us to the existence of evaluative properties, thereby undercutting the realist commitments inherent in evaluative thought itself. And because he thinks these explanations cannot in turn be undercut by others, he thinks whatever expressivisms they support could never be anything but local (Blackburn 2013: 77-9). We shall return to this disagreement between Blackburn and Price in a moment. Before pursuing it further, however, we should note that the premise on which it is based is one that Davidson quite emphatically *rejected*. Davidson did not agree with Price and Blackburn that scientifically informed beliefs about our capacities as human beings speak strongly in favor of metaethical expressivism. He thought they speak strongly in favor of a version of metaethical realism. Whereas Blackburn objects that Price's defense of global expressivism cannot possibly succeed, Davidson would have objected that it never even gets off the ground.

7

In order to understand why Davidson endorsed a version of metaethical realism, we need to consider how he thought externalism about content applies to evaluative beliefs.

The first point to stress here is that Davidson did think externalism about content applies to evaluative beliefs and not just to non-evaluative ones. This may come as a surprise to those enamored of orthodox expressivism. After all, as they

---

[29] As we shall see in section 8, this is not Price's only argument in favor of global expressivism; but he does often start with it, and it will help us to work through it as well.

see things, there is no need to explain the contents of people's evaluative beliefs in terms of their typical causes, since they are convinced that the contents of such beliefs can be adequately explained in terms of the contents of the pro-attitudes they express. As Davidson saw things, however, any such explanation would be incomplete, for he was convinced that it would leave us without a satisfactory explanation of how those pro-attitudes came to have the contents they do. In point of fact, he thought the contents of people's pro-attitudes are typically shaped by and sensitive to the contents of their evaluative beliefs, with the contents of people's earliest evaluative beliefs, like the contents of their earliest non-evaluative beliefs, being explained in terms of their typical causes.[30]

Now the suggestion that a property could be, as Davidson put it, "attitude-causing" yet still evaluative will strike many as a non-starter (Davidson 1995: 47). It is therefore important to remember how Davidson understood the interconnected notions of a causal relation, a causal law, and a causal explanation. In saying that evaluative properties are attitude-causing, he was certainly not suggesting that there are strict laws, couched in evaluative and intentional terms, linking events instantiating the evaluative properties to events instantiating their associated attitudes. On the contrary, he thought that, for an event instantiating an evaluative property to be causally related to an event instantiating its associated attitude, it is enough that there be lower levels of description at which strict laws do exist linking events describable as these two events are. And he thought that, for the one event also causally to explain the other, it is enough that there also be looser generalizations linking events describable in the same evaluative and intentional terms that they are.[31]

Given this understanding of the interconnected notions of a causal relation, a causal law, and a causal explanation, Davidson had the room he needed to distinguish the prescriptive authority of evaluative properties from their motivating force. Since the generalizations linking events instantiating evaluative properties with events instantiating their associated attitudes are never perfectly strict, the actual ramifications of evaluative properties will almost never reach anything like as far as they ideally should. On this score, Davidson's metaethical realism seems safe against arguments from queerness; it does not attribute to evaluative properties more motivating force than is plausible. Along another dimension, however, Davidson's metaethical realism may still be vulnerable to arguments from queerness, for it maintains that evaluative properties do have prescriptive authority, not

---

[30] Hence his insistence that the triangulation argument applies to evaluative beliefs as well as to non-evaluative beliefs. For extensive discussion and references to Davidson, see Myers and Verheggen (2016: ch. 6) and Myers (2017, 2020).

[31] In all these respects, Davidson's metaethical views were continuous with his anomalous monism in the philosophy of mind. He hoped to develop a non-reductive and non-revisionary naturalism covering both evaluative properties and intentional ones. For more discussion of his prospects, see Myers and Verheggen (2016: ch. 7) and Myers (2019, 2021).

simply over people's beliefs, but also over their motivations, and it might be wondered how higher level evaluative properties possessing prescriptive authority over people's motivations could possibly supervene on and be grounded in lower level non-evaluative properties lacking such authority over people's motivations. Yet evaluative properties would have to be grounded in non-evaluative properties if they are really to figure in causal relations and causal explanations.[32]

Although we believe Davidson's metaethical realism can be defended against such worries, we shall not explore this corner of his philosophy any further here.[33] Given how controversial metaethical realism remains, our argumentative purposes in this chapter will in fact be better served if we assume that metaethical expressivism is correct and consider whether this bolsters the case for global expressivism. As we saw in section 6, Blackburn denies that it does on the ground that there is no prospect of explaining scientific thought in terms that do not commit us to the existence of scientific properties. But do doubts about the *existence* of evaluative properties provide the only or even the best reasons to favor metaethical expressivism over metaethical realism? If they do, then the "no-exit" argument, as Blackburn (2013: 78) calls it, would seem to be quite telling; the best and perhaps only argument for metaethical expressivism would in effect be an argument against global expressivism. What we now need to consider, therefore, is why Price is not persuaded by this argument, and whether Davidson's theory of content puts him in a position to make a stronger case against global expressivism.

8

One way to understand why Price is not persuaded by Blackburn's no-exit argument is to note that there is an ambiguity in the claim that scientific properties must be invoked in the explanation of scientific thought. Clearly they must be invoked in explanations of the thinking of such thoughts; but must they also be invoked in explanations of their content?

Keeping this in mind, we can understand both why Price thinks, contra Davidson, that the case for metaethical expressivism is especially strong and why he thinks, contra Blackburn, that it bolsters the case for global expressivism. He thinks the case is especially strong because he sees no role at all for evaluative properties to play in explanations of evaluative thought, and so no need to

---

[32] As explained in Myers (2019), Davidson understood naturalism to require not simply that higher level properties supervene on lower level ones but also that they be grounded in them, a fact which left him with a "hard problem of prescriptivity" not unlike the "hard problem of consciousness" (or intentionality) familiar from his philosophy of mind.

[33] It might be more accurate to say we believe a position along broadly similar lines can be defended; Davidson's own views about events and causality would have to be updated in a number of significant ways.

wonder whether they simply help to explain the thinking of such thoughts or also help to explain their content. By contrast, while Price agrees that we cannot explain the thinking of scientific thoughts without invoking scientific properties, he does not see why scientific properties must be invoked in explanations of the content of scientific thought. He thinks the lesson we learn from the example of metaethical expressivism is that such explanations are otiose; they do no philosophically interesting work. And he thinks this lesson generalizes; it applies equally to the case of science even if scientific properties exist and evaluative properties do not.[34]

Of course, this generalization presupposes that, even in the absence of evaluative properties, evaluative thought would not be all that different from scientific thought.[35] Otherwise the alleged successes of metaethical expressivism would give us very little reason to believe that global expressivism could also succeed perfectly well. As Davidson saw things, however, there is no need for realists to get ensnared in this debate; for even if global expressivism might have been true, he thinks we know it in fact is false. We know this, he thinks, because we actively participated in the processes of triangulation through which the contents of our earliest beliefs were determined.[36] Certain causes of our earliest beliefs and not others emerged as typical and so as content determining as a result of choices we made. As Davidson saw things, therefore, it does not really matter whether an expressivist account of the content of scientific thought can be developed; for we know first-hand that any such account will be mistaken.[37]

As we understand him, Price would reply by denying that we know global expressivism to be false, since we cannot get outside our beliefs to confirm that it was often their causes that determined their contents. We may believe certain causes of our earliest beliefs and not others emerged as typical and so as content determining as a result of choices we made in the course of our triangulations with one another. For Price, however, this would simply be another belief of ours, not some unmediated insight into the nature and content of belief itself. Even if our interactions with one another played a part in determining the contents of our earliest beliefs, how could we confirm that the part they played was to make our beliefs sensitive to possible causes? As Davidson might have retorted, however: "Such a one may best be viewed as having knowledge he does not know he

---

[34] Macarthur and Price (2007: esp. §§7–9) provides a helpful account of Price's position on this point.
[35] As mentioned above, in note 28, Price advocates something like Blackburn's quasi-realism, which is in effect to say he believes this presupposition can be vindicated.
[36] Would Davidson have agreed that metaethical expressivism can also be disproved in this way? Davidson 1995 strongly suggests that he would have. This would still leave the puzzle about prescriptivity, but it would prevent the puzzle from sufficing to refute metaethical realism.
[37] In his (1999), Nagel suggests that Davidson's argument has the form of a *cogito*: I think; therefore I triangulate; therefore I have knowledge of other minds and our shared world. Davidson went along with this characterization of his argument in his (1999).

has: he thinks he is a skeptic. In a word, he is a philosopher" (Davidson 1983: 137).[38] In Davidson's view, this is one belief that we can know to be true even though we cannot get outside our beliefs to check.

Our allegiance here is to Davidson, but we will not spend any more time in this chapter trying to adjudicate this disagreement with Price. Our purposes in this chapter will have been served if we have shown that Davidson offers a version of neopragmatism that combines realism with an ironclad guarantee that our beliefs could not be largely false. Perhaps it will be wondered whether Davidson broke ranks with neopragmatism by allowing that some beliefs can be known to be true even though we cannot get outside our beliefs to check on their truth. But surely what is essential to neopragmatism is the idea that getting outside our beliefs is never a way to check on their truth, not that it is the only way to learn of their truth, and nothing Davidson has said in the course of developing his theory of content would seem to have broken ranks with that essential tenet. We know our beliefs to be in their nature veridical from within, by having been active *and knowing* participants in the processes of triangulation through which some causes and not others became determinative of their contents.[39]

9

Let us now return, very briefly, to the question we tabled earlier. Why did Davidson agree that truth is not a goal of inquiry? If, as he maintained, we can know, from within our beliefs, that they are in their nature veridical, why can we not build on this knowledge with a view to getting still closer to the truth?

As we saw in section 2, Davidson's worry appears to have been that we have no way of knowing how to go about this. We might hope to build on this knowledge by revising our beliefs in ways that will make the whole set of them more coherent, on the assumption that, since our beliefs are in their nature veridical, greater coherence among them would necessarily take us closer to the truth. Davidson's worry, however, appears to have been that there are many different ways in which we could increase the coherence of our beliefs, and that we would need to get outside our beliefs in order to determine which of them will take us closer to the truth. So the presumptive veridicality of belief does not take us very far; it vanquishes global skepticism, but otherwise leaves epistemology in the lurch.

But surely this is too quick. Before drawing such a pessimistic conclusion, we need to reflect on the fact that Davidson's reasons for concluding that beliefs are

---

[38] For a different reading of Price, one which narrows his differences with Davidson but puts his quietism at risk, see Simpson (2020).

[39] For further discussion of Davidson's arguments against skepticism about the external world, see Verheggen (2011) and Myers and Verheggen (2016: ch. 4).

presumptively veridical do not apply to all beliefs equally. The claim was never that belief contents are always fixed through triangulation; it was that they frequently are, and in particular that they are in the case of early beliefs, which anchor all of the rest. Moreover, even when the contents of beliefs are fixed through triangulation, the presumption of veridicality will not be equally noteworthy in every case; much will depend on how closely connected a belief is to others. All of this is just to say that Davidson's argument for the presumptive veridicality of belief is by no means as monolithic as our discussion of it in section 5 might have led one to suppose. This is something that it is important to bear in mind because coherentist epistemologies are at their most vulnerable when distinctions of these sorts are not drawn among the beliefs that are to be made more coherent. If all beliefs start out on an equal footing, the directive to increase their coherence is effectively empty; but the more distinctions among beliefs can be made, the greater bite the directive is likely to have.[40]

We will not pursue this thought any further here. Our point is simply to note that Davidson may have given up on his own argument too quickly. Given that we cannot get outside our beliefs, there is indeed a sense in which truths not currently known to us are neither "visible as a target" of inquiry nor "recognizable when achieved." But this need not prevent truths which are currently known to us from providing our inquiries with direction, and so does not prevent the discovery of more truths from being at least one goal of inquiry. Given the holistic nature of belief, we should not expect the resulting epistemology to yield detailed directives about how our beliefs should be revised. But that is no excuse for forsaking epistemology altogether, which is effectively what Davidson seems to have done.[41] On the contrary, prioritizing those of our beliefs that we know from our triangulations to be presumptively veridical, especially those with many close connections to others, we should look for ways to increase their coherence and, thereby, their chances of being true.

10

By way of conclusion, let us consider once again the kind of realism that has been rehabilitated via Davidson's arguments. As we have seen throughout this chapter, Davidson denied that thought and reality are entirely independent of one another, not on the ground that reality depends on thought, but on the ground that thought depends on reality. As a result, while he understood realism in terms of

---

[40] It is also worth noting that coherentist epistemologies need not be static. People continue to triangulate throughout their lives as they acquire new concepts and maintain or revise their current concepts under cross-examination by others.

[41] As we have seen, he was concerned to argue against broadly skeptical conclusions of various sorts, but not in favor of any normative epistemology.

the independence of reality from thought, he understood the nature of its independence differently than classical realists do. They understand it as allowing at least the in principle possibility that our beliefs could be largely false; Davidson understood it as requiring only that many of our beliefs are answerable to causes external to us.[42] But there is another way in which this independence might be understood, about which it would have been helpful if Davidson had said more. For some realists, such as Nagel (1986: ch. 1), have speculated that reality might also transcend thought, in the sense that some aspects of reality might be such that people could not even begin to form beliefs about them.[43]

It seems obvious that Davidson would have rejected any such transcendence thesis, although exactly why he would have done so is difficult to say. In rejecting talk of conceptual schemes, he clearly meant to reject the possibility that such things keep people from forming beliefs about certain matters. His view seems to have been that a creature who is capable of forming beliefs about anything is capable of forming beliefs about everything. But he would not have maintained that a creature who is capable of triangulating on some things is capable of triangulating on all things. People can triangulate only on things to which they are causally sensitive, and obviously they are not causally sensitive to everything there might be. So his triangulation argument alone does not rule out the transcendence thesis; any objections to it must come from a broader theory of belief.

Whether Davidson actually had an argument against the transcendence thesis and, if he did, how convincing it is are once again very interesting and important questions that we will not pursue any further in this chapter. Our point here has simply been to note that, while Davidson's theory of content certainly does rehabilitate realism, it still leaves us with much work to do, as both metaphysical and epistemological questions remain to be answered. One can agree with Davidson that classical realists exaggerate the extent to which reality is independent from thought, while still wondering whether and how some version of the transcendence thesis might turn out to be correct; one can agree with Davidson that "nothing can count as a reason for holding a belief except another belief," while still wondering whether and how the concept of truth can direct our inquiries from within our beliefs. Thus, much as we appreciate Rorty's (1987: 113) acknowledgement that "Davidson's work seems to me the culmination of a line of thought in American philosophy which aims at being naturalistic without being reductionist," we would add a caveat.[44] By demonstrating how fruitfully pragmatist insights can be applied to questions about content, Davidson did indeed

---

[42] This way of putting things would require delicate handling in the case of some social realities, but the many interesting and often difficult questions this raises are best left for another time.

[43] Very often, of course, realists have argued that reality is independent of thought in both the metaphysical and the transcendence senses.

[44] Rorty is to be commended, however, for highlighting the non-reductive character of Davidson's thought.

advance this line of thought a great distance; but its culmination seems to us still to be some way off.[45]

References

Amoretti, M. C. and Preyer, G. (eds.) (2011). *Triangulation: From an Epistemological Point of View*. Frankfurt: Ontos Verlag.

Blackburn, S. (2013). 'Pragmatism: All or Some?', in Price 2013.

Brandom, R. (ed.) (2000). *Rorty and His Critics*. Oxford: Blackwell.

Davidson, D. (1983). 'A Coherence Theory of Truth and Knowledge', in Davidson 2001a.

Davidson, D. (1987). 'Afterthoughts', in Davidson 2001a.

Davidson, D. (1988). 'Epistemology and Truth', in Davidson 2001a.

Davidson, D. (1991). 'Epistemology Externalized', in Davidson 2001a.

Davidson, D. (1995). 'The Objectivity of Value', in Davidson 2004.

Davidson, D. (1997). 'Indeterminism and Antirealism', in Davidson 2001a.

Davidson, D. (1999). 'Reply to Thomas Nagel', in Hahn 1999.

Davidson, D. (2000). 'Truth Rehabilitated', in Brandom 2000.

Davidson, D. (2001a). *Subjective, Intersubjective, Objective*. Oxford: Clarendon Press.

Davidson, D. (2001b). 'Externalisms', in Kotatko et al. 2001.

Davidson, D. (2001c). 'Comments on Karlovy Vary Papers', in Kotatko et al. 2001.

Davidson, D. (2004). *Problems of Rationality*. Oxford: Clarendon Press.

de Caro, M. and Macarthur, D. (eds.) (2010). *Naturalism and Normativity*. New York: Columbia University Press.

Hahn, L. (ed.) (1999). *The Philosophy of Donald Davidson*. Chicago and La Salle, IL: Open Court.

Kotatko, P., Pagin, P., and Segal, G. (eds.) (2001). *Interpreting Davidson*. Stanford: CSLI.

Levine, S. (2008). 'Rorty, Davidson, and the New Pragmatists', *Philosophical Topics* 36–1: 167–92.

Macarthur, D. and Price, H. (2007). 'Pragmatism, Quasi-Realism, and the Global Challenge', in Price 2011.

Misak, C. (ed.) (2007). *The New Pragmatists*. Oxford: Oxford University Press.

Myers, R. H. (2017). 'Holism in Action', in Verheggen 2017a.

Myers, R. H. (2019). 'Davidson's Meta-Normative Naturalism', *Journal for the History of Analytical Philosophy* 7: 48–58.

---

[45] Thanks to Joshua Gert, Muhammad Ali Khalidi, Sam Steadman, Olivia Sultanescu, and an audience at the University of Chicago for many very helpful comments on earlier drafts of this chapter.

Myers, R. H. (2020). 'Replies to Kirk Ludwig and Paul Hurley', *Dialogue: Canadian Philosophical Review* 59: 255–69.

Myers, R. H. (2021). 'Davidson's Meta-Normative Naturalism and the Rationality Requirement', in Yang and Myers 2021.

Myers, R. H. and Verheggen, C. (2016). *Donald Davidson's Triangulation Argument: A Philosophical Inquiry*, New York: Routledge.

Nagel, T. (1986). *The View from Nowhere*, New York: Oxford University Press.

Nagel, T. (1999). 'Davidson's New Cogito', in Hahn 1999.

Price, H. (2003). 'Truth as Convenient Friction', in Price 2011.

Price, H. (2011). *Naturalism Without Mirrors*, Oxford: Oxford University Press.

Price, H. (2013). *Expressivism, Pragmatism and Representationalism*, Cambridge: Cambridge University Press.

Putnam, H. (1978). *Meaning and the Moral Sciences*, London: Routledge.

Ramberg, B. (2000). 'Post-Ontological Philosophy of Mind: Rorty versus Davidson', in Brandom 2000.

Rorty, R. (1979). *Philosophy and the Mirror of Nature*, Princeton: Princeton University Press.

Rorty, R. (1986). 'Pragmatism, Davidson, and Truth', in Rorty 1991.

Rorty, R. (1987). 'Non-Reductive Physicalism', in Rorty 1991.

Rorty, R. (1991). *Objectivity, Relativism and Truth: Philosophical Papers*, vol. 1. New York: Cambridge University Press.

Rorty, R. (1995). 'Is Truth a Goal of Inquiry? Donald Davidson versus Crispin Wright', in Rorty 1998.

Rorty, R. (1998). *Truth and Progress: Philosophical Papers*, vol. 3. New York: Cambridge University Press.

Rorty, R. (2000a). 'Response to Davidson', in Brandom 2000.

Rorty, R. (2000b). 'Response to Ramberg', in Brandom 2000.

Rorty, R. and Price, H. (2010). 'Exchange on "Truth as Convenient Friction"', in de Caro and Macarthur 2010.

Simpson, M. (2020). 'What Is Global Expressivism?' *The Philosophical Quarterly* 70/278, 140–61.

Stout, J. (2007). 'On Our Interest in Getting Things Right: Pragmatism without Narcissism', in Misak 2007.

Verheggen, C. (1997). 'Davidson's Second Person', *The Philosophical Quarterly* 47/188, 361–9.

Verheggen, C. (2005). 'Stroud on Wittgenstein, Meaning, and Community', *Dialogue: Canadian Philosophical Review* 54: 67–85.

Verheggen, C. (2006). 'How Social Must Language Be?' *Journal for the Theory of Social Behavior* 36/2: 203–19.

Verheggen, C. (2007). 'Triangulating with Davidson', *The Philosophical Quarterly* 57/226: 96–103.

Verheggen, C. (2011). 'Triangulation and Philosophical Skepticism', in Amoretti and Preyer 2011.

Verheggen, C. (ed.) (2017a). *Wittgenstein and Davidson on Language, Thought and Action*, Cambridge: Cambridge University Press.

Verheggen, C. (2017b). 'Davidson's Treatment of Wittgenstein's Rule-Following Paradox', in Verheggen 2017a.

Verheggen, C. (2017c). 'Davidson's Semantic Externalism: From Radical Interpretation to Triangulation', special issue for the centenary of Donald Davidson's birth, *Argumenta* 3/1: 145–61.

Verheggen, C. (2021). 'The Continuity of Davidson's Thought: Non-Reductionism without Quietism', in Yang and Myers 2021.

Yang, S. C. and Myers, R. H. (eds.) (2021). *Donald Davidson on Action, Mind and Value*. Singapore: Springer.

9
What Is Linguistic Interpretation?

José L. Zalabardo

1. Pragmatist Accounts of Meaning Grounds

In metaphysics we often inquire into the ultimate nature of a specific region of facts.* We ask how things would have to stand in the world in order for, say, an ethical, causal, mathematical, or counterfactual fact to obtain. For each of these areas of metaphysical research, there is a corresponding area of semantic research, concerning the meaning of the linguistic expressions (or the content of the mental items) with which we represent the relevant facts. Thus, for example, corresponding to the metaphysical question, what is it for something to be good, we have the semantic question, what is it for the predicate "good" to have the meaning it has.

When we ask the semantic question, we aim to identify a ground for the meaning of the target expression, its *meaning ground*—what makes it the case that the expression has the meaning it has. This involves identifying necessary and/or sufficient conditions for a linguistic expression to have the meaning of the one we are interested in. Where should we look for the meaning grounds of linguistic expressions?

When we are interested in the meaning of the linguistic expressions with which we represent a region of facts, one obvious place to look for their meaning grounds is in the semantic links between the expressions and the region of the world they purport to represent. I'm going to refer to this approach as *representationalism*. On the representationalist approach, a sentence has the meaning it has as a result of its connection with the state of affairs it represents as obtaining. The sentence "Fido barks" has the meaning it has by virtue of its connection with the possible state of affairs, Fido's barking, that the sentence represents as obtaining. This sentence-state of affairs link can be treated as primitive or, more commonly, as the result of referential links between subsentential expressions and the items in whose combination states of affairs consist—individuals, properties, relations, etc. On this version of the view, the sentence "Fido barks" represents the state of affairs of Fido barking as a result of referential links between the name,

---

* I am grateful to Joshua Gert, Javier González de Prado Salas, Huw Price, and Matthew Simpson for their comments on this material.

José L. Zalabardo, *What Is Linguistic Interpretation?* In: *Neopragmatism: Interventions in First-Order Philosophy*. Edited by: Joshua Gert, Oxford University Press. © José L. Zalabardo 2023. DOI: 10.1093/oso/9780192894809.003.0009

"Fido," and the dog, Fido, and between the predicate "barks" and the property of barking.[1]

Now, if the facts represented by the sentences we are interested in call for a metaphysical account, a representationalist account of the meaning grounds of these sentences will have to be built on our metaphysical account of the facts the sentences represent. Thus, for example, on a representationalist account of the meaning ground of the sentence "stealing is wrong," the sentence would have the meaning it has as a result of referential links between the noun, "stealing," and the action, stealing, and between the predicate, "is wrong," and the property it denotes, as identified by our metaphysical account of the nature of moral facts.

There's a family of views according to which metaphysical questions concerning a range of facts are pre-empted or undercut by our account of the corresponding semantic questions. On this approach, the explanatory need that we might have tried to address with a metaphysical account can be addressed instead with the corresponding semantic account. Once we've provided an account of the meaning grounds of the expressions with which we represent the relevant family of facts, we've said everything a philosopher needs to say about these facts. Thus, for example, when applied to ethics, this approach dictates that once we have provided an account of the meaning grounds of ethical discourse, we don't need to provide, in addition, an account of ethical facts. The semantic account tells us all we need to know about the corresponding facts. I'm going to refer as the *pre-emption thesis* to the view that our account of the semantic grounds of a discourse pre-empts in this way a metaphysical account of the facts the discourse purports to represent.[2]

It should be clear that the pre-emption thesis is incompatible with a representationalist account of the meaning grounds of the relevant sentences. The pre-emption thesis concerning a discourse dictates that an account of the meaning grounds of the expressions of the discourse removes the need for a metaphysical account of the region of reality that the discourse purports to represent. But if our account of the meaning grounds of the expressions of the discourse is representationalist, it will presuppose the metaphysical account that we should be able to do without if the pre-emption thesis were correct. It follows that subscribing to the pre-emption thesis with respect to a discourse commits us to a non-representationalist account of the meaning grounds of its expressions.

Where else could we look for meaning grounds for a discourse? One unquestionable source of meaning grounds for some linguistic expressions is the way the expressions are used. Consider linguistic expressions like "hello," "mayday," or

---

[1] The mode of combination that the referents of the term are represented as exemplifying (here, the individual as instantiating the property) would also have to be fixed by the meaning grounds of the sentence. We'll leave this aspect of the problem to one side here.
[2] Terence Cuneo (2020) offers an interesting critical discussion of the pre-emption thesis in ethics. He uses the term *undercutting*.

"you're welcome." Clearly what makes these expressions have the meanings they have is not a semantic link to some region of the world. The most plausible account of their meaning grounds appeals to the way they are used. What makes "hello" have the meaning it has is the fact that it's used as a salutation or greeting, or to begin a phone conversation. If you know that "hello" is used like that, you know the meaning of the word, and any expression that is used in that way has the same meaning as "hello."[3]

That the meaning grounds of some linguistic expressions consist in the way they are used is hardly controversial. What's much less clear is that this approach can be successfully applied to sentences that appear to have the function of representing things as being a certain way. I'm going to use the label *pragmatist* for accounts of the meaning grounds of sentences with an ostensive representational function in terms of the way the sentences are used. Notice that pragmatist accounts have the same (semantic) subject matter as representationalist accounts. The difference registered by the labels doesn't concern their explananda but their explanantia. Representationalists seek to specify meaning grounds in terms of language-world relations; pragmatists aim to do it in terms of features of language use (see Price 2011a).

Pragmatist accounts of the meaning grounds of declarative sentences typically focus on two aspects of their use that we can label as *upstream* and *downstream* (see Brandom 2011: 49). They both involve the phenomenon of sincere assertion or acceptance of the sentence as true. Upstream features of the way a sentence is used concern the procedures used by speakers for deciding whether to accept it as true. Downstream features concern the consequences of accepting the sentence as true. The pragmatist's hope is that upstream and downstream features of the use of a sentence will provide its meaning ground.[4]

We can get a sense of how the pragmatist proposal would work by considering some ideas deployed by expressivist metaethicists in their account of ethical language (Ayer 1936; Stevenson 1944; Gibbard 1990, 2003; Schroeder 2008). Take the sentence "killing one to save five is morally right." Upstream aspects of the use of this sentence concern how speakers decide whether to accept it as true. On one simplistic but not altogether implausible account, we do this in terms of our moral sense. We accept the sentence as true just in case we feel moral approval towards the killing of one to save five. Downstream aspects of the use of the

---

[3] The link between meaning and use is one of the central ideas of Wittgenstein's later philosophy: "For a *large* class of cases of the employment of the word 'meaning'—though not for *all*—this word can be explained in this way: the meaning of a word is its use in the language" (Wittgenstein 2009: §43).

[4] The strategy for explaining the meaning of declarative sentences that Saul Kripke finds in the later Wittgenstein exhibits a parallel structure. It consists in providing answers to two questions: "first, 'Under what conditions may this form of words be appropriately asserted (or denied)?'; second, given an answer to the first question, 'What is the role, and the utility, in our lives of the practice of asserting (and denying) the form of words under those conditions?'" (Kripke 1982: 73).

sentence concern the consequences of accepting it as true. One consequence that stands out is the motivation to engage in or promote the action in question. A simplistic but, again, not hugely implausible pragmatist account of the meaning ground of the sentence would invoke these two aspects of its use. On this account, what makes the sentence have the meaning it has is (a) the fact that its acceptance is regulated by the speaker's sense of moral approval with respect to the killing of one to save five; and (b) the fact that its acceptance produces the motivation to perform or promote the action. On this account, the presence of these two features in the use of a sentence will be necessary and sufficient for the sentence to have the meaning that we attach to "killing one to save five is morally right."

Notice that subscribing to this account of the meaning ground of the sentence doesn't enjoin a commitment to an account in terms of (a) and (b) of the state of affairs that the sentence represents as obtaining. The pragmatist's goal is to specify what makes the sentence "killing one to save five is morally right" have the meaning it has. She's not aiming to specify, in addition, what would have to be the case for the sentence to be true—what would make it the case that killing one to save five is morally right.

Now, expressivists will add to this account of the meaning ground of the sentence their headline claim about its function. On this view, the function of ethical language is not to represent things as being a certain way, but to express the attitude of moral approval that regulates acceptance of ethical sentences. This second component of the view—the claim that the sentences of the discourse have a non-representational function—is widely seen by both supporters and opponents as a consequence of the first—the specification of the meaning grounds of the sentences in pragmatist terms. According to this line of thought, a pragmatist account of the meaning ground of a sentence is incompatible with ascribing to the sentence the function of representing the world. Hence, if the discourse is not to be treated as idle, a different, non-representational function will need to be found for it. Perhaps we'll be able to speak as if the discourse was in the business of representing, but this would have to be treated merely as a way of speaking, to be contrasted with the genuine representational role of sentences whose meaning grounds are specified along representationalist lines.[5]

There's a powerful line of reasoning in support of this position. If a sentence represents the world, there has to be a state of affairs that the sentence represents as obtaining, and the link to this state of affairs will be a necessary condition for the sentence to have the meaning it has. But if the sentence has a pragmatist meaning ground, then a feature of the way it's used will be a sufficient condition for the sentence to have the meaning it has. The problem is that these two claims

---

[5] Huw Price has argued that discourses with a primarily non-representational function can nevertheless be "descriptive, fact-stating, truth-apt, cognitive, belief-expressing, or whatever—and full-bloodedly so, not merely in some ersatz or 'quasi' sense" (Price 2011b: 136).

are incompatible—unless the sentence being used in that way is a sufficient condition for its link to the state of affairs it represents as obtaining.

This is a powerful challenge to the view that pragmatist meaning grounds are compatible with the function of representing the world. However, as I argue elsewhere (Zalabardo forthcoming), the challenge can be overcome. We can treat the way a sentence is used as a sufficient condition for the sentence's link to the state of affairs it represents as obtaining without extracting from the way the sentence is used a specification of the state of affairs playing this role that could sustain a representationalist account of the meaning ground of the sentence. This paves the way for treating sentences with pragmatist meaning grounds as successfully discharging the representational function, in whatever sense this function can be ascribed to any sentence. I'm not going to argue this point here, and I'm not going to assume it's correct. However, I'm not going to assume either that a pragmatist account of the meaning ground of a sentence forces us to ascribe to it a non-representational function. I'm going to discuss pragmatist accounts without making any assumptions about the consequences they may or may not have concerning the possibility of ascribing a representational function to the target discourse.

I've argued that the availability of a non-representationalist account of the meaning grounds of a discourse is a necessary condition for the pre-emption thesis to hold for the discourse—for the account of the meaning grounds of the discourse to pre-empt a metaphysical account of the region of facts that the discourse purports to represent. I have not argued, in addition, that it's a sufficient condition. Other obstacles stand in the way of the pre-emption thesis that fall outside the scope of this chapter.

2. Pragmatist Accounts of Interpretation

Lists of regions of reality that call for a metaphysical account often reserve a prominent place for facts to the effect that a sentence (or thought) represents things as being a certain way, like the fact that with the sentence "der Schnee ist weiß" (and the thought that it expresses), Kurt represents snow as being white. I'm going to refer to this phenomenon as *propositional representation*, and I'm going to concentrate on its linguistic version, leaving the mental aspect to one side. A metaphysical account of propositional representation would have to specify how things would have to stand in the world in order for Kurt's sentence to represent snow as being white. Discharging this task would normally require identifying a relation between sentences, on the one hand, and items in the world, on the other, that determines how sentences represent things as being. This relation would have to connect Kurt's sentence with the world in a way that makes it represent snow as being white.

As with other metaphysical problems of this kind, corresponding to the metaphysical question concerning the ultimate nature of propositional representation there is a semantic question concerning the meaning of the sentences with which we represent propositional-representation facts. I'm going to refer to the sentences with which we achieve this as *interpretations*. A typical interpretation is the sentence:

(S) "With the sentence 'der Schnee ist weiß', Kurt represents snow as being white"

Corresponding to the metaphysical problem of propositional representation, we have the semantic problem of identifying the meaning grounds of interpretations—specifying what has to be the case in order for an interpretation to have the meaning it has.

We can undertake this task using the representationalist strategy. This would involve treating the meaning of interpretations as arising from semantic relations they bear to the world—e.g. treating the meaning of (S) as arising from semantic relations it bears to Kurt's sentence, to the state of affairs of snow being white (or to its constituents) and to a relation between the former and the latter that determines how sentences represent things as being.[6]

However, here, as elsewhere, the representationalist approach is incompatible with the pre-emption thesis. An advocate of the pre-emption thesis with respect to propositional representation would have to find an alternative, non-representationalist account of the meaning grounds of interpretations. The pragmatist approach is a salient alternative, and this is the approach that I want to explore in the remainder of this chapter.

As we saw in the preceding section, the aspects of the use of declarative sentences typically invoked in pragmatist accounts of meaning grounds concern the speakers' acceptance of sentences as true. They include upstream features—related to the procedures that speakers employ for deciding whether to accept the sentences as true, and downstream features—related to the consequences of acceptance. The pragmatist's aspiration is to locate among these the facts that make it the case that a sentence has the meaning it has. My goal is to consider how this template could be applied to the task of providing a pragmatist account of the meaning grounds of interpretations.

The task can be understood in the following terms. An interpretation pairs a sentence with a possible state of affairs.[7] The state of affairs paired with a sentence

---

[6] The application of the representationalist approach to semantic discourse faces familiar puzzles, manifested in the fact that the term "represents" would have to be paired with a semantic relation by that very same relation. See Putnam (1978, 1981); Zalabardo (1998); Price (2011c: 193–5); Button (2013).

[7] Alternatively, interpretation can be construed as pairing sentences with sentences of the interpreter's language. It may turn out that the two approaches are ultimately equivalent, as it can be argued

by an interpretation is the state of affairs that the sentence represents as obtaining, according to the interpretation.[8] (S), for example, pairs Kurt's sentence with the state of affairs of snow being white. According to (S), snow being white is the state of affairs that Kurt's sentence represents as obtaining. Specifying the meaning grounds of interpretations requires identifying conditions under which a pairing of a sentence with a possible state of affairs is an interpretation, according to which the former represents the latter as obtaining. The pragmatist's claim, and our working hypothesis, is that these conditions can be found among upstream and downstream aspects of the practice of interpreting. Let me refer to any practice that produces and uses pairings of sentences with states of affairs as a *pairing practice*. The pragmatist hopes to find in our interpreting practice upstream and downstream features that can be plausibly regarded as necessary and sufficient for a pairing practice to count as producing interpretations. A pairing practice will produce interpretations of sentences as representing the states of affairs it pairs with them if and only if it exhibits these features. In the remainder of this chapter, my goal will be to develop a proposal for a pragmatist specification of the meaning grounds of interpretations, by identifying features of our interpretative practice that can plausibly play this role.

3. Meaning and Belief

One prominent consequence of accepting interpretations is the ascription of propositional attitudes, such as beliefs, desires, etc., to speakers. Ascriptions of propositional attitudes can of course also be based on non-linguistic evidence, but for linguistic creatures, what they say is the main source of information about what they believe, desire, etc.[9] I'm going to focus on the link between interpretation and belief ascription. The link is provided by the attitude of holding a sentence true.[10] When the interpreter believes that the speaker holds this attitude towards a sentence, she will ascribe to the speaker a belief in the obtaining of the state of affairs with which she has interpreted the sentence. If you believe that Kurt holds "der Schnee ist weiß" true, and you interpret the sentence as representing

---

that an interpreter can pair a sentence with a state of affairs only by pairing it with one of her sentences that represents the state of affairs as obtaining. The consequences of this are important and complicated. For the sentence-sentence approach, see Carnap (1956); Davidson (2001b); Field (2017).

[8] Pairing a sentence with the state of affairs it represents as obtaining might not amount to a full interpretation of the sentence, as sentence meanings are more fine-grained than states of affairs due to familiar Fregean considerations (Frege 1980). I'm not going to be concerned with this aspect of the problem here.

[9] For non-linguistic ascriptions of beliefs and desires, see Zalabardo (2019).

[10] The notion is of course central to Davidson's account of radical interpretation (Davidson 1973: 322), where it plays the same role that the notion of assent played in Quine's account of radical translation (Quine 1960: ch. 2).

the state of affairs of snow being white, you will ascribe to Kurt the belief that snow is white.

Determining whether a speaker holds a sentence true is not always straightforward. By asserting a sentence, a speaker presents herself as holding it true, but assertion is a voluntary act that can be performed for sentences that the speaker doesn't hold true. Only from sincere assertion does it follow directly that the speaker holds the sentence true.[11] The link from assertion to belief is always conditional on the assumption that the assertion is sincere.

This feature of our interpretative practice can be formulated as a condition that a pairing practice may or may not satisfy. Let's say that a pairing practice is *belief relevant* just in case it satisfies the following condition:

> The practitioners have identified an attitude that speakers can hold to sentences such that if the practitioners support a sentence-state of affairs pairing and they believe that a speaker holds this attitude towards the sentence, they will ascribe to the speaker the belief that the state of affairs obtains.

I'm claiming that our interpretative practice is belief relevant. I claim, in addition, that belief relevance should play a central role in any plausible pragmatist account of the meaning grounds of interpretations: a pairing practice should count as producing interpretations only if it is belief relevant.

Belief relevance is a downstream feature of our interpretative practice, but it has upstream consequences. For a restricted but important range of states of affairs, we have non-linguistic procedures for determining whether a subject believes in their obtaining. If the subject picks her umbrella when she leaves the house, this supports ascribing to her the belief that it's going to rain. This support will be conditional on hypotheses concerning her desires (e.g. that she doesn't want to get wet) but we can leave this complication aside for our present purposes. Now, suppose there are two rival interpretations of a sentence the subject holds true: according to one, the sentence represents the weather as being dry; according to the other, the sentence represents the weather as being wet. Her picking up the umbrella will give us a reason for favouring the second interpretation over the first—or if the first interpretation has considerable independent support, for giving up the claim that the speaker holds the sentence true.

If, as I'm suggesting, any interpretative practice has to be belief relevant, its procedure for selecting interpretations will also have to take this factor into account.[12] I'm going to argue next that there are other aspects of the procedure we

---

[11] Even sincere assertion is compatible with absence of belief, as the phenomenon of self-deception demonstrates. Here I will ignore this complication.

[12] David Lewis rightly accused W. V. O. Quine of failing to take account of this factor in his construal of our interpretative practice: "Too much emphasis goes to language as a vehicle for

employ for selecting interpretations that can also be plausibly included in their meaning grounds.

4. Compositionality

A declarative sentence represents things as being a certain way by representing a state of affairs as obtaining. On a standard metaphysical picture, states of affairs are produced by the combination of more simple items. Thus, for example, the state of affairs of Fido barking, on this picture, is produced when the individual, Fido, and the property of barking are combined with one another in the way that we call (monadic) instantiation—when the individual instantiates the property. Then all the states of affairs involving Fido will have a common constituent, and the same will go for all the states of affairs about barking.[13]

This metaphysical picture is not mandatory. One might hold instead that states of affairs are ultimate, irreducible units, rather than the result of combining more elementary items. On this picture, state of affairs 'constituents', such as the individual, Fido, or the property of barking, should be regarded as abstractions based on similarities between states of affairs—between the states of affairs that we describe as concerning Fido, or those that we describe as involving barking.[14]

These two metaphysical pictures offer different accounts of the relationship between the state of affairs of Fido barking, on the one hand, and the individual Fido and the property of barking, on the other. On the first picture, individual and property are the fundamental items, and the state of affairs is construed as produced by the combination of these. On the second picture, the state of affairs is fundamental, and individual and property are construed in terms of similarity relations between states of affairs. However, both approaches are compatible with the following claim:

CONSTITUENTS: the relationship between states of affairs and their constituents is essential to the identity of states of affairs.

According to CONSTITUENTS, Fido barking would not be the state of affairs it is if it didn't involve Fido and barking, whether we construe these as fundamental items or as resulting from relations of similarity between states of affairs. I'm going to assume that CONSTITUENTS is correct.

---

manifestation of belief and belief as manifest in language; not enough either to language as a social practice or to belief as manifest in non-linguistic behavior" (Lewis 1974: 341).

[13] In Zalabardo (2017), I refer to this view as the Combinatorial Account of Facts.

[14] I've argued that Wittgenstein's *Tractatus Logico-Philosophicus* (1974) advances this position (Zalabardo 2015: ch. 4; 2018). For this attribution, see also Skyrms (1981) and McCarty (1991). The position is also defended in Armstrong (1997).

Now, a system of propositional representation could have the following features:

a. The items with which states of affairs are represented as obtaining (e.g. sentences, or thoughts) are built from a common stock of constituents (or exhibit common features).
b. These constituents are paired with the constituents of the states of affairs that the system represents as obtaining.
c. The pairing of representational items with states of affairs is derived from the pairing of constituents of the former with constituents of the latter: a representational item represents as obtaining the state of affairs whose constituents are the items paired with the constituents of the representational item.[15]

Let's say that a system of propositional representation is *compositional* when it exhibits these features. It's clear that our representations of states of affairs in English and other natural languages is compositional in this sense. The sentence "Fido barks" represents Fido as barking as a result of a pairing between the name, "Fido," and the dog, Fido, and between the predicate, "barks," and the property of barking. The state of affairs the sentence represents as obtaining has as its constituents the items paired with the constituents of the sentence.

It has been argued that all human languages have to be compositional, or even that any system of propositional representation has to be compositional.[16] I find these claims very plausible, and I'm going to restrict my discussion of our procedure for selecting interpretations to the interpretation of compositional languages. My conclusions will only apply to the interpretation of compositional languages, whether or not these exhaust the range of actual or possible languages.

Our procedures for selecting interpretations of sentences typically exploit the compositional structure of these. We think that Kurt's sentence represents snow as being white because we think that "der Schnee" as meant by Kurt, refers to snow, and "ist weiß," as meant by Kurt, refers to the property of being white. Let's say that an interpretation procedure for a compositional language is *compositional* when its interpretations are selected in this way.

It's an interesting and difficult question whether an interpretation of a compositional language has to be compositional. Michael Dummett gives an example of

---

[15] This formulation assumes that each set of constituents can form (or be present in) at most one state of affairs. The fact that this assumption is wrong is a source of important difficulties that will not concern us here.
[16] Donald Davidson (2001c) has provided an argument for the view. Wittgenstein's *Tractatus* appears to defend the stronger claim that compositionality is essential to the very idea of propositional representation: "In a proposition there must be exactly as many distinguishable parts as in the situation that it represents" (1974: 4.04). On this point, see Bronzo (2011).

what a non-compositional interpretation of a compositional language would look like. He asks us to imagine that he hears a Basque sentence and is told that it means that the pigeons have returned to the dovecote, even though he cannot segment the sentence into components that he can recognize in other sentences (Dummett 1981: 308–9). According to Dummett, the knowledge of the meaning of the Basque sentence that we obtain in this way doesn't count as real understanding. I'm very sympathetic to Dummett's claim here, and to the general thought that a pairing practice has to be compositional in order to count as producing genuine interpretations. However, rather than offering support for this claim, I'm going to treat it as an assumption, I'm going to restrict my attention to compositional interpretations (of compositional languages). I'm going to describe our procedure for selecting interpretations of compositional languages compositionally. If all interpretations of compositional languages have to be compositional, this will count as our universal procedure for interpreting compositional languages. If, in addition, all systems of propositional representation have to be compositional, the procedure I'm going to describe will be our universal procedure for interpreting propositional representations.

5. Charity

I argued in section 3 that our interpretative practice is belief relevant and that this has consequences for the procedures we employ for selecting interpretations— how we interpret the sentences that a speaker holds true has to be contrasted with non-linguistic evidence concerning her beliefs. In what follows, it will be convenient for our purposes to consider also a parallel attitude of holding a sentence false. Now belief relevance will include also that interpreters have identified an attitude such that if they believe that a speaker holds this attitude towards a sentence they will ascribe to her the belief that the state of affairs with which they've interpreted the sentence doesn't obtain.

I want to consider next a family of characterizations of our interpretative practice according to which the interpretation of sentences that speakers hold true/ false plays a role that doesn't follow from belief relevance. They focus, not on whether the speakers actually have the beliefs ascribed in this way, but on whether the beliefs the speaker would have, if these ascriptions were correct, satisfy certain conditions. Let's say that a criterion for selecting interpretations is *doxastic* when it is based on conditions imposed on the beliefs that the speaker would have if the belief ascriptions generated by each interpretation were correct. I am going to argue that our procedure for selecting interpretations employs a doxastic criterion.

The view that our interpretative procedures employ a doxastic criterion is a central component of the accounts of translation/interpretation advanced by

W. V. O. Quine and Donald Davidson (see Quine 1960: ch. 2; Davidson 1973). The specific doxastic criterion that Quine and Davidson find in our interpretative practice is the principle of charity: we select interpretations with the goal of maximizing truth in the beliefs ascribed to the speaker as a result of each interpretation.[17] Satisfaction of the charity criterion is generally a matter of interpreting sentences that the speaker holds true with states of affairs that obtain and sentences that the speaker holds false with states of affairs that don't obtain. However, the ordering of interpretations according to the degree to which they satisfy the criterion is complicated. It's not simply a matter of how many of the sentences that the speaker holds true/false receive charitable interpretations. Some beliefs are more important than others. A set *A* of beliefs could provide a more accurate representation of the world than a set of beliefs *B* even if *B* contains more true beliefs and fewer false beliefs than *A*. Also, the ordering can only be partial. There are lots of cases in which neither of two sets of beliefs provides a more accurate representation of the world than the other.

It will be interesting to see how the charity criterion works in a very simple case. Let's suppose we are interpreting a very rudimentary language, all of whose sentences have a subject-predicate structure, with a predicate ascribed to a singular term. Let's suppose that all combinations of a singular term with a predicate produce a meaningful subject-predicate sentence in this language.

A compositional interpretation of this language will pair each singular term with an individual and each predicate with a property. As a result, each sentence of the language will be paired with a possible state of affairs. To apply the charity criterion to an interpretation, we would consider whether it pairs the sentences the speaker holds true with obtaining states of affairs and the sentences she holds false with non-obtaining states of affairs.

To see how this would work in more detail, suppose we have interpreted all the predicates of the language, and we need to select an interpretation for singular term "a." To apply the charity criterion, we would consider the "a"-involving sentences that that speaker holds true and those that she holds false, and the properties with which the predicates in these sentences have been interpreted. We would then pick as the referent of "a" the individual that is most accurately represented as instantiating the properties that the interpretation pairs with predicates in the held-true sentences and as failing to instantiate the properties paired with the predicates in the held-false sentences.

The points we made above about the ordering of interpretations generated by the charity criterion apply in this restricted scenario. The degree of satisfaction of

---

[17] Notice that the charity criterion is only effective for compositional interpretations. For a non-compositional interpretation the criterion can be maximally satisfied in each case by pairing every sentence that the speaker holds true with the state of affairs of snow being white. With the compositionality constraint in place these trivializing interpretations are no longer available.

the criterion by an interpretation of "a" won't be merely a matter of counting the "a"-involving held-true sentences interpreted with obtaining states of affairs and the "a"-involving held-false sentences interpreted with non-obtaining states of affairs. Also, we cannot assume that there will be a winner in each case. We can't rule out cases in which instantiating the properties paired with the predicates in the "a"-involving held-true sentences and failing to instantiate the properties paired with the predicates in the "a"-involving held-false sentences provides a maximally accurate description of more than one individual.

A similar procedure would be employed to select the interpretation of a predicate "P," assuming now that all the singular terms have already been interpreted. To apply the charity criterion, we would consider the "P"-involving sentences that that speaker holds true and those she holds false, and the individuals with which the singular terms in these sentences have been interpreted. We would pick as the referent of "P" the property whose extension comes closest to including the individuals paired with the singular terms in the "P"-involving held-true sentences and excluding the individuals paired with the singular terms in the "P"-involving held-false sentences. As before, this won't be simply a matter of how many of the relevant individuals each interpretation places in the right category. Also, we need to be open to the possibility that two or more properties satisfy the criterion to the maximum degree.

But these simplifications are artificial. We can't apply the charity criterion to the interpretation of predicates without applying it to the interpretation of singular terms and vice versa. We can apply the criterion only to an interpretation of all terms at once. In order to assess an interpretation according to the charity criterion, we would consider the states of affairs that would be represented, on that interpretation, by the sentences that the speaker holds true, and those that would be represented by the sentences she holds false. The degree to which the interpretation satisfies the criterion would be determined by how accurately the world is represented as involving the obtaining of the former states of affairs and the non-obtaining of the latter.

6. Permutations

The claim that our interpretative procedure is based on the principle of charity has received many objections. One prominent line of attack is most easily presented with respect to an account of the interpretation of predicates according to which they are paired, not with properties, but with sets of individuals—the individuals the predicate is true of (see Hochberg 1967). Consider the simple language introduced in the previous section, and take an arbitrary assignment of denotations to the singular terms of the language that pairs different terms with different denotations. Now, if "P" is a predicate of the language, consider the

"P"-involving sentences that the speaker holds true, and interpret "P" with the set of objects paired by the interpretation with the singular terms that figure in these sentences. If we do this for every predicate of the language, we get an interpretation on which all the sentences that the speaker holds true come out true and all the sentences she holds false come out false. The interpretation satisfies the charity criterion perfectly.[18]

Clearly our procedure for selecting interpretations doesn't generally favour candidates produced in this way. An interpretation of this kind can be built on any interpretation of the singular terms, but we do think that some interpretations of the singular terms are better than others. Furthermore, we routinely favour interpretations that result in the ascription of some false beliefs over those that produce only true-belief ascriptions.

One device that we use for selecting interpretations of singular terms is ostension. With an ostensive gesture, a speaker can point to the location of the referent of a singular term.[19] The procedure is not completely unambiguous—e.g. pointing at the statue is indistinguishable from pointing at the lump of clay—but it can rule out huge numbers of candidates. Notice also that we might occasionally accept an interpretation that pairs a singular term with an individual that wasn't in the location pointed at by an ostensive explanation. It's perfectly possible for a speaker to occasionally misidentify an object as the referent of one of her terms. This feature of our practice can be accommodated by the charity criterion. This can be achieved by treating ostensive explanations as on a par with sentences held true. Other things being equal, an interpretation that makes the ostensive explanation come out true would be preferred to one that doesn't, but the best overall interpretation could make an ostensive explanation come out false. Ostensive explanations of predicates are also possible. An ostensive explanation of a predicate will come out true on an interpretation when the ostended point contains an instance of the property with which the predicate is interpreted.

However, the cull of candidate interpretations that can be achieved by taking ostension into account will not completely solve the problem. For any interpretation of the singular terms that makes the ostensive explanations come out true, we can still use the procedure described to pair predicates with extensions in such a way that all the held-true sentences *and* ostensive explanations of predicates come out true and all the held-false sentences come out false.

Does the problem afflict also positions according to which predicates are interpreted with properties rather than sets of individuals? The answer depends on our view on which properties exist. Clearly, if we hold that for every set of individuals there is a property with that set as its extension, moving from extensions to

---

[18] A version of this argument can be found in Quine (1969). It was later used by Putnam in support of his conclusion that the ideal empirical theory must be true (Putnam 1978).

[19] See Quine's discussion of ostension in Quine (1969: 39–41).

properties won't improve our prospects. Even if we limit our commitment to finite sets of individuals the problem will persist. Beyond this, further restrictions on which properties are eligible as predicate referents will open the possibility of cases in which an interpretation that satisfies the charity criterion to a greater extent than any other will make some of the held-true sentences come out false.

One influential approach is to replace restrictions on which properties exist with a ranking of properties according to their degree of eligibility as predicates, and to use it alongside charity as an additional criterion for the selection of interpretations (Lewis 1984). On this approach, when two interpretations satisfy the charity criterion to the same extent, one will be preferable to the other if it pairs predicates with more eligible properties. Furthermore, an interpretation that loses out on the charity criterion might still be preferable overall, if its charity deficit is compensated for by a sufficient gain in the eligibility of its predicate referents.

7. Familiarity

I want to propose a different account of why we sometimes favour interpretations that don't satisfy the charity criterion to a greater extent than available alternatives. On this account, we prefer interpretations that pair terms with individuals and properties for which we have concepts. In general, we rank interpretations according to how easily we can define concepts for the individuals and properties they employ in terms of concepts we have.

We can illustrate how this consideration interacts with the charity criterion with an example discussed by Andrew Woodfield (1982: 276–7). As Woodfield explains, Spanish speakers are typically inclined to ascribe the predicate "rubio" not only to blond hair, but also to hair that is much too dark to count as blond. In light of this, the charity criterion would favour interpreting the predicate "rubio" as denoting the property of being either blond or light brown over interpreting it as denoting the property of being blond. Nevertheless, we may well prefer the latter interpretation even though it fares less well with respect to the charity criterion. I'm claiming that this is due to the fact that we have a concept denoting the property of being blond, whereas a concept for the property of being blond or light brown has to be constructed out of other concepts we do have. Notice that this preference would be hard to explain in terms of a notion of objective eligibility of properties, as the contrast between blond and not blond doesn't seem to be more natural or objective than the contrast between the hair shades to which Spanish speakers apply the term "rubio" and those to which they don't.

On an account of our interpretative practice that includes this, the problem considered in the previous section doesn't arise. The artificially constructed interpretations that guarantee maximal satisfaction of the charity criterion typically use as predicate referents properties for which we have no concepts, and constructing concepts for these properties in terms of concepts we have would involve highly complex definitions. This is the reason why they lose out to other interpretations that fare less well on the charity criterion.

So my proposal at this point is that our interpretative practice should be characterized as employing an additional criterion alongside charity, to which I'm going to refer as *familiarity*: select interpretations on the basis of how easy it is to construct, with our atomic concepts, concepts that refer to the properties and individuals each interpretation uses as referents. Thus, interpreting "rubio" as blond does worse than interpreting it as blond or light brown on the charity criterion, but better on the familiarity criterion.

The need to weigh up two criteria to select interpretations introduces another possible source of incommensurability between interpretations. When interpretation A does better than interpretation B on one criterion but worse on the other, it might not always be clear which of the two interpretations should be preferred all things considered.

8. Reference and Causation

There's an important family of cases that pose a problem for the charity criterion and can't be handled in terms of familiarity. Consider an otherwise normal English speaker who is unaware of the relevant biological facts and holds true sentences ascribing the predicate "is a fish" to singular terms that we have interpreted as referring to all types of swimming creatures, including both fish and marine mammals. Consider now the contest between interpreting "is a fish," as meant by her, as referring to the property of being a fish and interpreting it as referring to the property of being a swimming creature. Clearly, interpreting it as referring to the property of being a swimming creature does better on the charity criterion. It might do slightly worse on the familiarity criterion, but it's hard to see how this could outweigh the significant charity dividend.

I don't think we can avoid the conclusion that if our interpretative practice was governed by the charity and familiarity criteria we would prefer interpreting the predicate with the property of being a swimming creature to interpreting it with the property of being a fish. And yet, that doesn't seem to be the right interpretation. We can easily fill in the details of the case in such a way that it seems clear to us that the predicate should be interpreted with the property of being a fish and that we should ascribe to the speaker as a result false beliefs to the effect that marine mammals are fish.

A similar example can be obtained by adapting a case discussed by Saul Kripke, who asks us to imagine that, contrary to what most people think, Gödel was not in fact the author of the incompleteness theorem:

A man named 'Schmidt', whose body was found in Vienna under mysterious circumstances many years ago, actually did the work in question. His friend Gödel somehow got hold of the manuscript and it was thereafter attributed to Gödel.   Kripke (1980: 84)

Suppose we know these facts, but most other people don't. Consider now a speaker who is not aware of these facts and holds true the sentence "Kurt Gödel discovered the incompleteness of arithmetic." Suppose we have interpreted the predicate "discovered the incompleteness of arithmetic" as referring to the property of having discovered the incompleteness of arithmetic. Consider now the contest between interpreting the singular term "Gödel," as meant by this speaker, as referring to Gödel and interpreting it as referring to Schmidt. It is clear that the details of the case can be filled in in such a way that the latter interpretation is superior from the point of view of charity: the "Gödel"-involving sentence that the speaker holds true would come out true on the Schmidt interpretation but false on the Gödel interpretation, and there is no difference between the two interpretations with respect to the familiarity criterion. And yet, as Kripke argues, it would be wrong to interpret the speaker as referring to Schmidt by the term "Gödel." "Gödel," as meant by her, refers to Gödel, and the belief we attribute to her as a result of the "Gödel"-involving sentence she holds true is the false belief that Gödel discovered the incompleteness of arithmetic. Once again, the charity and familiarity criteria give the wrong results.[20]

Cases of this kind are usually considered in connection with the project of identifying representationalist meaning grounds for interpretations—by specifying what has to be the case in order for a sentence to represent a certain state of affairs as obtaining or for a term to have a certain referent. In this context, these cases are usually invoked in support of causal accounts of reference. On a familiar account of the reference of natural-kind terms, "fish" refers to the biological kind that's causally responsible for the surface features on the basis of which we decide to apply the predicate. And on an influential account of the reference of names, the referent of "Gödel" is determined by an act of baptism, in which a man received that name, to which our use of the name can be traced back through a chain of communication.

However, even if we don't think these ideas will ultimately sustain a successful representationalist account of the meaning grounds of interpretations, one might think that cases like these force us to adopt an account of our interpretative procedure according to which we assign referents to terms on the basis of causal relations between terms and referents. This would involve abandoning not only the charity criterion, but also the more general idea that we select interpretations on the basis of a doxastic criterion—in terms of the belief ascriptions generated by

---

[20] For another example of this phenomenon, see Grandy (1973: 445).

each interpretation, via the sentences that speakers hold true/false. I'm going to argue that the advocate of doxastic criteria doesn't need to concede defeat at this point. These cases do show that the charity criterion doesn't provide an accurate characterization of our interpretative procedure, but they can be successfully accommodated by a slightly different doxastic criterion.

9. Projection

Advocates of the charity criterion often emphasize the practical indistinguishability between charity and another doxastic criterion: select interpretations on the basis of the extent to which the beliefs attributed as a result of each interpretation agree with the beliefs of the interpreter.[21] The charity criterion and the agreement criterion are not equivalent. If the interpreter has false beliefs, the two criteria might generate different orderings of interpretations. However, interpreters will always obtain the same results with both criteria, since in order to determine the extent to which the beliefs attributed by an interpretation agree with how things stand in the world, all the interpreter has to go on is her own beliefs about how things stand in the world.

It follows that replacing the charity criterion with the agreement criterion would not give us any advantage in dealing with the cases we considered in the previous section. I'm going to argue, however, that a slight modification of the agreement criterion produces a doxastic criterion with the potential for accommodating the problematic cases. The proposal I want to explore is an instance of what Daniel Dennett has labelled *projective principles*. According to projective principles, Dennett writes, one should attribute to a creature in its circumstances "the propositional attitudes one supposes one would have oneself in those circumstances" (Dennett 1987: 342-3).[22] This approach readily suggests a doxastic criterion for selecting interpretations. According to the agreement criterion, as we've seen, we should select interpretations on the basis of the extent to which the beliefs attributed as a result of each interpretation agree with the beliefs of the interpreter. On what I'm going to call the *projection criterion*, we should select interpretations on the basis of the extent to which the beliefs attributed as a result of each interpretation agree with the beliefs the interpreter would have if she found herself in the speaker's epistemic situation.

---

[21] Davidson explains that the method of interpretation he describes proceeds by "assigning truth conditions to alien sentences that make native speakers right as often as plausibly possible, according, of course, to our own view of what is right" (Davidson 1973: 324). On the relationship between the two characterizations of the criterion, see Verheggen and Myers (Chapter 8, this volume).

[22] The approach can be traced back to Quine (1960: 219). Versions of the view have been defended by Grandy (1973) and Stich (1981, 1983).

We can easily see that the projection criterion gives the right results for the cases considered in the previous section. An interpreter who knows that dolphins aren't fish can easily recognize that if she found herself in the speaker's epistemic situation she would believe that dolphins are fish. Hence the projection criterion will favour interpretations that result in the ascription of this belief. The same goes for the Gödel/Schmidt case. An interpreter who knows that Schmidt proved the incompleteness of arithmetic realizes that she would believe that Gödel did if she found herself in the speaker's epistemic situation. Hence, other things being equal, an interpretation that ascribes to the speaker the false belief that Gödel proved the result would do better by the projection criterion than one that ascribes the true belief that Schmidt did.

It is interesting to consider the relationship between the projection criterion and the agreement criterion. When interpreter and speaker find themselves in the same epistemic situation, both criteria produce the same ordering of interpretations, since the beliefs I would have in the speaker's epistemic situation will be the beliefs I actually have. The more the epistemic situations of speaker and interpreter come apart, the more the interpretations favoured by the two criteria will differ from one another.

10. What Is (Compositional) Interpretation (of a Compositional Language)?

We now have the main ingredients of the proposal I want to make for a pragmatist account of the meaning grounds of interpretations. An account of the meaning grounds of interpretations needs to specify what has to be the case in order for a pairing of sentences with states of affairs to count as producing interpretations of the sentences as representing the states of affairs they are paired with as obtaining. A pragmatist approach would seek to accomplish this task in terms of upstream and downstream features of a pairing practice that can be regarded as necessary and/or sufficient for the pairings generated by the practice to be interpretations of sentences as representing the states of affairs they are paired with.

I've identified two features of our interpretative practice that can be plausibly included in the meaning grounds of interpretations. The first is belief relevance. The second is the selection of interpretations according to the projection and familiarity criteria. In terms of these features we can formulate a simple pragmatist account of the meaning grounds of interpretations, restricted, as explained in section 4, to compositional interpretations of compositional languages: interpretations have the meaning they have because they are generated by a belief-relevant pairing practice that selects sentence-state of affairs pairings according to the projection and familiarity criteria. Or to put it as an answer to the question in the title: linguistic interpretation, or, more precisely, compositional linguistic interpretation of a compositional language, is a belief-relevant pairing practice that uses the projection and familiarity criteria to select sentence-state of affairs pairings.

My discussion of these features of our interpretative practice can be seen as providing some motivation for the proposal, but it's clear that it falls well short of an adequate defence. Much more work would be needed to assert with some confidence that every pairing practice with these features generates interpretations and every pairing practice that generates interpretations will have these features. This is work that I'm not going to do here. What I want to do, in closing, is to highlight two important points about the nature of the proposal.

The first point I want to highlight is that I'm not proposing a representationalist account of the meaning grounds of interpretations. On the representationalist approach, the meaning grounds of interpretations would be specified by identifying the states of affairs they represent as obtaining. One might try to find states of affairs that would play this role among the factors we have discussed. The charity criterion could be put to this use. On the resulting proposal, the state of affairs represented by (S) consists in this: the compositional interpretation of Kurt's language that maximizes satisfaction of the charity criterion pairs "der Schnee ist weiß" with the state of affairs of snow being white. This proposal, as it stands, doesn't succeed, as it falls prey to the problems discussed in section 6. For any given interpretation of the singular terms (that makes the ostensive explanations come out true), we can manufacture an interpretation of the predicates that satisfies the charity criterion perfectly, but the sentence-state of affairs pairs that this interpretation produces do not seem to pair the sentences with the states of affairs they represent as obtaining. One might try to solve the problem with an objective eligibility ranking of potential referents. Now (S) would represent the following state of affairs: the compositional interpretation of Kurt's language that maximizes satisfaction of the criterion composed of charity and referent eligibility pairs "der Schnee ist weiß" with the state of affairs of snow being white. I'm not going to assess this approach here. What I want to emphasize is that it is fundamentally different from my proposal.

Notice that as we replace charity with agreement and then projection, and objective eligibility with familiarity, the resulting representationalist account loses whatever plausibility it might have enjoyed. Satisfaction of the charity plus eligibility criterion is an objective matter. The ranking of interpretations it generates is completely independent of the identity of the interpreter. By contrast, the ranking of interpretations generated by the agreement or projection criterion is radically dependent on who is doing the interpreting. If you and I have different beliefs, and would have different beliefs if we found ourselves in the speaker's epistemic situation, agreement and projection would favour different interpretations for each of us. The same goes for familiarity, for interpreters who have different conceptual repertoires.

It follows that a representationalist account of the meaning grounds of interpretations based on these criteria would result in a radically relativistic account of meaning. The same sentence would represent different states of affairs for different interpreters, and the question, which state of affairs a sentence represents as obtaining, could be made sense of only when relativized to an interpreter.[23] I regard this outcome as tantamount to a refutation of the view.

But this is not what I'm proposing. I'm not using features of our interpretative practice to specify the state of affairs that an interpretation represents as obtaining. I'm using them to specify what makes it the case that interpretations have the meaning they have—what makes it the case that pairing a sentence with a state of affairs has the character of an interpretation of the former as representing the latter. Given that this is our goal, there's no reason why we should expect that whenever these conditions are satisfied we will end up with the same interpretations. Interpreters can disagree with one another on which interpretations are correct and still count as interpreting. Specifying the meaning grounds of interpretations requires specifying who counts as interpreting. It doesn't generally require, in addition, specifying which interpretations are correct. If we adopt the representationalist approach, then our specification of who counts as interpreting will rest on a specification of which interpretations are correct. However, the pragmatist approach avoids this link. It specifies who counts as interpreting without specifying which interpretations are correct. Therefore, the fact that different interpreters might support different interpretations doesn't in principle entail that different interpretations are correct relative to different interpreters.

Notice also that, for a given interpreter, satisfying the conditions for counting as interpreting doesn't always single out a unique interpretation as the one she should endorse. If we were in the business of providing a representationalist account of the meaning grounds of interpretations, we would have to conclude from this that, even when relativized to a particular interpreter, interpretation is indeterminate—there is no fact of the matter as to which of several interpretations is correct. However, since we are operating within the pragmatist template, this conclusion doesn't follow. The pragmatist is not committed to the claim that if you satisfy the conditions that turn your pairings of sentences and states of affairs into interpretations, whatever interpretations you end up with will be correct.

The fact that we are not trying to specify the states of affairs that interpretations represent as obtaining also defuses a line of objection against the projection criterion. The problem is mentioned by Quine when he discusses what we've called projection principles: "Casting our real selves thus in unreal roles, we do not generally know how much reality to hold constant" (Quine 1960: 219). In order to

---

[23] Davison seems to have contemplated overcoming this obstacle by reference to the charitable interpretations that would be produced by an omniscient interpreter (Davidson 2001a).

apply the projection criterion, an interpreter needs to consider what beliefs she would have if she were in the speaker's epistemic situation. To perform this exercise, the interpreter needs to decide which aspects of her actual cognitive make-up she should include in the hypothetical scenario in which she finds herself in the speaker's epistemic situation. It seems likely that in many cases the question won't have a determinate answer, and any indeterminacy at this stage will result in indeterminacy concerning the extent to which different interpretations satisfy the projection criterion. Once again, this would be a disaster if we were in the business of providing a representationalist account of the meaning grounds of interpretations. For the pragmatist approach, by contrast, this outcome is not at all problematic. In order to determine whether someone counts as interpreting, we need to consider whether she is selecting interpretations on the basis of the beliefs she would have in the speaker's epistemic situation. So long as she does this, she will count as applying the projection criterion, independently of which aspects of her actual cognitive make-up she regards as included in the hypothetical scenario. This will affect which interpretations she endorses, but not whether she counts as interpreting, and the pragmatist's answer to the latter question does not require an answer to the former.

I'd like to end by reviewing briefly how things stand with respect to the pre-emption thesis. As I explained in section 1, vindicating the pre-emption thesis for a discourse requires providing a non-representationalist account of the meaning grounds of its expressions. In this chapter, I've outlined a proposal for how to achieve this with respect to interpretations. A pragmatist account of the meaning grounds of interpretations along the lines of what I'm proposing would not rest on a metaphysical account of the ultimate nature of meaning facts—of what makes a sentence represent a state of affairs as obtaining. This overcomes the immediate obstacle to the adoption of the pre-emption thesis for interpretations—the claim that our account of meaning grounds for interpretations removes the need for a metaphysical account of facts as to which state of affairs each sentence represents as obtaining. However, this isn't by any means the only obstacle that stands in the way of the acceptance of the pre-emption thesis, and I've said nothing here to address the remaining difficulties.

One important worry is the idea that adopting a pragmatist account of the meaning grounds of a discourse might force us to abandon the claim that the discourse performs the function of representing things as being a certain way. If this connection goes unchallenged, my account of the meaning grounds of interpretations would force us to give up the claim that they represent things as being a certain way, and to conclude that there are no facts to the effect that sentences represent states of affairs as obtaining.[24] This outcome would be counterintuitive

---

[24] Kripke (1982) openly accepts this outcome.

at best and incoherent at worst.[25] Removing this obstacle to the adoption of a pragmatist account of the meaning grounds of interpretations would require vindicating its compatibility with the thought that interpretations represent states of affairs as obtaining. I think this can be done, but I haven't tried to do it here.

References

Armstrong, D. M. (1997). *A World of States of Affairs.* Cambridge: Cambridge University Press.

Ayer, A. J. (1936). *Language, Truth, and Logic.* London: Victor Gollancz.

Boghossian, P. (1990). 'The Status of Content', *Philosophical Review* 99:157–84.

Brandom, R. (2011). *Perspectives on Pragmatism: Classical, Recent, and Contemporary.* Harvard, MA: Harvard University Press.

Bronzo, S. (2011). 'Context, Compositionality, and Nonsense in Wittgenstein's *Tractatus*', in *Beyond the Tractatus Wars*, R. Read and M. A. Lavery (eds.). Routledge: New York.

Button, T. (2013). *The Limits of Realism.* Oxford: Oxford University Press.

Carnap, R. (1956). *Meaning and Necessity.* 2nd ed. Chicago: University of Chicago Press.

Cuneo, T. (2020). 'Can Expressivism Have It All?' *Philosophical Studies* 177:219–41.

Davidson, D. (1973). 'Radical Interpretation', *Dialectica* 27:313–28.

Davidson, D. (2001a). 'A Coherence Theory of Truth and Knowledge', *Subjective, Intersubjective, Objective.* Oxford: Clarendon.

Davidson, D. (2001b). 'On Saying That', *Inquiries into Truth and Interpretation.* Oxford: Oxford University Press.

Davidson, D. (2001c). 'Theories of Meaning and Learnable Languages', *Inquiries into Truth and Interpretation.* Oxford: Oxford University Press.

Dennett, D. (1987). 'Midterm Examination: Compare and Contrast', *The Intentional Stance.* Cambridge, MA: The MIT Press.

Dummett, M. (1981). *The Interpretation of Frege's Philosophy.* Harvard, MA: Harvard University Press.

Field, H. (2017). 'Egocentric Content', *Noûs* 51 (3):521–46.

Frege, G. (1980). 'On Sense and Reference', in *Translations from the Philosophical Writings of Gottlob Frege*, M. Black and P. T. Geach (eds.). Oxford: Basil Blackwell.

Gibbard, A. (1990). *Wise Choices, Apt Feelings.* Oxford: Clarendon.

Gibbard, A. (2003). *Thinking How to Live.* Cambridge, MA: Harvard University Press.

---

[25] See Wright (1984) and Boghossian (1990) for the claim that the outcome is incoherent.

Grandy, R. (1973). 'Reference, Meaning, and Belief', *The Journal of Philosophy* 70:439–52.

Hochberg, H. (1967). 'Nominalism, Platonism and 'Being True Of'', *Noûs* 1:413–19.

Kripke, S. (1980). *Naming and Necessity*. Oxford: Blackwell.

Kripke, S. (1982). *Wittgenstein on Rules and Private Language*. Oxford: Blackwell.

Lewis, D. (1974). 'Radical Interpretation', *Synthese* 23:331–44.

Lewis, D. (1984). 'Putnam's Paradox', *Australasian Journal of Philosophy* 62:221–36.

McCarty, D. (1991). 'The Philosophy of Logical Wholism', *Synthese* 87:51–123.

Price, H. (2011a.) 'Immodesty without Mirrors: Makind Sense of Wittgenstein's Linguistic Pluralism', in *Naturalism without Mirrors*. Oxford: Oxford University Press.

Price, H. (2011b). 'Naturalism and the Fate of the M-Worlds', in *Naturalism without Mirrors*. Oxford: Oxford University Press.

Price, H. (2011c). 'Naturalism without Representationalism', in *Naturalism without Mirrors*. Oxford: Oxford University Press.

Putnam, H. (1978). *Meaning and the Moral Sciences*. London: Routledge & Kegan Paul.

Putnam, H. (1981). *Reason, Truth and History*. Cambridge: Cambridge University Press.

Quine, W. V. O. (1960). *Word and Object*. Cambridge, MA: MIT Press.

Quine, W. V. O. (1969). 'Ontological Relativity', *Ontological Relativity and Other Essays*. New York: Columbia University Press.

Schroeder, M. (2008). *Being For: Evaluating the Semantic Program of Expressivism*. Oxford: Oxford University Press.

Skyrms, B. (1981). 'Tractarian Nominalism (for Wilfrid Sellars)', *Philosophical Studies* 40:199–206.

Stevenson, C. L. (1944). *Ethics and Language*. New Haven: Yale University Press.

Stich, S. (1981). 'Dennett on Intentional Systems', *Philosophical Topics* 12:39–62.

Stich, S. (1983). *From Folk Psychology to Cognitive Science: The Case against Belief*. Cambridge, MA: MIT Press.

Wittgenstein, L. (1974). *Tractatus Logico-Philosophicus*, D. F. Pears and B. McGuinness (trans.), 2nd ed. London: Routledge and Kegan Paul.

Wittgenstein, L. (2009). *Philosophical Investigations*, 4th ed. Oxford: Blackwell.

Woodfield, A. (1982). 'On Specifying the Contents of Thoughts', in *Thought and Object: Essays on Intentionality*, A. Woodfield (ed.). Oxford: Clarendon Press.

Wright, C. (1984). 'Kripke's Account of the Argument against Private Language', *Journal of Philosophy* 81:759–77.

Zalabardo, J. L. (1998). 'Putting Reference Beyond Belief', *Philosophical Studies* 91:221–57.

Zalabardo, J. L. (2015). *Representation and Reality in Wittgenstein's Tractatus*. Oxford: Oxford University Press.

Zalabardo, J. L. (2017). 'Davidson, Russell and Wittgenstein on the Problem of Predication', in *Wittgenstein and Davidson on Thought, Language, and Action*, C. Verheggen (ed.). Cambridge: Cambridge University Press.

Zalabardo, J. L. (2018). 'The Tractatus on Unity', *Australasian Philosophical Review* 2:250–71.

Zalabardo, J. L. (2019). 'Belief, Desire and the Prediction of Behaviour', *Philosophical Issues* 29:295–310.

Zalabardo, J. L. (Forthcoming). 'Meaning-Ascribing Discourse: Assertibility Conditions and Representation', in *Kripke's 'Wittgenstein on Rules and Private Language' at 40*, C. Verheggen (ed.). Cambridge: Cambridge University Press.

10
Neopragmatism and Logic
A Deflationary Proposal

Lionel Shapiro

1. Introduction

Pragmatism about logic takes many forms. One concerns methodology: pragmatists argue that logical principles should be defended and criticized by looking to the consequences of accepting logical theories, in the context of our other commitments. It is in this sense that Susan Haack advocates a "pragmatist conception of logic." Opposing the view that "logical laws...have a special status which guarantees their certainty," she argues that "logic is a theory...on a par, except for its extreme generality, with other, 'scientific' theories," whence "choice of logic, as of other theories, is to be made on the basis of an assessment of the economy, coherence and simplicity of the overall belief set" (Haack 1974: 26).[1]

Distinct from this *methodological* pragmatism about logical inquiry is a pragmatism concerning the *subject matter* of logic. On this view, claims made using logical vocabulary concern our practices of inference or assertion. Versions of subject-matter pragmatism in the proof-theoretic tradition hold that logical consequence is a matter of norms governing inference (e.g. Prawitz 1985) or constraining combinations of assertion and denial (e.g. Restall 2005). But subject-matter pragmatism hasn't only been applied to predicates that express *logical relations*, such as '*x* is a logical consequence of *y*'. It's also been applied to *logical connectives*, such as 'if' and 'not'. On Robert Brandom's view, conditionals let us state claims whose truth, when they are true, is "implicit in" *features of our discursive practices*—specifically, in the relations of "material" consequence and incompatibility relations these practices institute. Such explicitation typically requires using conditionals with embedded negations or conjunctions (Brandom 1994: xix, 114–15, 2010: 354).

Here I'll defend a third form of pragmatism about logical discourse. This form is naturally accompanied by methodological pragmatism. Moreover, it agrees with Brandom in characterizing the role of logical vocabulary in terms of our

---

[1] Pragmatism about logic in this sense, which traces to W. V. Quine, has become known as "anti-exceptionalism" (Hjortland 2017).

practice of making and challenging assertions. However, it rejects subject-matter pragmatism about logical vocabulary. That is a consequence of the general program it exemplifies, one pursued by Huw Price under the labels "global pragmatism" (Price 1991) and "global expressivism" (Price 2004). Following Michael Williams (2010, 2013) and Joshua Gert (2018, 2023), who endorse Price's program, I'll call it "neopragmatism." Neopragmatists shift the target of philosophical explanation from the *objects* we think and talk about to the *functions of expressions and concepts* in our cognitive economy. In that sense, they count as "metaphysical quietists" (Macarthur and Price 2007). We should thus expect that when neopragmatism is applied to logic, it won't yield substantive claims about the nature of logical consequence, or about what features of our discursive practice the truth of a conditional is implicit in.[2]

In section 2, I lay out and motivate neopragmatism's commitments. Section 3 explains how logical vocabulary can be a target for neopragmatist theorizing, and how it has also been thought to pose obstacles to neopragmatist accounts of other vocabulary. The rest of the chapter argues that these obstacles can be addressed by adopting a neopragmatist perspective toward logical relations, such as logical consequence and inconsistency, and toward propositional content. Section 4 argues that neopragmatists should be deflationists about logical relations. This will justify dismissing a standard constraint on functional explanations of logical complexity, namely that they must account for logical relations. Section 5 proposes functional explanations on which logical connectives are used to convey that a speaker has certain dialectical dispositions. The proposal will violate a second widely accepted constraint according to which the function a connective serves in an assertion of a complex sentence must be explained in terms of the functions of other expressions in the sentence. In section 6, I argue that the seeming rationale for that constraint depends on understanding the neopragmatist's functional explanations as telling us what it is in virtue of which sentences have their propositional content. But this aim, I'll argue, is in tension with a neopragmatist approach to the function of content ascriptions. In short, the proposal will be deflationary in a more general sense: it aims to deflate some of neopragmatists' theoretical ambitions.

2. Neopragmatism

As Lewis Carroll's Walrus observes, we can "talk of many things." These aren't exhausted by the artifacts, stuffs, organisms, and persons he itemizes. Citing his

---

[2] I thus view neopragmatism about logic as at odds with Brandom's version of pragmatism about logic, though Brandom shares many neopragmatist commitments (cf. Brandom 2013). For an interpretation and critique of Brandom on logic, see Shapiro (2018).

"cabbages and kings," Wilfrid Sellars adds "numbers and duties, possibilities and finger snaps, aesthetic experience and death," and later the "particles, forces and fields" of physics (1960: 1, 20). According to Sellars, philosophy aims to perspicuously understand how such "radically different items" can "hang together," i.e. fit unmysteriously into an overall picture of how the world is.

In pursuit of this aim, we might attempt two kinds of *analysis*: uncovering relations of constitution among our concepts or meanings, or uncovering relations of constitution among the things talked of. One broad way to think of the pragmatist tradition inaugurated by C. S. Peirce is as recommending an alternative to either kind of analysis. This is the route of *explaining the functions* of concepts or linguistic expressions. What do we do with them that accounts for our having them?[3] Here I'll take no general position on language's role in the acquisition of conceptual capacities. However, since the logical concepts at issue are plausibly ones we only acquire in learning a language, I'll focus on linguistic expressions. While an expression may have multiple functions, I'll write "the function" rather than "the function or functions."

If the pragmatist approach is to yield insight into how what we talk of hangs together, this imposes a restriction on answers to its question about linguistic functions. The explanation of an expression's function shouldn't, in general, be that it's used to *represent or describe some constituent of reality*. For on such *representationalist* accounts, insight into the heterogeneity of discourse could only be supplied by metaphysical investigation of its multifarious objects (Price 2013: 184). The pragmatist's contention, by contrast, is that puzzles about how these objects hang together become tractable when we turn from metaphysical analysis to functional explanation of how vocabularies hang together in our discourse.

Nevertheless, it remains open to pragmatists to advocate a representationalist account of *some* kinds of propositional discourse (e.g. "ordinary empirical discourse"), while telling a different functional story about other kinds. That would be to espouse a *local* pragmatism. In the paradigmatic cases of normative and modal vocabulary, non-representationalist stories have usually invoked speakers' expressing attitudes other than belief. Thus local pragmatists tend to be local expressivists.[4] However, there are reasons to globalize pragmatism (Macarthur and Price 2007). One reason is that functional investigation of our talk of "reference" and "truth conditions" can support a *semantic deflationism* according to which such representational vocabulary is nowhere suited for explanatory work.[5] At the

---

[3] Rejecting "analysis" in favor of "explanation" is central to Price (1988). Elsewhere, he speaks of giving the "functions and genealogy of particular parts of language" and "asking how they arise, and what functions they serve in the lives of the creatures who employ them" (2011: 12; 1993: 79).

[4] Local pragmatism is influentially elaborated by Blackburn (1993) and Gibbard (2003).

[5] Price (2013) argues that other representational notions may be so suited; an example would be the notion of "mapping rule" from Millikan (1984). Shapiro (2020: 22–5) argues that *correct mapping* and *reference* needn't even be coextensive: we can expect cases where our predicate 'F' *is supposed to map onto* something other than the F things.

same time, semantic deflationism vindicates the univocal applicability of reference and truth talk to all uses of language that display the syntactic and pragmatic hallmarks of propositional discourse. I'll use "neopragmatism" for any approach that meets two conditions: it's globally pragmatist, in the above-characterized sense, and it embraces deflationism about truth and reference.[6] As I use the label, neopragmatism doesn't require that the functions of all expressions be explained in terms of the expression of attitudes.[7]

A key aim of neopragmatists has been to argue that an adequate explanation of the functions of our talk about (e.g.) numbers, duties, and possibilities undercuts the demand for a metaphysical story about what the truth of claims about them consists in. That would be a story that reduces facts about them to other facts. Such a demand is often motivated by a naturalism that insists that all facts be reducible to ones that can be stated using vocabulary of the natural sciences. Against this, Price advertises that his "functional standpoint" should

> undercut the *motivation* for reductionism: once we have an adequate explanation for the fact that the folk *talk of* Xs and Ys and Zs, an explanation which distinguishes these activities from what the folk are doing when they do physics, why should we try to reduce the Xs and Ys and Zs to what is talked about in physics?　1993: 76–8

For example, the explanation of why we speak of *morally wrong actions* (perhaps to encourage condemnation), *probable outcomes* (perhaps to coordinate degrees of confidence), and *truths* (perhaps to facilitate generalization) may prove fundamentally different from the explanation of why we talk of *molecules*. In this way, functional explanations can undermine the view that naturalistic reductions must in principle be possible on pain of eliminativism or fictionalism.

But the point isn't just that neopragmatism undercuts the demand for *naturalistic* reductionism. The promised "blocking of reductionist moves" (O'Leary-Hawthorne and Price 1996: 123–6) is more general, casting doubt on projects of reducing facts statable in a given vocabulary to facts statable in a vocabulary with a fundamentally heterogeneous function. Later, I'll argue that neopragmatists who stress this point as it applies to (e.g.) normative and modal discourse haven't drawn the proper consequences of applying it to discourse about propositional content.

---

[6] By embracing deflationism about truth, neopragmatists avoid what Sellars views as a failing of classical pragmatists: "I would argue that Pragmatism, with its stress on language (or the conceptual) as an instrument, has hold of a most important insight—an insight, however, which the pragmatist has tended to misconceive as an *analysis* of 'means' and 'is true'" (Sellars 1954: 213).

[7] Here I differ from Gert (2023). Price recognizes that his use of "global expressivism" could be misconstrued as endorsing the requirement (2013: 176).

3. Logic as Target and Obstacle

How might neopragmatism be relevant to the philosophy of logic? For one thing, logical discourse is as traditional a source of philosophical perplexity as any. Consider the claim that instances of disjunctive syllogism are valid. Or the claim that either there are gods or there aren't gods. Or, most venerably, the claim that Theaetetus is not flying. What, if any, domains or aspects of reality are limned by these claims? How does the subject matter of each hang together with the rest of what we talk of, and what are the implications for our ability to attain knowledge? Logical discourse appears a prime candidate for pragmatist exploration.

If we stick with Price's formulation, according to which pragmatists examine how the "folk *talk of* Xs and Ys and Zs," obvious targets would include talk of logically valid arguments and of logically inconsistent sets of sentences. (Here, the relevant "folk" consist almost entirely of those engaged in philosophy or mathematics.) Standard approaches to such *logical relations* have taken the form of reductive analyses, e.g. in model-theoretic or proof-theoretic terms. In section 4, I'll summarize a neopragmatist approach according to which when we talk about what sentences are logical consequences of what others, we're doing something very different from talking about either model-theoretic or proof-theoretic properties.[8]

Logical discourse isn't exhausted by talk of logical relations, however. That talk has features of linguistic expressions as its overt subject matter. By contrast, when using the disjunction 'Either it's raining or it's snowing' one no more talks about sentences than when using the constituent 'It's raining'. What, then, can be said about the subject matter that the use of *logical connectives* contributes to our discourse? On one representationalist view, the answer is that rather than let us talk of any Xs, Ys, and Zs, connectives let us talk of ontological "structure." While such structure is part of what makes true any sentences employing logical connectives, logically true sentences are said to be true wholly in virtue of that structure. Thus, according to Penelope Maddy, "the world has very general structural features" such that the "the core of our logic reflects" these features (2002: 76, 83; cf. Millikan 1984: ch. 14; Sider 2011).[9] In opposition to such a view, neopragmatists offer non-representationalist accounts of the function of logical connectives and operators in the tradition of Frank Ramsey (1927, 1929) on negation and quantifiers; and Gilbert Ryle (1950) and Sellars (1953) on conditionals.

Yet discussion of logical connectives by local and global pragmatists usually occurs in a different context. Rather than invoking functional explanations of

---

[8] Unlike model- and proof-theoretic accounts, the expressivism ("projectivism") about consequence of Field (2015) is congenial to the neopragmatist strategy.

[9] A complication is that Maddy rejects substantive notions of reference and truth; her "reflecting" is explained in "correlational" terms (2007: 195–6, 226n3).

logical connectives to resolve philosophical perplexities about (e.g.) negative and disjunctive states of affairs, such discussion focuses on connectives as posing a formidable challenge to functional explanations of other vocabulary. The challenge is due to Peter Geach, who criticizes advocates of pragmatist functional explanation for having overlooked it, thereby revealing that they have held "little regard for formal logic as a philosophical instrument" (1965: 461–5).[10]

The issue is that functional explanations typically concern assertions of logically simple sentences. An account of the function of 'wrong' might tell us that the function is served when (e.g.) an assertion of 'Torture is wrong' contributes to condemnation of torture. An account of the function of 'urgent' might tell us that the function is served when (e.g.) an assertion of 'Climate action is urgent' instigates expeditious action to address climate change. But pragmatists about wrongness or urgency must also explain what being able to assert *logically complex sentences* containing 'wrong' or 'urgent' does for us. To this end, the usual strategy has been to explain how each embedding context can serve its function in assertions where the embedded sentences contain 'wrong' or 'urgent' (e.g. Blackburn 1988; Schroeder 2008; Gert 2023; Sinclair 2021).[11]

In seeking to meet Geach's challenge this way, pragmatists have presupposed two criteria of adequacy on functional explanations of logical connectives. The first is a weak compositionality constraint on functional explanation.

Compositional Dependence of Explanation. Let S be a logically complex sentence containing atomic expression E. In explaining the function S's major connective serves in an assertion of S, we must make reference to E's function.[12]

For example, suppose we seek to explain the function 'not' serves in an assertion of 'Climate action is not urgent', or the function 'if' serves in an assertion of 'If climate change is causing famines, then climate action is urgent'. According to Compositional Dependence of Explanation, adequate explanations must ultimately

---

[10] Geach criticizes "some Oxford philosophers," and his paper cites or alludes to a handful of figures in Oxford ordinary-language philosophy. Presumably he wouldn't have made the same remark about the "Cambridge pragmatist" and logician Ramsey (see Misak 2016)!

[11] Price (1993: 65–6) argues that pragmatists have no problem accommodating logical complexity if they *look away* from their functional explanations and focus instead on the *propositional content* of sentences like 'Torture is wrong'. Still, he recognizes that pragmatists also owe an explanation of the *functions of logical embeddings*, such as conditionals. Part of that task, he says, is explaining "how the general function of the conditional serves the specific purposes of moral discourse, modal discourse, or whatever" (1993: 75–6). Here he endorses the similar view of Blackburn (1988: 185–6; Price 1993: 65n6).

[12] Following Millikan (1984), I am construing an expression's function as something whose performance accounts for the expression's continued use. This presents a problem for attributing functions to sentences, since these aren't generally kept in use by prior utterances. Still, if an expression is understood as having a "relational" function, one specified in relation to a context including the other constituents in a sentence (p. 80), we can say that it has an "adapted" function as a part of a particular sentence. Of course, like all functions, this one won't be *served* in every assertion of the sentence.

refer to the function of 'urgent', one it serves in logically simple assertions, e.g. of 'Climate action is urgent'. To be sure, a connective's function should be explained *in a uniform way* (cf. the "Generality Condition" of Sinclair 2021: 109). Thus there should be a parallel explanation of the function served by 'not' in an assertion of 'Climate action is not costly', one that appeals to the function of 'costly'. Still, notwithstanding this generic pattern of explanation, the specific function of 'urgent' must play a role in explaining the function 'not' serves in assertions of negations containing 'urgent'. One proposal would be that 'not' serves its function in an assertion of 'Climate action is not urgent' when that assertion counters the instigating of expeditious action to address climate change.[13]

Furthermore, local and global pragmatists have assumed that their theories are subject to a second criterion of adequacy deriving from logic:

Explanation of Logical Relations. Functional explanations for the logical connectives must explain the logical relations that obtain between (sets of) sentences.

Consider the facts that 'Climate change is not causing famines' is a *logical consequence* of the above negation and conditional, and that 'Climate action is not urgent' is *logically inconsistent* with 'Climate action is urgent'. To explain why these relations obtain without invoking truth conditions, pragmatists appeal to the functions served by 'if' and 'not'. Naturally, their aim in satisfying Explanation of Logical Relations has been more general, e.g. a system of functional explanations that "explains the applicability of first-order logic" (Gert 2023: 110). For this purpose, functional explanations for connectives will have to mesh appropriately with the kinds of explanations given for other expressions, such as atomic predicates.

Pragmatist approaches to language have struggled to meet the two constraints.[14] My contention will be that proper regard for the need to accommodate logical complexity doesn't require accepting Compositional Dependence of Explanation or Explanation of Logical Relations. Sections 4 and 6 will examine

---

[13] Lest Compositional Dependence of Explanation be construed as a stronger condition than it is, it may help to see how Gert (2023) satisfies it. According to Gert, an assertion of 'Climate action is urgent' expresses an attitude of "being for" some attitude u toward climate action. Then 'not' serves its function in an assertion of 'Climate action is not urgent' by making it the case that the assertion expresses being for the attitude $\neg u$ that's "paired" with u. This is another attitude toward climate action, a contrary of u, such that learning to use 'urgent' involves learning to associate the word with the pair $\langle u, \neg u \rangle$. Since $\neg u$ isn't a second-order attitude toward u, the attitude u needn't be playing any role in the mind of a *speaker* of 'Climate action is not urgent'. Still, the fact that 'urgent' contributes u plays a role for the *theorist* in explaining the function 'not' serves in an assertion of this particular sentence.

[14] For an overview of challenges facing various approaches, see Schroeder (2010: 139–41). Two recent attempts at meeting them, by a local and a global pragmatist respectively, are Sinclair (2021) and Gert (2023).

these constraints in reverse order, while section 5 will sketch an approach to logical connectives made possible by rejecting them.

4. Deflationism about Logical Relations

Deflationism about logical relations is motivated and elaborated in Shapiro (2011, 2022); I can only give a summary here. My concern will be to point to its dual status as an application of neopragmatism and a view with upshots for neopragmatism.

Consider first a familiar position endorsed by neopragmatists, a version of deflationism about truth. It starts with a functional proposal concerning why we have the predicate 'x is true', namely that it allows us to generalize in ways that would otherwise require quantification into sentence position (or, in finite cases, list-like specifications). We can say "Nothing the candidate said was true" or "Some instances of excluded middle aren't true."[15] Deflationists argue that for this function to be served, it suffices that the predicate obey an intersubstitutability schema:

(T) If S has the propositional content that p, then 'S is true' is intersubstitutable with 'p'.[16]

Henceforth, I make the simplifying assumption that the sentences discussed lack any context-sensitivity that prevents speaking of their being true or having a propositional content.

From the explanatory sufficiency of (T), deflationists draw an antimetaphysical conclusion. The functional explanation based on (T), they argue, doesn't depend on 'true' expressing a substantive property, whence we have no reason to think it expresses such a property. Here I'm taking a *substantive property* to be any property regarding which there's a uniform answer to the question "In virtue of what do the bearers of the property bear it?"[17] A theory on which truth is a substantive property may still count as *metaphysically quietist* about truth: a primitivist about truth will hold that the uniform answer may be "Never in virtue of anything!" But deflationism is a different kind of quietism about truth. According to

---

[15] Price (2003) argues that 'true' has the further function of expressing a norm that governs any assertoric practice. In such a practice, all that's required for a predicate to serve this function is satisfying something like (T). Shapiro (2021) agrees that (T) lets 'true' serve a further important function, one involved in recognizing an asserter's communicative authority, but argues that truth isn't a kind of correctness.

[16] To underwrite the claimed function, the intersubstitutability must extend to embedded contexts. However, we must exclude, at least, modal contexts that render relevant possibilities in which S has a different content.

[17] Shapiro (2022: 16n28) compares this conception with a similar one in Edwards (2013).

deflationists, the question "In virtue of what is S true?" can have answers, but only non-uniform ones. Here's one such answer: S has the content that climate action is urgent, and climate action is urgent.[18]

Deflationism about logical consequence can be presented in parallel fashion. It too starts with a functional proposal, this time concerning why we have the predicate '*x* has *y* as a logical consequence'. The proposal is that using this predicate lets us generalize in ways that would otherwise involve quantification into sentence position, specifically over sentences whose main connective is a *logical conditional* (also called an *entailment connective*). These are sentences such as 'If it's snowing then logically either it's raining or it's snowing'. Using a consequence predicate, we can say things like "Every sentence has as a logical consequence any disjunction with that sentence as a disjunct" and "She denied a logical consequence of something he asserted." The deflationist now argues that for this generalizing function to be served, it suffices that the consequence predicate obey an intersubstitutability schema:

(C) If S has the propositional content that *p* and S' the propositional content that *q*, then 'S has S' as a logical consequence' is intersubstitutable with 'If *p* then logically *q*'.

Like (T), this is a principle of linguistic ascent/descent: the consequence ascription is about *sentences*, while the logical conditional sentence isn't. Here I've limited myself to single-premise consequence. The extension to multipremise consequence, where the convenience of generalizing using consequence talk is most pronounced, is supplied in Shapiro (2022). The general deflationary schema specified there is also applicable to the relation of logical inconsistency—in place of a logical conditional, we would use a preclusion connective 'That *p* logically precludes that *q*'.

As in the case of truth, deflationists now draw an antimetaphysical conclusion. The functional explanation based on (C), they argue, doesn't depend on the predicate 'has as a logical consequence' expressing any substantive relation, whence we have no reason to think that it expresses such a relation. If it doesn't, the question "In virtue of what does S have S' as a logical consequence?" can have only *non-uniform* answers. Here's one such answer:

---

[18] According to Shapiro (2022, p. 17), the deflationist concludes that when a true sentence S has the content that *p*, what S is true in virtue of (besides having that content) is just *whatever (if anything) it is in virtue of which p*. This won't yet imply the additional claim that such a sentence is true (in part) in virtue of *its being the case that p*. It's not clear that the most parsimonious explanation of (T) involves this additional claim (I'm indebted to Susanna Melkonian-Altshuler for alerting me to the issue through her work in progress). But for present purposes, all that matters is that when accounting for S's being true, a deflationist needn't point to any fact about S other than its having the content it does.

(a) *S* has the content that climate action is urgent,
(b) *S'* has the content that it's not the case that climate action is not urgent, and
(c) if climate action is urgent then logically it's not the case that climate action is not urgent.[19]

Deflationism about logical consequence thus contrasts with substantive accounts of the nature of that relation, whether these be model-theoretic or proof-theoretic.

We're now ready to see why a deflationist about logical consequence should reject Explanation of Logical Relations as a constraint on functional explanations. Suppose someone demands to know *why facts (a) and (b) settle that S and S' stand in the relation of logical consequence*. If they're a substantivist about consequence, they won't regard the *non-metalinguistic* claim (c) as an adequate answer. For they'll want to understand the connection between facts (a) and (b) about the sentences and whatever *further fact about the sentences it consists in*, according to their theory of the consequence relation, for them to stand in that relation. And if their substantivist theory of logical consequence is part of a pragmatist approach, it will be natural to seek such an understanding in an account of the function of a negation connective. After all, the relation between *S* and *S'* is characterized by (a) in (b) entirely in terms of the involvement of such a connective.[20]

According to deflationism about logical consequence, by contrast, this explanatory demand would be illegitimate. It should help to compare deflationism about truth, where the analogous point is made by Paul Horwich (1995: 361–5). Suppose I ask why fact (a) is relevant to the fact that *S* is *true*. Deflationists who agree that climate action is urgent will be content to answer that this is because climate action is urgent. It's only substantivists about truth who will further want to understand the connection between fact (a) and whatever, according to their theory of the truth property, it consists in for the sentence to have the property of truth. My argument is that an analogous point applies to deflationism about logical consequence.[21]

---

[19] Why isn't the following uniform answer available: "*S'* expresses a proposition that's a logical consequence of the proposition expressed by *S*"? This just transfers the question about sentential consequence to propositional consequence, and logical deflationists will hold that the latter relation isn't substantive either. Crucially, according to logical deflationism, (c) doesn't state a *relation between propositions*, any more than 'Climate action is not urgent' states a *property of a proposition*.

[20] I've assumed the substantivist isn't a primitivist. But even a primitivist about consequence, e.g. an advocate of Field's (2015) expressivism, may wish to understand, in terms of *features of the negation connective*, why every sentence bears the consequence relation to its double negation. Compare: moral expressivism doesn't entitle those who condemn torture to dismiss a demand that they point to some *feature of torture* relevant to its being wrong.

[21] Båve (2013: 638) voices skepticism about Explanation of Logical Relations, citing Horwich. Here I've explained how deflationism about logical relations lets Horwich's argument be extended from *truth* to *logical relations*. Shapiro (2004: 150–3) defends the extension to "material" consequence.

Admittedly, neopragmatists who are deflationists about consequence might seek to defend Explanation of Logical Relations in a very different way. They could claim that understanding the functions of the connectives must suffice to tell us whether, e.g., *if it's not the case that torture isn't wrong, then logically torture is wrong*. But this would be a marked departure from what neopragmatists say about other vocabulary. A neopragmatist explanation of the function of 'wrong' isn't expected, even together with non-ethical facts about torture, to tell us whether torture is wrong. We should no more expect a neopragmatist approach to logical connectives to settle logical questions stated using them than we'd expect a neopragmatist approach to ethical predicates to settle ethical questions stated using them.

In short, if I'm right that neopragmatists should be deflationists about logical relations, they have no reason to accept Explanation of Logical Relations. According to that constraint, neopragmatists must show that their functional explanations for logical connectives can succeed in "accounting for the logical relations that hold among logically complex sentences" (Gert 2023: 107), such as the fact that S' is a logical consequence of S. But neopragmatists need no more show this than they need to show that their functional explanations for non-logical expressions help account for the *truth or falsity* of sentences containing those expressions.

The above exposition of deflationism about logical relations has incurred two debts. First, I haven't said what's meant in (C) by "intersubstitutable." The worry arises that in explaining the function of logical-consequence talk, I'm using the notion of logical consequence.[22] If "intersubstitutable" in (C) meant *logically equivalent*, talk of logical consequence would be performing explanatory work it might not be suited for by deflationary lights. Second, deflationism about consequence explains the function of the consequence predicate in terms of generalizations over sentences containing a connective 'if p then logically q'. What can neopragmatists say about that connective's function? Can they avoid explanatory appeal to a logical relation obtaining between two entities, the proposition that p and the proposition that q? I'll only make a partial payment on the second debt, while suggesting where to look for the remaining funds. The next section outlines a program for explaining the functions of sentential connectives, of which the logical conditional is an admittedly tricky example. In the course of this, the first debt will also be repaid.

---

[22] Or, at least, that I'm using a closely related notion—if consequence *in virtue of the behavior of the consequence predicate and logical conditional* doesn't count as *logical*.

5. Dialectical Disposition Expressivism about Logical Connectives

What does being able to form logically complex sentences do for us? Here I'll limit myself to types of complexity that are usefully regimented using connectives of propositional logic. No doubt even such forms of complexity serve multiple functions, as the English words 'and', 'or', and 'not' certainly do. My purpose is to identify plausible core functions so as to illustrate the potential of a kind of non-representationalist functional explanation.

The proposal will be a dialectical one, in that respect following Price's discussions of negation (1990, 1993, 2009).[23] More specifically, it's couched in terms of Brandom's view of propositional discourse as a "game of giving and asking for reasons" that centrally involves making assertions. In asserting, a speaker assumes responsibility to defend their assertion when challenged (or withdraw it), and licenses hearers to assert the same proposition. The speaker does the latter by making available to the hearer a way to meet her own responsibility when challenged: namely, to defer to the speaker's assertion (Brandom 1994: 171–2).

These are the only elements of Brandom's account I'll draw on. No use will be made of his notion of being *committed* to a proposition—including in virtue of having asserted other propositions that bear an inferential relation to it. I also depart from Brandom on what count as appropriate challenges and adequate responses. On his view, one way to challenge an assertion is to assert an incompatible claim (1994: 178). I make no explanatory use of any inferential or incompatibility relations (whether "material" or "formal"), since I believe neopragmatists should espouse deflationism about such relations. Instead, I'll talk only of a speaker's treating a performance as a challenge to their assertion, and treating another performance as a way to meet the challenge. But speakers also recognize challenges that *don't* involve asserting propositions. One way to challenge the assertion of a proposition can be to *reject* one or more other propositions. For present purposes, it should suffice to think of the act of *rejecting* the proposition that p as involving one's expressing that one is prepared to challenge assertions that p. One can also commit oneself not to challenge assertions that p; that is *conceding* that p (Walton and Krabbe 1995: 186).

Using these ingredients, we can explain the intersubstitutability claimed in schema (C). Suppose one understands S as having the content that p and S' as

---

[23] There's also contact with Gibbard's identification of "disagreement as the key" to logic (2003: 65) and Lance's interpretation of incompatibility using a "pragmatic relation of challenge" (2001: 443). Dutilh Novaes (2021) likewise discusses and develops a tradition that looks to dialogue to explain the functioning of logical vocabulary. Much of that tradition, though, has different aims. For example, the dialectical rules for connectives in Lorenzen (1960) are meant to underwrite intuitionistic logic. Dutilh Novaes's approach also has a non-deflationary flavor. She defends general principles connecting logical consequence to norms governing interactions between Prover and Skeptic (pp. 76–7). When C is a consequence of A and B, "Skeptic ought to see to it that, if he has granted A and B and Prover puts forward C, then he will grant C." The present proposal yields no such principles.

having the content that q, and that one's language has a logical conditional. Then one will be disposed in a certain way toward substitutions, in one's own speech or that of an interlocutor, of one of the following for the other:

a sentence with the content that *S has S' as its logical consequence*
a sentence with the content that *if p then logically q*.

Specifically, one will be disposed to treat such substitutions as making no difference to the game of giving and asking for reasons—to what one takes as a challenge to an assertion or to what one takes to be a way to meet such a challenge.

Turning at last to connectives, let's start with conjunction. My suggestion is that the expression regimented by 'and' in logician's English enables one to make an assertion by which one conveys that one has a certain dialectical disposition with regard to *that very assertion*.

> **Conjunction.** In asserting 'p and q', a speaker expresses her being disposed thus:
> (i) She's prepared to acknowledge an interlocutor's rejection of the claim that p as a challenge to her assertion, and to acknowledge an interlocutor's rejection of the claim that q as a challenge to her assertion.
> (ii) When an interlocutor has challenged her assertion, she's prepared to adduce, as a way to meet the challenge, any pair of available assertions that p and that q.

Here available assertions include any the speaker makes in the context of the challenge, but can also include assertions by others. An assertion by someone else counts as being available to the speaker provided she would be prepared to assert the same claim and defer to that speaker's assertion in meeting a challenge. Notice that the clauses don't say that the speaker expresses a disposition *not* to acknowledge other kinds of challenge to her assertion of 'p and q', or *not* to meet a challenge in other ways.

Why might it be useful to have a way to express this dialectical disposition? Suppose one defends the claim that r against an interlocutor's challenge by adducing dual assertions that p and that q. (Example: "Mine is the better plan for mitigating climate change. Here's why. First, it's more effective. Second, it's less costly.") One will then acknowledge an interlocutor's rejection of either claim as a challenge. But the conjunction connective facilitates dialectical engagement by allowing a further way for the interlocutor to challenge one's defense of the claim that r. For they may wish to challenge one's dual assertions that p and that q even if they're neither prepared to reject the claim that p nor prepared to reject the claim that q.[24] Conjunction allows the dialogue to take the form of one's assertion, and

---

[24] Though rejection needn't take the form of an assertion for which one assumes justificatory responsibility, one will still aim to avoid gratuitously rejecting propositions.

their subsequent challenge, of the proposition that *p and q*. ("It's more effective *and* less costly? Come on!")

Admittedly, we could obtain the same benefit if the game of giving and asking for reasons had as a distinct move the act of *rejecting a pair of propositions taken conjunctively*. But the story wouldn't end there. As we'll soon see, there would be a corresponding benefit to including an act of asserting a pair of propositions *taken disjunctively*. And now there would be pressure to recognize as a further primitive act the *disjunctive* asserting of one proposition together with a *pair of others taken conjunctively*. (And so on.) Having 'and' in our language allows us to stick instead with disjunctively asserting one proposition together with a second proposition that's a conjunction. Of course, provided we can also state disjunctive propositions, we can do without acts of asserting disjunctively *or* rejecting conjunctively.[25]

Unsurprisingly, a parallel functional story can be told about disjunction. Having a device regimented in logician's English as 'or' likewise enables the expressing of a dialectical disposition with regard to the very assertion that expresses the disposition.

Disjunction. In asserting 'p or q', a speaker expresses her being disposed thus:

(i) She's prepared to acknowledge an interlocutor's pair of rejections of the claims that p and that q as a challenge to her assertion.

(ii) When an interlocutor has challenged her assertion, she's prepared to adduce, as a way to meet the challenge, any available assertion that p, and likewise any available assertion that q.

Again, the clauses don't say that the speaker expresses a disposition *not* to acknowledge other kinds of challenge, or *not* to meet them in other ways.

As before, we can ask why it's useful to have a way to express this dialectical disposition. Suppose one's assertion that r has been challenged, and the situation is such that if one were prepared to adduce an assertion that p, or alternatively an assertion that q, one would be prepared to meet the challenge that way. (Example: I assert that some speaker's climate change skepticism needn't be taken seriously. I might defend this claim by asserting that they are ignorant, or by asserting that they are corrupt.) One may not be prepared to adduce an assertion of either proposition.[26] Nonetheless, one may be prepared to meet the challenge to one's assertion that r by sticking one's neck out and making oneself liable to a challenge by any interlocutor who rejects *both* the claim that p and the claim that q. The

---

[25] Thus "bilateralist" treatments of connectives (Rumfitt 2000), which invoke assertion and rejection, don't *additionally* invoke asserting disjunctively or rejecting conjunctively. (For related discussion, see Humberstone 2000: 367–70.) However, Lance (2001: 444) employs as primitive notions *asserting a sentence* and *challenging a totality of assertions*.

[26] This may be because one lacks warrant. Alternatively, one might know that one's interlocutor is unlikely to concede that p, and therefore be unwilling to adduce an assertion that p in defense of one's assertion that r.

disjunction connective allows this dialectical move to take the form of asserting the proposition that *p or q*. ("Either they are ignorant or they are corrupt.")

Concerning the function of negation, my proposal is as follows.

Negation. In asserting 'not *p*', a speaker expresses her being disposed thus:

(i) She's prepared to challenge any assertion that *p*.

(ii) When an interlocutor has challenged her assertion, she's prepared to adduce, as a way to meet the challenge, any available assertion she would acknowledge as a way to reject the proposition that *p*.

Negation thus provides a standardized means of rejecting a proposition by asserting another proposition (Price 1990, 1993: 70ff). As before, a key benefit is that such propositions can be deployed in assertions in which they are logically embedded. Without negative propositions, we'd again need to proliferate types of moves in the game of giving and asking for reasons, such as the disjunctive assertion of one proposition with a second *taken negatively*. With 'not', we can instead assert that *either p or not q*.

Clarifying this account of negation requires addressing an objection. Suppose a speaker asserts that *not p*, and is challenged by her interlocutor. According to (ii), it might seem, the disposition the speaker expresses includes being prepared to respond by adducing an assertion that *possibly not p*. After all, wouldn't she acknowledge that assertion as a way to challenge assertions that *p*? (See Incurvati and Schlöder 2017). Yet surely a speaker can't meet a challenge to her claim that *not p* by adducing the claim that *possibly not p*. What this objection reveals is that, on the current view, asserting that *possibly not p* isn't a way of challenging assertions that *p*. To be sure, it's a way of expressing that one isn't prepared to concede that *p*. But asserting that *possibly not p* falls short of challenging in the sense used here. In particular, it doesn't impose a burden on the asserter that *p* to defend their assertion on pain of having to withdraw it. On the present account, then, rejection (as expression of a disposition to challenge) is stronger than the "weak rejection" of Incurvati and Schlöder.[27]

I conclude my exposition of dialectical disposition expressivism by noting two issues that can't be pursued here. One is how to give functional explanations for additional connectives and operators—including the logical conditional used by logical deflationism to explain the function of the logical-consequence predicate.[28] Another issue is whether the same functional explanations could be exploited in

---

[27] Still, there remains a sense in which rejection is weak. There's no incoherence in rejecting the proposition that *p* without being prepared to assert, or even concede, that *not p*. (One might take this line with Liar propositions.)

[28] Shapiro (2018: 185–6) sketches an application to indicative conditionals, on which asserting 'If *p* then *q*' expresses a dialectical disposition with regard to the pair of propositions that *p* and that *q*. An assertion of 'If *p* then logically *q*' might then express that disposition with regard to all pairs sharing a logical form.

substantivist analyses of logical relations. Suffice it to say, I see no direct way to use the above expressive clauses for the connectives to generate a relation plausibly coinciding with even a weak notion of logical consequence.[29] In this respect the clauses differ from the "bilateral" *inference rules* of Rumfitt (2000), to some of which they bear a non-coincidental resemblance.

6. Neopragmatist Metasemantics?

The last two sections offered functional explanations for two kinds of logical vocabulary: the predicate 'is a logical consequence of' and the connectives 'and', 'or', and 'not'. The approach taken diverges from most pragmatist approaches to logic in rejecting Explanation of Logical Relations. I argued that neopragmatism motivates a deflationism according to which logical relations needn't be accounted for by the functions of connectives.

I turn now to a second divergence from other pragmatist approaches. This concerns Compositional Dependence of Explanation. According to this constraint, an adequate explanation of the function 'not' serves in an assertion of a given negation must draw on the functions of that sentence's non-logical expressions. Yet the above clauses for 'not *p*' make no reference to the *functions* of any vocabulary contained in the substituend for '*p*', instead taking into account only that it has the *content* that *p*. To assess whether that's a problem, let's ask why Compositional Dependence of Explanation might seem reasonable. One line of thought starts with an assumption about how two kinds of description are related: ascriptions of content and specifications of function.

> *Explanation of Propositional Content.* Pragmatists seek to explain what it consists in for a sentence to possess its propositional content by providing functional explanations for the sentence's constituent expressions.

As Amie Thomasson puts it, the pragmatist's "functional analysis" will "provide the basis for giving a meaning analysis" (2020: 79).[30]

---

[29] The clauses do yield that in certain cases there's a pragmatic tension in asserting a proposition while rejecting one of its consequences, e.g. asserting that *p and q* while rejecting that *p*. They also suggest that an idealized agent (who exhibits the dialectical dispositions they express and knows which dispositions they *would* express by an assertion) will take (e.g.) an interlocutor's assertions that *not p* and that *not q* as a challenge to their assertion that *p or (q and r)*. But there's no clear route to extending such pragmatic considerations to capture all cases of logical consequence or inconsistency. (Contrast the aim to "explain inconsistency as frustration of constitutive function" in Sinclair 2021: 268.)

[30] She clarifies, following Williams (e.g. 2010: 325, 2013: 138), that this may require specifying not just an expression's function, but aspects of its use that enable it to serve its function. I'll ignore this complication.

According to Explanation of Propositional Content, a pragmatist about urgency should wish to explain what it consists in for a sentence to have (say) the content *that climate action is not urgent*. And that's indeed a common ambition of local and global pragmatists. Sometimes it's formulated in terms of what constitutes the state of mind of someone who "accepts" the sentence. Expressivists thus wish to explain what *meaning* that climate action is not urgent consists in by explaining what it consists in to *think* that climate action is not urgent, which (they say) is what someone thinks when they accept a sentence with this meaning. Thus Mark Schroeder writes: "For each sentence [of *our* language—LS], 'P', an expressivist theory says what 'P' means by saying what it is to think that P" (2010: 74, 137). Once coupled with global non-representationalism, the project of Schroeder's expressivist becomes the project Gert (2023) calls giving a "neopragmatist semantics". Many would instead call it a project in *metasemantics*, if "metasemantics" is understood as concerning what it is in virtue of which expressions possess their content (e.g. Chrisman 2016 and Sinclair 2021).

Suppose that we accept Explanation of Propositional Content, and that our task as pragmatists is to explain why 'Climate action is not urgent' has the content it does. Presumably, we'll wish to explain this in terms of the function that 'not' serves in assertions of the sentence. For that to succeed, it won't suffice to specify this function in a way that takes for granted that 'Climate action is urgent' has the *content* that climate action is urgent. Rather, we'll ultimately need to make reference to the *functions* of that sentence's constituent expressions. On the other hand, if Explanation of Propositional Content is rejected, this allows for the functional explanations given for logical connectives in section 5, which invoked only the *content* of sentences in a connective's scope.

Why, then, have neopragmatists typically viewed their task as offering explanations of what it consists in for a sentence to have its propositional content? One cause, I think, has been a misunderstanding of how neopragmatists should employ the strategy, which they share with local expressivists, of turning attention to language or thought. Instead of explaining what it consists in for something to be morally wrong or possible, expressivists seek to explain the role 'morally wrong' or 'might' plays in our linguistic-cognitive economy. Consider how Seth Yalcin explains the strategy of "psychological ascent":

> It says: don't start with questions like this: What is the world like when 'It might be raining' is true?... But instead with questions like this: What is it to think it might be raining?   2022: 326–8

Similarly, Yalcin says, expressivists reject the task of explaining what the wrongness of breaking promises consists in, while instead providing "substantive" truth conditions for 'A thinks it's wrong to break promises'.

But this would be the wrong way for *neopragmatists* to understand the strategy of ascent. To see why, recall how that strategy figures in an early neopragmatist position, that attributed to Wittgenstein by Kripke (1982).[31] Take the sentence '2 + 3 = 5'. Instead of seeking a non-trivial explanation of what the world has to be like for this arithmetic sentence to be true, Kripke's Wittgenstein asks "What is the role, and utility, in our lives of our practice of asserting (or denying) the form of words?" (Kripke 1982: 73). It's tempting to assume that answering this question amounts to saying what it consists in for the sentence '2 + 3 = 5' to *have the meaning it does*, viz. that two plus three is five. But that isn't how Kripke conceives of functional explanations. After all, to answer the question "What does it consist in for a sentence to mean that two plus three is five?" would be to give a "straight" rather than "sceptical solution" to the very puzzle about meaning that is Kripke's topic. Rather than answer this question, Kripke *dismisses* it by applying the same strategy of linguistic ascent to the role in our lives of meaning talk. Hence his envisaged functional explanations for '+' and 'means' aren't intended as explanations of what it consists in for a symbol to mean *plus* or to mean *means*.

One would expect neopragmatists to be heirs to Kripke's Wittgenstein. As global pragmatists, they should apply to *propositional content* the same strategy of linguistic ascent they apply to *moral wrongness*. Surprisingly, neopragmatists seldom draw this analogy. Price is an exception (another is Warren 2018):

> There's an important difference between an approach which *analyzes* content, or meaning, in terms of use—which says what it is for an expression to have a particular content, in terms of how it is used—and an account which simply tells us how expressions are used, without thereby claiming to offer an account of *content*. For an account of the latter kind, ascriptions of content may figure as part of the explanandum. Part of the task of such a theory may be to explain the use, and function, of terms such as "content" and "meaning" in ordinary contexts. But...explaining the use of the term "content" is different from explaining what content *is*. A thoroughgoing non-representationalist view just tells us about use. It doesn't explain content by analyzing it in terms of use.
>
> Price (2004: 219; see also 2009)

We can press the point farther than Price does. Not only does the neopragmatist strategy not *amount* to explaining content as consisting in linguistic function; it should *undercut* such explanation. Like truth talk, content talk appears to exhibit a distinctive kind of function, very different from that of linguistic-function talk. Specifically, Brandom argues that content ascription serves to enable dialectical engagement: we report what someone asserted in order to defer to their testimony

---

[31] Miller (2020: 17n) draws the connection to Price's global pragmatism.

when challenged to defend our claims, or in order to clarify agreements and disagreements ("She said that climate change is a myth, but that's not true").[32] The functional distinctiveness of content talk should then result in "blocking reductionist moves" in the same general way that the functional distinctiveness of moral talk was supposed to block reductionist moves concerning moral properties. Price's guiding question is pertinent here: if our explanation of what the folk are doing when they talk of content distinguishes this from what we're doing when we explain linguistic functions, why should we try to reduce content to what we talk of when explaining linguistic functions?

Neopragmatism thus motivates rejecting Explanation of Propositional Content and the resulting demand for a function-based metasemantics. If that's right, we've found no reason why functional explanations for logical connectives should invoke the *functions* of expressions in their scope. When explaining the function 'not' serves in an assertion of 'Climate action is not urgent', neopragmatists needn't take into account anything about the constituent 'Climate action is urgent' other than that it has the content that climate action is urgent. Again, disallowing a role for content in functional explanations would make sense if those explanations were intended to yield metasemantic dividends. But neopragmatists should deny that they're so intended.

7. Conclusion

There are three ways in which this chapter has brought a neopragmatist perspective to bear on logic. Section 5 proposed explanations of the functions served in assertoric practice by the connectives 'and', 'or', and 'not'. The rest of the chapter has supported that proposal by applying neopragmatism in two additional ways.

The first additional application was to a different kind of logical vocabulary, namely predicates used to talk about *logical relations* such as logical consequence and incompatibility. By giving a deflationary explanation of the function of such talk, section 4 sought to undermine a widely held constraint on pragmatist explanations of the functions of connectives. This is that they must contribute (as Gert says) to "accounting for the logical relations that hold between logically complex sentences." But deflationists about *logical consequence* should no more require functional explanations of the connectives to explain what it takes for sentences to stand in the consequence relation than deflationists about *truth*

---

[32] Brandom (1994: ch. 8). Kripke hints at a related account of the function of 'means': in attributing meaning to someone's utterances, the community is "enabling him to engage in certain types of interactions with them that depend on their reliance on his responses" (1982: 109, 94–5). Lance and O'Leary-Hawthorne (1997: 64) argue that 'means' has a distinctive function in "mak[ing] communication, discussion, and argumentation possible."

require functional explanations of ethical vocabulary to explain what it takes for ethical sentences to be true.

The second additional application, in section 6, was indirect. I argued that when neopragmatists apply their methodology to ascriptions of *propositional content*, this should lead them to reject the task of giving constitutive explanations of what possessing a given content consists in. And I suggested that neopragmatists' acceptance of this task has been responsible for their embracing a second constraint. That constraint holds that a full explanation of the function a connective serves in an assertion of a given logically complex sentence must invoke functions of the sentence's atomic expressions.

I have aimed to show how neopragmatism yields reasons to dismiss both constraints, and that doing so makes room for new non-representationalist approaches to logic.[33]

References

Båve, A. (2013). 'Compositional Semantics for Expressivists', *Philosophical Quarterly* 63: 633–59.

Beran, O., Kolman, V., and Koreň, L. (eds.) (2018). *From Rules to Meanings*. New York: Routledge.

Blackburn, S. (1988). 'Attitudes and Contents', in Blackburn 1993.

Blackburn, S. (1993). *Essays in Quasi-Realism*. Oxford: Oxford University Press.

Brandom, R. (1994). *Making It Explicit*. Cambridge, MA: Harvard University Press.

Brandom, R. (2010). 'Reply to Bernhard Weiss's "What is Logic?"', in Weiss and Wanderer 2010.

Brandom, R. (2013). 'Global Anti-Representationalism?' in Price 2013.

Caret, C. and Hjortland, O. (eds.) (2015). *Foundations of Logical Consequence*. Oxford: Oxford University Press.

Charlow, N. and Chrisman, M. (eds.) (2016). *Deontic Modality*. Oxford: Oxford University Press.

Chrisman, M. (2016). 'Metanormative Theory and the Meaning of Deontic Modals', in Charlow and Chrisman 2016.

Dutilh Novaes, C. (2021). *The Dialogical Roots of Deduction*. Cambridge: Cambridge University Press.

Edwards, D. (2013). 'Truth as a Substantive Property', *Australasian Journal of Philosophy* 91: 279-94.

---

[33] I'm grateful to Joshua Gert, Özcan Karabağ, and Julian Schlöder for comments and suggestions, and to a UConn Logic Group audience for discussion.

Field, H. (2015). 'What Is Logical Validity?', in Caret and Hjortland 2015.

Geach, P. (1965). 'Assertion', *Philosophical Review* 74: 449–65.

Gert, J. (2018). 'Neopragmatism, Representationalism, and the Emotions', *Philosophy and Phenomenological Research* 97: 454–78.

Gert, J. (2023). 'Neopragmatist Semantics', *Philosophy and Phenomenological Research* 106: 107–35.

Gibbard, A. (2003). *Thinking How to Live*. Cambridge, MA: Harvard University Press.

Haack, S. (1974). *Deviant Logic*. Cambridge: Cambridge University Press.

Hájek, P., Valdés-Villanueva, L., and Westerståhl, D. (eds.) (2005). *Logic, Methodology, and Philosophy of Science*. London: College Publications.

Hjortland, O. (2017). 'Anti-Exceptionalism about Logic', *Philosophical Studies* 174: 631–58.

Horwich, P. (1995). 'Meaning, Use and Truth', *Mind* 104: 355–68.

Humberstone, L. (2000). 'The Revival of Rejective Negation', *Journal of Philosophical Logic* 29: 331–81.

Incurvati, L. and Schlöder, J. (2017). 'Weak Rejection', *Australasian Journal of Philosophy* 95: 741–60.

Kripke, S. (1982). *Wittgenstein on Rules and Private Language*. Cambridge, MA: Harvard University Press.

Lance, M. (2001). 'The Logical Structure of Linguistic Commitment III: Brandomian Scorekeeping and Incompatibility', *Journal of Philosophical Logic* 30: 439–64.

Lance, M. and O'Leary-Hawthorne, J. (1997). *The Grammar of Meaning*. Cambridge: Cambridge University Press.

Lorenzen, P. (1960). 'Logik und Agon', in Lorenzen and Lorenz 1978.

Lorenzen, P. and Lorenz, K. (eds.) (1978). *Dialogische Logik*. Darmstadt: Wissenschaftliche Buchgesellschaft.

Macarthur, D. and Price, H. (2007). 'Pragmatism, Quasi-realism, and the Global Challenge', in Price 2011.

Maddy, P. (2002). 'A Naturalistic Look at Logic', *Proceedings and Addresses of the American Philosophical Association* 76: 61–90.

Maddy, P. (2007). *Second Philosophy*. Oxford: Oxford University Press.

Millikan, R. (1984). *Language, Thought, and Other Biological Categories*. Cambridge, MA: MIT Press.

Miller, A. (2020). 'What Is the Sceptical Solution?', *Journal for the History of Analytical Philosophy* 8: 1–22.

Misak, C. (2016). *Cambridge Pragmatism*. Oxford: Oxford University Press.

O'Leary-Hawthorne, J. and Price, H. (1996). 'How to Stand Up for Non-Cognitivists', in Price 2011.

Plunkett, D. and Dunaway, B. (eds.) (2022). *Meaning, Decision, and Norms*. Ann Arbor: Michigan Publishing Services.

Prawitz, D. (1985). 'Remarks on Some Approaches to the Concept of Logical Consequence', *Synthese* 62: 153-71.

Price, H. (1988). *Facts and the Function of Truth.* Oxford: Blackwell.

Price, H. (1990). 'Why "Not"?', *Mind* 99: 221-38.

Price, H. (1991). 'Two Paths to Pragmatism', in Price 2011.

Price, H. (1993). 'Semantic Minimalism and the Frege Point', in Price 2011.

Price, H. (2003). 'Truth as Convenient Friction', in Price 2011.

Price, H. (2004). 'Immodesty without Mirrors: Making Sense of Wittgenstein's Linguistic Pluralism', in Price 2011.

Price, H. (2009). '"Not" Again', <https://philpapers.org/rec/PRINA>.

Price, H. (2011). *Naturalism without Mirrors.* New York: Oxford University Press.

Price, H. with S. Blackburn, R. Brandom, P. Horwich, and M. Williams (2013). *Expressivism, Pragmatism and Representationalism.* Cambridge: Cambridge University Press.

Ramsey, F. (1927). 'Facts and Propositions', in Ramsey 1990.

Ramsey, F. (1929). 'General Propositions and Causality', in Ramsey 1990.

Ramsey, F. (1990). *Philosophical Papers* (D. Mellor, ed.). Cambridge: Cambridge University Press.

Restall, G. (2005). 'Multiple Conclusions', in Hájek, Valdés-Villanueva, and Westerståhl 2005.

Rumfitt, I. (2000). '"Yes" and "No"', *Mind* 109: 781-824.

Ryle, G. (1950). '"If," "So," and "Because"', in Ryle 2009.

Ryle, G. (2009). *Collected Essays 1929-1968* (J. Tanney, ed.). Abingdon: Routledge.

Schroeder, M. (2008). *Being For: Evaluating the Semantic Program of Expressivism.* Oxford: Clarendon Press.

Schroeder, M. (2010). *Noncognitivism in Ethics.* Abingdon: Routledge.

Sellars, W. (1953). 'Inference and Meaning', *Mind* 62: 313-38.

Sellars, W. (1954). 'Some Reflections on Language Games', *Philosophy of Science* 21: 204-28.

Sellars, W. (1960). 'Philosophy and the Scientific Image of Man', in Sellars 1963.

Sellars, W. (1963). *Science, Perception, and Reality.* London: Routledge and Kegan Paul, 1963.

Shapiro, L. (2004). 'Brandom on the Normativity of Meaning', *Philosophy and Phenomenological Research* 68: 141-60.

Shapiro, L. (2011). 'Deflating Logical Consequence', *Philosophical Quarterly* 61 (243): 320-42.

Shapiro, L. (2018). 'Logical Expressivism and Logical Relations', in Beran et al. 2018.

Shapiro, L. (2020). 'Can Truth-Conditional Theorists of Content Do without "That"-Clause Ascriptions?', *Analytic Philosophy* 61: 1-27.

Shapiro, L. (2021). 'Truth's Dialectical Role: From Friction to Tension', *Inquiry*. DOI: 10.1080/0020174X.2021.1972834.

Shapiro, L. (2022). 'What Is Logical Deflationism? Two Non-Metalinguistic Conceptions of Logic', *Synthese* 200 (31): 1–28.

Sider, T. (2011). *Writing the Book of the World*. Oxford: Clarendon Press.

Sinclair, N. (2021). *Practical Expressivism*. Oxford: Oxford University Press.

Thomasson, A. (2020). *Norms and Necessity*. Oxford: Oxford University Press.

Walton, D. and Krabbe, E. (1995). *Commitment in Dialogue*. Albany, NY: SUNY Press.

Warren, M. (2018). 'Building Bridges with Words: An Inferential Account of Ethical Univocity', *Canadian Journal of Philosophy* 48: 468–88.

Weiss, B. and Wanderer, J. (eds.) (2010). *Reading Brandom*. Abingdon: Routledge.

Williams, M. (2010). 'Pragmatism, Minimalism, Expressivism', *International Journal of Philosophical Studies* 18: 317–30.

Williams, M. (2013). 'How Pragmatists Can Be Local Expressivists', in Price with Blackburn et al. 2013.

Yalcin, S. (2022). 'Modeling with Hyperplans', in Plunkett and Dunaway 2022.

PART IV
VALUE AND PRACTICE

11
Pragmatism in Practice

Simon Blackburn

1. Preamble

From the time of Socrates onwards philosophers have hoped that attention to features of the ways we think, or ought to think, would affect our practices. The ideas and theories people entertain certainly affect how they behave. We only need to think about highly contestable theories in the social sciences (Marx, Hayek) or biology and psychology (Darwin, Freud) to remember the wide influence theories have, while politics could almost be defined as the arena in which nebulous theories and ideas become fossilized into rock-hard, unassailable ideologies.

Naturally particular theories about particular matters need confronting on their own terms. But it may be harder to see how any highly general theory about meaning, truth, reason, facts, or metaphysics in general can have any effect on them. Yet pragmatism, in the sense in which philosophers think of it, is supposed to be just such a theory. And since its watchword is that the proof of a pudding is in the eating, it can hardly be happy to confess to its having little or no effect on the ways people think, and therefore the ways they behave. At the very least it must suppose itself to affect the climate in which theories grow, flourish, and die, and the climate in which they fossilize into dogma.

There is no doubt that pragmatists from Peirce, James, and Dewey to Rorty and contemporary neopragmatists have shared this self-image. Partly this is through a general commendation of scientific method, of open-minded and collaborative trial and error as the way to test and improve theories, and a corresponding mistrust of potential obstacles and enemies of open-minded and fruitful debate, such as apriorism and lapses into herd thinking. We might call this the educational promise of pragmatism. As the title of one of his earliest and best-known papers attests, Peirce himself supposed that once we have rational control of the 'ways to fix our ideas' truth can look after itself. We do not need to speculate about any imagined end of inquiry, although we can find ourselves frustrated by any lack of increasing consilience, nor do we need to begin by laying down *a priori* foundations for the procedures to follow in any such inquiry. The process is everything, and the product is just the result, or results, of the process. Of course, human beings will go on inquiring into issues that matter to them, whether in science, history, law, or government, with or without the bidding of philosophers. But with Peirce's orientation goes the downgrading of 'facts' as a useful topic for metaphysical speculation. What we accept as facts at any given time are just the results of the processes of inquiry at that times. The idea that truth is usefully described as correspondence with the facts is empty, for it is whatever our processes of inquiry lead us to at the time that we call the truth or, equally, the facts insofar as we take ourselves to have arrived at them. For a correspondence theory of truth to be useful we would need one way of settling what to believe and another, independent route to settling the facts, and then a third process of comparing the two. But this is not how we work, nor how we could work.

2. Awkward Customers

Along with the general orientation I have sketched, pragmatists have acknowledged that there are awkward customers in our thinking. In straightforward matters we have no difficulty in thinking of relevant states of affairs: the state of affairs of my being in a traffic jam, or riding a bicycle, or the world warming up, or lunch cooling down. But there are more awkward customers. We cannot so easily imagine the state of affairs making it true that people have some moral rights and not others, or that human happiness is the only good, or perhaps that it is not the only good. Ethics (I include morality under ethics) has been an awkward customer since the time of Plato, who resorted to the strange idea that a particularly impersonal and ascetic education, followed by many years of mathematics, might equip some small, favoured proportion of people to get it right: escaping from the world of illusion and detecting the Form of the Good. Others have suggested that the will of God mysteriously brings about ethical truth, although we are unfortunately unable to understand exactly what that will is, and yet others suggested that there should be an *a priori*, rational proof of ethical theories. But no such suggestions are particularly plausible.

The awkward credentials of ethics are matched by some other elements more closely involved in science. The modal vocabulary selecting what to regard as necessary or possible or impossible excites similar worries. So does the nature of chances and probabilities. I therefore find it salutary to compare what a pragmatist would say about ethical judgement and inquiry with what another great pragmatist, Frank Ramsey, said, initially, about probability. Ramsey wrote in opposition to Keynes, whose *Treatise on Probability* was started in 1906, and published in 1921, having been delayed not only by Keynes's work in economics, but also by the First World War. And just as Ramsey was a foil to Keynes, so, I shall argue, the right pragmatist approach to ethics should be seen as a foil to the ethical non-naturalism of G. E. Moore. Keynes and Moore each had what we might call an exalted view of the objects of such inquiry. Moore, like Plato looks beyond the natural world, the world of the senses and the sciences, in order to find a suitable subject matter for ethics. Keynes, influenced by Russell as well as Moore, looks to logical relations to deliver judgements of chance or probability. Both Moore and Keynes got a lot right about their subjects, but this conception of the reality they were concerned with failed to suggest a plausible story about the correct epistemology, or method of inquiry, to be pursued in either case. Since the case of Keynes is less familiar than the story about ethics, I shall begin by sketching that.

3. The Pitfalls of Realism (1) Probability, Chance, Laws

Should we be realists about chances and probabilities? Hume (1739/1975: 130) did not think so, holding that chance is nothing in itself, and 'what the vulgar call chance is nothing but a secret and conceal'd cause'. But in his *Treatise on Probability*, published in 1921, Keynes's positive view is that the theory of probability gets its subject matter by locating a rational relationship of partial implication, holding between some evidence, p, and some conclusion, q. This relationship is logically analogous to full implication, which at the time was of course being brilliantly illuminated with the advances made in formal logic by Frege and Russell. Keynes shared their objective and indeed Platonic views of mathematics and logic as themselves describing the relationships of abstract objects.

Nevertheless few writers have been as pessimistic as Keynes about revealing any such relationship. He constantly pillories those who, like Laplace or Quetelet, supposed that, *a priori*, mathematical reasoning by itself could conjure up probabilities. His skepticism is laid out early on, in the third chapter where he insists that 'We can say that one thing is more like a second object than it is like a third; but there will very seldom be any meaning in saying that it is twice as like. Probability is, as far as measurement is concerned, closely analogous to similarity (Keynes 1921: 28). The book is peppered with similar statements:

> I, at any rate, have not the same lively hope as Condorcet or even as Edgeworth of "illuminating the moral and political sciences by the torch of algebra."
>
> 1921: 316

> It would be very surprising, in fact, if logic could tell us exactly how many instances we want, to yield us a given degree of certainty in empirical arguments...Coolly considered, this is a preposterous claim, which would have been universally rejected long ago, if those who made it had not so successfully concealed themselves from the eyes of common sense in a maze of mathematics.
>
> 1921: 388–9

In the final section of the book he reminds us of Hume's problem of induction, and again pours cold water on the use of statistical methods:

> I do not myself believe that there is any direct and simple method by which we can make the transition from an observed numerical frequency to a numerical measure of probability... In the next chapters we will consider the application of general inductive methods to this problem, and in this we will endeavour to discredit the mathematical charlatanry by which, for a hundred years past, the basis of theoretical statistics has been greatly undermined.   1921: 367

But it is not as if he is about to give a better theoretical basis: the last chapter is pessimistic even about using "collections of facts for the prediction of future frequencies and associations." In short, Keynes had been driven to a very general skepticism about the empirical basis of judgements of chance. Indeed by the end of the *Treatise* it looks to modern eyes as though one last push might have brought Keynes to the point of skepticism about his logical quasi-numerical probability relations altogether.

The aspect of this story that I want to emphasize is the way in which an exalted view of the subject matter, be it a metaphysical view or an a prioristic view, readily tips into skepticism. This is perhaps an old story. After all exalted views about the nature of God—unchanging, beyond space and time, necessarily existent—opened the door wide to the religious skepticism of Hobbes, Hume, and many others.

Keynes deserves enormous credit for laying bare the epistemological difficulties of his quasi-logical relations of implication. But he didn't in the *Treatise* repudiate the ideal of the pure logical relation that got him into those difficulties. This last push was provided by the teenage Ramsey, whose flat denial of the existence of these logical relations, and the need for them, was first voiced directly after Keynes's book came out, and then repeated at length in his 1926 paper 'Truth and Probability'. By avoiding Keynes's logical relations and replacing them by personal credence or degrees of belief in propositions, Ramsey actually put the epistemology of probability on a more secure footing. By what we might call humanizing it, Ramsey opens more epistemological possibilities. So, for example, one of Keynes's important targets is the inversion of Bernoulli's theorem, whereby instead of deriving confidence in some frequency of results given a sequence in which each event has the same independent probability, we try to derive the probability from the observed frequency. As part of his campaign against the mathematicians such as Karl Pearson, Keynes rightly says that there is no mathematical or logical relation between the observation and the probability, if only because the frequency by itself cannot imply that we have a Bernoulli sequence, that is, a sequence of independent events each with the same probability. Ramsey says in effect that even if Keynes is right about this, nevertheless there may clearly be a good inductive reason for taking such a frequency as a guide to the future, which will be all that is required to identify and support a degree of confidence, increasing as the sequence grows longer and stabilizes around a frequency.[1] And it is these degrees of confidence that we express in terms of chance. Probabilities and chances are not independent topics; they appear only in the toolkit we have for creating and assessing our expectations.

Ramsey's method for thinking about this echoes that of C. S. Peirce, asking what is the ideal habit of distributing confidence, and answering that we can praise or blame a habit of belief formation accordingly as the degree of belief it produces is near or far from the actual proportion of cases in which the habit leads to the truth. You do worse insofar as you expect things to happen which seldom or never happen, or conversely ignore possibilities that are frequently realized. If things often happen, but not quite always, you do better by expecting them, but to some extent hedging your bets. Ramsey, like Keynes himself, salutes Hume on induction. But unlike Keynes he also embraces Hume's naturalized epistemology. Like other animals we naturally suppose that the past will be a guide to the future; science is the enterprise of finding the important ways in which this is so.

Why is there no logical inference from empirical data to chance? Because embracing a system with which to meet the future is having a definite practical disposition, akin to having a sentiment. Being aware of the past frequencies or the rest of a data set is one thing, but feeling its force, acting in the light of it, making it a part of the 'system with which you meet the future' is often quite another, however natural we may sometimes find it to move from the first to the second. I say 'often quite another' because it is wrong to deny that descriptions of how things stand themselves will have implications for the future. It is then an open question how much, not only of science, but of common-sense descriptions of the world around us should yield to a parallel pragmatist treatment. Wilfrid Sellars thought it should, describing for example the way in which counterfactual inference intertwines with almost all such descriptions (Sellars 1958). This is unfortunately not the place to explore that fascinating avenue.[2]

4. The Pitfalls of Realism (2): The Case of Ethics

The shift from Keynes's logicism to Ramsey's expressivism has been disguised and disfigured by the unfortunate title of "subjectivism" or "the subjective theory of probability," first used by De Finetti (1931/1989), and made common by Leonard Savage (1954). It cannot be overemphasized that Ramsey is not in any useful

---

[1] More accurately, the frequency coupled with evidence that the events are 'exchangeable': that is, there is no reason to think that particular subsets of events with different frequencies can effectively be predicted.
[2] I do so at more length in Blackburn (forthcoming).

sense a subjectivist. He knows we can subject our own distributions of confidence to doubt and hope for improvement (Ramsey 1926/1990: 93). Just as we grade people as unreasonable or not, so we grade the ways they respond to the world. Some habits are unfortunate, ill-thought out, careless, or, in the case of those that lead to conspiracy theories and cults, downright wicked. Others set us on the road to successfully navigating the future.

Of course, there is some latitude here: how quick or how slow should we be to take a result to have a wider significance? There is doubtless a range of permissible temperaments between on the one hand jumping too quickly to conclusions, and on the other hand ignoring evidence that is staring you in the face. It is true that subjects may differ in temperament, and if this is all that is meant by subjectivism we can admit it—but it is no more than the consequence of the fact that any belief or mental disposition is that of some actual or possible subject. It does not imply that anything goes, or that people can without fault litter the public square with ludicrous views. Neither does it imply that anyone is immune from criticism and correction, nor that it is sensible, or even consistent, to take a stand that permits us to ignore in advance the reasons others may give for querying our own judgement.

Any worry about a rampant subjectivism in the case of science and its elements is quickly met by the undeniable facts of consensus and progress. This is not so in ethics. Nevertheless, here many philosophers have hymned the objectivity of the facts of morality. They are to be independent of our desires and attitudes. They cannot be brushed away: the hardness of the moral 'must' is comparable to that of the logical 'must'. They are sculpted in cold marble and discovering them is one of the most important philosophical tasks.

It did not take a Keynes to voice doubts about this. A rationalist, *a priori* epistemology for ethics had been soundly rejected by generations of philosophers. But often enough the idea of a bulls-eye, a final, unarguable, complete theory still lived on. And the reason was that querying it is frightening or horrifying to many. The cold marble of truth is needed, they think, because denying it raises the frightening spectre of nihilism, skepticism, licentiousness, and immorality. Again the parallel with the death of God and the fears that aroused is obvious.

My own work in meta-ethics has been particularly directed against these fears. From the beginning the point of quasi-realism was partly to fend off skepticisms, such as John Mackie's "error theory," which implied that first-order moral thought would somehow be undermined by pragmatism. It is as if without the cold marble our practices are bound to crumble. In those debates the principal form pragmatism took was an expressive theory of moral and other kinds of discourse, and I have consistently argued that although this does not by itself solve first-order moral problems, neither does it close any doors to trying to do so. The appearance of Derek Parfit's *On What Matters* in 2011 could be taken to show how unsuccessful expressivists had been in trying to vaccinate the academic world against this misunderstanding, although I believe the decade since has done much to increase immunity to it. Indeed Parfit himself (2017: 165–224), having been implacably scornful of expressivism, came to a somewhat lukewarm recognition of its merits shortly before his untimely death.

I shall not rehearse the ins and outs of quasi-realism here. I have done so often enough. Instead I want to return to the question asked at the outset of this chapter: how much should we expect these high-level doctrines and disputes to affect practice? If the nihilists and skeptics were right, the answer would be a great deal, as confidence in any and every moral judgement flies out of the window. But I argue exactly the reverse. Insofar as pragmatism—here manifested as expressivism in judgements of chance and judgements of morality and ethics—has any first-order implications, I believe that it does so by bringing the epistemology of such first-order claims more firmly into focus, and more firmly down to earth, than philosophies that exalt the "realistic" nature of these judgements. It is in fact only their difficulties in making sense of the cold marble of realism that leads philosopher such as John Mackie (1977), Richard Joyce (2001), or Sharon Street (2006) to worry about the propriety of first-order judgements. But first I would like to detour through the case of a pragmatist who, unfortunately, fell into the same trap.

5. A Cautionary Tale

Richard Rorty famously connected his enthusiasm for various ideas he found under the umbrella heading of pragmatism with liberal democratic ideals, following in the path trodden by John Dewey. I am however much less sanguine about the refraction of difficult philosophical choices into the politics or ideology of an age. I like to illustrate such doubts with a salutary story. Bruno de Finetti shares with Frank Ramsey the distinction of having put expressive theories of probability firmly on the map. And his 'Probabilismo' manuscript shows that this was not for him an isolated doctrine, confined to the theory of probability and credence. He saw it as part of a more embracing pragmatism, with very definite moral and political consequences. He starts with a rousing pragmatist quotation from the Italian right-wing thinker Adriano Tilgher:

> Truth no longer lies in an imaginary equation of the spirit with what is outside it, and which, being outside it, could not possibly touch it. The absolute is not outside our knowledge, to be sought in a realm of darkness and mystery; it is in our knowledge itself. Thought is not a mirror in which a reality external to us is faithfully reflected; it is simply a biological function, a means of orientation in life, of preserving and enriching it, of enabling and facilitating action, or taking account of reality and dominating it.
>
> de Finetti (1989: 169, quoting Tilgher 1923: 49, 46, 23–4)

Apart from the last two words this might sound like a striking anticipation of Richard Rorty. But mark the sequel. Towards the end of his essay de Finetti writes:

> But where my spirit rebelled most ferociously and clashed against the concept of "absolute truth" was in the political field... Those delicious absolute truths that stuffed the demo[cratic] liberal brains! That impeccable rational mechanics of the perfect civilian regime of the peoples, conforming to the rights of man and various other immortal principles!   1989: 219

And referring to taking part in the march on Rome in October 1922 that brought Mussolini's Fascist party to power, he concludes: 'It seemed to me I could see them, these Immortal Principles, as filthy corpses in the dust. And with what conscious and ferocious voluptuousness I felt myself trampling them, marching to hymns of triumph, obscure but faithful Blackshirt!' (*219*). Like Tilgher himself, de Finetti took pragmatism to imply an exciting modernist destruction of outworn absolute moral, political, or rational principles, but then, alas, the welcome march of Mussolini's Fascism into the vacuum left when they have died. Tilgher and de Finetti saw themselves as having a philosophy that enabled them to overthrow the authority of traditional mores of social and political life, but only in order to worship a far more repugnant authority of their own.

Did pragmatism really open a space within which this catastrophe was more likely to happen? It ought to seem strange, as strange in fact as supposing that an expressivist theory of probability should lead to skepticism about ordinary first-order judgements of probability. But surely nobody would suppose that it implies a free-for-all in which there would be no fault in supposing that the chance of my walking to the nearby shops unaided is the same as the chance of my flying there unaided, or that the chance of my seeing a squirrel as I do so is no greater than the chance of my seeing a fairy. However much ferociously voluptuous pleasure anyone takes in trampling on well-attested judgements of chance, expressivism and pragmatism cannot be held to blame for their raptures. De Finetti may have thought that he was free to select his morality as he saw fit, but he did not think the same about judgements of probability. Pragmatists must remember Peirce's stress on actual processes of accepting and testing judgements, and not be seduced by abstract fears of metaphysical vacuums.

The view that morality is a matter of shared sentiment rather than otherworldly acquaintance with abstractions and reasons stands as Ramsey's view of chance did to Keynes's. It does not by itself dictate which moral views are correct, but it removes obstacles to understanding the actual dynamics of fixing on some and eschewing others. In morality it allows us to embrace the fact that sentiments become shared through human channels of imitation and persuasion, and to look askance at anyone sheltering under umbrellas of supposed authority or *a priori* principles. De Finetti was right to see that in this sense we are on our own, but wrong to derive from this his voluptuous sense of irresponsibility. For the populist Fascist atmosphere of the time unfortunately prevented him from exercising this freedom in a responsible, civilized, or decent way. He was ahead of his time in resembling the later addicts of Q-Anon and the rest.

6. Will Truth Out?

Ramsey's combination of expressivism with suitable epistemic seriousness, openness, and modesty may well have been buttressed by reading Peirce, whose collection *Chance, Love and Logic* had been given to him by its English publisher, C. K. Ogden, in 1923, shortly after his original attack on Keynes. It has recently been argued that Peirce's theory of scientific method and his championship of open, scientific inquiry give rise to at least one practical conclusion: a particular reason for respecting democracy. The idea is to identify democracy as not only possessing moral and practical advantages over other systems of government, but as something more like a necessary condition of satisfying one's own responsibility to the truth. The line of argument is presented by Robert Talisse (2013: 500): 'The thesis is that we have sufficient epistemological reasons to be democrats. The epistemological norms that we take ourselves to be governed by can be satisfied only under certain social conditions, and these social conditions are best secured under democracy'. The argument is intended to be non-consequentialist, and the idea is also presented by Cheryl Misak and Robert Talisse (Misak and Talisse 2021: 12) as follows:

> A true belief is one that would result in successful action, were we to continue to expose our beliefs to the tests of experience in complex ways, ways which need not involve our senses and which include the experience of being presented with reasons and argument. A true belief is the belief that would stand up to that robust kind of experience, if we were to pursue the matter as far as we fruitfully could. There is a built-in rationale here for democratic methods of inquiry and ways of living. If we want beliefs that would stand up to all experience, we had better take the experiences of all seriously.

And again (2021: 13):

> If we fail to take the views of others seriously, then we can be criticized for failing to aim at getting true beliefs. Put the other way, when we claim to hold genuine beliefs that are right or true, we commit ourselves to taking the experience of others seriously. This holds for physics as well as ethics. If we

refuse to look at results from Finnish labs, we are not genuine truth-seekers, and if we refuse to take seriously the experience of women, or of Muslim immigrants, or of trans people, we are not genuine truth-seekers. We can be criticized on these second-order grounds (of irrationality), as well as on first order grounds (of cruelty, failure of imagination, prejudice, or selfishness).[3]

The result is impressive enough, but does it stand up? It would be a shining example of pragmatism having a direct political consequence, and one which would be welcome to many of us. Although at the outset we might want to wonder to what extent the emphasis on these norms is peculiar to any one philosophical movement, such as pragmatism. There have indeed been philosophers who more or less ignored the social nature of inquiry: the tradition of individualism from Descartes through to Locke and beyond certainly obscured it. But once the social dimension has been pointed out, few philosophers if any would persist in thinking that the rational pursuit of inquiry is essentially private. Peirce may well have been one of the first to emphasize that it is not, but I cannot think that the insight remains the private property of any one school.

Let us sum up the various norms to be obeyed if we are responsible to the truth as the use of Right Reason in the context of inquiry. I think it is then useful to distinguish two steps. First, we recognize that Right Reason implies openness to reasons or experiences to which others may direct you. We can sum this up by saying that epistemological norms cannot often be obeyed in private: collecting and collating evidence is a social matter. At the very least, even for matters which we believe we can settle by ourselves, the question of whether others confirm or contest our view is bound to be relevant. Second, we should recognize that the openness to others requires a social setting. The second step says that this openness is at the very least more likely to exist under a democracy than any other form of government.

Unfortunately it appears to me that each step is in danger of weakening in the light of qualifications that quickly start to proliferate. Taking a rather different leaf out of Peirce's book, we should not copy the mistake made by Pontius Pilate, who troubled himself by airily asking what is truth, when he should instead have been concentrating on the case in front of him. We should think not so much of any abstraction, such as 'responsibility to the truth', but to the kinds of problems of responsibly forming and adjusting beliefs that arise *in medias res*. Then indeed Right Reason will typically require social resources. We may well need libraries, laboratories, personal anecdotes, and specialists of one sort or another to supplement our own epistemological resources which, meagre though they may be, will themselves have been nurtured and moulded in particular social settings. Thus

---

[3] I am grateful to Annabelle Lever for directing me to this literature.

far, we can and should agree with Talisse and Misak that Right Reason implies that we take the views of others seriously.

But not all others, all of the time. In an open society, anyone can have a view about almost anything, but not everybody is worth listening to. If I need an opinion on the safety of GM foods, I cannot rely on my own experiences, none of which I know to be relevant. I would need to take account of resources provided (however indirectly) by biologists, toxicologists, and agronomists. I would need to weigh their opinions, and insofar as consensus seems to have emerged I might find myself swayed in one direction or another. Right Reason would be satisfied, whereas it would not if I simply plumped for whatever Bob on my Facebook group says on the matter. But I wouldn't need to consult medieval historians, political theorists, or experts on the New Testament or palaeography. If any of those came forward to volunteer a view, I should doubtless listen out of courtesy, but it would be irresponsible to give it much weight. Hence, a good way to satisfy the demands of Right Reason is to restrict our confidence and our inquiries to areas in which, however indirectly, we take there to be social resources that properly confirm the answers we give. On other matters, we are cautiously to suspend judgement.

Peirce was also right that doubt is often uncomfortable. But that is only so when we want to find something out. And however curious we are, there are an indefinitely huge number of things about which we do not care at all. Speaking for myself I have no wish whatever to have beliefs about the private lives of footballers, or the names of winners of the Grand National from 1940 to 1980. It is not so much that I am in doubt about these things, and still less that I *feel* doubt about them. It is just that except for the purpose of providing philosophical examples, they do not swim into my consciousness at all. My responsibility to the truth does not stretch so far, so long as I am not stupidly confident of answers to these questions, while still having no evidence about them whatsoever. Right Reason cannot dictate the width of my interests, even if, given that I am a normal human being, it goes along with the awareness that some interests (sustenance, security, self-respect, health) are essential.

Hence I need not care if a social system shuts down or distorts some channels of information, so long as these are confined to things about which I do not care. It is of course possible that this could change. I might find a reason to want to know particular things about which I am at present unconcerned. And then I would be glad to live in a society where free and open access to reliable sources of information is at least possible, however expensive or arduous it might be. In Misak's example, if I decide I need to find out the nature of Bangladeshi society, I could only form opinions responsibly by listening to the voices of Muslim women as well as, or indeed in preference to, the voices of elderly male *mullahs*.

I think we can accept that dictatorships or totalitarian societies are very likely to block avenues of information whenever the truth is inconvenient to the beliefs, projects, or self-image of the government. But the demands of Right Reason can be met in such societies by leaving alone issues about which the government is likely to have poisoned the wells. Insofar as we are curious about them, we may find this frustrating, which indeed it is. But we also need to remember that when we think it likely that some power has disabled some avenues of inquiry, it is unlikely that Right Reason will tell people under its sway to open them. The government takes care to assure people, falsely, that Right Reason is fully satisfied by studying an official account of things. For example the Chinese Communist Party currently gives its population either no account or a false account of the events culminating in the Tiananmen Square massacre in 1989, and it suppresses sources of information that could tell its population that the official account is untrue, or remains true only by being entirely silent about the event. But this does not mean that Chinese people are unreasonable or unfaithful to the norms governing inquiry, if they attempt to master that piece of history. They will do so by listening to the experts (themselves unfortunately indoctrinated by the Party) and reading the textbooks, which of course will be similarly handicapped. The people may be suspicious but will have no way of knowing how far their handicaps extend.

I am not of course denying that we, in the open West, are in a better position to find out and know the truth on this and other such matters. In an open society it is much harder for anyone effectively and finally to block the emergence of the truth. If some power poisons the wells, it can eventually be brought to book.[4] Nevertheless many such avenues do get blocked in democratic societies as well. In a grand gesture of openness in the year 2000, the UK parliament passed a Freedom of Information Act requiring public bodies to answer requests for information that anyone may make. Nevertheless the government regularly impedes freedom of information citing any of a large number of get-out clauses. The USA has the admirable First Amendment to its constitution, a robust veto on Congress passing any law 'abridging the freedom of speech, or of the press' but the freedom this offers can scarcely be said to secure the epistemic health of its population. The wells are poisoned by individual agents and corporations, by people being muzzled by such things as non-disclosure clauses, by polarizations created or abetted by social media, by zealotries usurping the place of science, by limited education in public schools. These are serious obstacles to the deployment of Right Reason by many people in many democracies and across a frighteningly large range of issues.[5]

---

[4] As I write this the ghastly conspiracy theorist, Alex Jones, whose lies included the denial that the Sandy Hook school massacre had taken place, has been convicted and ordered to pay nearly $50 million to those bereaved by the event.

[5] Similar reservations have been voiced by Annabelle Lever (2021: 37): 'In short, the path from our individual interests in truth to a justification of democratic government is likely to be far longer and

We might hope that institutional pressures are too weak to assault the citadel of scientific integrity. But many examples suggest otherwise. The most salient is the familiar example of Big Pharma—the institutional corruption of science by the billions of dollars involved in the manufacture and selling of drugs. The medical writer Ben Goldacre (2008) reports that a meta-analysis of trials that are funded by pharmaceutical companies found that these are four times as likely than independent trials to give results favourable to the company. He also cites one set of fifty-six trials comparing different painkillers—ibuprofen, diclofenac, and so on. In every single trial the sponsoring manufacturer's drug came out better or at least equal to any other in the trial: the result being the logically impossible one that each of these drugs was better than any of the others. And then there are cases like that of Nancy Olivieri in Toronto who was sued, harassed, and disowned by her university for insisting on revealing the toxic side effects of a drug, deferiprone. The drug company was a major donor to the university's pharmacology research programme.[6] Cases like these might be met with the cheering thought that science is self-corrective, so that in the long run truth will out. But that cheery thought meets the brutal fact that scientific resources are finite, and less effort is directed to the less prestigious business of checking the results of others than to forging ahead with flashy results of one's own. And in any event, the passage of time covers many tracks, and we should remember Keynes's own pithy comment that in the long run we are all dead.

We might say that a society is epistemically healthy insofar as, across the widest possible range, it has the fewest possible obstacles to the open pursuit of the truth. But then I think it is not difficult to imagine a totalitarian society that enjoys better opportunities to use Right Reason than a democratic society gripped by the ailments I have mentioned, even if in the real world there have been very few, if any, examples.

To return finally to the more abstract philosophical issue: does pragmatism as a philosophy improve practice rather than impeding it? I hope I have shown that the terrain is not easy to traverse, and as with so many questions of an abstract kind, the answers may vary from case to case. But in spite of the inevitable setbacks, we can hope that the tide of Right Reason must rise relentlessly and eventually sweep away surviving jungles of unreason. And as it does so we can thank Peirce, Dewey, Ramsey, and many other pragmatists for their glorious successes in describing it, and abetting it.

---

more contingent than the Peircean justification of democracy implies. That path may even point in directions that are not especially liberal, constitutional or democratic, depending on how one defines terms and interprets empirical evidence and counterfactuals'.

[6] A summary can be found at https://jme.bmj.com/content/30/1/44

References

Blackburn, S. (forthcoming). 'Real Ethics', in P. Bloomfield and D. Copp (eds.), *The Oxford Handbook of Ethics*, Oxford: Oxford University Press.

de Finetti, B. (1931/1989). 'Probabilism', M. Di Maio, M. Galavotti, and Richard Jeffrey (trans.), *Erkenntnis* 31: 169–223.

Goldacre, B. (2008). *Bad Science*, London: Harper Collins.

Hume, D. (1740/1975). *A Treatise of Human Nature*, ed. L. A. Selby-Bigge, 2nd ed. revised by P. H. Nidditch, Oxford: Clarendon Press.

Joyce, R. (2001). *The Myth of Morality*, Cambridge: Cambridge University Press.

Keynes, J. M. (1921). *A Treatise on Probability*, London: Macmillan and Co.

Lever, A. (2021). 'Democracy and Truth', *Raisons Politiques* 81/1: 29–38.

Mackie J. (1977). *Ethics, Inventing Right and Wrong*, New York: Penguin Books.

Misak, C. and Talisse, R. (2021). 'Pragmatism, Truth, and Democracy', *Raisons Politiques* 81/1: 11–27.

Parfit, D. (2017). *On What Matters*, vol. 3, Oxford: Oxford University Press.

Ramsey, F. P. (1926/1990). 'Truth and Probability', in D. H. Mellor (ed.), *Philosophical Papers*, Cambridge: Cambridge University Press, 52–94.

Savage, L. J. (1954). *The Foundations of Statistics*, New York: John Wiley.

Sellars W. (1958). 'Counterfactuals, Dispositions, Causal Modalities', in H. Feigl, M. Scriven, and G. Maxwell (eds.), *Minnesota Studies in the Philosophy of Science*, vol. 2, Minneapolis: University of Minnesota Press.

Street, S. (2006). 'A Darwinian Dilemma for Realist Theories of Value', *Philosophical Studies* 127/1: 109–66.

Talisse, R. (2013). 'Sustaining Democracy: Folk Epistemology and Social Conflict', *Critical Review of International Social and Political Philosophy* 16/4: 500–19.

Tilgher, A. (1923). *Relativisti contemporanei*, IVth ed., Rome: Libreria di scienze e lettere.

12
Pragmatism and the Ontology of Art

Robert Kraut

> The aesthetician, if I understand his business aright, is not concerned with dateless realities lodged in some metaphysical heaven, but with the facts of his own place and his own time.
>
> R. G. Collingwood (1939: 325)

In his groundbreaking formalist manifesto *Art* (1913), Clive Bell (1958) laments the dearth of outstanding work in aesthetic theory. His diagnosis—invidious and potentially offensive, but perhaps correct—is that artistic sensibilities and analytical skills are separable, often occurring in one another's absence: would-be aestheticians sensitive to the arts are often poor theorists, thus fostering bad theories; and theorists skilled in rigorous theory construction often lack artistic sensitivity, thus depriving them of urgently relevant data.

It is ironic that Bell himself falls short on the theoretical side. The alleged data purportedly explained by his "aesthetic hypothesis"—viz. "the peculiar emotion provoked by works of art" and the (alleged) fact that art "transports us from the world of man's activity to a world of aesthetic exaltation"—are problematic at best (Bell 1958: 27) His "isolationist" conception of art and aesthetic experience is notorious:

> to appreciate a work of art we need bring with us nothing from life, no knowledge of its ideas and affairs, no familiarity with its emotions... For a moment we are shut off from human interests; our anticipations and memories are arrested; we are lifted above the stream of life. 1958: 27

Such a conception is out of phase with the realities of artworld experience and practice. Most people—ranging from philistines to highly cultivated aesthetes—regard artworks as essentially embedded in cultures and histories.

Bell's inquiry might have been different. Had he been moved by the spirit of pragmatism—in one of its many guises—he might have proceeded thus:

(1) Begin by recognizing that the artworld contains not only participants whose reactions to artworks involve transfigurative aesthetic emotions but also a wide range of people—varying in sophistication and familiarity

Robert Kraut, *Pragmatism and the Ontology of Art* In: *Neopragmatism: Interventions in First-Order Philosophy*. Edited by: Joshua Gert, Oxford University Press. © Robert Kraut 2023. DOI: 10.1093/oso/9780192894809.003.0012

with artworld history and culture—whose reactions to artworks differ from those privileged by Bell. Resist at the outset the exclusivist temptation to acknowledge some but not all artworld phenomena as worthy of theoretical accommodation.

(2) Building upon observation of actual critical practice (rather than *a priori* reflection upon aesthetic concepts), acknowledge that the historical context of production might be inseparable from the artwork itself, thereby undermining the isolationist picture conveyed by Bell. Grant that the artworld contains controversies about the artistic significance and value of various objects, performances, and achievements, and that such controversies are part of the data to be explained.

(3) Then turn a theoretical eye upon this dizzying array seeking to articulate the principles and norms sustained within actual practices of artistic creation, interpretation, evaluation, and commodification. Avoid bias in specifying the relevant data: the goal is to articulate and explain what actually occurs in the artworld, not what—according to some antecedently favored theory—ought to occur in the artworld.

Pragmatism recommends directives (1)–(3) as the canonical method for constructing a theory of art. Work by Arthur Danto (1964, 1981) and George Dickie (1974a, 1974b, 1984) explicitly conforms to such a model; and John Dewey's (1934) account of art and its significance remains a paradigm of pragmatist theorizing in this domain. But much work in aesthetic theory runs afoul of such methods and constraints, thereby lapsing into implausibility.

The goal here is exploratory: to observe the impact of pragmatist doctrine and method in theorizing about various aspects of the arts. Two strategies often prompted by pragmatist agendas—"institutional" theories of art and expressivist semantics for art-critical discourse—are shown to face serious obstacles. But—on the positive side—it emerges that pragmatist indictments of metaphysics justify skepticism about the ontology of art, thereby validating one strain of "neopragmatist" anti-representationalism. Pragmatist theories of art thus garner mixed reviews, depending upon the variety under consideration.

1

Precise specification of *pragmatism* would be helpful, but difficult to provide: a wide range of views tend to appear under the pragmatist rubric.[1] Frequently it involves little more than homage paid to the work of James, Peirce, and/or Dewey.

---

[1] A systematic effort to articulate the core features of pragmatism—if such there be—is provided in Kraut (1990).

More robust versions stress views about truth and reference (e.g. rejection of truth-as-correspondence-to-reality, or a more thoroughgoing deflationism about semantic discourse); other versions foreground the primacy of institutional norms, rejection of representational theories of mind and language, the significance of justificatory holism, inferentialist theories of conceptual content, and/or the folly of seeking to "ground" institutional practices in facts about confrontations with ontological realities which make normative demands. More radical versions challenge the very notions of *correspondence, accurate representation,* and *adequately capturing the world* (see, e.g., Rorty 1972).

Contemporary pragmatism—often dubbed 'neopragmatism'—opposes the idea that legitimacy—or illegitimacy—of institutional practices consists in conformity—or non-conformity—to requirements issuing from objects, properties, states of affairs, or categories that demand compliance. It is people, not objects, that make demands, and whose patterns of behavior constitute the ultimate grounds of normativity; thus Rorty (1982: 165):

> [pragmatism] is the doctrine that there are no constraints on inquiry save conversational ones—no wholesale constraints derived from the nature of the objects, or of the mind, or of language, but only those retail constraints provided by the remarks of our fellow inquirers.

This theme, conjoined with anti-representationalism—viz. the denial that a privileged word-world relation of "reference" or "representation" plays a key role in understanding language use—constitutes the strain of neopragmatism explored in what follows.

2

There could be a concern as to whether 'pragmatism' names a substantive doctrine or a methodological canon. C. S. Peirce, e.g., interested in clarification of concepts we already possess, sought to determine the practical consequences attendant upon application of a given concept:

> Consider what effects, which might conceivably have practical bearings, we conceive the object of our conception to have. Then our conception of these effects is the whole of our conception of the object.   Peirce (1878: 132)

This amounts to a theory of conceptual content in terms of practices and activities. Other characterizations treat pragmatism as a methodology which privileges social-institutional practices both as primary data and primary explanans. Simon Blackburn, e.g., is driven by pragmatist sentiment to eschew (where possible) explanations in terms of word/world correspondence relations and representational semantics, opting instead for expressivist strategies:

> You will be a pragmatist about an area of discourse if you pose a Carnapian external question: how does it come about that we go in for this kind of discourse and thought? What is the explanation of this bit of our language game? And then you offer an account of what we are up to in going in for this discourse, and the account eschews any use of the referring expressions of the discourse... Instead the explanation proceeds by talking in different terms of what is *done* by so talking. It offers a revelatory genealogy or anthropology or even a just-so story about how this mode of talking and thinking and practicing might come about, given in terms of the functions it serves. Blackburn (2013: 75)

Obviously there are objects and properties constraining human practice; pragmatism is not idealism.[2] But the pragmatist puzzles about the nature of such constraint, and seeks to understand the human condition not by privileging correspondence relations with objects, but by exploring the fabric of inferential connections and institutional practices associated with any given region of conceptual space.

There could also be a concern about whether the pragmatist aesthetician, having identified the relevant institutional facts and communal norms sustained within the artistic community, is then obligated to "dig deeper" and identify properties which putatively explain those facts and norms. This additional step involves an effort to locate underlying causal determinants of the institutional facts: an inference to the best explanation. But the posited explanatory properties—whether Bell's significant form, Plato's mimetic resemblance, Tolstoy's emotional expressiveness, or the Christian theologian's Presence of the Holy Ghost—might have no place within the pragmatist agenda. Less controversial explanatory properties—those involving, e.g., social cooperation, evolutionary forces, or strategic solutions to institutional coordination problems—might find place among the pragmatist's acceptable explanans; often it is unclear which explanatory resources are acceptable to the pragmatist, and why.

Above all, the pragmatist insists that inquiries into the nature of art are significantly different from inquiries into the essence of physical interactions (wherein underlying microstructures are posited to explain observables). Aesthetics is not chemistry. But the pragmatist also insists that if putative *grounds* of artworld phenomena are identified, the posited underlying properties and relations cannot be mere idle redescriptions (perhaps in richly metaphysical language) of the institutional facts: they must do explanatory work.

---

[2] Misguided conflations of pragmatism with idealism are explored in Kraut and Scharp (2015).

Possible pragmatist credo: focus upon patterns of social behavior, within which norms of action are upheld; pay no mind to the explanatory grounds beneath. Possible rejoinder: why?

Pragmatism gives pride of place to the articulation and explanation of the principles sustained within institutional practice. But in the realm of aesthetic theory it is conspicuous that traditional theorizing often ignores the realities of history and society; such theories fail—by pragmatist lights—to accommodate relevant data.

Examples of such infractions are plentiful. Consider Leo Tolstoy's (1896) "infection" theory of art—a paradigm instance of bad theorizing—which insists upon the transmission of sincerely experienced feelings and the lowering of affective boundaries between artist and audience. The resulting theory disenfranchises an enormous swath of generally accepted artists and artworks of Tolstoy's time (viz. those celebrated by elite social classes): for they fail to meet his stipulated conditions. But those conditions find insufficient ground in actual artworld practice.

Another such infraction is R. G. Collingwood's (1938: esp. ch. VI) theory of art in terms of *emotional expression*, where this latter concept is understood by Collingwood as emancipation from the helpless state of not knowing one's own mind. Collingwood regards genuine art ("art proper") as essentially bound to this self-clarificatory process; objects or events that fail to conform to this model fall by the wayside as either non-art or, in some cases, "counterfeit art." But once again something has gone wrong. Grant that clarification of an artist's own emotional state plays a role in the production of certain artworks: the paintings of Jackson Pollock come to mind as resulting from such a profoundly introspective process. But elevating this dynamic self-clarificatory enterprise to an essential condition of artistic production results in a theory that disenfranchises much of what routinely qualifies as art. The theory has lost touch with the data. Given Collingwood's credo voiced in the epigraph above, this is especially ironic.

There are more recent infractions. Monroe Beardsley (1958, 1979), seeking an account of artistic value, identifies a particular set of phenomenological responses to art, which responses are tied to perceptually discernible features of artworks. But Beardsley's strategy ignores art-critical realities insofar as it overlooks the significance of non-observable properties; here is Henry Pratt's gloss:

> Beardsley associates artistic value with disinterested attention to perceptually accessible properties of artworks, which necessitates disregard both for the conditions under which the works were produced and for the works' representational content. While some artworks can be evaluated fairly under such requirements, particularly those whose value derives from formal features, the actual practices and standards typical of art evaluation do not fit comfortably with Beardsley's view.   2012: 596

Tolstoy, Collingwood, and Beardsley fail by pragmatist lights; but they also fail by the lights of *any* acceptable theory construction, insofar as the theorist's task is to explain and predict observables. In what, then, does the uniquely pragmatist methodology consist? It is unclear how it contrasts with its alleged rivals. Perhaps it is a matter of what counts as relevant data, or what counts as an explanation. But clearly the pragmatist regards any theorizing that distorts the shape of the practice, or ignores subtleties visible from within, as inadequate. And here loom puzzles, prompted by the pragmatist's avowed efforts to accommodate "the realities of the practice." Surely only *relevant* realities merit attention; but it is unclear what counts as relevant, or why, and thus what constitutes *data* in the pragmatist's inquiry.

Related to questions about relevant data are questions about the scope and limits of the practice to be observed and explained. "Institutional" theorists—notably Danto and Dickie—often refer to "the artworld," as though there exists a relatively cohesive (though perhaps "informal") identifiable institutional structure (perhaps indistinct around the edges) on which to focus. Others dispute the assumption. If an artwork's socio-cultural and economic context of origin is deemed relevant to the interpretive enterprise, it is not obvious (without begging questions about the nature of art) how much of the passing institutional show qualifies as belonging to the pragmatist's targeted domain. Talk of "artworld practice," like talk of "relevant data," appears vacuous, pending further directives.

3

Possible procedure: look to savvy non-philistines when seeking to determine the nature of art; try to discover the norms and assumptions operative in description, interpretation, and evaluation of artworks; study interactions and disagreements among art critics, their descriptions of artworks, their patterns of approval and censure, their willingness to display a given object in a museum or present a sonic event in a concert hall. On the basis of such data determine what sort of thing an artwork might be, and what sorts of things aesthetic properties might be, in order to best explain social-institutional artworld practices. Basically: focus upon the experiences and behavior of those who understand the subject matter; ignore the rest of the population as irrelevant philistines.

But here looms circularity.[3] The problem is articulated by Ryan Michael:

> Discussions of pragmatism in aesthetics often tell us to look to the practices of qualified experts...The first thing we want to know is what certifies them as experts if not the ability to identify and discern the real features of artworks

---

[3] This is not news: circularities looming in the area are frequently noted by aesthetic theorists. See, e.g., Kivy (1967).

successfully. If real aesthetic properties are what explains it, then it seems that our aesthetic theories shouldn't be grounded in the attitudes of experts and deflated into the social practice, but should instead focus upon the deeper reality that those practices and attitudes point toward. If it's not that, we want to know how to carve out the relevant data or practices.

Private correspondence (October 18, 2019)

Michael's concern is that the pragmatist's insistence upon the primacy of practice is illusory: unless the ontology of art and aesthetic properties is already in place, circumscribing the class of relevant experts is not possible. Social practice—or, more precisely, canons of relevance for delineating social practice—cannot be regarded as the ground of ontology. It is the other way around: efforts to extrapolate the ontology from the practice are already contaminated with assumptions about the ontology.

The predicament is clear: without prior specification of the nature of artworks and aesthetic properties, the portions of social practice relevant to resolving philosophical questions about the arts cannot be circumscribed in any principled way. So much for the primacy of practice over ontology.

This pragmatist-unfriendly conclusion rests upon a fundamental assumption about the relation between properties and practices: viz. that the requisite properties are not themselves practice-dependent. But suppose it could be demonstrated that the properties enlisted to circumscribe the relevant community are *socially constructed*: that is, dependent upon practices within some specified population. Such dependence might take various forms: constitution, response-dependence, conferral, reification of norms, or yet some other variant.[4] However construed, such dependence would endow the specified population with ontological priority, insofar as reference to the properties would involve implicit reference to the population that constitutes them. The entities enlisted to delineate relevant practices would constitute no departure—*pace* Michael's earlier misgivings—from the primacy of institutional practice.

Put this another way. If aesthetic properties—the coherence of a symphony, the mystery of a painting, the energetic tension of an improvised jazz solo—are, as a matter of metaphysical fact, somehow dependent upon subjective or institutional phenomena (e.g. matters of collective taste), then references to such properties constitute no departure from the pragmatist's privileged resources: invoking such properties in explanations or justifications of artworld practice remains consistent with pragmatist agendas. On the other hand, if such properties are mind-independent, practice-independent existents, then—depending upon their

---

[4] For a good discussion of the possibilities, see Sveinsdottir (2013); see also Haslanger (1995).

constitution—the pragmatist might eschew their deployment in explanatory and/ or justificatory endeavors.

The upshot is that a careful inquiry into the metaphysics of aesthetic properties is imperative. Pending such inquiry it is unclear whether references to such properties in delineations, explanations, or justifications of artworld practices run afoul of pragmatist constraints.

4

Insistence upon the primacy of practice in theorizing about art faces a familiar challenge: viz. to circumscribe the relevant institutional structure without assuming the very notions that prompt the inquiry. Call this the "relevant community" problem. It is not unique to pragmatist aesthetic theory; familiar instances of the problem arise elsewhere.

It is most familiar in moral theory. Consider traditional portrayals of "moral relativism," wherein the standards of morality are claimed to be relative to cultural norms sustained within relevant social structures. Such relativism requires that relevant social structures be specified without begging questions about the "objectivity" or "universality" of morality, lest the relativist sentiment be undercut (as J. L. Austin (1962: 2) famously said, "There's the bit where you give it, and the bit where you take it back"). But the theory faces an immediate challenge, as W. T. Stace picturesquely notes:

> Does the American nation constitute a "group" having a single moral standard?... Perhaps every town and village has its own peculiar standard... "In Rome do as Rome does" may seem as good a rule in morals as it is in etiquette. But can we stop there? Within the village are numerous cliques each having its own set of ideas. Why should not each of these claim to be bound only by its own special and peculiar moral standards? And if it comes to that, why should not the gangsters of Chicago claim to constitute a group having its own morality, so that its murders and debaucheries must be viewed as "right" by the only standard which can legitimately be applied to it?
>
> Stace (1937: 52–3; see also Rachels 2009)

Stace's point bears less on the plausibility of moral relativism than on its very intelligibility: for if "relative to *what*?" finds no principled answer, it is not clear what remains of relativism: it appears to collapse into individualistic subjectivism. Thus it is, perhaps, with pragmatist efforts in other areas: e.g. efforts to illuminate aesthetic concepts in terms of social practices. Without some principled procedure for circumscribing the institutional practices relative to which aesthetic theories are to be formulated and assessed, it is not clear what remains of the pragmatist's strategy. The predicament goes beyond morality or aesthetics: *any* strategy invoking relativity requires clear delineation of the relata, lest the strategy be vacuous.

The problem might be tractable;[5] but if, as the pragmatist alleges, key notions deployed in connection with the arts are best understood in terms of social/institutional practices, it is vital to determine which practices are relevant, and why.

The most sustained effort to engage the problem of "relevant artistic community" is provided in George Dickie's "institutional" theory of art, which seeks to elucidate the nature of art by reference to social institutions. In response to allegations that his account suffers from circularity, Dickie responds thus:

> If, in the end, the artworld cannot be described independently of art, that is, if the description contains references to art historians, art reporters, plays, theaters, and so on, then the definition strictly speaking is circular. It is not, however, viciously so, because the whole account in which the definition is embedded contains a great deal of information about the artworld...What is important to see is that art is an institutional concept and this requires seeing the definition in the context of the whole account. I suspect that the "problem" of circularity will arise frequently, perhaps always, when institutional concepts are dealt with.
>
> 1974b: 48

Grant with Dickie that not all circularities—or interdependencies—are malignant; properties frequently travel in holistic bundles. Circularities are inevitable. Some circularities are benign (see Humberstone 1997; Keefe 2002). But some are not. The pragmatist seeking to ground aesthetic phenomena in institutional practices has yet to provide a non-question-begging account of which practices are relevant, and why (see Wieand 1981).

Institutionalism, traditionally conceived, is a descriptive theory: facts about art and aesthetic properties are identified with facts about activities and verdicts within institutional structures. It is a *reductive* theory. Whether an object or event satisfies Dickie's conditions is an objective, factual matter. As Dickie (1974b: 48) put it, "a work of art in the classificatory sense is an artifact upon which some person or persons acting on behalf of a certain social institution (the artworld) has conferred the status of candidate for appreciation." The theory appears acceptable by pragmatist lights—provided we have some non-circular justification for picking out just the participants focused upon by Dickie.

But controversy looms. Here is a critical assessment by Richard Wollheim:

> Does the art-world really nominate representatives? If it does, when, where and how do these nominations take place? Do the representatives, if they exist, pass

---

[5] The literature addressing such issues is extensive. See the helpful bibliography provided by Chris Gowans (2019) in his excellent SEP survey of moral relativism. See also MacFarlane (2014) for overviews and careful consideration of challenges.

in review all candidates for the status of art, and do they then, while conferring this status on some, deny it to others? What record is kept of these conferrals, and is the status itself subject to revision? If so, at what intervals, how, and by whom? And, last but not least, Is there really such a thing as the art-world, with the coherence of a social group, capable of having representatives, who are in turn capable of carrying out acts that society is bound to endorse? 1987: 15

Other writers voice similar misgivings about the existence of institutional structures and patterns of representative authorization sufficiently robust to do the work required by Dickie's theory.[6]

One way of confronting these problems is to change the subject: shift from an inquiry into the nature of artworks and aesthetic properties to an inquiry into the role played and purposes served by *recognizing* an object or event *as* an artwork. Perhaps the locution "Duchamp's *Fountain* is a work of art" serves not to state a fact—the nature of which continues to elude theorists—but rather serves to express an attitude or commitment to engaging a specific inverted urinal in certain ways. The nature of the alleged attitude or commitment would then require specification: the stimuli that prompt it, the situations that merit it, the patterns of behavior mandated or prohibited by it, the position occupied by the attitude within the larger institutional scheme. But theoretical attention would shift from the nature of aesthetic facts to the nature of aesthetic attitudes and commitments.

Another face of pragmatism thus emerges—perhaps the most familiar in the current climate: the face of nondescriptivism, which involves abandoning representationalist paradigms and instead focusing upon the social-institutional roles played by the targeted regions of discourse—in this case, thought and talk about artworks. Pragmatist credo: de-emphasize denotations of expressions, extensions of predicates, truth conditions of assertions. Shift emphasis from "What is art?" and "What kinds of properties are expressed by aesthetic predicates?" to "What role is played by aesthetic concepts and discourse within the larger pattern of human affairs? What is a person *doing* in designating an object or event as an artwork, or in conferring the status of *artwork* upon an item?"

5

In 1949, Arnold Isenberg published "Critical Communication," which attempted a detailed analysis of the structure and function of art criticism and stressed the influence of art-critical concepts upon the process of perception:

---

[6] See, e.g., Khatchadourian (1979). Dickie's theory evolves in response to such objections; later versions abandon the notions of *status conferral* and *acting on behalf of* as "too formal." See Dickie (1983).

> the critic…gives us directions for perceiving, and does this by means of the idea he imparts to us, which narrows down the field of possible visual orientations and guides us in the discrimination of details, the organization of parts, the grouping of discrete objects into patterns…This [critical] remark shifts the focus of our attention and brings certain qualities which had been blurred and marginal into distinct consciousness.   1949: 336

In other words: art criticism is primarily in the business of *shaping and altering* aesthetic perception. Attributions of aesthetic properties to artworks serve to *guide* viewers and listeners toward noticing certain features rather than others, and toward unifying observable features in certain ways. One might say that such apparent property attributions, despite surface appearances, are not property attributions at all: they are invitations rather than descriptions. The daunting challenge is to then explain the semantic realities of art-critical discourse against the backdrop of the ontological belt-tightening that accompanies Isenberg's non-descriptivist explanatory agenda.

Isenberg's claim is that the critic who speaks of, e.g., "what the artwork expresses" is issuing an invitation to experience the work in one way rather than another—to travel through the city, as it were, via a given route, attending to certain structures and conditions. The profoundly important question is whether the critic's interlocutor should embrace these travel recommendations, and what might be gained by doing so. After all, every critic, musicologist, or art historian is motivated by interests, goals, artworld orientation, and research agendas; a critic's recommended approach to the work might or might not optimize others' aesthetic utilities. And perhaps the word 'invitation' distorts the dynamic of critical dialogue: 'bullying' or 'manipulation' might more accurately describe the process. Nevertheless, Isenberg's theory is a bold gesture toward an expressivist explanation of aesthetic discourse—an explanation that does *not* involve the metaphysical nature or epistemic accessibility of aesthetic properties, because—on this view—there are none.

The challenge here is to improve on intelligibility. Directives and invitations require descriptive content; it is unclear that an invitation to focus upon the existential dread present in Munch's *The Scream*, e.g., can be understood without assuming the presence of that feature in the artwork. This reintroduces a descriptive component and renews the incentive to discover the nature of expressed existential dread. Nevertheless Isenberg's account comports with the pragmatist urge to downplay representational considerations and foreground the *action-guiding aspects* of the thought and talk under analysis.

Several years later Morris Weitz (1956) published "The Role of Theory in Aesthetics," claiming that efforts to articulate necessary and sufficient conditions for proper application of the concept *art* are misguided. Weitz's anti-essentialist argument—inspired by Wittgenstein's discussion of games—is generally deemed unsuccessful, flawed by undue restriction of the discussion to observable, non-relational properties. More significant, however, is Weitz's positive suggestion about the role played by aesthetic theories, which—he claims—serve not to identify the essence of art—for there is none—but rather to highlight features of objects or events that might be overlooked, given the momentum of entrenched art-critical norms of the day. Bell's formalist theory, e.g., is a directive to stop looking for representational content in Cezanne's works and instead focus upon formal/structural features internal to the work; Tolstoy's expressionism is a directive to stop regarding artworks primarily as a means to pleasure and instead focus upon their capacity to generate communal solidarity grounded in shared feelings. And so on. Thus construed, aesthetic theories are not in the business of stating facts about essences; the theories serve rather to redirect mindsets of those seeking to engage artworks properly. The role of theories in aesthetics is to move critical attention away from certain features and toward others; their primary function is directive, not descriptive.

Weitz's explanation of aesthetic theories fosters the view that despite overblown essentialist pretensions and aspirations to specifying defining properties, such theories constitute vital contributions to the practices of description, interpretation, and evaluation in the arts. The theories provide valuable "recommendations to attend in certain ways to certain features of art." The kinship with Isenberg's theory is obvious (though Weitz himself makes no reference to it).

The upshot is that both Isenberg and Weitz offer theories plausibly regarded as implementations of a neopragmatist perspective: both gesture toward expressivist explanations of aesthetic discourse, explanations that do *not* turn upon the metaphysical nature or epistemic accessibility of aesthetic properties.

6

We engage some objects and events as *art* and others not. The process does not appear unprincipled and random—especially when viewed against the backdrop of the history of art. The pragmatist seeks an understanding of what is going on when thus engaged.

Possible strategy: begin with the observation that there is *something it's like* to view artworks correctly; then identify and describe the psychological state characteristic of such viewing: call that state "the aesthetic attitude." Then suggest that designations of an object as *art* are manifestations of that attitude toward it—or, more plausibly, manifestations of the stance that such an attitude is *merited*. What appeared to be a description is, rather, an expression of an attitude or—relatedly—an endorsement of the appropriateness of occupying that attitude.

The existence of a distinctly aesthetic attitude has long been disputed; if there is such an attitude it is not clear how best to characterize it: "psychical distance," "disinterestedness," and/or preoccupation with beauty are among the traditional (discredited) candidates; but alternatives should be explored.[7] The upshot is that the question "What is art?" is replaced by the question "What is it to *see something as art*?" or "What is it to *take something to be art*?" or "What is it to *confer upon something the status of an artwork*?" Focus is shifted away from questions about ontology to questions about attitudes and individual and/or institutional behavior. Perhaps this spells victory for those who regard "the ontology of art" with suspicion.

Thus the aesthetic attitude is back on the scene; the task is to characterize it. Begin by observing that the competent consumer of art *notices* certain properties and *ignores* others: it is an attitude of selective sensitivity. Such selectivity is necessary, not sufficient: presumably it must be conjoined with other psychological states definitive of the aesthetic attitude. But sensitivity to which properties? Obviously, aesthetic properties. And which are those? Walton (1970: 337) provides directives:

> I will continue to call tension, mystery, energy, coherence, balance, serenity, sentimentality, pallidness, disunity, grotesqueness, and so forth, as well as colors and shapes, pitches and timbres properties of works of art, though "property" is to be construed broadly enough not to beg any important questions. I will also, following Sibley, call properties of the former sort "aesthetic" properties…[8]

A similar inventory (based upon the "usual enumerative induction") of aesthetic attributes is provided by Jerrold Levinson (1984): "gracefulness, mournfulness, balance, sublimity, garishness, sobriety, flamboyance, gaiety, eeriness, etc."

The current effort to characterize the aesthetic attitude builds upon the notion of an *aesthetic property*—without any pretense of effectively defining the class of such properties. Thus equipped, characterize the *aesthetic attitude* as requiring heightened attention to such properties and inattention to others. Finally—in a bold expressivist leap—explain characterizations of an object as *artworks* as expressions of the stance that such an attitude toward the object is merited. Such a theory highlights the functional role played by a certain perennially puzzling fragment of discourse: in Peirceian fashion, the concept *art* is revealed to be an action-guiding mechanism that prompts selective attention toward some properties and away from others.

---

[7] A canonical explication of modes of "disinterest" and "psychical distance" allegedly constitutive of the aesthetic attitude is provided in Bullough (1912). The classic challenge is provided in Dickie (1964); a powerful response to Dickie is provided in Kemp (1999).

[8] See also Sibley (1959, 1965). Helpful discussion of whether evaluative responses are partly constitutive of aesthetic properties is provided in Goldman (1993).

7

A summary of the current strategy is helpful: (1) begin with the observation that there is something it's like to view artworks correctly; (2) identify and describe the psychological state characteristic of such viewing. Call that state "the aesthetic attitude"—the nature of which is initially left unspecified; (3) offer a semantic hypothesis about aesthetic assertions: e.g. designation of an object as *art* functions as a manifestation of the aesthetic attitude toward it (or: as an endorsement that such an attitude is merited). The hypothesis dictates, e.g., that "Duchamp's *Fountain* is an artwork" is not, despite appearances, a description; it is an expression of a specific non-cognitive vantage point; (4) characterize that vantage point as one which involves, *inter alia*, selective attention to aesthetic properties; (5) characterize those properties—and thus the aesthetic attitude—without begging questions about the ontology of art or the constitution of the artworld community.

But something has gone wrong. The aesthetic attitude as currently conceived—viz. as requiring selective attention to aesthetic properties—assumes the notions to be illuminated. The problem emerges on two fronts.

First: consider artworks that push the boundaries of entrenched methods, styles, and concepts. The avant-garde—without which the evolution of art history cannot be understood—dares the viewer and critic to experience objects and performances in ways that diverge from previous modes of aesthetic engagement. Such works cannot be understood and appreciated in terms of properties hitherto regarded as "aesthetic." The bewildered viewer, lacking a clear precedent, does not know *how* to experience the work. In such cases it is unclear what the aesthetic attitude amounts to: a viewer whose experience of art is restricted to Impressionist and Cubist genres, e.g., is ill-equipped to properly experience work by Jasper Johns or Robert Rauschenberg. New items must be added to the list of properties toward which the attentive attitude is appropriately directed; and old ones must be deleted from the list. Duchamp's *Fountain*, e.g., is best seen as an iconoclastic harbinger of challenges to the very contrast between art and non-art; it is mischievous philosophical commentary, not properly engaged by confining attention to traditional aesthetic properties (viz. coherence, melancholy, balance, energy, serenity, etc.). The alleged "aesthetic attitude"—which requires selective attention to properties hitherto regarded as "aesthetic"—is *not* the proper attitude with which to view readymades or other instances of Dada.

Thus the problem: insofar as experiencing the work as art requires selective attention to specific properties, it is unclear how to specify those properties without already assuming *Fountain* to be an artwork, and without assuming that certain properties render it such. The ontology of art is back in the driver's seat.

Put another way: updating the alleged aesthetic attitude so as to include the appropriateness of its directedness toward new properties and predicates—and exclude the traditional ones—requires principled justification; but it is unclear how such justification might be provided without begging questions about the essence of art or the necessary and sufficient conditions for an object's qualifying as an artwork. The expressivist neopragmatist, intent upon moving from "What is art?" to "What is it to experience an object as art?" is forced to circle back and focus upon the ontology of art: an endeavor she hoped to sidestep by focusing instead upon the ideology of the aesthetic attitude and the predicates relevant to art-critical discourse.

Second problem: the aesthetic attitude as currently conceived violates the non-circularity constraint in a more fundamental way, given the very nature of aesthetic properties.

To see this, consider the view—advocated by Walton (1970)—that aesthetic properties such as tension, mystery, sentimentality, grotesqueness, and so forth occur in an artwork partly in virtue of the *artistic category* to which the work belongs. A painting might, e.g., be energetic relative to the category of Impressionist paintings, but bland and lethargic relative to the Futurist category; a music performance might be incoherent as Hard Bop but totally cohesive as Avant-Garde Jazz; a rock performance might be "muscular and sledgehammer" as Seattle Grunge but weak and ineffectual as Gothic Metal; and so on. Aside from occasional indeterminate cases, there are facts of the matter about the category to which a work belongs: there is a way to get it right. It is therefore vital to determine the conditions for correct categorization.

One criterion for whether a work W belongs to category C is this:

> the fact, if it is one, that C is well established in and recognized by the society in which W was produced. A category is well established in and recognized by a society if the members of the society are familiar with works in that category... roughly if that category figures importantly in their way of classifying works of art.   Walton (1970: 357)

This criterion clearly requires identification of the relevant "society." Here again a relevant community problem arises, analogous to that confronting the moral relativist in specifying relevant communal norms.

The problems are analogous but not identical. Here an analogy is helpful. Assigning a work to the correct artistic category is no more problematic than assigning an utterance to the proper language. Semantic interpretation of linguistic behavior depends, in part, upon the language to which an utterance event belongs: whether the inscription 'rot' denotes a color or state of deterioration depends upon the language in which it occurs. Likewise: a sequence of pitch-time events might qualify as powerfully energetic or incoherent, depending upon whether the embedding musical performance is traditional Bebop or Harmelodic Funk (which lacks a tonal center). The symmetry between ascribing semantic content and attributing aesthetic properties is irresistible.

It is also comforting to the pragmatist. Here, despite decades of controversy among linguists and philosophers, one can comfortably invoke the behavioral view of language and meaning deployed by Quine: a view grounded in Dewey's pragmatist conception of language as "a social art" consisting of dispositions to respond observably to socially observable stimuli (see Quine 1960: esp. chs. 1 and 2). Artistic categories are no more problematic than natural languages. Walton himself encourages the analogy in citing art historian Heinrich Wölfflin's observation that "pictures of different epochs, placed side by side... speak a different language" (Wölfflin 1929: 228).

But despite the alleged helpfulness of the analogy between artistic genres and natural languages, the linguistic model of artistic categories is misleading. Languages have finite, determinate lexicons; artistic categories do not. Languages have recursive syntactic rules; artistic categories do not. Doubtless the pragmatics of natural language foster a sense of resonance between the linguistic and the artistic: both are rule governed and highly context sensitive. But such similarities might be superficial at best.[9] Moreover the proposed analogy is dangerous: if, as Quine famously suggests, natural language translation is subject to indeterminacy—and thus "no fact of the matter" as to what an expression means (beyond correlations with stimulatory input)—then the language/art analogy dictates that a similar indeterminacy infects the attribution of aesthetic properties. This flies in the face of the prevalent intuition that artworks do, as a determinate factual matter, possess certain aesthetic properties and lack others.[10]

Walton's theory of aesthetic properties prompts questions about attributions of aesthetic properties and possible hidden parameters lurking in the background.[11] The significance of such parameters comes into focus when the aesthetic situation is viewed within a wider pragmatist context.

Expressivist explanations of a circumscribed region of discourse—in the artworld or anywhere else—require ingredients. A thoroughgoing expressivism about moral discourse, for example, requires a well-defined set of sentiments and/or stances—call it the *projective base*—elements of which are (according to the theory) expressed in moral indicatives. When Hume speaks of "gilding and staining natural objects with the colors borrowed from internal sentiment," he assumes the existence of sentiments sufficiently rich to do the job, and "colors" which—whatever their origin—are sufficiently real to get smeared onto the world. The expressivist, in suggesting that indicatives formulated within a given fragment of discourse serve to manifest stances, express commitments, or evince non-cognitive

---

[9] A helpful discussion of the aptness of linguistic models in the domain of music is Jackendoff (2009); see Raffman (1993).
[10] This is controversial: there is ongoing dispute about whether aesthetic properties fall on the "objective" or "subjective" side of the metaphysical divide. For exploration of the divide and its significance within artworld discourse, see Kraut (forthcoming).
[11] A helpful systematic study of Walton's theory is provided in Laetz (2010).

attitudes, needs a rich story about those stances, commitments, and attitudes: a story which does not backhandedly assume the discourse under analysis.

But the ingredients deployed by the current effort to explain aesthetic discourse as an expressive mechanism violate this requirement: the proposed projective base—which requires selective attention to aesthetic properties—assumes the very notions it was invoked to illuminate. Other characterizations of the aesthetic attitude fare no better.[12]

The upshot is that the pragmatist expressivist makes no progress in providing non-circular explanation of the aesthetic concepts she seeks to clarify. Nothing is gained if the problems and counterexamples associated with efforts to pinpoint the essence of art reemerge in efforts to pinpoint the essence of aesthetic properties or the essence of the aesthetic attitude. Transposing the inquiry from the ontology of art ("What is art?") to the ideology of artistic discourse ("Which predicates designate aesthetic properties?") or the constitution of the aesthetic attitude ("What is it to view objects as artworks?") offers no illumination of the problematized aesthetic concepts.

8

Nondescriptivism reflects one strain of neopragmatist thought: the urge to downplay representational elements in discourse and instead foreground institutionally upheld normativities. That strain is well described by Robert Brandom:

> there is an approach to language, shared by Dewey and the later Wittgenstein, which attributes little or no importance to the notion of truth. According to this view, language is best thought of as a set of social practices. In order to understand how language works, we must attend to the *uses* to which its sentences are put and the circumstances in which they are used.   1976: 137

If, as Dickie (1974b: 49) insists, "there is no reason to think that there's a special kind of aesthetic consciousness, perception or attention," nor any reason to countenance "a special kind of aesthetic appreciation," then efforts to pin down a characteristically aesthetic attitude and portray aesthetic claims as expressing that attitude are doomed. The psychological ingredients required by this form of expressivism do not exist.

---

[12] Cf. Danto's (1964) suggestion that seeing something as art involves experiencing it through "an atmosphere of artistic theory...a knowledge of the history of art...." But neither "history of art" nor "artistic theory" is conceptually separable from "art"; without prior specification of the extension of 'art', the touted attitude is unintelligible.

This is a blow to the anti-representationalist element of neopragmatism, which seeks to portray aesthetic discourse as a nondescriptive mechanism that serves to manifest uniquely aesthetic attitudes and/or commitments. But other aspects of pragmatism—those which foreground skepticism about metaphysics—remain viable, thereby challenging the legitimacy of an "ontology of art."

Here is Peirce's customary dismissiveness about metaphysics:

> It was in the earliest seventies that a knot of us young men in Old Cambridge, calling ourselves, half ironically, half defiantly, 'The Metaphysical Club'—for agnosticism was then riding its high horse, and was frowning superbly upon all metaphysics—used to meet, sometimes in my study, sometimes in that of William James.   Peirce (1974: 5.12)

More recently Huw Price, a strong contemporary voice of pragmatism, rails against "metaphysics, or at least a distinctively misguided and self-inflicted kind of metaphysics, to which philosophy has long been subject" (Price 2011b; Macarthur and Price 2007). Simon Blackburn (2007) shares the sentiment:

> [Huw Price and David Macarthur] say that for the pragmatist the crucial thing is not to answer questions about the function of language in ways that encourage metaphysics. On this I am entirely at one with them.

Similar sentiments are voiced by Mark Johnston (1993: 85):

> Let us say that metaphysics in the pejorative sense is a confused conception of what legitimates our practices; confused because metaphysics in this sense is a series of pictures of the world as containing various independent demands for our practices, when the only real legitimation of those practices consists in showing their worthiness to survive on the testing ground of everyday life…

Note that Johnston's target is *not* the ontological respectability of certain entities; it is, rather, what Brandom (2009: 134) calls "the metaphysical strategy for grounding normative appraisals of different forms of life."

Recall the pragmatist rallying slogan: it is people, not objects, that make demands, and whose patterns of behavior toward one another constitute the ultimate grounds of normativity. Thus the legitimacy of institutional practices consists not in their conformity to requirements issuing from metaphysical facts that demand compliance. As Michael Williams (2010: fn. 4) puts it, "Pragmatism is 'anti-metaphysical' in its hostility to postulating supernatural entities to guide human practices." The key word here is 'guide': the pragmatist alleges that metaphysical entities fail to "confer the required privilege on our practical concerns" (Johnston 1993: 591).

If this be the pragmatist objection to metaphysics, it appears unfair—perhaps even confused. Most metaphysicians have little interest in "legitimating" social practices: the goal is to specify what the world is like—including the entities it contains—and to provide systematic articulation of its most basic features. The pragmatist—at least, the one sketched above—apparently misunderstands the metaphysician's job description.[13]

But the skepticism is not without merit. A cursory survey of work in "the ontology of art" prompts suspicion that candidates for "the kinds of things artworks *are*" or "the ontological nature of art" are no more than projections of biases about the properties of artworks which, for whatever reason, are deemed (by some select community) to be important. If this be ontology, the pragmatist demurs.[14]

9

Pragmatism suffers from a curious ambivalence. On the one hand, the normative power of ontology is frequently questioned; on the other hand, no sensible person—pragmatist included—would deny that ontology *prima facie* earns its normative keep. Folk wisdom dictates that it is because of what Picasso's *Guernica is* that its proper understanding requires familiarity with Spanish iconography and the horrors of war. It is because of what Stravinsky's *Petrushka is* that it can be performed simultaneously in widely separated venues; it is because of what Vermeer's *Christ and the Disciples at Emmaus is* that Van Meegeren's forged copy of it lacks the aesthetic value of the original; it is because of what Daniel Burnham's Flatiron Building *is* that its proper restoration precludes the use of certain materials; it is because of what the Byrds' rendition of "My Back Pages" *is* that its lacking frenetic, improvisational interplay is no mark against it. In each such case, interactions with artworks are answerable to norms of correctness, and artworld ontology purports to identify the *grounds* of such correctness by specifying the demands that flow from artworks in light of their ontological natures. Surely the pragmatist is obliged to find such patterns of explanation and legitimization acceptable: they are, after all, familiar trappings of customary artworld practice. If 'the primacy of practice' is more than a hollow slogan, the widespread custom of grounding normativity in ontology must surely be accommodated.

---

[13] It is doubtful that all forms of pragmatism rule out the legitimacy of metaphysics; much depends upon one's preferred meta-metaphysics, wherein the interpretation of ontological constructions and metaphysical theorizing is provided. See Kraut (2016). A distinct conciliatory strategy consists in establishing that a form of metaphysical realism is sustained within some of our ordinary discursive practices, thereby revealing the consistency of neopragmatist anti-representationalism with various forms of ontology; see Rydenfelt (2021).

[14] A systematic denunciation of the ontology of art is provided in Kraut (2012).

Put this another way. Despite pragmatist resistance to the idea that normative constraints emanate from objects and events around us, we are inclined to say, following Wittgenstein (1984: 7), that "the work of art compels us...to see it in the right perspective." Such compulsion surely derives, *pace* the pragmatist, from the nature of the artwork. But this flies in the face of pragmatist insistence that no guidance or compulsion emanates from objects (including artworks) themselves: objects have causal but not justificatory impact. Thus the dialectical tension: despite pragmatist misgivings about the normative power of objects, customary artworld practice favors the *priority of ontology* (hereafter 'PO'): as Christopher Bartel (2011: 384) describes it, "we must first understand what kind of thing a musical work is before we can know how to evaluate it correctly." Andrew Kania (2008: 20) echoes the sentiment

> [a listener] cannot evaluate something without evaluating it as a particular kind of thing, and thus to evaluate it correctly, one must evaluate it as the kind of thing it actually is.

Surely this is correct.

Few would deny, e.g., that the music of James Brown should be appreciated for *what it is*—metrically intricate Funk—and not criticized for lack of lyricism or harmonic complexity. Brown's work must be heard and assessed *properly*: the genre to which the music belongs dictates the standards of propriety. Insofar as PO enshrines this connection, it is unimpeachable: ontology provides grounds for deploying one set of norms rather than another when engaging and critically assessing artworks.

There are innumerable such cases wherein specific norms are claimed to flow from the ontological facts. An art critic—pragmatist or otherwise—should be able to insist (in good conscience) that paintings are essentially historical artifacts, and infer that proper engagement with paintings therefore requires familiarity with aspects of their context of origin. In such a case, a favored artworld ontology ("artworks are essentially historically situated artifacts") fosters commitment to a specific mode of criticism (e.g. the "historical" criticism practiced by art historian Michael Baxandall 1985). This appears unproblematic, even by pragmatist lights. But this inference from ontology ("Here is what a painting *is*") to normativity ("Here is how it is *proper* to engage, interpret, and/or evaluate a painting") offends the neopragmatist. Unfortunately, the grounds for such offense remain unclear.

10

Suspicion about the legitimacy of ontology belongs to a venerable pragmatist tradition, wherein efforts to "ground" institutional practices in facts about confrontations with ontological realities are deemed futile. The world does not tell us how to think about it; nor does it offer us reasons to behave one way rather than another. The world offers no guidance. The pragmatist eschews portrayals of institutional practices as efforts to conform to the dictates of objects and their properties, because objects and their properties do not dictate how to correctly engage them. This is the force behind Rorty's frequent exhortations to replace "Confrontation" with "Conversation."

In the context of aesthetic theory, this anti-metaphysical sentiment surfaces as the conviction that an "ontology of art" is legitimately able to do one of only two things: (1) provide codification of majority verdicts about correctness, rather than providing legitimizing grounds of such correctness; (2) provide a causal explanation—not a justification—of the shape of artworld practice. The pragmatist insists upon a contrast between *summarizing* communal response and *legitimizing* it; insofar as ontology does only the former, it is dispensable and replaceable by empirically grounded descriptions of the structure of art-critical practice. As for (2), if ontology is enlisted to do causal explanatory work, it is vital to distinguish real from pseudo-explanation.

It is not clear how the pragmatist's anti-metaphysical sentiment, however well- or ill-motivated, sits consistently with the ongoing deployment of PO in artworld contexts. PO enshrines a deeply embedded aspect of artworld practice; as such it should be analyzed, rather than impugned, by the pragmatist. But pragmatist misgivings about the legitimacy of ontology pull toward treating it as problematic. Thus the dialectical instability.

Unfortunately, the basis of pragmatist misgivings remains unclear. Perhaps a generalized skepticism about ontology is the moving force; or perhaps the skepticism results from a thoroughgoing naturalism that tends to permeate much contemporary neopragmatist thought. Huw Price's pragmatism, e.g., deploys a principle of "subject naturalism": a view not only about the primacy of science and the overlap of science and philosophy, but about the methodology of "beginning with what science tells us about ourselves," as natural creatures in a natural environment (Price 2011a: *passim*). The upshot is a preference for functional/genealogical accounts of various linguistic/conceptual domains; clearly Price's theorizing favors the explanatory respectability of familiar portions of the causally animated environment and looks askance at items which are less obviously physicalistically respectable (thus his earlier indictment against "metaphysics"). Caution is thus required in disentangling pragmatism from the naturalism that often permeates it.

Nevertheless, the noted ambivalence in the neopragmatist assessment of ontology has dramatic counterparts in other areas—e.g. the notion of "linguistic correctness" and its foundations. Sabina Lovibond (1983: 167) suggests a relevant contrast:

> In relation to the community itself, then, as distinct from its constituent members, linguistic rules are not prescriptive but descriptive. They are abstract representations of what is actually done by speakers: representations, in other words,

of particular aspects of the use of language. As such, they are *read off from* the various collective practices which constitute linguistic behavior; they do not *govern* those practices *qua* collective.

Here Lovibond is addressing the normative status of linguistic rules. At first glance, one thinks of the rule as wielding the power to guide behavior. Rules are *prescriptive*: normative constraints flow from them. Rules *dictate* the standards against which linguistic correctness is measured. But if, as Lovibond suggests, linguistic rules are "abstract representations of what is actually done by speakers," the apparent prescriptive power of the rules vanishes: the prescriptive work is done not by the rule itself, but by some more basic imperative that prescribes conformity to communal uniformities ("Do as others do"). Thus construed, the linguistic rule is itself normatively inert: the information it provides does not go beyond that provided by sociologists and astute observers of actual cultural uniformities. Pragmatist skepticism about PO derives from precisely such considerations.

As an artworld case in point, consider Jerrold Levinson's (1980) efforts to specify "what a musical work is." Drawing upon various entrenched intuitions—that musical works are created rather than discovered, that cultural/historical contexts are relevant to the individuation of compositions, and that means of performance (e.g. choice of instrumentation) are integral to a work—Levinson (1980: 6) concludes that "a musical work is more than just a sound structure *per se*." His solution to "the ontological question" is to regard musical works as "indicated types," which pack into their essential natures the very information that Levinson (and many others) regard as vital in our interactions with musical works. Indicated types, unlike types *simpliciter*, conveniently contain in their canonical designations parameters that reflect those factors judged vital.

But it is not clear how Levinson's "ontology of musical works" adds anything—other than new notational devices—to the information already implicit in the individuative requirements sustained within the relevant community. The claim that "Works produced by different composers are different works" is neither explained nor illuminated by ascending to "ontological mode" and claiming that works are partly constituted by historical etiology. The ontology is redundant: it adds nothing to the (alleged) individuative data with which the inquiry began.

Redundancy itself is not damaging; often it is valuable to render underlying uniformities explicit. A perspicuous grammar for a natural language, e.g., simply articulates and systematizes what is already there; this echoes Lovibond's point above.[15] The damage occurs—according to the pragmatist—in the illusion that the ontology places normative constraints upon institutional practices. This is precisely the illusion that Wittgenstein seeks to dispel concerning the meaning of

---

[15] Thanks to Joshua Gert for suggesting the analogy.

an arithmetic expression and the norms that dictate the correct way to add.[16] Levinson's discussion, e.g., suggests that correct individuative procedures are dictated by the ontological nature of musical works. But an alternative order of explanation—preferred by the pragmatist—is that the ontology is itself a projection of entrenched individuative practices and cannot be invoked to legitimize them.

The motivation for neopragmatist qualms about ontology finally emerges. Steven Levine (2019: 22) provides a clear characterization:

> For Rorty, objective reality cannot dictate to us how we should represent it because it is mute—i.e., it does not speak and offer reasons to us. This is something that only we do in the intersubjective space of giving and asking for reasons.

The key idea—applied within the aesthetic domain—is that an "ontology of art" depicts artworks as placing rational constraints upon us, whereas—the pragmatist insists—the only source of such constraints is the demands we place upon ourselves.

This leaves a puzzle. If, as suggested earlier, ontology somehow encodes representations of artworld norms—rather than justifications for their adoption—then pragmatists (especially those who, in Rorty's phrase, "wish to reduce objectivity to solidarity") should feel no qualms about PO (see Rorty 1991). It is only when ontology is construed as a justificatory ground of extant communal norms, rather than as a summary or codification of those norms, that PO strikes the pragmatist as misguided. But a curious ambivalence infects the pragmatist's attitude toward PO because there is no settled view about whether appeal to the ontology of artworks violates pragmatist tenets.

Put this another way. The pragmatist suffers the pangs of contradictory forces. On the one hand, PO is part of the very practice which the pragmatist seeks to accommodate and understand: it should thus be treated as part of the data to be explained, not a disease to be cured. On the other hand, traditional pragmatist rejection of metaphysics fosters doubts about PO. Thus there remains a curious instability in pragmatist skepticism about artworld ontology.

11

Three broadly pragmatist themes have emerged in the context of aesthetic theory:

---

[16] The point is forcefully developed in discussions of "the rule following argument"; see Kripke (1982) and the torrent of reactions to Kripke's discussion. Thanks to Joshua Gert for stressing the utility of the comparison.

(1) The viability and utility of expressivist semantic strategies in connection with artworld discursive practice. Such strategies are motivated by the anti-representationalist wing of neopragmatism.
(2) The rejection of theories that selectively ignore aspects of actual institutional practice. Again Collingwood (1938: 325): "The aesthetician... is not concerned with dateless realities lodged in some metaphysical heaven, but with the facts of his own place and his own time." Collingwood's remark is intended not as a description, but as a methodological imperative.
(3) The questionable status of the ontology of art. Insofar as ontology summarizes collective practices it is unable to provide justificatory and/or explanatory underpinnings for those practices. The very idea of ontology is problematic; to repeat Rorty's (1982: 165) refrain:

> [pragmatism] is the doctrine that there are no constraints on inquiry save conversational ones—no wholesale constraints derived from the nature of the objects, or of the mind, or of language, but only those retail constraints provided by the remarks of our fellow inquirers.

Insofar as the ontology of art violates this condition (if it does), the pragmatist dismisses it as unacceptable. But additional arguments are required: the pragmatist's preferred meta-metaphysics—which treats ontology as providing "constraints on inquiry" and thus violating basic assumptions about the grounds of normativity—itself demands critical study.

Other themes merit pragmatist attention. The very idea of an "aesthetic emotion"—a psychological state regarded as uncontroversial by Clive Bell—requires the existence of a recognizable qualitative experience, the nature of which requires aesthetic concepts for its accurate characterization. But this idea flies in the face of Rorty's radical insistence that qualitative experiences as such do not privilege specific vocabularies as adequate to their intrinsic nature. As Rorty (1970: 118) puts it,

> The trouble with this view is that "adequate to" is an empty notion. There is no criterion for the adequacy of a bit of language to a bit of non-linguistic awareness. Indeed, the notion of a non-linguistic awareness is simply a version of the thing-in-itself—an unknowable whose only function is paradoxically enough, to be that which all knowledge is about.

If this is right, then the search for a vocabulary and conceptual repertoire *adequate to* the intrinsic nature of aesthetic experience is misguided: there is no intrinsic nature to be captured. And if this is so, then significant questions arise about the justificatory grounds for adopting one way of thinking about art rather than another. Rorty's recommendation is that "we should let a thousand vocabularies bloom and then see which survive." The surviving vocabularies are not those which accurately represent the subject matter—the very notion of "adequate representation" has been impugned—but rather those vocabularies favored by constraints imposed by institutional systems within which artworld experience, interpretation, and evaluation are embedded. Therein lies the soul of neopragmatism in the realm of the arts.

The upshot of this inquiry is that neopragmatism earns mixed reviews in the context of artworld theory and practice. But pragmatism—neo- or otherwise—is not a theory: it is a set of directives for the construction of theories. The pragmatist insists that institutional practices—artworld and otherwise—are not "guided" by determinate ontological realities: normative forces are instituted by communities, not imposed upon them by ontological facts that demand compliance. The legitimacy of our practices—artworld and otherwise—is grounded not in accurate representation, but in the contribution made by such practices to survival and flourishing within the larger scheme of things.[17]

References

Aikin, S. and Talisse, R. (eds.) (2023). *The Routledge Companion to Pragmatism*, New York: Routledge.

Austin, J. L. (1962). *Sense and Sensibilia*, Oxford: Oxford University Press.

Bartel, C. (2011). 'Music without Metaphysics?', *British Journal of Aesthetics* 51; 383–98.

Baxandall, M. (1985). *Patterns of Intention*, New Haven and London: Yale University Press.

Beardsley, M. (1958). *Aesthetics*, New York: Harcourt, Brace and Company.

Beardsley, M. (1979). 'In Defense of Aesthetic Value', *Proceedings and Addresses of the American Philosophical Association* 52: 723–49.

Bell, C. (1958). *Art*, New York: Capricorn Books.

Blackburn, S. (2007). 'Pragmatism: All or Some?' Lecture presented at a conference on 'Expressivism, Pragmatism, and Realism', Sydney, August 2007: 2.

Blackburn, S. (2013). 'Pragmatism: All or Some?', in Price 2013.

Brandom, R. (1976). 'Truth and Assertibility', *Journal of Philosophy* 73: 137–49.

Brandom, R. (2009). *Reason in Philosophy: Animating Ideas*. Cambridge, MA: Harvard University Press.

Bullough, E. (1912). '"Psychical Distance" as a Factor in Art and as an Aesthetic Principle', *British Journal of Psychology* 5: 87–98.

---

[17] I am grateful to many students, colleagues, and friends for discussion and/or correspondence; thanks to Cheryl Misak, Henrik Rydenfelt, Amie Thomasson, Guy Rohrbaugh, Ryan Michael, Zoe Ashton, Marc Lange, David Macarthur, and Allan Silverman for helpful challenges and suggestions. Special thanks to both Tristram McPherson and Joshua Gert, whose critical scrutiny of earlier drafts led to improvements in clarity of arguments and positions.

Collingwood, R. G. (1938). *The Principles of Art*, Oxford: Oxford University Press.

Daly, C. (ed.) (2015). *The Palgrave Handbook of Philosophical Methods*, London: Palgrave Macmillan.

Danto, A. (1964). 'The Artworld', *Journal of Philosophy* 61: 571–84.

Danto, A. (1981). *The Transfiguration of the Commonplace*, Cambridge, MA: Harvard University Press.

Dewey J. (1934). *Art as Experience*, New York: Minton, Balch and Company.

Dickie, G. (1964). 'The Myth of the Aesthetic Attitude', *American Philosophical Quarterly* 1: 56–65.

Dickie, G. (1974a). *Art and the Aesthetic: An Institutional Analysis*, Ithaca, NY: Cornell University Press.

Dickie, G. (1974b). 'What is Art? An Institutional Analysis', in Dickie 1974a: 19–52.

Dickie, G. (1983). 'The New Institutional Theory of Art', *Proceedings of the 8th Wittgenstein Symposium* 10: 57–64.

Dickie, G. (1984). *The Art Circle: A Theory of Art*, New York: Haven.

Goldman, A. (1993). 'Realism about Aesthetic Properties', *Journal of Aesthetics and Art Criticism* 51: 31–7.

Gowans, C. (2019). 'Moral Relativism', *The Stanford Encyclopedia of Philosophy* (Summer edn), Edward N. Zalta (ed.), <https://plato.stanford.edu/archives/sum2019/entries/moral-relativism/>.

Haldane, J. and Wright, C. (eds.) (1993). *Reality, Representation, and Projection*, New York: Oxford University Press.

Haslanger, S. (1995). 'Ontology and Social Construction', *Philosophical Topics* 23: 95–125.

Houser, N. and Kloesel, C. (eds.) (1992). *The Essential Peirce*, Vol. 1, Bloomington, IN: Indiana University Press.

Humberstone, I. L. (1997). 'Two Types of Circularity', *Philosophy and Phenomenological Research* 57: 249–80.

Isenberg, A. (1949). 'Critical Communication', *Philosophical Review* 58: 336.

Jackendoff, R. (2009). 'Parallels and Nonparallels between Language and Music', *Music Perception* 26: 195–204.

Johnston, M. (1993). 'Objectivity Refigured: Pragmatism without Verificationism', in Haldane and Wright 1993: 85–130.

Kahn, S. (ed.) (2009). *Exploring Philosophy: An Introductory Anthology*, New York: Oxford University Press.

Kania, A. (2008). 'New Waves in Musical Ontology', in Stock and Thomson-Jones 2008.

Keefe, R. (2002). 'When Does Circularity Matter?' *Proceedings of the Aristotelian Society* 102: 253–70.

Kemp, G. (1999). 'The Aesthetic Attitude', *British Journal of Aesthetics* 39: 392–99.

Khatchadourian H. (1979). 'Review of George Dickie, *Art and the Aesthetic, an Institutional Analysis*', *Noûs* 13: 113–17.

Kivy, P. (1967). 'Hume's Standard of Taste: Breaking the Circle', *British Journal of Aesthetics* 7: 57–66.

Kraut, R. (1990). 'Varieties of Pragmatism', *Mind* 99: 157–83.

Kraut, R. (2012). 'Ontology: Music and Art', *The Monist* 95: 684–710.

Kraut, R. (2016). 'Norm and Object: How Sellars Saves Metaphysics from the Pragmatist Onslaught', in O'Shea 2016: 60–80.

Kraut, R. (Forthcoming). 'Artworld Practice, Aesthetic Properties, Pragmatist Strategies', in Aikin and Talisse forthcoming.

Kraut R. and Scharp, K. (2015). 'Pragmatism without Idealism', in Daly 2015: 331–60.

Kripke, S. (1982). *Wittgenstein on Rules and Private Language*, Cambridge, MA: Harvard University Press.

Laetz, B. (2010). 'Kendall Walton's "Categories of Art": A Critical Commentary', *British Journal of Aesthetics* 50: 287–306.

Levine, S. (2019). *Pragmatism, Objectivity, and Experience*, Cambridge: Cambridge University Press.

Levinson, J. (1980). 'What a Musical Work Is', *The Journal of Philosophy* 77(1): 5–28.

Levinson, J. (1984). 'Aesthetic Supervenience', *Southern Journal of Philosophy* 22: 93–110.

Lovibond S. (1983). *Realism and Imagination in Ethics*, Minneapolis: University of Minnesota Press.

Macarthur, D. and Price, H. (2007). 'Pragmatism, Quasi-Realism, and the Global Challenge', in Misak 2007: 91–121.

MacFarlane, J. (2014). *Assessment Sensitivity: Relative Truth and Its Applications*, Oxford: Oxford University Press.

Misak, C. (ed.) (2007). *New Pragmatists*, New York: Oxford University Press.

O'Shea, James R. (ed.) (2016). *Sellars and His Legacy*, Oxford: Oxford University Press.

Peirce, C. S. (1878). 'How to Make Our Ideas Clear', in Houser and Kloesel 1992: 124–41.

Peirce, C. S. (1974). *Collected Papers of Charles Sanders Peirce*, Vol. 5, ed. C. Hartshorne, P. Weiss, and A. W. Burks, Cambridge, MA: Harvard University Press.

Pratt, H. (2012). 'Artistic Institutions, Valuable Experiences: Coming to Terms with Artistic Value', *Philosophia* 40: 591–606.

Price H. (2011a). *Naturalism without Mirrors*, Oxford: Oxford University Press.

Price, H. (2011b). 'One Cheer for Representationalism?', in Price 2011a: 304–22.

Price, H. (ed.) (2013). *Expressivism, Pragmatism, and Representationalism*, Cambridge: Cambridge University Press.

Quine, W. V. O. (1960). *Word and Object*, Cambridge, MA: MIT Press.

Rachels, J. (2009). 'The Challenge of Cultural Relativism', in Kahn 2009: 245–55.

Raffman, D. (1993). *Language, Music, and Mind*, Cambridge, MA: Bradford/MIT Press.

Rorty, R. (1970). 'In Defense of Eliminative Materialism', *The Review of Metaphysics* 24(1): 112–21.

Rorty, R. (1972). 'The World Well Lost', *Journal of Philosophy* 69: 649–65.

Rorty, R. (1982). 'Pragmatism, Relativism, Irrationalism', *Consequences of Pragmatism*, Minneapolis: University of Minnesota Press: 160–75.

Rorty, R. (1991). 'Solidarity or Objectivity?', *Objectivity, Relativism, and Truth: Philosophical Papers*, Vol. 1, Cambridge: Cambridge University Press: 21–34.

Rydenfelt, H. (2021). 'Realism without Representationalism', *Synthese* 198: 2901–18.

Sibley, F. (1959). 'Aesthetic Concepts', *The Philosophical Review* 68: 421–50.

Sibley, F. (1965). 'Aesthetic and Nonaesthetic', *The Philosophical Review* 74: 135–59.

Stace, W. T. (1937). *The Concept of Morals*, New York: Macmillan.

Stock, K. and Thomson-Jones, K. (eds.) (2008). *New Waves in Aesthetics*, New York: Palgrave Macmillan.

Sveinsdottir, Á. K. (2013). 'The Social Construction of Human Kinds', *Hypatia* 28(4): 716–32.

Tolstoy, L. (1896). *What is Art?*, trans. A. Maude, New York: Funk and Wagnalls Company, 1904.

Walton, K. (1970). 'Categories of Art', *The Philosophical Review* 79: 334–67.

Weitz, M. (1956). 'The Role of Theory in Aesthetics', *Journal of Aesthetics and Art Criticism* 15: 27–35.

Wieand, J. (1981). 'Can There Be an Institutional Theory of Art?', *Journal of Aesthetics and Art Criticism* 39: 409–17.

Williams, M. (2010). 'Pragmatism, Minimalism, Expressivism', *International Journal of Philosophical Studies* 18: 317–30.

Wittgenstein, L. (1984). *Culture and Value*, Chicago: University of Chicago Press.

Wölfflin, H. (1929). *Principles of Art History*, trans. M. D. Hottinger, New York: Henry Holt and Co.

Wollheim, R. (1987). *Painting as an Art*, London: Thames and Hudson Ltd.

13
The Subject Matter of "Subject Matter" and General Jurisprudence

Stefan Sciaraffa

The Hartian legal positivist holds that the law or, in other words, the set of legally valid norms of any legal system, comprises all and only those norms recognized by criteria of legal validity accepted in common by the system's officials. In addition, the Hartian positivist holds that the legal obligations, requirements, liabilities, powers, and so on within any legal system are those entailed by this set of legally valid norms as applied to the relevant facts (Hart 2012).[1] This position is a form of positivism, for it insists on a sharp distinction between what the law is and requires and what the law, as a matter of political morality, ought to be and ought to require. By contrast, Dworkinian theory takes the seemingly conflicting non-positivist position that the laws of any legal system are all and only those norms that satisfy the politico-moral test of integrity, and, as such, are norms that legal officials are *prima facie* justified in enforcing. On this view, a community's laws are all and only those norms that follow from the conceptions of justice, fairness, and due procedure that best fits and justifies the political decisions (e.g. legislative enactments and judicial decisions) that the community's officials systematically enforce. The Dworkinian further holds that the legal obligations, requirements, liabilities, powers, and so on within any legal system are entailed by the norms that satisfy this Dworkinian politico-moral test of integrity (see Dworkin 1986, 2013; Waluchow and Sciaraffa 2016).

Hart's and Dworkin's respective theories appear to be rival accounts of a shared subject matter. Nonetheless, Hart (2012: 240–1) insists that his and Dworkin's "theoretical enterprises" are distinct, and he characterizes Dworkin's theory as "in essence a theory of adjudication presented as a theory of law" (2013: 509). Likewise, a number of prominent contemporary supporters of a broadly Hartian approach to jurisprudential theory embrace Hart's characterization of Dworkin's theory. For example, Wil Waluchow (1994: 42–6) argues that Dworkin comes "perilously close" to collapsing the distinction between a theory of law and a theory of adjudication, and Brian Leiter (2007: 158) states that Dworkin "by limiting

---

[1] For recent defenses of positivist legal theory within the Hartian camp, broadly construed see e.g. Waluchow (1994); Raz (1994: esp. ch. 10); Leiter (2007: esp. ch. 6); and Gardner (2012: esp. ch. 2).

Stefan Sciaraffa, *The Subject Matter of "Subject Matter" and General Jurisprudence* In: *Neopragmatism: Interventions in First-Order Philosophy*. Edited by: Joshua Gert, Oxford University Press. © Stefan Sciaraffa 2023.
DOI: 10.1093/oso/9780192894809.003.0013

his account of law only to those cases where the exercise of coercive power in accordance with law can be morally justified, has, plainly, changed the topic."

In a similar vein, David Plunkett and Timothy Sundell (2013: 276) are open to the claim that Hartian and Dworkinian theorists speak to different topics, theoretical enterprises, or (in the terms I use throughout the following) subject matters. Plunkett and Sundell forefront the distinction between two kinds of conflicts—object-level and metalinguistic disputes. Speakers engage in an object-level dispute when they exchange incompatible assertions about the object of a shared concept or, in other words, about a shared subject matter. Parties to a metalinguistic dispute express incompatible claims about "which of various competing concepts is best suited to play a given functional role in organizing our thought, talk, and practice" (Plunkett and Sundell 2013: 276).

In summary, Plunkett and Sundell are open to the following characterization of the debate between the Hartian positivist and Dworkinian non-positivist:

Metalinguistic Dispute (MD):

(1) Dworkinian non-positivist and Hartian positivist legal theorists use shared legal terms, such as "law," "legal requirement," "legal liability," and so on, to set out the key tenets of their respective theories, but they do not thereby address a shared subject matter with legal terms and, hence, they are not embroiled in an object-level dispute.

(2) Hartian and Dworkinian theorists are embroiled in a metalinguistic dispute about the concept that ought to guide both camps' use of legal terms, such as "law," "legal requirement," "legal liability," and so on in their talk, thought, and practice.

Notably, Hart, Waluchow, and Leiter are not merely open to accepting MD; they are committed to it.

MD presupposes that the subject matter that speakers address with a term is one thing and the concept that speakers ought to take as a guide when using the term is another. Because it strikingly parallels legal positivism, I refer to this presupposition as metasemantic positivism. The first objective of the following is to explicate and defend a qualified version of the following metasemantic non-positivist thesis. Insofar as speakers address a subject matter with a term, that subject matter is the object of the concept that the speakers ought to take as a guide when using the term. To this end, I marshal a variant of neopragmatic metasemantic theory, pragmatic inferentialism. I argue that the subject matter that speakers address with their terms is the object of the concept that the speakers ought, as a matter of sound coherentist, hermeneutic reasoning, to take as a guide for using the term. In summary, I argue that the metasemantic positivist's sharp distinction between object-level and metalinguistic dispute cannot be maintained;

for metalinguistic disputes bleed through to the object level. Sections 1 and 2 are devoted to this attempted contribution to the philosophy of language.

A second objective is to undercut and replace the characterization of the dispute between the Hartian and Dworkinian theorist set out in MD. I argue that metasemantic non-positivism is true and, hence, MD must be false. For MD presupposes the truth of metasemantic positivism and the falsity of metasemantic non-positivism. I further argue that Hartian and Dworkinian theories generally speak to different subject matters, but, contra MD, not always. As I argue, Hartian theory generally speaks to a descriptive subject matter, Dworkinian theory generally speaks to a normativist subject matter, but, sometimes, the Hartian strays into the Dworkinian, normativist occasion for the use of legal terms.[2] Section 3 is devoted to this attempted contribution to general jurisprudence.

A third overarching objective of the following discussion is to contribute to our understanding of how word-meaning and the content of thought is collective and normative and to explain how it is possible for individuals to exchange assertions and think thoughts without fully grasping the meaning of the assertions exchanged or the content of their thoughts.[3] I pull together the threads of this objective in the chapter's concluding section.

1. Pragmatic Inferentialism

Pragmatic inferentialism is a variant of neopragmatic metasemantic theory. It is also a key pillar of the metasemantic non-positivist account of subject matter that I discuss in the next section. In this section, I rehearse three defining theses of neopragmatic theory and then turn to a number of features that distinguish the pragmatic inferentialist variant of neòpragmatism.

1.1 Three Defining Neopragmatic Theses

Neopragmatic theory holds that declarative statements, assertions express propositions, and that the content of any proposition is determined by the role

---

[2] As understood here, a descriptive subject matter is the object of a descriptive concept—i.e. a concept that enables speakers to describe some aspect of mind-independent reality. By contrast, a normativist subject matter is construed here as the object of a normativist concept—i.e. a concept that enables speakers to evaluate prospective responses of a certain kind (perhaps intentional actions or attitudes of endorsement, to name two possibilities) in immediate prelude to instantiating the most highly evaluated response. See section 3 for further discussion.

[3] Compare Burge (1979: 73–4).

the proposition plays as premise and conclusion in a space of reasons. A proposition's address in the space of reasons is determined by two components. The first comprises the conditions that are reasons for accepting or asserting the proposition (the conditions of warranted assertion). The second comprises the consequences for which the proposition is a reason (the warranted consequences of assertion).[4]

For example, the conditions that warrant assertion of the proposition "The cat is on the mat" might include a cattish perception under standard conditions or testimony from a reliable observer of cats on mats. That I experience this cattish perception and my friend Bob tells me that he too sees the cat on the mat are two distinct defeasible reasons for accepting the proposition that the cat is on the mat.

A warranted proposition might be a reason for a number of kinds of consequences, including asserting or accepting other propositions or adopting other mental attitudes, such as an intention to act or an endorsement or negative assessment of some item. For example, a roughly Dworkinian gloss on the meaning of legal terms holds that "A's action is legally prohibited" uttered by a legal official purports to warrant (to be a reason for) (1) acceptance of the proposition that A ought to be held legally accountable for the prohibited action and (2) the official's intention to do her part in the collective task of ensuring that A is held accountable.

A second defining neopragmatic thesis holds that the meaning of any subsentential subject or predicate term is to be explained by reference to the rules of use for the term. Michael Williams's (2013) Explanation of Meaning as Use (EMU) is a schematization of this approach that comprises two components.[5] The first is a curated report of the rules (specifying conditions and consequences of application) that, as a matter of sociolinguistic fact, by and large guide speakers' use of the explanandum subsentential expression, such as "cat," "mat," "legally required," "law," and so on. The rules for the use of a term are derived by abstracting from the rules of use for assertions that contain the explanandum term. The second component of Williams's EMU is an account of the explanandum term's function derived by reflecting on the rules that by and large guide the term's use with the following question in mind: given that these are the rules that by and large govern the use of this term, what is it used for, or, in other words, what is the term's function?[6]

---

[4] For the seminal statement of this neopragmatic inferentialist metasemantic theory, see Brandom (1998). See also Williams (2013) for a pithy schematization.

[5] See also Brandom (1998: esp. ch. 6) on the derivation of the content of subsentential singular terms and predicates by way of adducing their systematic contribution to the content of sentences.

[6] See e.g. Williams (2013), Thomasson (2020: 54), and Kohler (forthcoming) for rival accounts of the functional component of the neopragmatic EMU. The hermeneutic conception of function that I give below is yet another rival account.

1.2 The Pragmatic Inferentialist Variant of Neopragmatic Theory

Pragmatic inferentialism is a variant of neopragmatic theory, and as such, it subscribes to the two key theses discussed above. In addition, it introduces a number of distinctive elements, including the ideas of semantic potential, hermeneutic function, hermeneutic meaning, and hermeneutic EMU.

Semantic potential. A semantic potential is a resource shared by a linguistic community.[7] The members of a community who share such a resource roughly converge in associating some term with a distinctive configuration of conditions and consequences of application or, in other words, rules of use for the term. Moreover, they are mutually aware that they and the other members of the community by and large converge with respect to the rules of use that they associate with the term. As I shall explain below, semantic potentials are linguistic resources that the members of a linguistic community tailor to the demands of particular occasions of use for the term in question.

Hermeneutic function. To reason about a term's hermeneutic function is to reason in a coherentist way about what speakers ought to use the term for on a particular occasion. This coherentist reasoning involves two main components. The first is reasoning about the rationale that would rationalize and unify the chain of meaning-constituting inferences associated with the term. For example, one might argue that the chain of inferences from a cattish perception (condition of application) to an assertion that X is a cat to the further assertion that X is a mammal (consequence of application for "cat") is unified and rational because chains of inferences of this form (and variations thereof) enable speakers to track and exchange information about cats. The second component of coherentist reasoning about a term's hermeneutic function concerns the discursive values relevant to the particular occasion of the explanandum term's use. Discursive values are goods at stake in particular occasions of use that speakers can collectively realize by way of convergently tailoring the semantic potential of an explanandum term in service of those values and exchanging assertions with one another in accordance with the tailored rules of use.

To illustrate, consider Amelia Bedelia, a recurring character in an eponymous series of children's books. Pursuant to a chore list that asks her to dress the turkey and dust the furniture, she puts doll clothes on the turkey and sprinkles dusting powder on the couch. The funny thing about Amelia Bedelia is that she is really bad at adducing what she and her interlocutors ought to use key terms for in particular contexts. She fails to see that in the context of receiving food preparation instructions, she and her interlocutors have reason (based in the discursive values relevant to that context) to converge in tailoring the semantic potential of terms such as "dress __" or "__ is dressed" to the function of describing a food

---

[7] Compare Bach (1994) and Rayo (2013).

item, say, a turkey, that is prepared for cooking rather than outfitted for a child's tea party. Similarly, she fails to see that in the household cleaning context, she and her interlocutors have reason to use terms such as "dust __" or "__ is dusted" to describe items that have been cleansed of rather than coated with dust. By contrast, speakers from a very young age typically get the joke about Amelia Bedelia, for they are able to adduce the contextually sensitive hermeneutic functions of key terms, such as "is dressed," "__is dusted," and many others besides.

Hermeneutic EMU and hermeneutic meaning. The pragmatic inferentialist EMU specifies the hermeneutic function of an explanandum term, and it replaces Williams's curated sociolinguistic report of the rules of use by and large followed with respect to the explanandum term with a specification of the rules of use that would enable the term to fulfill its hermeneutic function. That is, the pragmatic inferentialist EMU gives the hermeneutic meaning of an explanandum term by giving the rules of use that enable the term to fulfill its hermeneutic function.[8] For example, if the hermeneutic function of the term "__is dressed" is to enable speakers to describe game that has been prepared for cooking, then a condition of application for that term might be that the game in question has been properly cleaned and seasoned, and a consequence of application might be that the object in question is ready to put in the oven. For it might be that these rules of use enable speakers to describe and exchange information about objects that have been prepared for cooking.

2. The Subject Matters of "Subject Matter"

Price (2003: 175) speculates that the speakers of any linguistic community regularly observe the following norm:

> (Truth) If not-*p*, then it is incorrect to assert that *p*; if not-*p*, there are *prima facie* grounds for censure of an assertion that *P*.

He presents this norm in a descriptive rather than a prescriptive register. That is, he presents Truth as a description of a norm that speakers are by and large committed to following and, hence, regularly follow. In this same descriptive register, he conjectures as follows:

> [The Truth norm] makes what would otherwise be no-fault disagreements into unstable social situations, whose instability is only resolved by argument and consequent agreement-and it provides an immediate incentive for argument, in that it holds out to the successful arguer the reward consisting in her community's positive evaluation of her dialectical position.   Price (2003: 181)

---

[8] Compare Thomasson (2020: 4).

Here, Price seems to have a Rousseauvian motivational picture in mind.[9] The members of linguistic communities are abidingly motivated both to avoid the disesteem of being found to have asserted P without good reason and to secure the esteem of being found to have asserted P with good reason. Because they are also abidingly subject to epistemic challenge by one another by dint of the regularly observed Truth norm, they regularly engage in sustained reasoned argument.

As Price (2003: 182) recognizes, he supplies no more than a coarse-grained account of the Truth norm that elides important finer grained details. The detail I seek to clarify here concerns the subject matter of the assertion described by the Truth norm's antecedent—namely, the interlocutor's assertion that P which is incompatible with the hearer's belief that ~P. The key issue is the proper characterization of the subject matter of the interlocutor's assertion. For there are numerous conceptions of subject matter, and, accordingly, there are numerous conceptions of the conditions in which the Truth norm's antecedent is satisfied—i.e. conditions in which the subject matter of the interlocutor's utterance is P, which is incompatible with ~P, rather than P*, which is compatible with ~P.[10] Immediately below, I distinguish the speaker-understanding, hermeneutic, and conventional conceptions of subject matter. This discussion sets the stage for the argument that there is an important, recurring occasion for the use of the term "subject matter" in which participants in the Truth norm ought to adopt the hermeneutic conception of subject matter.

2.1 Three Conceptions of Subject Matter

The speaker-understanding conception of subject matter glosses the interlocutor's assertion and its subsentential elements or, in other words, its component terms in accordance with the speaker-understanding conception of meaning. To illustrate, consider Tyler Burge's rheumatologist who joins in the medical community's consensus that arthritis is a condition that only afflicts the joints. Imagine further that the rheumatologist's patient makes the seemingly conflicting claim that his arthritis has spread to his thigh (Burge 1979: 77). The speaker-understanding conception characterizes the meaning of the patient's claim in terms of the patient's understanding of what he has said. From this perspective, the patient asserts the proposition P^* (his tharthritis, a condition that afflicts joints and muscles, has spread from his joints to his thigh).

---

[9] See Neuhouser (2008) for discussion of Rousseau's account of the drive for self-esteem (*amour propre*).
[10] As coined by Christine Tiefensee (2021), a metaconceptual device is a second-order concept whose function is to explicate and codify patterns and norms of inferential reasoning. The concept "subject matter" is one such metaconceptual device. For this concept explicates and codifies an element of the inferential reasoning that leads the participant in Price's Truth norm from the cognition of some utterance to the inference that the utterance ought to be censured and challenged.

Note that if we construe the subject matter of the patient's utterance in accordance with the speaker-understanding conception of its meaning, his utterance would not satisfy the Truth norm's antecedent *vis-à-vis* the doctor's commitment to ~P. For the doctor's commitment holds that the patient's arthritis, a condition that afflicts only the joints, cannot spread to the patient's thighs, whereas the speaker-understanding conception of subject matter attributes P^* to the patient—the assertion that his tharthritis, a condition that affects both joints and muscles, has spread to his thigh.

The hermeneutic conception of subject matter construes the subject matter of the interlocutor's assertion and its component terms in accordance with the hermeneutic conception of the assertion's meaning. For illustrative purposes, let us stipulate that the rules of use for "arthritis" by and large followed by medical practitioners is the most useful vehicle for effective diagnosis and treatment and that these rules of use facilitate the communication of information about arthritis, a condition that afflicts only the joints. Let us further stipulate that on the typical occasion in which a rheumatologist and patient use the term "arthritis" to discuss the patient's health, the relevant discursive values are the realization of these medical benefits. Hence, the hermeneutic function of the term on these occasions is the patient's and doctor's exchange and tracking of information about the condition, arthritis, as understood by the medical community of the time. In this case, the hermeneutic meaning, and, hence, the hermeneutic conception of the subject matter of the patient's statement that his arthritis has spread to his thigh would be that his arthritis, a condition that afflicts only the joints, has spread to his thigh.

Note that if we construe the patient's utterance in accordance with the hermeneutic conception of its subject matter, the patient's utterance would satisfy the Truth norm's antecedent *vis-à-vis* the rheumatologist's commitment to ~P. For the subject matter of the patient's utterance "arthritis" would be construed as a condition that afflicts only the joints, and his assertion would be construed as the proposition P (his arthritis has spread to his thigh) *vis-à-vis* the rheumatologist's commitment to ~P (the patient's arthritis has not spread to the patient's thigh).

The conventional conception of subject matter construes the subject matter of an assertion and its component terms in accordance with the meaning that speakers by and large attribute to the expression in question. To illustrate, it might be that the larger community's convention for the use of the term "arthritis" mirrors or is tethered to the medical community's practice of using the term to refer to a condition that only afflicts the joints. If so, then the conventional conception of subject matter would construe the rheumatology patient's assertion as the claim that his arthritis, a condition that only afflicts his joints, has spread to his thigh. Moreover, construed in accordance with this conception, the patient's assertion would satisfy the antecedent of the Truth norm *vis-à-vis* the patient's doctor.

2.2 Hermeneutic Reasoning about the Conception of Subject Matter That Speakers Ought to Adopt

With the foregoing three conceptions of the subject matter of an assertion and component terms in hand, we can now consider which, if any of these three, aptly characterizes the assertion that figures in the Truth norm's antecedent. In other words, we might ask how we *qua* students of Price's Truth norm ought to use the term "subject matter" when further refining Price's (2003: 175) account of the Truth norm's antecedent. The three possibilities under consideration are:

Speaker-understanding Truth norm. If not-p, then it is incorrect to assert p, where one asserts p by uttering an assertion with the speaker-understanding subject matter of p; if not-p, there are *prima facie* grounds for censure of an assertion with the speaker-understanding subject matter of p.

Hermeneutic Truth norm. If not-p, then it is incorrect to assert p, where one asserts p by uttering an assertion with the hermeneutic subject matter of p; if not-p, there are *prima facie* grounds for censure of an assertion with the hermeneutic subject matter of p.

Conventional Truth norm. If not-p, then it is incorrect to assert p, where one asserts p by uttering an assertion with the conventional subject matter of p; if not-p, there are *prima facie* grounds for censure of an assertion with the conventional subject matter of p.

In what follows, I appeal to the pragmatic inferentialist premise that we ought to use a term—in this case, the term "subject matter"—in accordance with its hermeneutic function to adjudicate between these three seemingly rival accounts of Price's Truth norm.

To prevent confusion, I should emphasize that the idea of hermeneutic function comes in at two places in the following pragmatic inferentialist argument. The first instance of this idea is located at the level of the pivotal question that queries the hermeneutic function of the term "subject matter." The second instance of this idea comes in at the level of a candidate answer to this pivotal question. According to this candidate answer, the hermeneutic function of the term "subject matter" is to communicate information about the hermeneutic meaning of an expression, where hermeneutic meaning is understood in terms of the rules of use for the expression that facilitate the expression's realization of its hermeneutic function. As noted above, a second candidate answer is that the hermeneutic function of the term "subject matter" is to communicate information about the speaker-understanding of an expression, and a third candidate answer is that the hermeneutic function of "subject matter" is to communicate information about the expression's conventional meaning.

Recall that properly reasoning about how speakers ought to use some expression entails reasoning in a coherentist, hermeneutic fashion about the rationale that would unify and rationalize the rules of use for the expression on particular occasions of use as well as the discursive values relevant to such occasions. Accordingly, to determine the hermeneutic function of the expression "subject matter" on occasions in which the expression is used to clarify and refine our understanding of Price's Truth norm, we must pause to clarify key details of this occasion of use. Closer inspection reveals two distinct kinds of Pricean occasions of use and, concomitantly, two distinct sets of discursive values that respectively yield different hermeneutic functions.

On the first kind of Pricean occasion, quasi-social scientific theorists seek to refine Price's Truth norm in a descriptive register. In such contexts, the predominant discursive value is the accurate prediction of the circumstances in which speakers censure and challenge one another's utterances. Perhaps further empirical inquiry would reveal that the interpretation of utterances in accordance with the conventional meaning (rather than the hermeneutic meaning or speaker-understanding) conception of subject matter is much more useful for the purposes of predicting whether a speaker who takes it that not-P will censure and challenge interlocutors' utterances. If so, then the discursive value of predicting Truth norm related behavior would favor using "subject matter" to track and describe the conventional meaning of interlocutors' assertions.

Another set of discursive values emerge from the speaker's role as a participant in the practice of Price's Truth norm. The key feature of this speaker-participant occasion of use is the practical upshot of judgments about the subject matter of an assertion—namely, if the subject matter addressed by the assertion is P and $\sim P$, then the censure and challenge of the assertion is *prima facie* warranted. The following passage from Price is suggestive of what the relevant discursive values might be in the participant-speaker occasion of use:

> If reasoned argument is generally beneficial-beneficial in some long-run sense-then a community...who adopt this practice [the Truth norm] will tend to prosper, compared to a community who do not.   2003: 181

There is much that can be said about the benefits realized by any community robustly disposed to observe Price's Truth norm and concomitant practice of sustained reasoned argument. For present purposes, I focus on one benefit in particular—the Millian good of greater understanding of important truths facilitated by a robust practice of appealing to reasons to defend and challenge one another's assertions. This discursive value uniquely supports the use of "subject matter" to track and communicate information about the hermeneutic rather than conventional or speaker-understanding conception of the subject matter of interlocutors' assertions.

To help see why, consider again Burge's scenario in which a patient relays his fear that his arthritis has spread to his thigh. Now imagine further the possibility that the hermeneutic meaning of the term "arthritis" on such medical occasions of use is constituted by the rules of use that enable the users of the term on those occasions to exchange and track information about the condition, arthritis, a conditions that afflicts only the joints. For by using the term in accordance with this function, the speakers realize the discursive values of effective medical diagnosis and treatment.

By this same token, speakers in this medical community have reason to follow and hold other caregivers and patients accountable to the hermeneutic meaning of "arthritis" or, in other words, censure and challenge uses of the term "arthritis" that run afoul of the conditions and consequences of application specified by the term's hermeneutic meaning. The members of the medical community realize the discursive values of effective medical diagnosis and treatment by observing and holding one another accountable to the rules of use that constitute the hermeneutic meaning of "arthritis"; they also thereby develop their collective understanding and knowledge of a store of important truths—truths crucial for effective medical diagnosis and treatment.

Speakers who followed a norm of censuring and challenging assertions for violations of the rules of use specified by the speaker-understanding conception of the assertion's meaning would not thereby maintain and develop a store of important truths. For example, Burge's rheumatologist would not censure or challenge her patient's assertion that his arthritis had spread to his thigh, thereby depriving the patient of an opportunity to replace his concept of tharthritis and accompanying tharthritis-oriented beliefs with a more useful set of arthritis-oriented concepts and truths.

A parallel argument applies to a practice of censure and challenge revolving around conventional meaning. To put the point abstractly, the rules of use that a community by and large associates with a term is not yet tailored to the demands of the discursive values relevant to a particular occasion of use, whereas the rules of use specified by the term's hermeneutic meaning are so tailored. Accordingly, a practice of censuring and challenging violations of conventionally accepted rules of use would impede rather than further the production of important truths insofar as the conventional meaning of the term in question differs from its hermeneutic meaning.

At this point, I am able to summarize the pragmatic inferentialist case for metasemantic non-positivism. On occasions of the Pricean speaker-participant kind, speakers have abiding reason to use terms such as "subject matter" to collectively track and exchange information about the hermeneutic meaning of interlocutors' assertions and those assertions' component terms. Thus, they have reason to use the term "subject matter" to track the meaning that ought to guide speakers' utterances of assertions and use of component terms, and, hence, a qualified version of metasemantic non-positivism is true. For (as coined above) the defining thesis of metasemantic non-positivism holds that insofar as speakers address a subject matter with a term, that subject matter is the object of the concept that the speakers ought to take as a guide when using the term.

3. The Subject Matters of General Jurisprudence

As discussed above, Hart, Waluchow, Leiter, and other Hartian-minded legal theorists subscribe to the characterization of the dispute between Hartian and Dworkinian theory that I have named MD. Moreover, Plunkett and Sundell are open to the possibility that MD aptly characterizes this dispute. At this point, the pragmatic inferentialist argument against MD has come into view.

This argument rests on two main premises. First, the proponents of MD inhabit a Pricean speaker-participant (as opposed to a Pricean descriptive) occasion for the use of the expression "subject matter," for their judgments about the subject matter of Dworkinian theory are a prelude to object-level censure and challenge. That is, the proponents of MD refrain from engaging in an object-level dispute with Dworkinian theory's use of legal terms for the explicitly stated reason that Dworkinian theory uses such terms to address a subject matter that differs from the object of Hartian legal theory. Second, on any such speaker-participant Pricean occasion of use, the subject matter addressed with a term is the object of the concept that the term's users ought to take as a guide, or so I have argued. On the basis of this metasemantic non-positivist foundation, the pragmatic inferentialist concludes that the Dworkinian and Hartian address a shared subject matter with legal terms insofar as they ought to take a shared concept as a guide for their use of legal terms.

The key point is that if the pragmatic inferentialist conclusion defended above is true, at least one of MD's two theses must be false. For MD holds that the Dworkinian and Hartian alike ought to take a shared concept (namely, the Hartian positivist's concept) as a guide for the use of legal terms and that the Dworkinian and Hartian address distinct subject matters with legal terms. Whereas, the pragmatic inferentialist conclusion implies that if the Dworkinian and Hartian ought to take a shared concept as guide for the use of legal terms, then they use legal terms to address a shared subject matter.

With this argument against MD in place, I now turn to a pragmatic inferentialist alternative to MD's characterization of the dispute between Hartian and

Dworkinian theory. To this end, I say a few preliminary words about the semantic potential of the legal terms whose subject matter is in question, and then I explicate and defend an account of the hermeneutic function and, hence, the hermeneutic meaning of legal terms on the occasions in which Hartian and Dworkinian theorists, respectively, use the terms.

3.1 The Semantic Potential of Legal Terms

As a preface to answering the question "What is law?," Hart enumerates features of the legal system that "[a]ny educated man might be expected to identify…"

> They comprise (i) rules forbidding or enjoining certain types of behaviour under penalty; (ii) rules requiring people to compensate those whom they injure in certain ways; (iii) rules specifying what must be done to make wills, contracts or other arrangements which confer rights and create obligations; (iv) courts to determine what the rules are and when they have been broken, and to fix the punishment or compensation to be paid; (v) a legislature to make new rules and abolish old ones. Hart (2012: 3)

From the perspective of pragmatic inferentialism, Hart's description of what almost any educated person knows about the law is a partial statement of the warranted consequences that almost any educated person associates with legal terms, and, as such, it is a partial statement of legal terms' semantic potential. If X is law then X is a rule (i) forbidding or enjoining certain types of behavior under penalty, (iv) adjudicated by courts, and (v) enacted by a legislature. Moreover, if X is law, then X might belong to any number of categories, including rules that (ii) require people to compensate those they injure or (iii) specify what must be done to make wills, contracts, or other arrangements.

Hart's foundational idea of a secondary social rule of recognition is informative with respect to a second aspect of the semantic potential of legal terms—namely, the conditions of application commonly associated with a legal term. According to Hart, a social rule is a pattern of behavior generally followed by a group, where at least a threshold number of the group's members must bear a kind of mental attitude, the internal point of view, that takes the pattern of behavior as its content. This attitude is normative in the following sense. The agent gripped by the internal point of view holds that she and her fellow group members ought to conform to the pattern in question, and, accordingly, she is robustly disposed to conform to the pattern, to criticize those who deviate, and to be receptive to others' criticisms for her failures to conform (Hart 2012: 57). Hart's theory of law centers around a particular kind of social rule that he refers to as a secondary rule of recognition.

As Hart (2012: 94) puts it, this rule enumerates the "feature or features possession of which by a suggested rule is taken as a conclusive affirmative indication that it is a rule of the group" or, in other words, a legally valid rule of the system. In any mature legal system, the rule of recognition comprises numerous clauses specifying multiple indications of legal validity (e.g. being a legislative enactment, executive order, constitutional provision, or court holding). From the perspective of pragmatic inferentialism, Hart's rule of recognition doubles as an aspect of the semantic potential for legal terms. For the rule of recognition comprises criteria of validity or, interchangeably, conditions of application that the members of the community by and large associate with legal terms, such as "is law," "is legally valid," and so on.

3.2 The Hermeneutic Function of the Hartian Use of Legal Terms

With the foregoing sketch of the semantic potential of legal terms in mind, consider the following passage from Hart's *The Concept of Law*:

> [M]ost of the features of law which have proved most perplexing and have both provoked and eluded the search for definition can best be rendered clear, if these two types of rules [primary rules and secondary rules, such as the rule for recognizing the legal system's rules described above] and the interplay between them are understood. We accord this union of rules a central place because of their explanatory power in elucidating the concepts that constitute the framework of legal thought.   2012: 81; bracketed content added

In a postscript to this work, Hart expands on his methodological approach:

> My aim in this book was to provide a theory of what law is which is both general and descriptive. It is *general* in the sense that it is not tied to any particular legal system or legal culture, but seeks to give an explanatory and clarifying account of law as a complex social and political institution with a rule-governed (and in that sense 'normative') aspect. This institution, in spite of many variations in different cultures and in different times, has taken the same general form and structure.   2012: 239–40

Later in his career, Hart adds that he seeks "to provide an illuminating form of description of a specific type of social institution which will bring out clearly certain salient features of the institution which, given the general human condition, are of universal importance" (2013: 504–5).

If we view these passages together through a pragmatic inferentialist lens, it appears that Hartian legal theory seeks to elucidate the community's shared legal conceptual resources in service of the discursive value of illuminatingly describing certain recurrent and important forms of social institutions. Insofar as the value of theoretical illumination is the discursive value germane to the occasion in which descriptive-minded theorists use legal terms, the theorists inhabiting that context have reason to follow and hold one another accountable to a concept, i.e. to the concept's constitutive rules of use, that would serve these goals.

Arguably, Hart's conventionalist theory of law specifies the conditions of application of a concept that would serve these descriptive goals. Hart's theory is conventionalist, for it holds that all and only those norms validated by criteria by and large accepted in common by the system's officials are legally valid.[11] In other words, this theory specifies conventionalist conditions of application. On this view, assertions of the form "X is legally valid" are warranted only if X satisfies criteria that the relevant system's officials accept in common.

In support of Hart's conventionalist theory, the pragmatic inferentialist can press three points. First, insofar as a community's legal officials converge in accepting particular criteria of legal validity from the internal point of view, they are systematically and robustly disposed to enforce the set of norms so identified. Second, by dint of legal officials' robust disposition to enforce this set of norms, the set of norms is causally potent. Third, social rules of recognition and the causally potent set of norms picked out by such rules are, as Hart would put it, important, recurring features of social institutions. Thus, theorists have reason to bend their shared stock of legal conceptual resources into a Hartian conventionalist content. By following the conventionalist modulation of the conditions of application commonly associated with legal terms, theorists track and communicate information about important, recurrent features of social institutions, and they thereby realize the discursive value of theoretical illumination.

Note that this pragmatic inferentialist reading of Hart's theory draws it closer to the naturalized approach to jurisprudence that Brian Leiter has recently defended. As he and Alex Langlinais describe this approach: "[T]he 'folk' concept of the phenomenon ought to be revised in light of whatever refined understanding of the phenomenon is explanatorily and predictively fruitful" (Langlinais and Leiter 2016: 13). Leiter argues that because the Hartian account of law is explanatorily and predictively fruitful whereas Dworkinian accounts are not, the folk concept of law ought to be revised to conform to the Hartian positivist account.[12]

---

[11] A stronger version of conventionalism would require that most or all the system's officials accept the system's criteria of validity at least in part for the reason that their fellow officials accept those criteria. See Marmor (1998). For a defense of the weaker conventionalist reading, see Dickson (2007).

[12] See Leiter (2007: 187–99 and 2015).

Pragmatic inferentialism could in principle join Leiter in this conclusion, with two qualifications. First, pragmatic inferentialism would reject Leiter's seeming presupposition that there is a privileged, univocal construction of the meaning of legal terms; rather, pragmatic inferentialism allows that there might be myriad modulations of the semantic potential of legal terms, each of which is tailored and applicable to particular occasions of use. Second, pragmatic inferentialism would replace Leiter's thought that there is a folk concept of law in need of revision with the crucially different notion of a semantic potential that serves as a template from which particular fine-grained concepts can be fashioned to fit the discursive demands of particular occasions in which the term associated with the semantic potential is used.

In summary, I have argued that the hermeneutic meaning of legal terms on the Hartian occasion of use comprises those rules of use that enable theorists to track and communicate information about a particular set of important, recurrent features of social institutions. I have further argued that the Hartian conventionalist elucidation of the conditions of application are rules of use of this kind. Insofar as these arguments are sound, the subject matter of Hartian legal theory is fixed by this descriptive hermeneutic function and the complement of rules of use that enable speakers to realize this function.

3.3 The Hermeneutic Function of the Dworkinian Use of Legal Terms

The following passage contains the foundational premise of Dworkin's defense of his theory of law:

> Our discussions about law by and large assume, I suggest, that the most abstract and fundamental point of legal practice is to guide and constrain the power of government in the following way. Law insists that force not be used or withheld, no matter how useful that would be to ends in view, no matter how beneficial or noble these ends, except as licensed or required by individual rights and responsibilities flowing from past political decisions about when collective force is justified.
> Dworkin (1986: 93)

With this premise putatively established, Dworkin further argues that it is necessary to engage in politico-moral reasoning about this set of rights and responsibilities that flow from a political community's past political decisions to determine what the laws of that community are.

Pragmatic inferentialism provides resources for fortifying Dworkin's foundational premise.[13] Pragmatic inferentialism locates the Dworkinian theorist in

---

[13] See Dickson (2001: 108–10) for a withering critique of Dworkin's defense of this premise.

relation to the occasion in which officials issue legal judgments (i.e, judgments of the form "X is the law or legally valid"). As a matter of longstanding and nigh immutable collective practice, legal officials' publicly stated legal judgments about what is and is not law are immediate preludes and guides to state-enforcement action. Thus, legal officials by and large cannot, as a practical matter, pronounce that "X is law" and then effectively insist that X not be enforced.[14] In light of this characterization of the legal officials' occasion for the use of legal terms, the pragmatic inferentialist defense of the foundational Dworkinian premise holds that politico-moral considerations are abidingly salient on the legal officials' occasion for the use of legal terms. For the abidingly relevant issue on such occasions of use relates to the justification of the officials' collective enforcement actions. On such occasions, legal officials have reason to use legal terms to cooperatively track and communicate information about those norms that they, as a matter of politico-morality, would be justified in collectively enforcing.

As understood here, a subject matter is normativist if it is the object of a normativist concept—i.e. a concept that enables speakers to evaluate prospective responses of a certain kind (perhaps intentional actions or attitudes of endorsement, to name two possibilities) in immediate prelude to instantiating the most highly evaluated response. The subject matter of Dworkinian theory is normativist in this sense, for it is the object of a concept that enables legal officials to track and communicate information about norms that the officials would be justified in enforcing as immediate prelude and guide to subsequent collective enforcement actions. On this view, the hermeneutic meaning of legal terms uttered by the Dworkinian theorist comprises rules of use that enable the legal official to realize this normativist, hermeneutic function.

3.4 The Subject Matters of Hartian and Dworkinian Legal Theory

If the foregoing characterization were perfectly accurate, then Hartian and Dworkinian theory would always address distinct subject matters. However, things are not so cut and dried. For the Hartian sometimes strays into the legal officials' occasion for the use of legal terms. For example, in a well-known debate with Lon Fuller, Hart (1983: 75-7) cast doubt on the wisdom of a German postwar court for putatively appealing to considerations of justice to invalidate a Nazi-era German law, thereby running foul of the dictates of his conventionalist theory. More recently, Brian Leiter (2009: 1224) has defended the thesis that when judges issue opinions out of step with Hart's conventionalism, they are acting either disingenuously or in error. In such instances, the Hartian uses legal terms to censure and challenge legal officials' claims about the law, and, in such a case,

---

[14] Cf. Hart (1983: 72-8) and Gardner (2012: 51-2).

the Hartian has reason to use legal terms in accordance with the hermeneutic meaning of legal terms that governs the legal officials' occasion for using those terms. Thus, the Hartian and Dworkinian theorist speak to the same subject matter in instances of this kind.

To be sure, nothing in the foregoing is meant to imply, much less establish, that when the Hartian strays into this Dworkinian terrain, the Hartian's criticisms of legal officials' appeal to politico-moral considerations when making legal judgments are misguided. For it might be that the abidingly predominant discursive values germane to the legal official's normativist context are rule-of-law values relating to the stability of expectations, and these rule-of-law values would arguably support using legal terms to identify and communicate information about the set of rules recognized by an established, publicly known, conventional rule of recognition.[15] Rather than taking sides in the debate, the foregoing discussion clarifies a proposed frame for assessing the force of Hartian criticisms of legal officials. So framed, the pivotal question is whether the Hartian who strays into the Dworkinian normativist context subjects legal officials to rules for the use of legal terms appropriately tailored to that occasion for the use of legal terms. It might turn out that in such contexts, legal officials have reason to hew to Hartian conventionalist conditions of application for legal terms. Alternatively, they might have reason to hew to Dworkinian conditions of application, or they might have reason to observe some other set of conditions unimagined by either Hartian or Dworkinian theorist. In any case, pragmatic inferentialism holds that to adjudicate between these possibilities, the theorist must engage in the hermeneutic, coherentist reasoning described above.

3.5 A Hermeneutic Caveat

At this point, it is important to register a crucial qualification of the pragmatic inferentialist account of hermeneutic function and meaning. Namely, it should not be assumed that on all occasions in which speakers exchange assertions, those assertions and their component terms serve a hermeneutic function and, hence, bear a hermeneutic meaning. For it might be that there is no rationale that would unify and rationalize the rules of use for the assertions' key terms on the occasion of use in question.

For the purposes of illustrating this abstract claim, let us stipulate that oftentimes some version of non-positivist legal theory is correct. That is, groups of legal officials oftentimes have reason to use legal terms to track norms that

---

[15] Compare Dworkin (1986: ch. 4).

satisfy some set of politico-moral considerations in prelude to their collective enforcement of those norms. Perhaps, the relevant politico-moral considerations are grounded in the Dworkinian value of integrity or, alternatively, some other constellation of politico-moral values—say, the values of respect and relational equality realized by converging in the enforcement of a democratic legislature's enactments. Let us further stipulate that a necessary enabling condition of this non-positivist hermeneutic function is that the non-positivist use of legal terms facilitates officials' convergent enforcement of norms that realize the relevant politico-moral values.

Now, consider that in the American antebellum South, legal officials habitually used legal terms to track and identify applications of norms that constituted and regulated the institution of slavery. Presumably, the enforcement actions guided by such norms failed to realize any politico-moral value, for any such value would be undercut by the egregious injustice and disvalue of perpetuating slavery. For example, irrespective of the democratic pedigree of slavery-instituting norms, the collective enforcement of such norms would not realize the values of egalitarian respect and relational equality. In such a context, it might be that legal terms bear a non-positivist hermeneutic function and meaning that implies that the era's chattel-slavery constituting enactments were not legally valid.

An alternative and more radical possibility is that the politico-moral values that would underwrite the non-positivist hermeneutic function are undercut in the chattel-slavery context. For it might be that legal officials have reason to use legal norms to identify norms that realize politico-moral values only insofar as doing so effectively facilitates the officials' subsequent collective enforcement of those norms. Moreover, it might be that in the context of deciding cases related to the entrenched institution of chattel slavery, there is no set of politico-moral value realizing norms that could win sufficient convergence among the antebellum community of legal officials. On such an occasion of use, there would be no non-positivist hermeneutic function for legal terms—no reason to use legal terms to track norms that realize the relevant constellation of politico-moral values. Moreover, on such occasions, the use of legal terms might not realize a hermeneutic function of any sort—normativist, descriptivist, or otherwise. For there might be no function of any sort that would both rationalize and unify the semantic potential of legal terms and serve discursive values relevant to the chattel-slavery occasion for the use of legal terms.

To be clear, legal officials might be unaware that they have traveled beyond the discursive space of hermeneutically meaningful legal discourse. Moreover, in such contexts, legal terms and statements would be meaningful in other (non-hermeneutic) senses of the term. For example, legal terms might bear a conventional or speaker-understanding meaning. Perhaps, more interestingly, they might bear an expressivist meaning. That is, the legal official might use legal terms to exert expressivist or emotivist influence on her interlocutors in accordance with normative attitudes that the official endorses.[16] The crucial point is that insofar as legal officials find themselves outside the bounds of hermeneutically meaningful legal discourse, their legal statements lack a hermeneutic meaning. Moreover, on such hermeneutically meaningless occasions, officials' legal statements could not even in principle satisfy the Truth norm's antecedent, at least not from the participant's (as opposed to the descriptive theorist's) point of view described above. For this norm's antecedent is satisfied from the participant perspective only if ~P, and a speaker utters an assertion with the hermeneutic subject matter of P. Yet, on the occasions we are considering, officials' legal statements lack any hermeneutic meaning. Thus, the expressivist user of legal terms would be outside the jurisdiction of the Truth norm, and, hence, her expressivist locutions would not be truth-apt—at least not in the pragmatic inferentialist's sense of the term.

4. Conclusion

In summary, I hope to have now realized three main objectives. The first was to explicate and defend metasemantic non-positivism. To this end, I have argued that on participant Pricean occasions of use, speakers ought to use the term "subject matter" to identify and communicate information about the hermeneutic meaning of one another's assertions. In other words, I have argued that such speakers ought to use "subject matter" to refer to the concepts that speakers ought to take as a guide for their use of their terms.

Second, I have appealed to pragmatic inferentialist resources to argue for an alternative to the characterization of the dispute between Dworkinian and Hartian legal theory set out in MD. According to this pragmatic inferentialist alternative, the Dworkinian theorist uses legal terms on occasions of use (the legal officials' occasion for the use of legal terms) in which the hermeneutic function and meaning of those terms is normativist, and hence, the Dworkinian addresses a normativist subject matter with legal terms. By contrast, the Hartian

---

[16] See Toh (2011) for a discussion of a kind of legal expressivism modeled after Gibbard's metaethical expressivism. When a term has a hermeneutic function, the function is limited to a particular occasion of use, and all parties to that occasion of use have reason to use the term in a cooperative, communicative project that realizes the discursive values relevant to the occasion. Moreover, they each have reason to use the terms in accordance with a hermeneutic conversational scoreboard defined by these rules of use, and, concomitantly they each have reason to hold one another accountable in accordance with this shared scoreboard. A speaker might use a term in a way that realizes the expressivist end of influencing the interlocutor, and she might have reason to use a term in this expressivist way, but this would not yet be to have a hermeneutic reason that requires each party to a linguistic exchange to hold herself and her interlocutors accountable to a shared conversational scoreboard for the use of the term.

by and large uses legal terms on occasions in which the hermeneutic function and meaning of those terms is descriptive; hence, the Hartian addresses a descriptive subject matter. Thus, the Dworkinian and Hartian at times talk past each other when they seem to be engaged in a substantive object-level dispute.

However, at crucial moments, the Hartian strays into the Dworkinian occasion of use (i.e. the legal officials' occasion of use), and in those moments, the Hartian uses legal terms to address the normativist subject matter of Dworkinian theory. This alternative characterization of the dispute between Hartian and Dworkinian theory is offered as a frame for adjudicating this dispute rather than as premise that directly supports either side. To be sure, I have argued that the pivotal question queries the hermeneutic function of legal terms and that on a key type of occasion for the use of legal terms, the legal official's occasion for use, legal terms serve a normativist hermeneutic function. That said, further auxiliary argument is required to determine whether this normativist hermeneutic function yields Hartian positivist or Dworkinian non-positivist legal concepts.

The third and overarching objective of the foregoing discussion is to further our understanding of the collective and normative nature of word-meaning and conceptual content. I have broached the key idea above. Namely, on many occasions in which we exchange assertions, there is a hermeneutic conversational scoreboard that governs our use of the key terms in question and associated thoughts. This conversational scoreboard comprises the rules of use, the hermeneutic meaning that would enable speakers to realize the hermeneutic function of the terms used on particular occasions of use.[17]

A key feature of any such hermeneutic scoreboard is that a speaker is accountable to and bound by the scoreboard's constitutive rules of use by dint of her capacity and commitment to modulating the rules of use for terms and assertions on the fly in coordinated mutual anticipation with other similarly situated speakers. These rules of use comprise schedules of the reasons (e.g. perceptions and warranted acceptance of other propositions) that warrant the application of terms and the consequences (acceptance of other propositions, adoption of emotional attitudes, and so on) for which statements applying the terms are reasons. Pragmatic inferentialism makes explicit and articulates the hermeneutic, coherentist reasoning that guides speakers in such mutually anticipatory modulations of their shared terms' rules of use.

Word-meaning construed in terms of hermeneutic meaning is normative and collective in a number of ways. First, the semantic potentials of the terms that are the objects of hermeneutic reasoning are instilled by way of a common socialization into a linguistic community. Second, the hermeneutic reasoning is a prelude to joint-action. That is, to reason about the hermeneutic meaning of a term on an

---

[17] See Brandom (1998: 141–43) for a seminal discussion of the idea of conversational scorekeeping. See also Chrisman (2021).

occasion of use is to reason about what a group of speakers including oneself is normatively committed to using the term to do. Another way to put this point is that for the most part, discursive values are not realized by individual speakers. Rather, they are realized by a community of speakers universally bound by and generally compliant with a shared conversational scoreboard—a scoreboard ultimately fixed by the form of hermeneutic reasoning described above. In such a context, each party to the linguistic exchange has reason to hold herself and her interlocutors accountable to a shared conversational scoreboard specifying rules of use that the group must follow in order to realize the relevant discursive values. Third, as Price notes, the utility of these conversational scoreboards is dramatically augmented by a constellation of strategically interrelated linguistic dispositions— namely, the disposition to challenge and censure assertions that one takes to be in violation of the hermeneutic conversational scoreboard, the commonplace aversion to being publicly shown in violation of some such scoreboard, and the no less commonplace desire to win the public esteem of successfully defending one's reasoned position in accordance with the scoreboard.

In this same vein, pragmatic inferentialism explains the collective and normative nature of the individual speaker's concept possession. Although there are many senses in which a speaker might be said to possess or master a concept, pragmatic inferentialism forefronts the speaker's possession of the concept that is the hermeneutic meaning of some term. In short, a speaker possesses a concept in this sense only if there is a term that has a hermeneutic meaning on a particular occasion of use, and the speaker has a threshold disposition to engage in coherentist reasoning about the term's hermeneutic function and the rules of use that would support speakers' realization of that function. Key elements of any such threshold disposition are a sufficient grasp of the semantic potential of the term in question and a threshold capacity to engage in sound coherentist reasoning about a term's hermeneutic function and its supporting rules of use. Because a speaker can only possess a hermeneutic concept insofar as there is some term that has a hermeneutic meaning, concept possession in this sense is essentially a collective and normative phenomenon. For the hermeneutic meaning of a concept is collective and normative in the ways described immediately above.

Pragmatic inferentialism also explains how one might possess a concept despite failing to fully grasp the concept. A speaker possesses a hermeneutic concept by dint of her threshold disposition to engage in coherentist reasoning about a term's hermeneutic function, irrespective of whether she has successfully exercised that disposition. A related felicitous feature is that it provides guidance for achieving such mastery. That is, it enjoins the speaker to engage in sound coherentist reasoning about the hermeneutic function and meaning of the term in question.

Notably, this gap between concept possession and concept mastery allows for the possibility that the members of a group of speakers might each possess some key concept or set of concepts that are the hermeneutic meanings of the key terms of assertions that they regularly exchange with one another, and yet they might be guided by divergent conceptions of the fine-grained rules of use for the terms as well as the terms' hermeneutic function. For illustrative purposes, consider again the occasion in which legal officials exchange legal judgments that are immediate preludes and guides to subsequent state-enforcement actions.

As Hart has argued, a key condition of the existence of any legal system is that the officials of the system by and large converge with respect to the criteria of legal validity that they accept (see Hart 2012: 116–17). Pragmatic inferentialism glosses these criteria as rules of use (particularly, conditions of application) for legal terms, and it allows that legal officials might bring a wide variety of fine-grained conceptions of these rules of use to their exchange of legal judgments and subsequent enforcement actions. Pragmatic inferentialism introduces the further possibility of reflective officials who have an idea of what they and their fellow officials ought to use legal terms for and, accordingly, follow a particular set of conditions of application for legal terms that they take to be consistent with this idea. To be sure, pragmatic inferentialism allows that there might be many such reflective officials with a variety of conceptions of the hermeneutic function of and hence fine-grained rules of use for legal terms.

The foregoing plurality of conceptions among legal officials regarding the hermeneutic function and rules for the use of legal terms is compatible with the existence of a Hartian legal system. To be sure, too much divergence in this plurality of conceptions would fatally disrupt a legal system. However, there might be pressures that stabilize and preserve their collective convergence, while allowing for significant fine-grained differences between individual officials and moments of legal judgments. As Hart (2012: 203; see also Dickson 2007) speculates, the officials of a system might be motivated to hew closely to convention by a wide variety of motivations, including "calculations of long-term interest; disinterested interest in others; an unreflecting inherited or traditional attitude; or the mere wish to do as others do," to name just a few possibilities.

In summary, pragmatic inferentialism frames a hermeneutic question for legal theory and practice. It asks the theorist and participant whether on occasions in which legal officials exchange legal judgments in prelude to collective enforcement of the judgment, the legal terms used in those judgments bear a hermeneutic function and meaning. It allows that the answer to this question might be globally in the negative, globally in the affirmative, or punctuatedly in the affirmative for some, but not all, occasions. In a similar vein, pragmatic inferentialism allows that the hermeneutic function might vary across the occasions in which legal officials use legal terms. Insofar as officials' legal statements realize a hermeneutic function, pragmatic inferentialism provides a descriptive account and prescriptive guide of how we do and should go about deepening our understanding of the function and meaning of those terms as well as the legal practice in which assertions featuring those terms are exchanged. Moreover, the legal officials' occasion of use is a participatory Pricean occasion in which the shared disposition to follow and hold one another accountable to a shared hermeneutic conversational scoreboard fuels the collective project of deepening our grasp of legal practice and the meaning of legal terms.

References

Bach, K. (1994). 'Conversational Impliciture', *Mind & Language* 9: 124–62.

Brandom, R. (1998). *Making It Explicit*, Harvard University Press.

Burge, T. (1979). 'Individualism and the Mental', *Midwest Studies in Philosophy* 4: 73–122.

Cappelen, H., Gendler, T., and Hawthorne, J. (eds.) (2016). *The Oxford Handbook of Philosophical Methodology*, Oxford University Press.

Chrisman, M. (2021). 'A Peircean Inferentialist Alternative to Expressivism about Normative Vocabulary', in Shafer-Landau 2021.

Dickson, J. (2001). *Evaluation and Legal Theory*, Hart Publishing.

Dickson, J. (2007). 'Is the Rule of Recognition Really a Conventional Rule?', *Oxford Journal of Legal Studies* 27: 373–402.

Duarte d'Almeida, L., Edwards, J., and Dolcetti, A. (eds.) (2013). *Reading HLA Hart's The Concept of Law*, Oxford University Press.

Dworkin, R. (1986). *Law's Empire*, Harvard University Press.

Dworkin, R. (2013). *Justice for Hedgehogs*, Harvard University Press.

Gardner, J. (2012). *Law as a Leap of Faith*, Oxford University Press.

Hart, H. L. A. (1983). 'Positivism and the Separation of Law and Morals', *Essays in Jurisprudence and Philosophy*, Oxford University Press.

Hart, H. L. A. (2012). *The Concept of Law*, 3rd ed., Oxford University Press.

Hart, H. L. A. (2013). 'Answers to Eight Questions', in Duarte d'Almeida et al. 2013.

Kohler, S. (Forthcoming). 'What is Neo-Pragmatists' Function?', *Australasian Journal of Philosophy*.

Langlinais, A. and Leiter, B. (2016). 'The Methodology of Legal Philosophy', in Cappelen et al. 2016.

Leiter, B. (2007). *Naturalizing Jurisprudence*, Oxford University Press.

Leiter, B. (2009). 'Explaining Theoretical Disagreement', *University of Chicago Law Review* 1215–50.

Leiter, B. (2015). 'Marx, Law, Ideology, Legal Positivism', *Virginia Law Review* 101: 1179–96.

Marmor, A. (1998). 'Legal Conventionalism', *Legal Theory*, 4(4): 509–31.

Neuhouser, F. (2008). *Rousseau's Theodicy of Self-Love: Evil, Rationality, and the Drive for Recognition*, Oxford University Press.

Parish, P. (1963). *Amelia Bedelia*, Harper & Row.

Plunkett, D. (2016). 'Negotiating the Meaning of "Law": The Metalinguistic Dimension of the Dispute over Legal Positivism', *Legal Theory* 22: 205–75.

Plunkett, D. and Sundell, T. (2013). 'Dworkin's Interpretivism and the Pragmatics of Legal Disputes', *Legal Theory* 19: 242–81.

Price, H. (2003). 'Truth as Convenient Friction', *Journal of Philosophy* 100: 167–90.

Price, H. (2013). *Expressivism, Pragmatism and Representationalism*, Cambridge University Press.

Rayo, A. (2013). 'A Plea for Semantic Localism', *Nous* 47: 647–79.

Raz, J. (1979). *Authority of Law*, Oxford University Press.

Raz, J. (1994). *Ethics in the Public Domain*, Oxford University Press.

Shafer-Landau, R. (ed.) (2021). *Oxford Studies in Metaethics*, Oxford University Press.

Thomasson, A. (2020). *Norms and Necessity*, Oxford University Press.

Tiefensee, C. (2021). 'Metasemantics for the Relaxed', in Shafer-Landau 2021.

Toh, K. (2011). 'Legal Judgments as Plural Acceptances of Norms', *Oxford Studies in the Philosophy of Law*, Vol. 1, Oxford University Press.

Waluchow, W. (1994). *Inclusive Legal Positivism*, Oxford University Press.

Waluchow, W. and Sciaraffa, S. (2016). *The Legacy of Ronald Dworkin*, Oxford University Press.

Williams, M. (2013). 'How Pragmatists can be Local Expressivists', in Price 2013.

14
Pragmatism and the Prudential Good

Diana Heney

Methodological pragmatism flows from what founder Charles Sanders Peirce described as its "principle and method of right thinking" (1997 [1903] (CP): 70)—the pragmatic maxim, which tells us to "look to the upshot of our concepts in order to rightly apprehend them" (CP: 5.3). In this chapter, I argue that methodological pragmatism yields some first-order constraints on how an individual can conceive their own prudential good. I begin by raising questions about philosophical engagement with the notion—and the pursuit—of well-being, the better to have our explanatory quarry in view (section 1). I then introduce methodological pragmatism, with an emphasis on its model of inquiry and its approach to promoting conceptual clarity (section 2). I bring those methodological devices to bear on the concept of well-being, through a consideration of practices of valuing-as-good evidenced in our use of the concept in philosophical traditions (section 3) as well as in contemporary human rights discourse (section 4). While important questions about the most effective model of well-being remain (section 5), I conclude that the pragmatist can offer a set of resources for approaching these questions.

1. Preliminaries

The question of what makes a life go well for the person living it is a perennial philosophical concern. It is also, as pragmatist C. I. Lewis suggests, an existential predicament: "How to cook up a good life, out of whatever ingredients, or of the ingredients found in the cupboard, is indeed the practical problem of every man. But it would be an utterly hopeless problem if he did not know what manner of thing he was wishing to achieve" (1970 [1950]). We have before us nothing less than the practical problem of every person.

Any serious discussion of well-being raises multiple questions. I count at least three: first, what are the methods of investigation that allow us to answer the question of what makes a life good for the person living it? Second, what is it that makes a life good for the person living it? And third, do we see a convergence on unified answers that suggests a concept amenable to theorizing, or responses so disparate that to attempt a theory of well-being would be a non-starter? In more straightforward terms, and to deploy Lewis's metaphor: how can we learn the recipe for well-being? What is the recipe for well-being? If there is such a recipe, is there just one or should we recognize a range of variations?

Before we explore the path pragmatism opens up for us in approaching these questions, it will be helpful to have the gist of common philosophical accounts of well-being before us. The term 'well-being' picks out the prudential good for an agent—that which makes her life good in the living of it.[1] Philosophical theories of well-being fall into two broad camps: subjectivism and objectivism. On a subjectivist account, what is well-being relevant is particular to individual subjects, who are the authority on their own well-being and perhaps also the origin of its constitution. The most robust versions of subjectivism have both epistemological and ontological commitments: agents have unique first-personal access to knowledge of what contributes to their own good, as well as the power to deliberately constitute it. The latter addition means that subjectivism (in some forms) is not exclusively about epistemic access, but is subject-centered in a deeper way, as agents have the power to determine what that good consists in. On an objectivist account, what is well-being relevant is not particular to individuals, but is instead indexed to the kind of thing that we are. The most robust versions of objectivism also have both epistemological and ontological commitments: agents can be mistaken about what is well-being relevant for them and potentially learn from others; and the good for our kind is not up to us to choose as individuals.[2] While agents may have the power to choose to pursue their own good, they do not have the power to write their own recipe for the good life.

An example to illustrate the contrast may be helpful. Suppose Will tells us that pleasure makes him happy, and that pursuing his own well-being thus requires that he make choices that promote pleasurable experiences. Further, Will is inclined to regard other people as being not at all like himself. Many others, in his view, find their happiness elsewhere. Indeed, Will tells us that he has reacted against his boring parents and their insistence that cultivating virtue is the key to well-being by choosing to be a hedonist—he has committed himself to finding happiness always and only in pleasure. By contrast, Wilma tells us that pleasure makes her happy, but thinks that this is just because all animals (including rational ones) are made happy by pleasure. It is not up to her, on Wilma's view, whether or not pleasure makes her happy. The subjectivist Will is inclined to

---

[1] I do not propose here to work out a stance on the relation of the prudential good to the moral good, only to work to clarify what we talk about when we talk about well-being.

[2] Aristotle has perhaps the best-known account of fallibility with respect to one's own well-being. In *Nicomachean Ethics* (*NE*), bk 1, ch. 10, he advocates for the need to take the long view, and not judge in the moment how one's well-being stands: "let us grant that we must wait to see the end, and must then count someone blessed, not as being blessed [during the time he is dead] but because he previously was blessed" (*NE* I, 10, §7). He even goes so far as to suggest that whether one could be said to have lived a flourishing life could change after one's death, depending on what one's descendants do with the legacy of one's life.

regard himself as having written his own recipe for well-being; the objectivist Wilma believes that everyone is working with the same recipe.[3]

How should we think about the choice between subjectivism and objectivism about well-being?[4] This is not merely a theoretical choice-point but also a choice which has significant practical bearing on how we conceive of our own good, and how that conception guides our actions. Our choices of plans, projects, and pastimes are informed by what we think will enhance our quality of life. It also impacts how we think about the welfare of others, who are all, alike, facing the practical puzzle of how to live.

My strategy in what follows will be to focus primarily on objectivism. This is because objective list theorists often claim a kind of commonsensical authority for their view, and pragmatists likewise often present their approach as a kind of "ordinary reflection systematized" (Tiller 2008). As Guy Fletcher puts it, if we can ask people "what they want for themselves, for their loved ones, and for their friends and they will likely suggest a few things," such as "health, friendships, romantic relationships, pleasure and enjoyment, happiness, achievement, knowledge" (2015: 148). If we equip ourselves with pragmatist methods and do not find adequate reason to continue to pursue the objectivist program, this will serve as a kind of *reductio* argument, and serve to push the agenda toward searching for a satisfying subjectivist account.

Bernard Williams described the question of how to live *well* as Socrates's question, but also as always our question (1985: 1). What is it to say that it is "our" question? One possibility is to say that this question—which I have described as our practical puzzle—is shared by those with whom we share the capacity for deliberating about what to do. "Our question" is ours because it arises for us characteristically.[5] As a turn to pragmatism will make clear, seeing "our question" as amenable to inquiry means seeing it as a community question, one which may arise for each of us but also for us together.[6] This is one reason why it may be illuminating to connect our discussion of well-being with the contemporary human rights discourse: doing so enlarges the conversation, as it encourages us to focus on the possibility of general conditions conducive to human well-being,

---

[3] For the sake of keeping the example brief, suppose further that Will and Wilma are not concerned about becoming trapped on hedonic treadmills with the incline turned up to 11 or perturbed by the possibility of a paradox of happiness-as-pleasure whereby one cannot successfully pursue it directly.

[4] One strategy which I do not consider here is to try to achieve a hybrid account. I find this unpersuasive for reasons presented in Hurka (2019), which roughly distil to: what is really doing the explanatory work in such accounts is the objective element(s).

[5] The Wittgensteinian pragmatist will make this point in terms of *life-form*: "an ethically-saturated counterpart to the biological concept of a species" (Congdon forthcoming: 5). Thompson (2008: 62) puts the point in pragmatist-friendly terms: "our question should not be: What is a life-form, a species, a *psūche?*, but: How is such a thing described?"

[6] I have argued the pragmatism leads us to cosmopolitanism on epistemic grounds, because knowing better requires knowing together (Heney 2020a).

conditions of the sort that can be recognized, codified, and protected in a rights schema.[7]

2. Methodological Pragmatism

Historical pragmatists and their contemporary counterparts have many "in-house" disputes. I do not wade into such disputed waters here. This is not merely because to do so would take us too far from our present investigation, but also because the strongest point of agreement between historical and contemporary pragmatists and neopragmatists is method, which is the jumping off point needed to see what headway can be made from this perspective on questions of well-being.[8] Pragmatists of all stripes have shared what Hilary Putnam called its central emphasis: "the primacy of practice" (1995: 52). While the focus may have shifted to strongly emphasize linguistic practice as 20th-century pragmatists joined their contemporaries in taking the linguistic turn, we can nonetheless see pragmatists in general as having common cause in seeking methods that allow us to interrogate and understand core aspects of our shared lives and projects. In this section, I draw from various classical and contemporary pragmatist thinkers whose work bears on the presentation of pragmatist methods.

In approaching our questions about well-being, pragmatism offers methodological assistance in two main ways. First, it calls us to refocus our attention on what we are doing when we engage in an inquiry of practical importance, such as when we inquire into the sources of well-being. Second, it offers a framework to clarify our concepts through an investigation of their weight-bearing place in our practices.

Let us begin with inquiry. What is it that we do when we inquire? What makes inquiry as an activity different from wishing or speculating? Pragmatists espouse an embedded model of inquiry, and espouse its use widely. To say that it is 'embedded' means simply that the impetus for inquiry arises in human lives as a result of friction between endorsed beliefs and the evidence of experience, between previously successful habits and new situations that challenge them. When we inquire, we are moved to do so by doubt that presents itself in the course of living, not by wishes or speculations. Real doubt arrests action, and whenever this occurs, it is to inquiry that we should turn. As John Dewey expressed this thought, "Inquiry is the life-blood of every science and is

---

[7] While other accounts of the nature and status of human rights are obviously possible, I am interested in how such rights are articulated in practice: in lists that are not only structurally analogous to objective list theories of well-being, but also offer many content 'matches'. I return to and develop this parallel in section 4.

[8] The point here is not to minimize the substantive differences between particular pragmatists on particular points, but simply to indicate that I will steer around them in the work I attempt here.

constantly employed in every craft, science, and profession" (1986 [1938]: 12). For any hypothesis sensitive to evidence and argument, inquiry is a suitable path.[9]

Further features of pragmatist accounts of inquiry include an emphasis on lived experience, the demand to own uncertainty, and the opportunity to build consensus. These are not mere platitudes for the pragmatist, but features of inquiry that shape its progress.

To emphasize lived experience means that that inquiry begins from, and proceeds through, the failures and fresh efforts of actual people.[10] As Peirce put this point, we do not start an investigation from "vagabond thoughts that tramp the public roads without any human habitation," but rather "must begin with men and their conversation" (CP: 8.112). In situating inquiry as a process undertaken by an agent embedded in a context, we see that experience is relevant both as an impetus to inquire and as instrumental in securing the goods of inquiry. It also helps us to get a fix on what the explanatory focal points are—what, exactly, we are trying to explain or vindicate in practice.

The experimentalism of pragmatist methodology comes packaged with fallibilism. This demands of us that we own our uncertainty where appropriate, and work toward building consensus. We may be wrong, and may need to revise beliefs, and the recognition that this is so is often prompted by the conversations Peirce alluded to as our starting place. Through such conversations, being part of a community is liable to offer plenty of opportunities for inquiry—if we are willing to take the evidence and experience of others on board as relevant and informative. Taking others seriously is part and parcel of being an inquirer, as is trying to find answers that we can rest satisfied with. As Joe Heath has framed it, we know that we are in business with others, and we take the expectation of convergence as a normative presupposition of inquiry (Heath 1998).

This demand for convergence is rooted in our need to work together—a purpose at once prosaic and profound. Federico Lijoi points out that taking the experimental mindset of pragmatism on board allows us to convert "a threat into an opportunity": the threat of dealing with disagreement into the opportunity to learn from others (2021: 63). When it comes to the question of how to live well, the forcefulness of such a threat is not to be taken lightly. Not knowing how to pursue one's own good can be doubt-inducing and action-inhibiting to a severe degree. The opportunity, if we have the good fortune to have the time and tools to

---

[9] Of course, we may not realize that a belief we hold is a hypothesis sensitive to evidence and argument. But when the settled becomes unsettled, trying to dispel doubt by 'doubling down' on the belief in question through tenacious adherence is, Peirce says, no more effective than an ostrich putting its head in the sand to deal with an oncoming predator (CP: 5.377).
[10] It is perhaps worth noticing that such failures occur in all sorts of endeavors, and can in such cases be the impetus to turn to inquiry as a method. Failures can also occur *within* the practice of inquiry, as when a community of inquiry is too small to have canvassed salient phenomena.

turn to inquiry, is also not to be taken lightly.[11] Well-being matters. The pragmatist picture would have us see doubt about how to live as real and arresting, and any attempt to find a stable answer to questions of how to live as embarking on a process of inquiry.

This is, in some sense, a realist picture: our beliefs about what makes a life go well are rationally answerable to real phenomena. It is also a historically dynamic picture, as our engagement with the concept of well-being and with the use of the language of rights to attempt to secure well-being shapes and reshapes our social organization as our situations evolve.[12] While we are trying to capture the facts of the matter, what those facts concern is the human experience of flourishing. This suggests that we are dealing with an interactive phenomenon, one for which a strict focus on reference is not a good model. As Ian Hacking memorably put it, we carve nature at the joints we put there—though our categorization is tracking something real, it is nonetheless inevitably ours. "A realistic account is one which dispenses with myth and metaphor, and which instead places human beings—finite, fallible, and yet extraordinarily functional—at its heart" (Methven 2015: 51).[13]

In addition to this general account of inquiry, pragmatism offers us a second instrument, which is an account of meaning that centrally involves the pragmatic maxim. Originally presented in Peirce's "How to Make Our Ideas Clear," the pragmatic maxim expresses the centrality of a term's use in determining its meaning.[14] We arrive at the maxim in the context of unpacking what it is to have mastery over a concept. To understand it fully, Peirce stipulates, we must have a clear and distinct perception of the concept. A distinct perception is evidenced by having a grasp on the concept's instantiation—being able to sort cases from non-cases. A clear perception makes that grasp articulate in the form of a definition (even if such a definition is incomplete or nominal). But full mastery requires more yet: it requires understanding the function a term or concept has in our linguistic practices. To achieve that level of clarity, we must "Consider what effects, that might conceivably have practical bearings, we conceive the object of our conception to have. Then, our conception of these effects is the whole of our conception of the object" (CP: 5.402). Peirce later reinterpreted the maxim in his injunction that we must "look to the upshot of our concepts in order to rightly apprehend them"

---

[11] That not everyone has such affordances is one driver in pivoting from thinking about well-being to thinking about rights. I return to this point in the discussion of attempts to codify human rights in section 4.

[12] This way of articulating the balance of realism with a historically dynamic understanding of our language use is drawn from Congdon (forthcoming: 2–3).

[13] Quoted in Misak (2016). I agree with her assessment there: "this is as good a description of pragmatism as any" (2016: 88). It is worth noticing that the pragmatism Methven is describing is that of Frank Ramsey. For more on Ramsey's "realistic spirit," see Methven (2015).

[14] For a discussion of how this conceptual investigation plays out with respect to the concept of truth in the pragmatist tradition—one of the most (in)famous applications of the pragmatic maxim—see Heney (2015 and 2022).

(CP: 5.3). As we see in the later version of the maxim, Peirce shifts his focus from the objects of our conceptions to the concepts themselves, and how those concepts are weight-bearing in practice. He insisted that correct identification of instances (grasping) and clarification (definition) remain important to rounding out our understanding of a term, even though he regarded the pragmatic grade of clarity as most important of all.

Crucially, meeting the pragmatic standard does not mean merely figuring out how I, myself, use a word. Cheryl Misak has explained the process of pragmatic elucidation in terms that help us to see that it is a fundamentally social endeavor. It is not merely a matter of asking ourselves "what do I mean by this?," but of considering "the commitments we undertake when we assert or believe" (2000: 73).[15] Such commitments are not inert private resolutions, but reveal themselves in our actions and habits. These actions and habits can be assessed by others as well as by ourselves; in enacting them, we make ourselves responsible for their upshots. They also reveal themselves as useful or misguided in the ways they support us, or fail to support us, in coping with the world in which we find ourselves. Pragmatism portrays human life and language use as social and engaged, not solipsistic, and as responsive to and reflective of the context in which it functions. Humanizing truth does not imply abandoning a standard of objectivity. Rather, we can talk of truth and good in human terms that are responsive to the kind of thing that we are without losing sight of the fact that we are a kind of thing.

Recall that our first question concerned what methods of investigation will allow us to answer the question of what makes a life good for the person living it. A turn to pragmatism supplies methodological tools for approaching the question of how to live: an account of inquiry as a communal business embedded in, and responsive to, our experience, along with a way of orienting ourselves toward the practical meaning of our weight-bearing concepts. We are now in a position to turn toward concrete territory, to see whether an investigation of the pragmatic elucidation of "well-being" supports subjectivism or bears out a form of objectivism. We have our second question firmly in view: what is it that makes a life good for the person living it? For the pragmatist, this question is inseparable from the way that the ideal of flourishing functions—that is, from the practical significance of the concept of well-being.

3. A Model of Things from the Middle of Things

As we have seen, considering the nature of inquiry and our way of articulating meaning illuminates the social nature of human lives, inquiries, and language use.

---

[15] For more on the pragmatic elucidation of 'truth', see Misak (2004 [1991]). For accounts that emphasize the place of reality in Peirce's account of truth, see Lane (2018) and Howat (2018).

Starting out from a pragmatist position, we see that inquiry is a situated process: we can only find a model of things from the middle of things. An investigation into human well-being is an inquiry, and thus an empirical business guided by the conviction that there is something to get right—some agreement to work toward. Like any other concept that is weight-bearing in human conversation and coordination, the concept of 'well-being' is amenable to investigation along multiple grades of clarity. We defined it earlier in a preliminary way: the term "well-being" picks out the prudential good for an agent, that which makes her life good in the living of it. To pursue the pragmatic grade of clarity, this section considers the concept as it functions in practice. This elucidation requires two steps: first, I will explain Richard Boyd's account of homeostatic property clusters in order to suggest that "well-being" can be modeled as a property cluster term; second, I explore how typical objective list theorists' inclusions can be construed as an elucidation of the property cluster term "well-being." This yields substantial agreement on a cluster of things or states of affairs repeatedly offered as co-extensive with how people understand the prudential good. That is, the convergence and consensus-building expected from a shared inquiry do in fact arise in conversations about how to live a good life, which points toward the possibility of an informative objectivist account of well-being.

In "How to Be a Moral Realist," Boyd (1988: 308) espouses holism in exploring the symmetry between our epistemic access in scientific domains and in the moral domain, noting that for both "improvements in knowledge can be expected to produce improvements in method." While advocating naturalistic explanation across domains, Boyd takes care to point out that a naturalistic explanation need not be atomistic or reductive. It can be pragmatic: "a wide variety of terms do not possess analytic or stipulative definitions and are instead defined in terms of properties, relations, etc. which render them appropriate to particular sorts of scientific or practical reasoning" (1988: 320–1). Boyd (2002: 44) describes "reference [as] a dialectically complex process, of which exactly determinate reference for particular terms is a special case." Even while strictly determinate reference is rare, this process view is still motivated by desire to achieve correspondence "between the use of [...] terms and causal structures" (2002: 53). Boyd maintains that tracking the reference of terms, including homeostatic property cluster terms, requires a representationalist semantics "positing some sort of *correspondence* between internal representational structures and features of the empirical world" (2002: 57).[16]

---

[16] One might say that being a bit vague about correspondence is a pragmatist family tradition: Peirce allows that there is a "nominal" sense in which truth can be defined in correspondence terms, but swiftly goes on to insist that this is *merely* nominal, and that a full grasp of the concept of truth requires seeing how we use it in practice.

Boyd is interested in the possibility that "good" in the moral sense is a property cluster term that picks out those things which satisfy important human needs. Such needs are what he calls "homeostatically clustered." They tend to have an intertwined character, arise or achieve satisfaction together, and also not to come into conflict with one another in practical settings (1988: 329–30). As he puts it, "The question of just which important human needs there are is a potentially difficult and complex empirical question," but it is one that we can nonetheless gain traction on. Here is Boyd's initial gloss on an answer:

> There are a number of important human goods, things which satisfy important human needs. Some of these needs are physical or medical. Others are psychological or social; these (probably) include the need for love and friendship, the need to engage in cooperative efforts, the need to exercise control over one's own life, the need for intellectual and artistic appreciation and expression, the need for physical recreation, etc.   Boyd (1988: 329)

Because he develops a form of consequentialism, the identification of moral goodness with those things conducive to welfare allows Boyd to complete his own shift from second-order concerns about epistemic access to the moral domain to an empirically resourced first-order account of the moral good.[17]

I suggest that we extend the thought to the prudential good as well, and avail ourselves of part of Boyd's explanation for the realistic character of moral terms. His task is to make moral realism plausible, while we are interested in the plausibility of its prudential cousin—well-being objectivism. The apparent plurality of goods involved in an objective list theory all answer to the concept of "well-being" because "good" in the prudential sense is a property cluster term. But we do not need to go so far in the correspondence direction as Boyd thought we must. As Heath (1998) has put it, we need not think of ourselves as examining a given discourse to see whether it is objective or whether it is about the world. Rather, what we need to satisfy our pragmatist aspirations is convergence on a core of understanding that serves the practical purposes to which we put the concept of well-being.

This is, in fact, what non-monistic objective list theories offer.[18] Objective list theorists claim that what impacts our well-being is a list of things objectively relevant to well-being for creatures of our kind. Whether we actively or currently

---

[17] As mentioned in section 1, we have resolved here to remain neutral on the relationship between the moral good and the prudential good, as the latter is our animating interest.

[18] While it is worth noticing that an objective list could be monistic—this would allow us to understand hedonism as an objective list with one item on it: pleasure!—the majority of philosophers who espouse this view enumerate multiple possible contributions. Still, it is important to see that hedonism is not structurally opposed to objective list theory in a way that marks it out as a different *kind* of theory. For more on this point, see Fletcher (2015), which helpfully traces out the influence of Parfit (1984) in treating them as different kinds of theories.

desire them, those things or states of affairs would actually contribute to our well-being if we had them. If we recall the questions that arose earlier (section 1), we see that objectivists can avail themselves of the pragmatist response to the first question: what are the methods of investigation that allow us to answer the question of what makes a life good for the person living it? The pragmatist response: individual inquirers can test hypotheses about what makes a good life in their own experiments in living, but such experiments always occur within the context of a community that provides the threat and the opportunity of occasion to revise away from accidental idiosyncrasy. Elizabeth Anderson presents an early account of the function of such experiments as occurring in the work of John Stuart Mill, who "claimed that evidence for the superiority of one conception of the good over another can be found in experiments in living" (1991: 14). Anderson articulates the connection between this idea and the pragmatist account of inquiry beautifully, and in terms especially suited to reflection on well-being:

> A person may enter a period of crisis if, having faithfully followed the recommendations of the conception of the good under reasonably favorable conditions, she experiences her life as one of suffering rather than one of flourishing. This crisis has two dimensions: it is a crisis of life, since she is not realizing what she can recognize as good; and it is a theoretical crisis, since the theories linked with her conception of the good cannot account for her felt suffering. The experience of crisis prompts a twofold quest, for a way of life which relieves the suffering and sets new goals she recognizes as worthwhile, and for a new theory which can explain the failures of the old way of life and the successes of the new.
>
> Anderson (1991: 23–4)

The results of such experiments are the empirical resource we need to underwrite well-being as a property cluster term. We do not need to go further, or attempt to pull back a curtain to causal structures, to secure the reference of the term. Indeed, we should resist attempts to do so, as seeking the sources of well-being in causal structures rather than human experiences pushes the concept too far into purely intellectual territory, when the question before us—and our need to answer it—is essentially practical.

Communities of inquirers can enumerate viable hypotheses by pursuing a collective exercise in conceptual clarity. These methods are effective if they lead us to answers to the second and third questions: what can make a life good for the person living it, and is there convergence on unified answers? Objective list theorists have answered both questions together: a bunch of things, and yes. Importantly for our investigation here, a consideration of actual objective lists *demonstrates* the 'yes': many of the same things appear on objective lists over and over again, for over 2,000 years. From a pragmatist perspective, this is not an accidental feature of philosophical reflection on the good life, but an indication that the term as it is deployed succeeds in tracking reliable convergences. This may sound high-minded and distant from the first-personal existential dread of trying to get one's own life on track. But when it comes to well-being, the kinds of things proposed on philosophers' objective lists are simply the things that people value-as-good, and have had success in organizing their own lives around.[19]

Consider some of the inclusions that we see on proposed objective lists over and over again: "pleasure, friendship, and knowledge" (Lin 2018), "loving relationships, meaningful knowledge, autonomy, achievement, and pleasure" (Rice 2013), "achievement, friendship, happiness, pleasure, self-respect, virtue" (Fletcher 2015). These goods are non-instrumentally valuable in a human life, according to those who defend their place on the list: good not merely for bringing about something else (such as pleasure), but really good on their own and good for the kind of thing we are.

Notice, too, that the idea that we can identify meaningful convergence does not require us to engage in any deep metaphysics of the human. A distinction made by Crisp (2006), amplified by Fletcher (2013), shows that theories of well-being may be either enumerative or explanatory: enumerative theories identify *what* is well-being relevant, explanatory theories tell the story of *why* something is well-being relevant. Methodological pragmatism orients us toward providing an enumerative theory which vindicates itself in practice, rather than an explanatory theory that explains why something enhances human well-being. For this project, we need be committed only to the idea that humans are a kind of creature capable of reflecting on their own good beyond mere noticing of individual patterns of aversion and attraction.[20]

Still, such patterns are important, for the phenomenon in question—a good life—cannot be understood apart from human experience. To borrow a term offered by Joshua Gert, we are engaged in an exploration that involves "human responses in such a central way" that it should be understood as "response-featuring" (2012: 36). Gert presents an analysis of the domain of color that articulates how "uniformity of response might help to explain the presence of a certain kind of term in the language" (2012: 37). When it comes to well-being, we are engaged at the level of what is valued-as-good, and so here too our responses matter—not merely as individuals, but as a socially situated and intertwined collective. Nor is there any great mystery about how we shift from social collaboration to individual reflection (or vice versa) in the conversation about well-being.

---

[19] As Josh Gert pointed out to me, it's an interesting asymmetry that the motivation to inquire into well-being could be construed as negative—existential predicament!—but the things that appear on lists are all *goods*. The recent rise in attention to ill-being could conceivably shift this conversation in interesting ways.

[20] This does not necessarily mean that there is no point in seeking an explanatory theory (though some pragmatists are sufficiently anti-metaphysical to take this additional step), only that the order of explanation for the concept in use, in practice, calls out for an enumerative theory—and, as we shall consider in section 4, social melioration.

It is, like any conversation, normatively constrained in a way that requires us to "ascribe value to those judgements we are prepared to make ourselves" (Price 1988: 205). Similarly, we ascribe disvalue to those judgments we regard as incompatible with our evidence and experience—we regard them as false. We do not see it is as a matter of mere individual expression, but rather as a truth-apt assertion, when someone claims that something is essential to living a good life. When a right that protects something widely accepted as essential for well-being is infringed upon, we do not regard that as a matter of merely individual concern.

Further, we are prepared to ascribe value to more than one judgment about what makes a good life. We recognize a plurality of reasonable contenders. As our consideration of objective list theories has shown, "well-being" admits of robust consensus despite the abundance of items on such lists and the possibility of variation between some pairings of lists. To build on Gert's analysis: this suggests that a term can pick out something that is both conceptually complex and response-featuring.[21] Thus, our well-being is "up to us" in the sense that our needs and responses help to delineate the proper application of the concept.

But in another sense, it is not up to us—that is, it is not up to *each* of us, in isolation. This brings us, at last, back to the dispute between subjectivist accounts of well-being and objective list theories. Recall that on strong subjectivist views, agents have a kind of individual normative authority to determine all the practical ends particular to their own singular set of values. In other words, an agent could write the recipe for their own well-being from scratch. From a linguistic perspective, they could assert "to me that term refers only to such-and-such, and no one can tell me otherwise." Such an account would not only *feature* the agent's response, but make the accuracy of the use of the term *dependent* on it. It would render such an agent incorrigible, because their own claims about the good for them would not be open to the kind of doubt that spurs one to seek evidence beyond the edges of one's own experience. But the pragmatist emphasis on experience and on the embedded nature of inquiry does not radically individualize a sphere of value for each valuer. Instead, it positions us as capable of offering one another threats to our beliefs and opportunities to improve on them.

A consideration of philosophical objective lists suggests that we can find stable loci when we consider how "well-being" functions in practice. Objectivists explain this as a convergence on what matters. Such a convergence needn't provide a perfect or exhaustive grasp in order to be, nonetheless, a meaningful consensus. The subjectivist thus acquires a burden of proof: to explain convergence away or problematize it. As I have indicated, this is unappealing from a

---

[21] The sort of complexity I have in mind is a kind of internal heterogeneity, of the sort that would be best captured by an explanation in terms of paradigmatic core and reasonable penumbra—rather than, say, an explanation in terms of necessary and sufficient conditions. I allude to this in section 5, though I do not develop this proposal in any detail in this project.

pragmatist perspective, because it forecloses the possibility of inquiry as a method for learning about well-being.

But it is not enough to generate a problem for the would-be subjectivist. We should expect more. If there are features of a human life that are predictably well-being relevant for diverse individuals, convergence should obtain beyond philosophical practice and it should inform our efforts to live well and reflect on the welfare of others. Let us now consider a candidate conversation: contemporary human rights discourse.

4. A Brief Case Study: Codifying Human Rights

The idea of well-being does work for human communities in practice, because it captures the suite of needs that we ourselves believe must be met in order to live a good life as the kind of creature we are—and because we care about others leading good lives, too. This gives us a reason to prefer an account that advances the work rather than undermining it. It also means that our need to justify some mutually intelligible account of the prudential good is a practice-improving need, not a practice-originating need. When we have a practice that is woven into the fabric of our shared discourse, we are trying to ensure that what we have is fit for purpose.[22] The standard of explanation to which we hold ourselves in such cases is that of vindicatory explanation (Wiggins 1990–1). Wiggins offers this standard as an alternative to causal explanation, which seeks to link cause and effect in a necessary relation. By contrast, vindicatory explanation affirms a conclusion as defensible in comparison with the alternatives. Wiggins discusses beliefs, which are vindicated when there is simply "nothing else to think" but that they are true.

What could vindicate the objective list theorist's approach in practice? One answer is the existence of a practice that relies on objective list theory, and which we could not excise from our shared life without significant cost to human well-being. To stress the sort of justification we are seeking, such vindication is pragmatic—there is "nothing else to think" but that we should be invested in engaging in organizational practices that stand to enhance well-being. One such organizational practice is our ongoing attempts to codify human rights. This is a context where we see the idea of well-being operating at a theory-practice nexus, as what such rights are *for* is the protection and enhancement of the opportunities people have to live a life that's good for them. Many people are imperiled with respect to their own well-being not because they are existentially unmoored, but

---

[22] For a more extended discussion of what it means to take a "practice-first" frame, see Heney (2020b). In that essay, I also say more about pragmatic vindication, and how it relates to shared practices.

because they lack access—through no fault of their own—to the basic necessities that undergird any sustainable pursuit of a good life.

The project of codifying a list of internationally recognized human rights that governments and institutions should be in the business of honoring and promoting has been an animating project for seventy-five years. Beginning with the United Nation's 1948 "Universal Declaration of Human Rights" (UDHR), there have been a number of attempts to express rights that should be protected because the benefits conferred by such protection are well-being relevant. An example of such refinement is at hand even within the UN's own codification processes. The 1948 UDHR lasted less than twenty years as the document-of-record by the UN's own lights: in 1966, the General Assembly ratified the International Covenant on Economic, Social, and Cultural Rights (ICESCR) and the International Covenant on Civil and Political Rights (ICCPR) which have been folded together with the UDHR to form the UN's bill of human rights. The UDHR itself ranges widely, including rights to non-interference and recognition, as well as positive rights to rest and leisure (A.24); education (A.26); and participation in the cultural life of one's community (A.27). Article 25 makes the relation of the rights package developed in the declaration to the pursuit and enhancement of well-being explicit, stating that "Everyone has a right to a standard of living adequate for the health and well-being of himself and his family." One function of statements aimed at the international community is to serve as a call to recognize the situations of others, including distant others, and their own grappling with Socrates's question.

Despite this laudable aim, human rights discourse is also often marked by disagreement. Interestingly, the style of disagreement in some ways mirrors internal disputes among objective lists theorists: advocates of the project of codifying human rights agree that it is a necessary project, but have differences in emphasis with respect to what is most important. In the international conversation on human rights, these differences arise in part from the fact that competing codifications have been crafted from multiple cultural contexts. One important question advocates of human rights have thus faced in the late 20th and early 21st centuries is whether there is a "legitimacy dilemma" in human rights discourse. The situation is well-framed by Abdullahi Ahmed An-Na'im:

> If we take the UN Charter and the Universal Declaration of Human Rights as the starting point of the modern movement for the promotion and protection of human rights, we will find it true that the majority of the peoples of Africa and Asia had little opportunity for direct contribution to the formulation of these basic documents. Since the majority of the peoples of these two continents were still suffering from the denial of their collective human right to self-determination because of colonial rule and foreign domination at the time, they were unable to participate in the drafting and adoption processes.
> 2016 [1990]: 69

The legitimacy dilemma arises in part because of the particular historical context of the UN's crafting of the original Declaration, but also because there have since been additional documents introduced into the international conversation on rights and well-being.

One competitor to the UN's codifications is the Banjul Charter, adopted in 1981 by a collective of African heads of states and governments, which came into force in that region in 1986. As Simeon Ilesanmi points out, this document was meant to supplement, not replace the UN documents, offering "cultural reasons to justify [...] a less vacuous, more focused regional experiment in moral and political innovation" (2016 [1997]: 76). The authors of the Banjul Charter were thus concerned not to deny the rights set out by the UN, but to insist on a more nuanced and regionally informed take on specific rights—such as the right to development and self-determination—needed to address the damaging legacy of colonialism in Africa.

A second competitor is the Bangkok Declaration (1993), which was "the first organized expression of Asian opposition to the UDHR" (Bell 2016 [2006]: 90). As was the case with the Banjul Charter, the Bangkok Declaration demands a recognition of the historical exclusion of representation from Asian countries in the crafting of foundational UN documents. A key similarity with the Bangkok Declaration is that it emphasizes that a narrowly Western accounting of human rights leaves out features that could aid in advancing those rights. Daniel Bell argues that there are "positive reasons in favor of drawing on the resources of indigenous cultural traditions to persuade East Asians of the values of human rights" (2016 [2006]: 91). Learning from the history and practitioners of such traditions, such as Confucianism, may provide a case for widening the scope of fundamental human rights to reflect what is centered as well-being relevant in those traditions. Teruhisa Se and Rie Karatasu argue, for example, that there could be a "right to be brought up in an intimate community" (Se and Karatsu 2004).

The legitimacy dilemma must be taken seriously, as must the contexts in which competing codifications have emerged. Efforts to make sense of human rights are potentially "a significant site for intercultural encounters that include both conflict and dialogue" (Flynn 2016: 15). Like any conversation that spurs inquiry, the international conversation around human rights offers both threats and opportunities of the sort that arise when we widen the scope of inquiry and demonstrate a willingness to take the experience and evidence of others on board.

What is crucial for connecting a philosopher's objective list and human rights advocacy is the following observation: competing documents coalesce around certain clusters of rights, namely the need to honor self-determination, cultural goods, education, and support for not just individuals but also their family structures. In an attempt to delineate that to which humans are entitled in the pursuit of a good life, human rights theorists functionally generate stable loci.[23] The best explanation for this is that a realistic interpretation fits our way of using the concept of human rights to protect and enhance well-being. But we must remind ourselves that "realistic" here need not mean timeless or eternal, for the sense of objectivity we are operating with in a pragmatist account is understood as a standard within, not apart, from our practices. In his nuanced approach to intercultural dialogue on human rights, Flynn stresses the importance of not overstating the kind of objectivity we are capable of. As he argues, philosophers "must appreciate the dynamic nature of these debates along with the local and global contexts in which they are situated" (Flynn 2016: 16). This means that what appears at one time as an overlapping consensus achieved by theorists advocating for human rights from different cultural starting points should not be reified as "The List," but considered open to continued critique—further inquiry—as doubt dictates.[24]

There remains much to be said about how to understand iterations of objective lists with significant, but incomplete overlap, as we might think of different human rights schemes. But we can say at least this much: we can be informed by our earlier treatment of well-being as a property cluster term. Advocates of different schemes of human rights do not disagree about the importance of formalizing recognition of such rights to promote well-being, but about where the emphasis lies for people of different regions based on their historical, social, economic, and political situation. Flynn draws our attention to the legacy of colonialism and global inequality, which have created "deep asymmetries in power that cannot remain in the background if the intercultural dialogue on human rights is to be fully open, inclusive, and symmetrical" (2016: 16). This helps us to see that context matters for which property within the cluster most demands attention for a group of people.

In order to satisfy the aims of inquiry—which are our aims, in seeking to determine how to live, individually and together—it is necessary that we broaden the scope of the conversation. The objectivist is in a position to argue strenuously for the need for intercultural dialogue, as it is only dialogue at the most inclusive international level that provides the most serious threat—and

---

[23] That the job of the rights schema is to protect against threats to well-being and enhance it for all is sometimes made explicit, as at UDHR Article 25, which invokes the well-being of a person and their family as the grounds for protecting rights that enable access to all that is necessary for an adequate standard of living.

[24] This may sound unremarkable, but it in fact cuts against the very formulation of the UDHR, which was set out "as a common standard of achievement for all peoples and all nations," fit for "universal and effective recognition and observance." While there have been supplements to the UDHR in the form of subsequent international covenants (such as the International Covenant on Economic, Social and Cultural Rights of 1966), it has never been revised. The UN also appears to believe that the original continues to be fit for purpose, as they prominently declare on their website that the UDHR is the "most translated document in the world" (see https://www.ohchr.org/en/universal-declaration-of-human-rights).

the best opportunity—to improve our defense of human rights as a mechanism to support human well-being in practice. Human rights discourse operates on the presumption that there is something to get right with respect to promoting well-being for humans based on what we as a kind need to foster a life good for us in the living of it.

5. A Lingering Question

I have drawn on pragmatist methods to assess what's at stake in the philosophical dispute between objectivism and subjectivism, focusing on our engagement with ideals of the good as a form of inquiry, on the need for conceptual clarity around the term "well-being," and on what a pragmatic elucidation of that term suggests: that objective list treatments of the concept both offer internal convergence and coalesce with what is meant to be protected and promoted as well-being relevant by diverse human rights documents.

There remains a lingering practical question for how to move forward in first-order investigations of the good life. The fact that our assessment of things as good for us clusters around stable loci does not tell us *how* those goods relate to one another, and how that relational structure should guide attempts to promote or enhance well-being. As Crisp puts it, "there is nothing to prevent an objective list theorist's claiming that all that the items on her list have in common is that each, in its own way, advances well-being" (Crisp 2021). While there is nothing to prevent this, it would prove less useful for action-guidance than a model that had something to say about the relation of items within the list. This is not to say that we must seek an undergirding ontology to explain *why* things are on the list, only that for those things accepted as being on the list, we can benefit practically from having a sense of how to pursue them given the real constraints on the promotion of well-being, such as limited time and resources. Modeling an objective list theory of well-being admits of many possibilities, which I merely sketch here.

One possibility is that the objective list should be seen as hegemonically organized. On such a model, a number of things or states of affairs are well-being relevant, but some *one* feature is so critical that it carries the day in determining the valence of a life's quality for the person living it. One likely version of such an account places pleasure and the absence of pain in the role of hegemon.

A related but distinct second option is that the objective list could be seen as prioritarian, where some things have higher priority or more central importance than others, but not in the "swamping" way a hegemonic account would indicate. One possible version of such an account could prioritize friendship, which may not position someone to overcome the bad-making effects of pain or lack of access to basic health care, but could perhaps aid in coping through absences or events deleterious to overall well-being.[25]

A third possibility is that the objective list should be regarded as giving the necessary and sufficient conditions for well-being, such that each and every inclusion on the list would need to be satisfied in order for a person to live a life good for them. On some readings, perfectionist accounts of the human good hold this high standard, though on other readings, perfectionism sets the ceiling but not the floor—it gives an ideal based on our kind to strive for, but allows that a less that complete satisfaction of that ideal can still be a good life for the person living it.

My own hypothesis—here merely ventured, not defended—is that a paradigm-based explanation of well-being best captures the centrality of some features and the fluidity of electing variable ends as ways of meeting them. This is consonant with "well-being" taken as a property cluster term, and allows that emphasis on various things within the cluster can be intelligible as a pursuit of the good life. To appeal once more to recipe talk, that such features contribute to the goodness of a good life does not itself convey to us proportion, weight, or fixity of the ingredients. And yet, it still requires the presence of at least enough of a subset of ingredients. With a set of standard ingredients, there may be room for a non-standard addition or modification while still satisfying the paradigmatic core, and even room for personal preference in determining ratios. Consider chocolate cake. It can be made vegan, gluten-free, flourless—but not chocolate-less. You can hide zucchini in it and still call it chocolate cake. You can add more or less of things, within reason: adding three eggs instead of two makes it a richer cake; adding twelve eggs instead of two leads to a chocolate omelet. On a paradigm-based account, recipes for well-being seem to be like recipes for chocolate cake: variations in individual construction occur and are intelligible *as* variations around a shared core.

6. Conclusion

What I have been most concerned to demonstrate is that methodological pragmatism offers both a set of resources for approaching questions about the prudential good and at least the beginnings of answers. This is because taking pragmatism on board frames the objective list in humanistic terms—it is *our* objective list. This helps us to see that our epistemic access to it is natural and not

---

[25] Friendship may seem an odd choice, but its centrality to human life has historically been of great interest to philosophers. Consider the large portion of Aristotle's *Nicomachean Ethics* that concerns the forms of friendship and how each fits into a flourishing life; or Montaigne's *Of Friendship*.

mysterious, that our ability to work to individualize it is real but limited, and that our recognition of others as relevantly similar to ourselves in respect of their well-being should move us to appreciate the possibility and the urgency of meeting the basic needs enshrined across a diversity of human rights codifications. We can know what is good for us, we have some—but only some—power to choose how to pursue a good life, and we know that working with others is a prerequisite to any sustainable pursuit of a life good in the living of it.

References

An-Na'im, A. A. (2016 [1990]). 'Islam, Islamic Law, and the Dilemma of Cultural Legitimacy for Human Rights', reprinted in L. May and J. Delston (eds.), *Applied Ethics: A Multicultural Approach*, Routledge, 84–91.

Anderson, E. (1991). 'John Stuart Mill and Experiments in Living', *Ethics* 102(1): 4–26.

Aristotle (1999). *Nicomachean Ethics*, 2nd edition, trans. and ed. T. Irwin, Hackett Publishing Company. = *NE*.

Bell, D. (2016 [2006]). 'Asian Justifications for Human Rights', reprinted in L. May and J. Delston (eds.), *Applied Ethics: A Multicultural Approach*, Routledge, 106–16.

Boyd, R. (1988). 'How to Be a Moral Realist', in G. Sayre-McCord (ed.), *Essays on Moral Realism*, Cornell University Press, 181–228.

Boyd, R. (2002). 'Truth Through Thick and Thin', in R. Schrantz (ed.), *What Is Truth?*, De Gruyter, 38–59.

Congdon, M. (forthcoming). *Moral Articulation: On the Development of New Moral Concepts*.

Crisp, R. (2006). *Reasons and the Good*, Oxford University Press.

Crisp, R. (2021). 'Well-Being', *The Stanford Encyclopedia of Philosophy* (Fall 2021 Edition), ed. Edward N. Zalta <https://plato.stanford.edu/archives/fall2021/entries/well-being/>.

Dewey, J. (1986 [1938]). *Logic: The Theory of Inquiry*, in J. A. Boydston (ed.), *The Later Works of John Dewey 1925–1953*, Southern Illinois University Press.

Fletcher, G. (2013). 'A Fresh Start for the Objective List Theory of Well-Being', *Utilitas* 25(2): 206–20.

Fletcher, G. (2015). 'Objective List Theories', in G. Fletcher (ed.), *The Routledge Handbook of Philosophy of Well-Being*, Routledge, 148–60.

Flynn, J. (2016). *Reframing the Intercultural Dialogue on Human Rights: A Philosophical Approach*, Routledge.

Gert, J. (2012). *Normative Bedrock: Response-Dependence, Rationality, and Reason*, Oxford University Press.

Heath, J. (1998). 'A Pragmatist Theory of Convergence', *Pragmatism, Canadian Journal of Philosophy*, supplementary volume 24: 149–75.

Heney, D. (2015). 'Reality as Necessary Friction', *Journal of Philosophy* 112(9): 504–14.

Heney, D. (2020a). 'A Peircean Argument for Epistemic Cosmopolitanism', *Yearbook for Practical Philosophy in a Global Perspective*, No. 4: *Normativity Beyond Borders*, Verlag Karl Alber.

Heney, D. (2020b). 'On Moral Architecture', in D. Kaspar (ed.), *Explorations in Ethics*, Palgrave Macmillan, 141–68.

Heney, D. (2022). 'Truth, Pragmatic Theory of', *Routledge Encyclopedia of Philosophy*. Routledge.

Howat, A. (2018). 'Misak's Peirce and Pragmatism's Metaphysical Commitments', *Transactions of the Charles S. Peirce Society* 54(3) (Summer): 378–94.

Hurka, T. (2019). 'On "Hybrid" Theories of Personal Good', *Utilitas* 31(4): 450–62.

Ilesanmi, S. O. (2016 [1997]). 'Civil-Political Rights or Social-Economic Rights for Africa?', in L. May and J. Delston (eds.), *Applied Ethics: A Multicultural Approach*, Routledge, 74–87.

Lane, R. (2018). *Peirce on Realism and Idealism*. Cambridge University Press.

Lewis, C. I. (1970 [1950]) 'The Empirical Basis of Value Judgments', in J. D. Goheen and J. L. Mothershead, Jr (eds.), *Collected Papers of Clarence Irving Lewis*, Stanford University Press, 175–89.

Lijoi, F. (2021). 'Forming New Ends Creatively', in R. Frega and S. Levine (eds.), *John Dewey's Ethical Theory: the 1932 Ethics*, Routledge, 60–78.

Lin, E. (2018). 'Welfare Invariabilism', *Ethics* 128(2): 320–45.

Methven, S. J. (2015). *Frank Ramsey and the Realistic Spirit*, Palgrave Macmillan.

Misak, C. (2000). *Truth, Politics, Morality*, Routledge.

Misak, C. (2004 [1991]). *Truth and the End of Inquiry*, Oxford University Press.

Misak, C. (2016). *Cambridge Pragmatism: From Peirce and James to Ramsey and Wittgenstein*, Oxford University Press.

Parfit, D. (1984). *Reasons and Persons*, Oxford University Press.

Peirce, C. S. (1997 [1903]). *Pragmatism as a Principle and Method of Right Thinking: The 1903 Harvard Lectures on Pragmatism*, ed. P. A. Turrisi, SUNY Press. = CP.

Peirce, C. S. (1931–58). *Collected Papers of Charles Sanders Peirce*, Harvard University Press, 8 vols.: vols. 1–6 ed. C. Hartshorne and P. Weiss; vols 7–8 ed. A.W. Burks.

Price, H. (1988). *Facts and the Function of Truth*, Blackwell.

Price, H. (2003). 'Truth as Convenient Friction', *Journal of Philosophy* 100(4): 167–90.

Putnam, H. (1995). *Pragmatism: An Open Question*, Wiley Blackwell.

Rice, C. M. (2013). 'Defending the Objective List Theory of Well-Being', *Ratio* 26(2): 196–221.

Se, T. and R. Karatsu (2004). 'A Conception of Human Rights Based on Japanese Culture: Promoting Cross-cultural Debates', *Journal of Human Rights* 3(3): 269–89.

Shapiro, L. (2021). 'Truth's Dialectical Role: From Friction to Tension', *Inquiry*. DOI: 10.1080/0020174X.2021.1972834.

Thompson, M. (2008). *Life and Action: Elementary Structures of Practice and Practical Thought*, Harvard University Press.

Tiller, G. (2008). 'George Santayana: Ordinary Reflection Systematized', in Cheryl Misak (ed.), *Oxford Handbook of American Philosophy*, Oxford University Press, 125–43.

United Nations (1948). 'Universal Declaration of Human Rights', available at: <un.org>.

United Nations (1966). 'International Covenant on Economic, Social and Cultural Rights', available at: <un.org>.

Wiggins, D. (1990–1). 'Moral Cognitivism, Moral Relativism and Motivating Moral Beliefs', *Proceedings of the Aristotelian Society* 91: 61–85.

Williams, B. (1985). *Ethics and the Limits of Philosophy*, Routledge.

Wittgenstein, L. (2009). *Philosophical Investigations*, 4th edition, ed. J. Schulte, trans. P. M. S. Hacker, Wiley Blackwell.

Index

For the benefit of digital users, indexed terms that span two pages (e.g., 52–53) may, on occasion, appear on only one of those pages.

actions, basic 125–6
aesthetic attitude 286–9
aesthetic properties 281–2, 287
agency 34, 36–40, 46, 60–2
agreement 173–4, 178–9
Anderson, Elizabeth 336–7
anthropology 185
Armstrong, David 218n.14
assertion 4–5, 173–4, 176, 246
anti-essentialism 285–6
anti-realism 6
anti-representationalism 277
artworld, the 280
Ayer, A. J. 212–13

Bangkok Declaration 342
Banjul Charter 342
Bartel, Christopher 294
Beardsley, Monroe 279
Bell, Clive
  formalism 275
  isolationism 275
Bernoulli's theorem 264–5
bifurcation 5, 174n.5
Bird, Alexander 44–6
Blackburn, Simon 5–6, 11–12, 17, 25–6, 46, 71, 198–200, 199n.28, 202–4, 277–8, 292
Boghossian, Paul 232n.25
Boltzmann, Ludwig 31–2, 58
  Boltzmann-Schuetz proposal 31–2, 40–1, 58–9
Boncompagni, Anna 43–4
Boyd, Richard 334–6
brains in vats 175–80, 183, 186
Brandom, Robert 24, 29, 46–7, 49, 212, 235–6, 246, 252–3, 291–2
Bronzo, Silver 219n.16
Burge, Tyler 309
Button, Tim 215n.6

Callender, Craig 30, 57, 59
Cambridge Pragmatism 25
Cappelen, Herman 73–4
Carnap, Rudolph 80–1, 83–4, 101–2, 215n.7

Carroll, John 128n.11
Cartwright, Nancy 37–8, 129–31
Cassirer, Ernst 8, 112–13, 113n.20
causation 4–5, 18, 24, 36–8, 179–80
  general 118–19, 129–31
  practical relevance for 36–8
  singular 118–19, 135–6
  temporal character of 38–40
causal laws 130
causes
  as determinants of evaluative contents 200–2
  as determinants of non-evaluative contents 190, 195–9, 202–4
ceteris paribus laws 129n.12
chances 81–2, 89–90, *see also* probability
charity criterion 220–2, 226–7, *see also* principle of charity
Chirimuuta, Mazviita 5, 8, 15–17
Clark, Andy 51–2
clarity, grades of 332, 336
coherence
  and interpretation 193–4, 194n.12
  and truth 189n.3, 190–1, 204–5
Collingwood, R.G. 279, 298
color 11
compositional interpretation procedures 219–20
compositional systems of propositional representation 219
conditional, logical 243, 245–7, 249–50
confidence 264–5
consensus 332, 334–5, 339–40, 342–3, *see also* agreement
consequentialism 336
content, propositional *see* propositions
control 144–5, 147, 150–1, 160, 162–4, *see also* standby control
convention 141–2, 161
convergence 328–9, 332–40, 344
conversational scoreboard 323
coordination 142, 161, 164–5, *see also* agreement
correspondence, *see also* truth as correspondence
  and interpretation 193–4
Craig, Edward 25
Cuneo, Terence 211n.2

Danto, Arthur 276
Davidson, Donald 6, 16, 189–207, 215n.7, 216n.10, 219n.16, 220–1, 227n.21, 230n.23
DCOP (decision crowds out prediction) 38
de Finetti, Bruno 267–9
defeasibilty 144, 158–9, 162–3
definition 6
deflation 3–5, 17, 173, 182, 186
  logical 236, 242–6, 249–50, 253–4
  semantic 237–8, 242–4
democracy 269
demystification 12–13
Dennett, Daniel 24, 54–6, 227
deontic modality *see* modality, deontic
descriptive concept 305n.2
  descriptive legal concept 316–18, 322–3
descriptivism 171–2, 175, 182–4
Dewey, John 6, 261–2, 276, 290, 331–2
Dickie, George 276, 283
disagreement 170, 332–3, 341, *see also* dispute, object level
dispute, object-level 304, 314
disquotation 192n.7, 193
discursive values 307–8
  legal practice and 318–19
  medical practice, arthritis, and 313
  Millian, and truth-norm 312–14
  social-scientific 316–18
disposition 41–2, 49, 179–81, 183, 185–6
doubt 331–3, 339, 342–3
doxastic criteria 220, 226–7
Dummett, Michael 219–20
Dworkin, Ronald 303, 318

e-representation 75n.7, 82, 87n.29
easy ontology 83, 90–1
Eddington, Arthur 25n.1, 30–1, 33n.7
eligibility 224, *see also* reference magnetism
embedding problem *see* Frege-Geach problem
emotion, aesthetic 298
epistemology 3, 262–5, 267
  social 270–1, *see also* misinformation
ethics 262–3, 265–7
Euthyphro question 34–7, 42, *see also* explanation, direction of
evaluative beliefs and/or properties 199–203
evolution 9–12, 176
expectation 42, 264–5
experience, lived 332
experimentalism 332
experiments in living 336–7
explanation 3–4
  direction of 14, 40
  vindicatory 340

of meaning as use (EMU) 305–6, *see also* hermeneutic EMU.
expressivism 5, 17, 198–204, 212–13, *see also* pragmatism
dialectical disposition 236, 246–50
global 23–4, 26, 235–8
legal 321–2
local 237–8, 251
moral 93–4
recipe for 26–7
semantics, virtues of 284, 291
externalism 194n.11, 195–8, 200–1

fallibility 7–8, 13, 185, 332
familiarity 225
Field, Hartry 215n.7
Fletcher, Guy 330
Flynn, Jeffrey 342–3
Frege, Gottlob 216n.8
Frege-Geach Problem 80–1, 123–4, 127, *see also* logical embedding, problem of
function 306, *see also* hermeneutic function.
future-facing character
  of language 26n.2
  of thought 51

games
  baseball 3–4
  chess 3–4
Geach, Peter 239–40
genealogy 10–12, 141–2, 164
Gert, Joshua 240–1, 245, 251, 253–4, 338–9
Gibbard, Allan 127, 212–13, 322n.16
globality 5
grammatical metaphor 76–8, 82–5
Grandy, Richard 226n.20, 227n.22
grounding 130

Hacking, Ian 333
Halliday, Michael 4, 13–14, 75–6, 78–9, 82–3
harmony *see* agreement
Hart, H.L.A. 303–4, 319–20
Hartle, James 59
Heath, Joseph 336
Hegel, Georg Wilhelm Friedrich 101, 113–15
Heidegger, Martin 8
Heney, Diana 5–8
hermeneutic EMU 307–8
hermeneutic function 307–8, *see also* function
  of "dress" and "dust" 307–8
  of "subject matter" 310–14
  of legal terms (Hartian) 316–18
  of legal terms (Dworkinian) 318–19

hermeneutic meaning 307-8
  of "dress" and "dust" 307-8
  of "subject matter" 310-14
  of legal terms (Hartian) 316-18
  of legal terms (Dworkinian) 318-19
hermeneutic reasoning 307-8
Hochberg, Herbert 222-3
Hohwy, Jakob 51-2
Horwich, Paul 244
human rights 330-1, 340-6
  legitimacy dilemma for 341-2
humanoid 142-3, 148-52, 154-64, 166
Hume, David 24, 43, 54, 119, 130-1, 265
Husserl, Edmund 8

idealism 114-15
ideational macro-function 75-6, 80-1, 85-6, 88, 91
illusion 179-80
indexicals 24, 29-30
inference tickets 44-5, 47
inquiry 261-2, 328, 330-7, 339-40, 342-4
  as embedded 331-2, 334, 339
interpersonal macro-function 76, 78-81, 85-6, 88-9, 91
interpretation 171-2, 184, 186-7, 193-5, 197-8, 198n.22, 215
interpretationism 197-8
Isenberg, Arnold 284-5
Ismael, Jenann 30, 40n.16, 59, 101

James, William 6, 23-4, 28, 176, 261-2
Johnston, Mark 292
joint activity 142, 151-60, 163-4

Kania, Andrew 294
Kant, Immanuel 101, 114n.23
Kant-Sellars thesis 46-7, 49
Keynes, John Maynard 262-5
Kneale, William 35
Kraut, Robert 3
Kripke, Saul 46, 181, 212n.4, 225-6, 231n.24, 252-3

Lange, Marc 131n.14
language
  as a naturalistic phenomenon 3-4, 172-3
  as a social practice 3-4, 6-7, 9, 13-15, 173, 176, 178-81, 331, 333-4, 339
  congruent 75n.7, 82-3, 87-9, 91-4
  functions of 13-14, 70-1, 73-86, 235-7, 240-3, 245-54
    in childhood language 75
    in mature language 75-6
  learning 13-14

laws of nature 131-5
legal expressivism *see* expressivism, legal
legal non-positivism 303
legal positivism 303
Leiter, Brian 303-4, 319-20
Levine, Steven 297
Levinson, Jerrold 287
Lewis. C.I. 328-9
Lewis, David 30, 36, 46, 84, 89-90, 170-2, 186-7, 217n.12, 224
Lijoi, Federico 332-3
linguistic analogues to artistic categories 289-90
location problems *see* placement problems
logic 17
logical consequence *see* logical relations
logical connectives 235-6, 239-43, 245-51, 253-4
logical embedding, problem of 240-1, *see also* Frege-Geach Problem
logical relations 235-6, 239, 241-5
Lovibond, Sabina 295-6

Macdonald, Margaret 45n.18
Macro-functions of language 75-6,
  see also ideational macro-function, interpersonal macro-function, textual macro-function
Maddy, Penelope 239
manifest image 28, 54-6, 114
Marion, Mathieu 44
mathematics 263-4
Mccarty, David 218n.14
meaning 4
meaning ground 210
Mellor, D.H. 25, 35-6
memory 25, 60-2
Merleau-Ponty, Maurice 8, 112
meta-policies 125-7
metalinguistic dispute 304, 314-15
metaphysics 3-5, 7, 11, 13, 15-16, 170, 172, 180, 184, 261-2
  pragmatist dismissals of 268, 292
metasemantics 251, 253
metasemantic non-positivism 304-5, 312-15
metasemantic positivism 304-5, 312, 314-15
Michael, Ryan 280-1
Mill, John Stuart 336-7
Millikan, Ruth 237-40
mind-independence 8, 16
mirror of nature 98-100
Misak, Cheryl 25, 36, 45n.18, 51, 269-70, 334
misinformation 271-3

modal discourse
   acquisition and development of 77–8
   functions of 78–86
   varieties of 71–3
modality
   deontic 72–3, 77, 84–5
   epistemology of 70, 87, 92–4
   facts about 70, 87–9, 92
   flavors of 72, 77
   metaphysical 72, 91n.35, 92–3
      puzzles about 70–1, 87–95, 262–3
   natural modals 118–19, 136–7
Modal properties 70, 78, 81–2, 87–93
modeling 344–5
mood system, functions of 76, 78–81, 85
moral sense 212–13
motivation 212–13
Myers, Robert 6, 18, 227n.21

Nagel, Thomas 189n.1, 203n.37, 205–6
naturalism 11, 13, 17–18, 172–3
   subject 28
naturalness *see* reference magnetism
necessity
   logical 134
   metaphysical 134
   nomic 131–2, 134n.16
Newcomb problems 37–8, 39n.14
no exit problem 187, 202
nondescriptivism *see* expressivism, semantics, virtues of
non-naturalism 13, 17–18
normativist concept, *see also* subject matter, normativist
   defined 305n.2, 318–19
   subject matter 318–19
   normativist legal concept 319–20, 322–3
Nozick, Robert 92

objectivism 329–30, 334, 336, 344
objectivity 334, 342–3
ontology
   of art 293–4
   of music 296
   priority of 294
open-mindedness 261–2, 269–70
ostension 223

pairing practice 215–16
   belief-relevant 217
Parfit, Derek 266–7
past, the 177–8
pattern 142–3, 147–65
Peirce, Charles 6, 25, 45n.18, 51, 176, 261–2, 269–71, 277, 292, 328, 332–4

Pettit, Philip 6–7, 9–13, 18
placement problems 26–7, 91
Plunkett, David 303–4
pluralism 5
policies 123n.4, 124–6
possibilities 73, 77–8, 81–4, 89–91
possible worlds 70, 73–4, 77–8, 81–2, 84, 87–93
practical relevance constraint 27, 30, 40, 42, 46
   for causation 36–8
   for probability 34–6
pragmatic
   elucidation 334–5, 344
   grounds 27
   inferentialism 307–8, 322–5
   maxim 328, 333–4
   vindication 340–1
pragmatism 212
   American 114–15
   educational promise of 261–2
   global 23–4, 26, 55–7, 103–4, 114–15, 235–42, 251–2
   local 237–42, 251
   methodological 235
   political influence of 270
   subject matter 235–6
Pratt, Henry 279
pre-emption thesis 211, 231
Predictive Processing Framework 51–5
prescriptivism, moral 80–1
Price, Huw 5, 8–9, 16–17, 70, 74, 82, 98n.1, 99n.3, 115, 173, 189–207, 212, 213n.5, 215n.6, 235–8, 240, 252–3, 308–9
   rejection of metaphysics 292
   subject naturalism 295
primitivism, color 102–4
principle of charity 193–4
probability 262–6
   practical relevance for 34–6
   temporal character of 40
projection criterion 227, 230–1
property cluster term 334–7, 343, 345
propositions 17, 175, 214, 236, 238, 250–4
Putnam, Hilary 56, 170–2, 175, 182–3, 185–7, 215n.6, 223n.18, 331

quasi-realism 5, 173–4, 199n.28, 203n.35, 266–7
quietism 15–17, 103–4, 107, 199, 204n.38
Quine, W.V.O. 216n.10, 217n.12, 220–1, 223nn.18,19, 227n.22, 230–1, 290

Ramsey, Frank 25, 33–4, 36–9, 44, 51, 60–1, 239–40, 262–6
realism 13, 15, 17, 171, 185, 333, 336, 342–3
   classical (a.k.a. metaphysical) 189–90, 198–200, 205–7

metaethical 200–2, 203n.36
scientific 98n.2, 106, 106n.11, 108n.14
vs. antirealism 189–90, 197–200
vs. transcendence 206–7
reality 15–17, 172
reason 271–3
reductionism 238, 252–3
reference 3–4, 9, 174, 333, 335, 337
magnetism 4–5, 170–87
robust 4–5, 180, 182, 184–6
theories of 181–4
causal 226
vs. the referent 182–3
rejection 246, 248–9
relativism 185–6
relevant community problem 282–3
representation 15, 17–18, 184
representationalism 210–11, 229, 237–9
responsibility 14, 120–7, 135–6
causal 120
moral 125–7
revisionism 3–4
Roberts, John 14, 18
Rorty, Richard 190–4, 199n.24, 206–7, 261–2, 277, 297–9
Rousseau, Jean-Jacques 308–9
Rovelli, Carlo 32n.6, 58n.29, 59n.32, 61n.37
rule 6–7, 10, 174–5
basic 141–6, 148, 151, 157, 162–4, 166
following 50, 141–2, 144–8, 150–2, 158–60, 163–4, 166–7
Russell, Bernard 25, 60–1
Ryle, Gilbert 44–5, 47, 72, 80

Sartorio, Carolina 136n.18
Schroeder, Mark 212–13, 240–2, 251
Schroeter, Laura 181n.9
Sciaraffa, Stefan 6–7
science 8, 11–12, 16–17
scientific image 28, 54–6, 114
Sellars, Wilfrid 24, 28, 45, 47, 54, 236–9, 265
semantic potential 307
of "dress" and "dust" 307–8
of legal terms 315–16
sensitization 142–3, 148–54, 156–66
Shapiro, Lionel 12–13, 17
skepticism 6, 11–12, 170–1, 175, 179–80, 187, 264
skill 7, 10, 178–80
Skyrms, Brian 218n.14
Stace, W.T. 282–3
standby control 144–5
starting points 8–10, 16, 187
Stevenson, C.L. 212–13
Stich, Stephen 227n.22

subject matter 6–7, 303–5, 309–11
conventional conception 310–11
descriptive 316–18, 322–3
hermeneutic conception 310
normativist 319–20, 323
subject-understanding conception 309–10
subjectivism 265–6, 329–30, 334, 344
substantive
property or relation 242–4
truth condition 251
Sundell, Timothy 303–4
Systemic Functional Linguistics 73–8, 82–3

Talisse, Robert 269–70
Taylor, Charles 98–100, 112n.19, 113n.21
textual macro-function 76, 83–6, 86n.28, 88–9
theory 261–2
enumerative 338
explanatory 338
influence of 261
thermodynamics, second law of 32n.6, 40–1, 58–9
Thomasson, Amie 4–5, 9–10, 12–14, 18, 250
Tilgher, Adriano 267
time
block view of 48
direction of 30–3
flow of 30
passage of 30
physics of 57–9
present moment of 30
Toh, Kevin 322n.16
Tolstoy, Leo
infection theory of art 279
expressionism 279
triangulation 142–3, 148, 161–2, 193, 195–8, 198n.22, 201n.30, 202–6
trivial inferences 82–4, 86, 90–1
truth 3–4, 6, 18, 170, 172–3, 176, 180–1, 334, *see also* coherence, correspondence
and the end of inquiry 192
aptness 321–2
as correspondence 172–3, 192–3, 198n.23, 261–2
as a goal of inquiry 189–91, 193, 204–5
assessment 5, 173–8
concept of
Davidson's 189–90, 192–8, 206–7
epistemic 189–90, 192, 198–9
Price's 190–3
radically non-epistemic 185–6, 189
Rorty's 190, 192–3
sui generis nature of 192–3
vs. warranted assertibility 191–2, 196

truth-norm 308–9, 312
  speaker-understanding 311
  hermeneutic 311
  conventional 311

unbreakability 133–4
uncertainty 332
Universal Declaration of Human Rights (UDHR) 341–2
use 211–12
usefulness 6, 174–6

Verheggen, Claudine 6, 18, 227n.21
veridicality of belief 198–9, 204–5

Walton, Kendall
  categories of art 287, 289
Waluchow, Wil 303–4

Weitz, Morris *see* anti-essentialism
Wiggins, David 340
Williams, Bernard 330–1
Williams, Daniel 24, 52–4
Williams, Donald 48–9
Williams J.R.G 184
Williams, Michael 26, 292, 305–6
Wittgenstein, Ludwig 6–8, 17, 212n.3, 218n.14, 219n.16, 294
Wollheim, Richard 283–4
Woodfield, Andrew 224
words 4, 16–17, 25, 43–5, 49, 51, 176
Wright, Crispin 232n.25

Yalcin, Seth 251

Zalabardo, José 4